T0354514

A NEW FATHERLAND

DISCUSSION BETWEEN BICYCLES

JOSEPH ADLER

TORONTO, CANADA 2013

Order this book online at www.trafford.com
or email orders@trafford.com

Most Trafford titles are also available at major online book retailers.

Printed in the United States of America.

ISBN: 978-1-4669-7114-1 (sc)
ISBN: 978-1-4669-7113-4 (e)

Trafford rev. 06/20/2013

 www.trafford.com

North America & international
toll-free: 1 888 232 4444 (USA & Canada)
phone: 250 383 6864 ♦ fax: 812 355 4082

CONTENTS

First Part

Second Part

Third Part

It contains the list of published articles in major
newspapers and magazines from Canada and abroad
and the letters of support from outstanding personalities
for the proposed concept of the BICYCLE EXPRESSWAY
SYSTEM. The respective articles and letters follow in
CHRONOLOGICAL ORDER as they were printed and
received by Joseph Adler.

 # INTRODUCTION

This book is a real story about an attempt that has been a long and difficult struggle to improve one important aspect of life in the human society. What is quite particular and interesting is that everything is told and accurately expressed not by human beings but by bicycles. In this story, the bicycles can think, and think well, they talk among themselves, have a sharp sense of observation and they are watching carefully the human beings and the many aspects of their society with the objectivity and impartiality that only an observer from outside of the human species can have.

Being close to the reality of the everyday life of the human beings as a mean of transportation but being not responsible for the human beings actions and the respective consequences and, as bicycles, not accountable for their opinions to any human authority, the bicycles do not have any fear or concern in expressing their opinions freely without restrictions, with total openness, sincerity and objectivity, regardless of the position of the person they are talking about or the subject or the situation they are presenting or discussing. The fears and reservations the human beings have in this regard, are totally strange to them.

The initial subject of discussion at the first bicycle reunion is the true story about the development and promotion of an original, visionary and sustainable concept for the radical improvement of urban transportation by implementing a system of expressways exclusively for bicycles, elevated above the street level, covered and without uphill slopes, which will create excellent conditions of safety and convenience for the mass use of bicycles. This will tremendously reduce the dependency on cars, the traffic congestion, the air pollution, the number of traffic accidents, the waste of precious time and it will increase the general level of health at the same time with significant economic advantages.

All the promotional actions by the engineer, author of the concept, as meetings with various officials, authorities and personalities, presentations at International Conferences and Seminars, articles in major newspapers and other publications in several countries, interviews by major Radio and TV networks, received letters of support as well as setbacks and negative attitudes at some contacted organizations, are real and truthfully related.

Together with relating the complete story of the promotion of the proposed concept, from the beginning when the idea was born, the bicycles talked about many subjects, giving their own objective interpretation and explanation of many aspects of life in the human society. The range of the subjects discussed at the three bicycles reunions is very wide and includes various aspects of social organization, politics, arts, sports, religion, and of course, urban transportation and the potential role of bicycles, especially after the implementation of the concept of the Bicycle Expressway System.

The disputes among bicycles about their differences in opinions are solved peacefully, politely and thoroughfully, as should always be among humans. No one unclear item is left behind until it is completely clarified. The questions asked by junior bicycles with little life experience are genuine even if sometimes amusing, and the answers by the bicycles with more life experience are well documented, clear and complete. Being at all times very close to the humans and being very observant, the bicycles achieved a perfectly clear understanding of the problems existing in the human society and figured out the required solutions in a clear and feasible way, in which unfortunately, the human beings have proved themselves unable to understand and to act.

The sharp but realistic criticism based on pure logic and rational thinking and not on prejudices of any kind, would be very useful for the human beings for improving their own life in a major way, if they only could be aware of the opinions expressed by the bicycles and if they were able to translate them into their human society life.

ACKNOWLEDGEMENT

Many thanks to those visionaries, in modest or very high positions, who helped genuinely and substantially to promote the concept of the Bicycle Expressway Systems in Canada and in other countries.

Even if, for the reasons explained in this book, the concept has not yet been implemented, there is hope that one day, the wisdom will prevail, and with the strong wind of necessity blowing in the same direction, the vision of today will be the reality of tomorrow.

ACKNOWLEDGEMENT
TO ENA VASQUEZ

I would like to express in these few words but full of profound sentiments, my recognition and thanks for all her valuable and affectionate contribution during many years to the promotion of the idea, which is the subject of this story. Also, her generous, dedicated and meticulous help of high competence, was essential for the correction of the text for the English and Spanish editions of the book, for its publication, and cannot be overestimated.

ACKNOWLEDGEMENT
TO NINA ADLER

Many thanks to my very young but very skilled daughter Nina Adler for her precious help in handling the computer tasks connected with the review and the correction necessary for the high quality of publishing the book.

Dear Reader,

The story in the book that you have in your hands, regardless of the fact that everything is told by bicycles, is far from being a fiction. The subject of the book is very realistic and of tremendous practical value for improving the urban transportation in a radical way. To prove this, after you finish reading the story presented by bicycles, please find attached the real letters of support from outstanding personalities received by the author of the book, Joseph Adler, who is also the author of the Bicycle Expressway Systems concept which is described in detail in the book. Also attached are articles published in major publications in several countries.

All the received letters and published articles are presented in the attached ANNEX not in order of considered importance but in CHRONOLOGICAL order in which the articles were published and the letters were sent.

 # FIRST PART

What the bicycles think about the present conditions of urban transportation and of their own bad situation.

Recently, in an unspecified place in the world, let's say in a parking lot for bicycles, the following discussion between bicycles took place in an informal reunion.

— Dear sisters, said a bicycle with an extensive experience of travelling in many places, please think about this: the cars and other motorized vehicles have the supremacy of the roads in cities and of the highways outside of the cities, the pedestrians have the sidewalks, the trains have their own railroads, the subway trains have their exclusive tunnels, the planes have their airports and the air corridors for their flights, but we, the poor bicycles, who provide so many good services in silence and with humility, have nothing. In all the places, in any country, we are treated with defiance, arrogance and dislike or even hate by the cars which in many occasions kill us when we are using the same roads with them, and with a feeling of nervousness and hostility by the pedestrians when, being desperate because of the deadly danger on the roads, we use very carefully, the sidewalks.

— All this is very true, answered back at the same time three bicycles, with a feeling of sadness in their voice.

— Not only this, intervened a bicycle which just returned from a trip in France, not only that the different modes of transportation have their own ways in accordance with the respective category as trains, cars or planes, but there are exclusive ways even within the same category. In France, for instance, the trains of high speed or TGV, for "trains a grande vitese", have their own exclusive lines which no other trains can use.

— Exactly the same is the case in my country, Japan, where no other train uses the rails of the Sun Can Sen, a very rapid train which moves with 250 kilometers per hour.

— I can confirm this, said a bicycle which in spite of her youth and elegant aspect which among bicycles also, some times is considered a sign of superficiality, gives the impression that knows a lot of what happens in the world. It is very good that the human beings who sometimes are intelligent and rational beings, had succeeded to create those trains which save lots of time but I want to mention that this achievement was possible only because they had constructed also those special rails exclusively for the rapid trains. However, unfortunately, all the time saved by travelling in these trains is lost from the moment the travellers enter the streets of the city after leaving the train station. During peak hours, ten kilometers per hour for the motorized urban traffic is considered the average speed and the situation is not very different at other hours. We, the bicycles, can circulate more rapidly than this but there are so many cars in the streets and many streets are so narrow, that it is not only difficult but also very dangerous for us to be there. There are many traffic accidents and a significant number of them are fatal.

— You talk about Tokyo, Japan, but there is no difference from what happens in Paris, France, in Frankfurt or Berlin in Germany or in London, England, said a bicycle, which obviously knows well the large cities of Europe.

— The situation is identical also in New York and in other cities of North America, including Canada, added a bicycle with twelve speeds, a Yankee which travelled a lot in North America and it seems that she knows well what she is talking about, and in addition that it is not possible to move at our maximal speed level, is also not possible to breath. The air is so polluted and there is such a noise in the streets that there is no more desire to live in the large cities. Unfortunately, there is no other alternative, at least for the great majority of people.

— If you talk about North America, do not forget please, to include Mexico not only Canada. I am from Mexico and the situation in the great majority of our cities can only be worse.

— It seems to me, I could even say that I am sure, that there are two categories of human beings: one very intelligent that builds with such a precision, elegance and functional logic the planes and the trains of large capacity and high speed and the cars, and other category, totally fool, of which are those in charge of the cities, especially of the large ones. All the cities are non-functional, or better to say, anti-functional, they occupy a large area and continue expanding, wasting an unbelievable great area of productive land, much more than it is necessary for living with all modern comfort, transforming a field of agricultural land in a field of houses in so many cases ugly, with narrow streets without green space. On the other hand, in the center of the city, in a very limited space, are concentrated high-rise buildings, very close one to another, canyon style without enough natural light and nice view to enjoy.

— And for moving in these cities, interrupted other bicycle very interested in this discussion, the human beings in their irrational behaviour, succeeded to convert a very valuable invention if it is used in moderation, a product of those few intelligent human beings, the car, in the greatest foolishness of the twentieth century in the urban transportation. Instead of reconstructing, concentrating and modernizing their cities, they multiplied the car in millions of copies, of all imaginable models and sizes and suffocated the streets of their own cities with an invasion of cars for which the cities in no way are prepared. At the end, instead of moving faster, the urban transportation with its permanent congestion transformed itself in a serious problem. And there are many traffic accidents, every day.

— And now, continued the idea the bicycle which talked before, the result is that it is much more difficult to travel, to breath because the air is polluted with so much gas and to hear because of the high, permanent noise in the streets. And we, the bicycles could help so much to improve the urban transportation!

— Some idiots or criminals insist that we, the bicycles, must share the streets with the cars, buses, trucks and other motorized vehicles!

Debate about the relationship between bicycles and cars.

They don't think how vulnerable we are in these conditions! got nervous a bicycle that before didn't say anything. And other fools think that if they paint a white line on the pavement of the streets to mark a space presumably for bicycles only, we will be well protected and that this is the solution! said in the same bad mood the same bicycle and after a very short pause, continued her vehement protest: what narrow minds! They cannot understand that this only creates more problems than it solves, increases the congestion of the motorized traffic because, the space which is given to us, the bicycles, is taken from them, the cars, the width of the street being the same. Look, in the great majority of streets there are no more than two lanes for cars in each direction, and usually three in the main streets but the traffic is much more intense there. Well, what happens when an urban planner, how they are called, in charge with the bicycle traffic, thinking in his stupidity that he makes us a favor, creates with a white line on the asphalt a lane for us. A bicycle needs only half of the width of a lane for cars, it is true, but the remaining half of the lane is of no use for the cars and then for the motorized traffic an entire lane is lost. Then, follows with her invincible logic the bicycle, for the same motorized traffic in the same street the number of lanes is reduced from three to two and from two to one. The immediate consequence of this is the terrible increment of congestion in the remaining lanes.

— My friend, intervened a bicycle closely parked to the speaking bicycle, all that you said is right, but why you are so concerned about the fate of the cars? Do you think that they are concerned about us? I came recently from the countryside and I recognize that I didn't have the opportunity to see those streets with a lane for us, but it seems to me that the idea of that urban planner, which you call stupid, of creating a protected space for us in the streets with intensive traffic, is not so bad. At least we will be secure in the street, true?

— No, it isn't true, replied right away the other bicycle, and it is not true for more than one reason, but at first I would like to tell you that if I called that planner stupid, this is not to offend him personally. I don't know him, he might be a very nice and capable person in other directions, but in this case he is certainly stupid, it means from the scientific point of view, as opposite to the notion of intelligence. Someone intelligent takes decisions that give positive results; in this case the results are not only negative and dangerous but instead of improving the existing situation it makes it worse. But well, if you don't like the word "stupid", we can replace it with the words "limited in his thinking", or we could say that not the person but the policy is stupid.

— Of what policy are you talking about?

— Of the policy of integrating the bicycle traffic with the car traffic in the same streets and pretending that the safety for the bicycles can be achieved by dividing the street with a line of white paint on the pavement and nothing else.

— This is clear, the enunciation is very clear and precise but I would like to know exactly what are the reasons on which this enunciation is based, please, insisted the bicycle from the countryside with the fervor of a lawyer hired by the cars confronting a false accusation.

Nonetheless, it seems that the other bicycle, the attacker, was very well prepared for this unexpected intervention, and more than that, instead of feeling offended, launched a powerful counterattack with a more than obvious pleasure.

— My dear interlocutor, I like that you are so combative and frank in your suspicion. You talk like this because you are a newcomer to the city, when you will have more kilometers in town, you will talk as I am talking because you will then know better the reality. Here are the direct answers to your questions:

— number one: we and they, it means bicycles and cars in the same streets with heavy traffic is an explosive mixture, very dangerous even with the separating lines because when a bicycle doesn't follow the circulation rules and collides with a car or bus, only the bicycle suffers and nothing happens to the car or bus, also, when a car, even a small one, collides with a bicycle, nothing happens to the car and less than nothing to the bus but for the bicycle, in the great majority of cases this collision is fatal, and there are so many cases when the motorized vehicles do not respect the rules.

— number two: in addition to the conscientious violations of the law by the drivers, there are many cases of involuntary errors called human errors from which also, the white line on the pavement not only cannot protect us as a wall or other physical protection, but it gives the illusion, a false impression of safety. For instance, in the case of an accident between two cars in their lane immediately at the left of the white line, nobody can stop one or both cars in their uncontrollable movement to enter the space reserved for bicycles at the right of the white line where the bicycles are still very vulnerable. Imagine for one moment how a bicycle will feel, let's say how you will feel during an intense traffic with cars and buses passing at high speed at a quarter of a meter and sometimes only a few centimeters from you, during the night, when it rains, when it is foggy, when it snows, is windy, or more, during any possible combination of these factors.

— My friend, I am scared even at listening to this, excuse me please, that simply by my ignorance I didn't think about all this, said the bicycle from countryside.

— I didn't finish yet, was the short but authoritarian answer of the other one and after that she continued her demonstration as the movement of a tank:

— number three: when there is a significant congestion of motorized traffic in the only one or in the two lanes available for this traffic and a free space some times available between bicycles on the other side of the white line, there will always be a temptation to use it for by-passing and sometimes even for parking. This is not a theoretical speculation, it is a real situation observed as a daily routine in the cities where there are lanes for bicycles in the streets.

— number four: talking about the main streets which represent the main problem of the joint traffic of bicycles and cars, surely there is there a heavy motorized traffic and it is assumed also, I don't believe it but it is assumed by the advocates of this joint traffic, that there will be many bicycles also if these lanes for bicycles are created. Now imagine please, two situations: what happens when one or some bicycles want to turn left at an intersection and what happens when one or some cars want to turn right at an intersection. In the first case, the bicycles must get out of their protected space and mix with the intensive traffic of cars, buses ant trucks which circulate with a legal speed of fifty or sixty kilometers per hour and many times, as everybody knows it, more than this. Other possibility is to stop at the intersection, wait for the stoplight to change and after that to continue their trip to the left. It is good when there are only one or two bicycles which want to turn and there are not others behind which want to continue their trip straight. If there are, all others must stop and wait until the bicycles which want to turn, can pass, because those which want to turn usually do not have any additional space for waiting without inconveniencing the others. In the second case, when a car wants to turn right, it must cross the white line and the protected space for the bicycles. It is good if there are no bicycles at that moment, but if there are, all the motorized traffic behind the turning car must stop or the bicycle traffic must stop and wait until the turning car or cars, pass. There is not only the inconvenience but there is also a great danger for accidents, and for bicycles, they could be fatal.

— All what you have said is very reasonable, entered the discussion a sports bicycle which until then was listening only, but in this case we cannot travel in the streets knowing very well that always there will be cars in the streets. What should we do?

— I didn't say that we cannot travel, what I said is that a line painted on the asphalt doesn't represent a real protection, generally gives us, how I said before, only a false sense of security, and only in few cases, when there is good weather and few cars in the streets, we can say that in principle, it is better with this line. But by all means, this is not the solution for a great number of bicycles in the main streets. Nevertheless, it is much better for us to travel in the secondary streets, the risk there is much less. It is true that these streets are good for local trips of short distance, for longer trips it takes too much time for reaching the same point, many of them being winding, without good connections. For this reasons everybody prefers the main streets for long trips.

Immediately after the last word of the speaking bicycle, a ring of a bicycle bell from behind, called the attention of all others. How it was proved a second later, by this signal the respective bicycle asked permission to talk without delay.

— I didn't want to interrupt you before, said this new speaker to the previous one, but I am sure that there is a reason for this policy of these separating or protecting lines, or white lines on the pavement how you call them, which policy you do not want or you cannot explain to us. I respect your opinion but not instead of a clear explanation to what I will ask you and to what I will say concerning the massive future use of bicycles in cities including the main streets.

The radical tone of this bicycle was like a cold shower for all bicycles of the audience, which continued to grow because no one of the newcomers quit and the discussion became passionate.

— I like that you smile when you answer the questions, she continued, but look, I warn you that I am not from the countryside, my cyclist is a journalist and I am well informed about things that other bicycles do not know much or do not know anything, for instance the discussions at a high level in a municipal committee in charge with the urban transportation.

The last words of this bicycle—journalist provoked a shock, a commotion, seemingly unanimous, judging by the general roar of wheels changing their position. The arrogant observation about the bicycle that came from the countryside and her manner of talking with the same arrogance about her knowledge and relations, made a very unfavorable impression. Meanwhile it seemed that a feeling of concern about what the bicycle—journalist will say, was present. All were sympathizing with the bicycle criticizing the white lines as a solution for the safety and convenience of the bicycles because all that she said makes lots of sense, but who knows, maybe the journalist really has a valuable argument in spite of her arrogance. Poor defender of our rights! some of the bicycles present at this discussion were thinking. What will she respond to the journalist?

In waiting for the continuation of this verbal battle, the silence that took place was interrupted only by the mild sound of some newcomer bicycles parking as close as possible to the last two speakers, for better listening.

Eventually, the bicycle, let's say the defender, said:
— My esteemed journalist, I don't know what you will tell us but I am afraid that I cannot compete with your erudition and experience. By the way, do you use frequently the new protected lanes in the center of our city? Now I am ready to listen to you.

— Ah, don't worry if you cannot answer to my argument, at least I will be glad to clarify the issue, said the journalist with a protecting and superior condescending tone of a millionaire who renounces to the debt of few cents from his poor friend, evidently not understanding the sarcasm of the defendant. Related to your question, she continued, I must say that I don't like the congestion of the center and fortunately I can avoid it because my cyclist goes to his work by car, but every Sunday, when there is good weather, in the summer, we go for at least two or three hours in the large park close to the house, I repeat, each Sunday and sometimes even in other days of the week in the afternoon when there is not much traffic in the streets up to the park.

— How nice! exclaimed with the same sarcasm the bicycle defender, and tell me please what is your information, I believe so precious. All of us are listening to you.

After a pause for effect, the bicycle—journalist started talking:

— We, the bicycles, will conquer the city, all cities, and the lanes for the bicycles are the first step in this direction. It is true that there are many problems with them and thinking about what you have said, it is true that the problems cannot be solved at present but the idea and the hope is that starting with these lanes, more and more bicycles will be in the streets and consequently less and less cars will be there. This is to say that little by little we will push the cars out of the streets. More bicycles will be in the streets, more difficult will be the life for cars there. Eventually, they will be an insignificant minority and we, the bicycles, will be able to travel in all the streets in full safety and will have a very happy life, of which we think and wish today. Few of us today but many tomorrow, this is the meaning of this first stage for conquering the streets of the city. Do you understand now that in long term there is a good reason for this policy of the urban planners? triumphed proudly at the end of her speech the journalist, looking with defiance initially at her interlocutor and after that, around to all other bicycles.

Now the most waited moment arrived. Will the defender or other bicycle answer? Or there is nothing to answer? We will see, all the bicycles were thinking. During this time of waiting, not only that all the bicycles became totally silent but it seemed that even the light afternoon breeze stopped among the surrounding trees.

— This issue is exactly my point number five, about which I want to talk in continuation, addressed suddenly the defender to the journalist. You interrupted me but thanks for your help, you talked very well precisely about what will never happen. Do you like to die? asked unexpectedly the defender.

— To die? Who wants to die? For what to die?

— For the noble cause of bicycles in their fight against the cars in the streets of the city! responded the defender with emphatic irony. Let me explain with facts and some theory. In the present situation in all large cities of the world, in the developed countries as well as in the poorest countries, or developing ones, the number of utilitarian bicycles in the urban transportation is insignificant, except China which for historical reasons represents a special and very interesting case about which we will talk later in due detail. Now I want to say only that presently China is well in her way of creating the same terrible problems with the urban transportation as other countries and it moves in this direction with great speed.

— And nobody can stop or at least control this process? asked a bicycle.

— Nobody. Not because this process is uncontrollable, certainly can be controlled and very well. It didn't fall from the sky on the head of the poor human beings, which in this way became victims of a new situation. They, the human beings themselves, are the authors of this process and considering their poor minds, what can we expect? But let me continue my idea.

And the bicycle which is called by everybody the defender, continued:

— All of us know that in normal conditions of operation and safety, the bicycle has uncontested qualities as a mode of urban transportation, as the flexibility in time and space, what means the convenience of using it from door to door, saving energy, a maximal economic efficiency, it is very fast if considering the required time from door to door, it is very healthy, totally silent and non pollutant, very easy to park and maintain. With all these advantages by comparison with any other mode of urban transportation, how one can answer the question why there are not more bicycles on the road today, with or without the protecting white lines, moreover that these lines are now in many streets? There are not more bicycles in the streets because in spite of the enumerated advantages, and always accompanying them, there are grave risks, many times deadly. But there is a number of bicycles that defy these risks and the implacable statistics of traffic accidents, many of them deadly, which repeat themselves and are growing each year. Nobody obligates these bicycles to take the present risk in the streets and at the same time nobody interdicts to other ones to join those already in the streets. Why don't they join them? The answer is very simple: they don't join them because in the present situation the streets are very dangerous and inconvenient for bicycles. More bicycles in the streets signify more risk and, as our journalist, nobody wants to die. Until that day when there will be so many bicycles and so few cars travelling in the city, without accidents and without danger, it will be a transition period during which, in accordance with the scenario presented by you, the defender addressed again to the journalist, there will be more and more bicycles in the same streets with still enough cars, in the same unfavorable traffic conditions. Question: what is more probable to happen to the number of accidents for us in this period, it will be the same, less or more? Don't forget that in the large cities for each bicycle in the street there are not less than one hundred cars. This means that if the number of bicycles doubles, the number of cars can be reduced only with one percent and that with an acceptable approximation, we can say that if the number of bicycles increases ten times or by one thousand percent, this may result in a reduction of no more than ten percent in the number of cars. Assuming that a bicycle more in the street means one car less, although there are cars with two or three passengers. Well, knowing this, the correct assumption is that the number of accidents, and for us these accidents are so often deadly, will increase in this period of transition until that time when the traffic accidents will disappear. For sure, not all of us will die in this action of eliminating the cars, but only one thousand of us, or one hundred, well, let's say that no more than ten and at the extreme, one, only one bicycle, and looking around at all bicycles continued with other question: I would like to know, there is here a voluntary, one, only one who would like to die for the better future for us?

— I don't want to die, I want to live in safety and enjoy my life even if I have to travel only around my house and nothing else said a bicycle, rebelling.

— It is a great foolishness to take a risk which is more than moderate.

— Where there is a deadly danger, certainly it is not for me, said other bicycle.

— Only if one of us turns really crazy can think to fight with the cars for the supremacy of the streets. We don't have any chance in such an action and in what concerns me, I prefer a peaceful solution. I know from my own experience what means travelling very close to a car! Thanks for your offer to die as a glorious volunteer in the fight with the cars but I don't take it! was the comment of a bicycle which, judging by her wise talk and the number of kilometers travelled, has a valuable experience.

— I am realist, says other bicycle, I don't believe that it will ever be possible for us to expel the cars completely or the majority of them, from the streets, this is only a dream and it is not worth to take the risk with our lives for this.

— If the situation and our fate cannot be improved without this great and obvious danger to fight against the cars, it is better to live with the present restrictions instead of dying, continued on the same issue, other bicycle.

— Very well, it is right what all of you are saying, intervened the bicycle defender, you who do not want to put your lives in danger by fighting against the cars, but I didn't hear anybody who wants to be part of the future statistics of dead and injured ones. If there is any, I would like to hear her opinion.

For a while a total silence dominated the audience.

— Nobody? asked again the defender.
The same silence continued.
— Now I think that the conclusion is very clear. Nobody wants to die or get injured, and exactly for this, the foresight of our friend, the journalist, will never be realized. I think also that the very idea of a city completely without cars, is not realistic. At this stage of development of the civilization, we cannot assume that the cars will disappear. I agree that it is possible to reduce their number in the favor of bicycles but only if better conditions for bicycles are created.

The situation of urban transportation in China and the position of the bicycles.

— With regard to the integration of bicycles and cars in the same streets, I would like to refer to what is going on in China from where I returned recently, after living there for several years. As all of us know, China is a country where the absolute domination of bicycles, even in large cities, is an everyday fact. At least this was until two or three years before. Since then, a phenomenon opposite to the one which we discussed here, namely the conquest of cities by bicycles, occurs. There, the powerful offensive of the cars against the bicycles takes place now. Everyday more and more cars appear in the streets of Beijing, Shanghai, Canton, where I know the situation by my own experience. I am informed that the same thing happens in other cities too. Now the cars are not yet a majority but there are already numerous traffic accidents unknown before, resulting in tens of thousands of dead and injured per year, and many of these victims are our sisters, the bicycles. This demonstrates once more that it is a very unfortunate situation when we must fight even with a small number of cars. I am not of the opinion that the proposal or the idea of the journalist bicycle of imposing ourselves in the streets of the city confronting the cars, is feasible . . . ! We are so fragile in comparison with the cars!

— I want to complete what our sister from China just said. The new situation in the urban transportation in China and the invasion of cars is not the result of a lost battle by us in the fight against cars, it is the result of the policy of the human beings, whose limitations in their thinking many times have very grave consequences. For several decades China was an exception from the rule. The bicycles represented the main mode of transportation in the cities. This was the result of the policy of the Government of those times. The buying power of the population was very low but almost equal for all, nobody could afford to buy a car. A visitor in a large city could see rivers of bicycles and the few cars were the official ones. At present the policy of the new Government is totally different, there is a big difference in the standard of living, the poor continue being poor without any possibility to buy a car but the new local rich and the foreigners working with the investing companies from other countries, fill the streets with their cars. Today a visitor can see rivers of cars and much less bicycles. The mentality also changed. The bicycle is today a symbol of poverty and the car a symbol of richness and everybody dreams to buy a car. In short time all these enthusiasts of transporting themselves in their own cars will see the other side of this pleasure, when the streets of the city will be suffocated with cars.

— I am sure that they will see this other side, was the comment of a bicycle that couldn't abstain from making it.

— You have all the reasons to be sure, responded the defender and after that she continued:

— At the end of my answer to the journalist I want to mark and underline an essential argument of which it seems that our sister forgot completely. This argument consists in our limitations. We, the bicycles, have many qualities and advantages for the urban transportation, this is evidently true, but we are not all powerful.

The modern, civilized society with a high level of living and technology cannot be called so, if suddenly all the cars and other motorized vehicles which represent a danger to us disappeared and all the tasks of transporting in the cities rely only on our bicycle wheels. In this scenario nobody will be happy, neither the human beings nor we. The elementary objectivity obligates us to recognize that the cars and other motorized vehicles help us a lot. Look what happens in the very poor countries where a car is a very rare thing. The poor bicycles transport all the cargo. Would we like this for us? For sure not! So it is better to be careful when some of us think to eliminate the cars from the streets of the cities. The car doesn't have to be our enemy, must and can be our friend! This may seem strange but it only seems. A serious, in depth analysis can demonstrate this.

These words so pacifist, shocked the audience in its belligerent tendency against the cars as natural enemies of the bicycles. Exactly this thinking was expressed by a bicycle a bit rebellious to the idea of peace with cars.

— My friend, it seems to me that I didn't understand well, you say that we, the bicycles, must and can be friends with them, the cars, when they cause so many problems and are such a great and permanent danger to us in the street?

— You understood very well, I said it and repeat it. And to the even greater surprise for the audience, she added:

— The cars can be our friends, this is a possibility depending of the circumstances, but the reality is that they are our relatives, and much closer relatives than you think, they are our brothers.

— What?

— Brothers, the children of the same parents.

— My friend, by no means I want to offend you but it seems to me that something wrong happened to you.

The defender smiled and with a disarming calm, continued:

— I guess that you need an explanation.

— Surely, please, responded immediately the bicycle, very intrigued.

— Well, they, the cars and we the bicycles are the children of the same parents, the creators of both of us, and the parents are the intelligence of those very intelligent human beings who invented us, build and perfected us, not to be enemies but to collaborate and to be of much use in the society, everyone in its specific field of action for which it was created. If the cars would be able to do everything, including what we, the bicycles, do, we wouldn't be necessary and we would not have been invented. If we could do everything, including what the cars can do, the cars wouldn't have been invented. But each has its well-defined limits, don't forget this.

A roar of approval demonstrated that the reasoning of the defender was well understood by the audience of bicycles.

— Very well, responded the other bicycle, in a calmer mood but not totally convinced, in this case how it can be explained that the brothers kill the sisters, it is to say that the cars that you say are our brothers, kill and hurt us in the street, if we are their sisters?

— This is true, responded without pause the defender, but you are talking only about the effect but not about the cause of that effect. The fact is, how you said, we are killed in the street but the cause is not the cars but the actions of the human beings which are guilty twice.

— It means?

— Directly, the human beings who drive the cars, the drivers, who due to the malfunctioning of their minds, are provoking the accidents in the street, and indirectly, those human beings responsible with the urban planning and the control of the traffic in the city. Not the cars had built the cities how they are, prone to accidents, but the human beings. And in order to be objective in our judgment, not only bicycles die but also cars and human beings, and many more than bicycles. The cause? The human beings. The cars are not suicidal, or criminals but the human beings are. In their stupidity, they get intoxicated with alcohol, with drugs, talk on their cellular phones when they drive, do not pay due attention to the traffic rules and signs, to the operation of the vehicle, they drive when they are very tired and fall asleep while driving, and so the accidents happen and many times these stupid people die, which is not so bad, but also the respective cars and other human beings and cars which are innocent, die.

The three enemies of the bicycles.

This discussion about the relation between bicycles and cars was a real debate involving real cases in life, passion, animosity, words and opinions pro and contra and explanations with objective and rational arguments, without the subjective approach, which usually gives the false sense of reason. To the end, this realistic interpretation and without passion prevailed and all the bicycles agreed that it is more reasonable to qualify as enemies not the cars themselves but the motorized traffic which includes also the actions and the faults of the human beings. With this very important aspect clarified, the discussion continued with the same interest about the same subject.

— My friend from China, intervened a bicycle in a calm and rational manner but not without pride that she was going to justify, your information is very relevant and I agree with you completely. However,

I would like to tell a few words about what you called our fragility. It is true that we are fragile but this is, as you said, only when we compare ourselves with the weight of the cars. Except this, we are very resistant and we achieve our mission circulating and travelling for decades and tens of thousands of kilometers without problems and with little maintenance. And if you want to know, in this relative fragility resides our power! We are vulnerable by a car this is true, but at the same time we are fifty to one hundred times lighter than a car and the same times cheaper, we are much easier and efficient in operation and maintenance. And as fragile as you say we are, we last much longer in time than a car. For instance, I am on the road for more than twenty years, I am in good shape and I am able to function perfectly. Show me please, how many cars of the same age can you count on the road today? if you cannot find them, look for them, do you know where? in the garbage! A new car, well preserved, without being used even one single day, after fifteen or even ten years, has no value if you want to sell it, even if it is in perfect condition. The first question for its evaluation is of what year is the car. If the answer is fifteen years or close to this number of years, nobody wants to waste time to inspect it. But a new bicycle after the same number of years has the same value, nobody asks about the age, only about the condition. Well, now it is clear that at least in this regard, we the "fragile" are much more resistant in time than the cars, so robust! Therefore there are two aspects about our "fragility", true?

— It is true what you are saying, responded a very timid bicycle, thanks for your reasoning which gives us a very tonic perspective.

— My sisters, it was heard again the voice of the defending bicycle, in support of what I said before, I want to finalize, following with my point number six which is the last one. We had talked a lot about our difficult life in cities as they are at present, but all was related to the cars as the only responsible for all our difficulties. According with the story presented by our friend the journalist, all this difficulties will disappear when the cars as our enemies, will disappear. True? Nothing is farther from reality.

— What do you mean? hurried the journalist.

— I mean that, talking about enemies, we the bicycles have three of them in our daily life. The cars, or how it was clarified before, better said the motorized traffic, is one of them, clearly the most dangerous one but not always an enemy, and paradoxically, an enemy with which, in principle, perhaps one day in the future, it is possible to reach an agreement, I don't know now how, but in principle it is possible. With the other two enemies, unfortunately, no agreement and even no dialogue is and will ever be possible. One of these enemies is the unfavorable climate conditions as rain, snow, ice on the road, wind, fog, many times combined with the darkness of the night, or on the other hand, with too much sun and heat during the summer. The other enemy is the difference in elevation in the city, the streets with steep slopes too difficult for us. Against these enemies, which in many places and occasions prevent us from circulating, the white lines on the pavement are of no use, even in a festive day when there are no cars in the streets.

— What you are saying makes lots of sense, but of what help are for us the urban planners with their white lines? asked with indignation a bicycle.

— Of no help, was the quick answer of another bicycle.

— Your explanation is very precise and impossible to be ignored, intervened other bicycle from the audience, but in this case, what is the solution for us?

— Frankly, I don't know, responded calmly the defender, but what is for sure is that the policy of white lines and nothing else, for us is closer to a farce than to be of any help.

The story of the Cuban bicycle.

A robust bicycle, with one single speed, signaled that she wanted to talk and without wasting time, she started:

— I want to confirm what our friend defender just said, with a vivid and relevant example. I am from a very nice and interesting country in many aspects but of a special interest in what concerns the development of the utilitarian cycling. My country is Cuba where few years ago a bicycle in the streets of Havana was a rare thing, usually lost among a multitude of cars and trucks. The human beings treated us as Cinderella, without love and without respect. When I think about those days from today's perspective, I cannot restrain myself from smiling at the irony of life! How everything changed in a way simply unimaginable in such a short time! For sure this is a unique story in the world and in the history of bicycles. Soon after the fall of the Soviet Union followed the crisis of imported oil, with devastating effects for the entire motorized population: cars, buses, trucks, motorcycles. For the urban transportation this was a real disaster. Then, Fidel thought about us and he decided that we were the solution for saving the fatherland from a general and imminent economic crisis. The decision was taken to replace the cars and buses the great majority of which were paralyzed, with us, the bicycles. A policy of massive immigration of our sisters from China was put in place very rapidly and therefore today there are hundreds of thousands of bicycles in the streets of Havana and other places and this number is growing fast everyday. Suddenly we were transformed as by magic, from Cinderella into the Queen of the road. In an incredible short period, our force and usefulness were demonstrated with total clarity and eloquence. Today we are the Number One in the urban transportation in a country not only without cycling tradition like Holland in Europe or China in Asia but the opposite, with a strong tradition in copying the North American style of living, meaning to move around essentially in cars. Now the streets are silent and the air is clean, the contamination of the environment was reduced dramatically.

All the bicycles were listening with great interest to this story so original, and after a short pause the Cuban bicycle continued:
— These are the good news. Unfortunately, there is also very sad news. Although the motorized transport was reduced to a minimum

and the number of bicycles increased to a level, which corresponds to the last part of our journalist dream, the number of accidents between the bicycles and the remaining cars, with very many fatal cases for us, increased also in an unexpected manner. And I want to underline that those accidents occurred not during a war against the cars to conquer the city streets, as the very optimist journalist suggested, but during a period of peace, after the cars were forced out of the streets not by bicycles but because of lack of gasoline. It is easy to imagine how would be the situation in normal conditions. This is one aspect. Now, after our victory against the cars obtained so easily, due not to us but to the decision of Fidel and to the lack of gas, we have problems with the other two enemies about which the sister defender spoke. There are streets with slopes steep enough to make it difficult for us to go up and not without danger going down, and during the rainy season it is difficult to travel long distances. The same can be said when it is too much sun. But with these enemies we cannot fight, we must put up with them. This is what I wanted to tell you. Thanks a lot for your attention.

— Thanks to you, our sister from Cuba for such interesting information, said a bicycle.

— I also thank you, added the defender.

So happened that the very close neighbour of the Cuban bicycle was a sportive one with twelve speeds, of a nice blue color with some special bags attached behind the saddle, signaling that she is prepared to travel long distance. Looking with sympathy at her attractive but not so modern neighbour, she started to talk immediately after the defender said her last word.

— I agree with all what the two sisters have said, the defender and the Cuban, and I can confirm that the same difficulties for us are present not only in countries with scarce economic resources or with a special situation as in Cuba but also in countries well developed. I am from Canada, a country with lots of gas and many cars. Always where and when there are many cars there is a permanent danger for accidents for us, and how our defender sister commented, totally independently of traffic conditions, in many cities we have problems with the differences in elevation and with weather conditions. There are many months with rain, snow and wind, and when this is combined with streets with steep slopes, there is not a great pleasure to travel. When this is further combined with the intensive motorized traffic, it is better to stay home.

A roar of approval followed this conclusion of the Canadian bicycle. Afterwards, she continued:

— I remember very well the Sunday of nine of June, one thousand nine hundred and ninety one, when I participated at a cycling event in Toronto, the largest city in my country. The event in which ten thousand bicycles participated, was organized in a large section of the Don Valley highway, in the East side of the city. In that day the car traffic was closed completely and all six-car lanes were reserved exclusively for us, the bicycles. But do not imagine even for a moment that the authorities closed the car traffic, even for a few hours, because of their love for bicycles, no, this happened only because the highway was closed for that weekend for repairs and a businessman decided to use that occasion and the bicycles for fund raising for a humanitarian cause, at least theoretically, surely with a benefit for the organizers. But this is a secondary matter. What I want to say is that, in that summer Sunday so nice, with a blue sky above us and without any other mode of transportation around, not even pedestrians, it seemed that all the conditions for traveling by bicycle were ideal.

It seemed, and this was so but only in the first part of the trip, in the flat section of the highway. The first hill to climb diminished rapidly the speed of advancing and the initial enthusiasm. The descend that followed was of much help for the moral of cyclists and for the confidence in our strength. But this didn't last for long. All was lost when climbing the second hill, longer and with a steeper slope. Few of us, with a terrible effort arrived at the top, all others stopped much before, to be more precise, this happened between Eglinton Avenue and York Mills Avenue at the top. This experience was the proof of our limitations, of that we were not created for climbing slopes except when they are very moderate. In this we cannot compete in any way with the cars. But in a flat street we are wonderful. Understanding this truth means to be realistic.

After other pause, probably necessary to come back from that past time to the present, she continued:
— I can imagine how difficult would be to go to work everyday in these conditions, and if it is possible to eliminate the cars from the street by decree, or assuming that ten thousand bicycles can force out a car from the street, what can a decree, or ten thousand bicycles do against a street with a steep slope? Really, the difference in elevation to climb, the steep slopes, is a powerful enemy with which is not possible to negotiate. It is true, our friend the defender is so right when she says that the cars, or better to say the motorized traffic, is not our only enemy, certainly the most dangerous but perhaps not the most powerful neither the most inevitable. It can be easily understood what happens to us when these two enemies unite against us, moreover in combination with the third enemy about which our sister, the defender, spoke, sometimes the unfavorable weather. For all these reasons, there are relatively few bicycles and plenty of cars in the street. But I am sure that there are so many people who would like to travel in the city using the bicycle instead of the car. If somebody could change the natural conditions and those of the motorized traffic, I am sure that we will be in more demand . . . . finished talking the Canadian bicycle dreaming about a miracle for bicycles in the future.

The fourth enemy. The amusing story of the bicycle from Jamaica.

— Don't be so sure, was the immediate reaction of a bicycle until then quiet, the human beings are so many times, or may be functionally stupid, that at least I, cannot expect much from them. I agree completely with everything that was said here about the three enemies of ours, the motorized traffic, the slopes and the unfavorable weather but I want to mention other enemy, also very powerful, and it is the mentality of the human beings related to us, more precisely, of many of them. I lived in Kingston, the capital of Jamaica for many years and I know, by my own experience, all the dangers connected with the motorized traffic, which is terrible there, and all the natural difficulties as very many streets with slopes, the rainy season, but there is also, perhaps in this country more than in other places, a very disgraceful attitude of many human beings towards us. The bicycle is considered the transportation mode for the poorest of the poor and the car is not only a mode of transportation but firstly a symbol of class, of social status. I remember some situations, comic and embarrassing but significant for exemplifying this attitude. I would like to present to you these situations, but to understand them well it would be necessary a little more of your time.

— Doesn't matter, go ahead, was the collective answer of the bicycles.

— Thanks, in this case listen to me. My cyclist is an engineer from Canada who worked for several years in Kingston. He is white. This is important because in the local philosophy, to be white means to be rich, and if one is rich, the only mode of transportation acceptable to the society is the car, and not a cheap one, the more expensive and newer, the better, and even better is a luxurious one. The most frequent question when talking about a person not known by the interlocutor is "What car is he driving?"

We lived at that time in an apartment at fifteen minutes of pedaling to the beautiful Botanical Garden and almost each Sunday morning we went there to exercise and go around on the quite lanes without being scared by the cars and trucks. Coming back home, we always stopped at a fruit stand from where we bought a slice of fresh watermelon. The vendor, a very kind man, knew us well and served us immediately very nicely. In a weekend, maybe one year later, my cyclist couldn't go to the Garden on Sunday and decided to go on Saturday but because of the motorized traffic more intensive in the street, he chose to use his big car and with me well installed on the rack behind, we went up to the parking lot at the entrance to the Botanical Garden. Everything was as usual and when returning home, as before, we stopped at the fruit stand in front of the same vendor. He came close to the car to take the order and when he recognized my cyclist seated in the car, as his valuable client, a very happy and natural smile appeared on his face and he exclaimed with amazement and satisfaction that could not be hidden: "Ah, you have a car also! How nice!" He was happy that his permanent client was not a poor who traveled by bicycle only because he didn't have a car. I can imagine what a total confusion was before in his head, how come this white, who obviously is an intellectual, a professional, is so poor that doesn't have a car. I, as witnessing this scene, felt immediately very humiliated for all previous times when we stopped there only the two of us, my cyclist and myself. And who knows, I thought after, how many others had the same impression. This embarrassing feeling lasted until next week. On Sunday we stopped as usual to buy the slice of watermelon and I felt directly that the same smile and consideration were addressed not only to my cyclist but to me too. I wasn't anymore a poor one transporting a poor man, but a rich bicycle, very special, transporting maybe an eccentric, but an eccentric with a big car, and not a poor one. Since that day, I recognize that I have a feeling of envy mixed with a feeling of respect for the car of my cyclist but only for him, and on other hand, he never puts me in danger and he is good to me. I am not afraid of him, because he could be dangerous for me only if both of us travel on the same street at the same time but this never occurs. When I am on the road with my cyclist, he is parked in front of the house, when he is on the road, I am in the house. But I am very scared by other cars and certainly the same happens with all other cars and bicycles. It is a very interesting relationship and I would be so happy, and for sure all of us would be, if a solution without confrontation were possible.

— What an interesting story! said rapidly a bicycle utilizing a short pause after the last word of the speaking bicycle. Continue please, our sister from Jamaica.
— This is exactly my intention! replied the Jamaican, kindly smiling. Other example of prejudice. In one of the nice summer afternoons, during a short ride in the quiet streets in an area of middle class, when we were passing in front of a house with a garden, I heard a girl of eight or ten years standing at the gate suddenly shouting: "Mammy come fast to see a white man on a bicycle!" I leave the conclusion of the exclamation of this little, innocent girl, to you.

Other time, meeting a colleague from work on the street, my cyclist stopped to have a chat with her. During the conversation, she asked about a book. My cyclist said that he has it and he could bring it in one hour and asked if there is where to park the car. She said no, but that is a parking place farther on the street.
— Then I will come by bicycle, said my cyclist.
— No, don't come by bicycle, protested without delay the colleague.
— Why? asked surprised my cyclist
— Because is not possible! What will my neighbors say if they see that I have a visitor coming to my house on a bicycle!
This response came as a shock to both of us, my cyclist and me. An abysmal difference of mentality was discovered in a few words.

— Very well, answered my cyclist and shortly after, we came home. My cyclist didn't leave the house neither with me nor with the car.

— This is all, concluded the Jamaican. Don't you think that this mentality is also a powerful enemy of us?

— Certainly, exclaimed at the same time a group of bicycles.

— Without any doubt, said others convincingly.

— Many thanks for your contribution to this discussion, sounded the voice of the defender. I spoke about three enemies thinking of physical enemies, which can be seen, touched or felt, as a car, the rain, a street with slope, the wind, but really, the enemy number four, the insane mentality, exists although cannot be seen or touched and I have to say that, without exaggeration, this enemy may be more difficult to fight than the others, because great and frightening can be many times the stupidity of these human creatures.

What the bicycles think about the intelligence of the human beings.

This reflexion generated an avalanche of comments and thoughts not much favorable to the human beings. And unfortunately for them, it seems that very many if not all of these comments and conclusions are invincible arguments, the result of the careful observation and silent, well documented study during a long period of time.

— I am of the opinion, started to comment a bicycle, that we don't have to be surprised by all these problems, which in fact are created by the human beings. If our life is so difficult and very many times so dangerous, they are responsible. If our potential, which is so great and could be utilized in such a valuable manner in their very society, is not utilized, it is their fault. But, being realist, what can we expect from them? They are a very primitive species, inferior to many animals, the behavior of which is only instinctive but much more logical, if it can be said so, and for sure inferior to us, the bicycles. There are many examples to prove this! They, the human beings which pretend to be intelligent, rational and of high morality, kill each other not only in isolated cases in the streets or in their houses, but also in large numbers, by millions, in organized actions called wars. This never occurred in the whole history of bicycles or in the life of animals of the same species. Also, they use drugs, get drunk with alcohol and after become violent and do not know anymore what are doing, they are wasting an immense quantity of valuable resources to destroy their own environment. Also, these creatures smoke.

— This is not true, interrupted a sportive bicycle of blue color, probably suffering of spirit of instantaneous contradiction, only the chimneys and the old locomotives smoke because they eat carbon and petroleum and burn them for living, the human beings eat other things.

— In this regard you are right, but you do not know everything because you are very young. How many kilometers do you have?

— I have two thousand kilometers.

— Well, I have more than forty thousand. I traveled much and I know well the world from close and from far away and I tell you that yes, there are many human being which smoke exactly as you said very well, as chimneys and old locomotives, destroying little by little themselves in this way and making sick others around them. I see that you don't understand what means that these creatures smoke. Let's me explain to you.

— Please, said with a more humble tone, the blue bicycle.

— They put dry plants called tobacco, in paper tubes, which they put with one end in their mouth and set fire to the other end, inhaling in their lungs all the toxic fumes. In our mentality of simple bicycles such an action is unimaginable, it is like putting ourselves sand in the bearings of our wheels instead of fine oil. I wonder if there is any bicycle that thinks that the same human beings care about us, the bicycles, and will create better conditions for us and for them with the same action. I don't believe it.

— Yes, there is not much intelligence in these human beings. The cars that they use in an increasing number each year, are not only the worse enemies of us, the bicycles, when we travel in the same streets but also in very many cases, the enemies of the human beings. However, they continue to use them like maniacs, intervened in the discussion a bicycle with much experience in the street. She continued:

— I remember that accident caused by a car when I was seriously hurt and almost lost one wheel. Fortunately, a good mechanic repaired me well and now I can function without problems. But my poor cyclist, who is very careful, fell and was hurt in many places. He was transported in emergency to a repair shop for human beings which is called hospital and there the mechanics for them who are called doctors, repaired him during two weeks. Definitely, we, the bicycles and the cars in the same streets are a very dangerous mixture. It is so bad that we don't have our own ways where we could travel safely, we are always like Cinderella, always as a very poor relative without rights in the big family of transportation modes! And what is sadder is that there isn't any hope for a better life.

It seems that all the bicycles became sad thinking about what the bicycle with a big life experience just said. For a while nobody interrupted the absolute silence. Finally, a bicycle decided to express her opinions about the dangers of urban life:

— It is true that we have problems with natural causes, I remember for instance, when a friend of mine was destroyed, poor one, years ago, by a wall, which fell on her during an earthquake, but the great majority of accidents are caused by the human beings.

— My friend, said a bicycle of a nice green color, equipped with many accessories for security on the road, all that the sister who spoke before me said, is true. It is clear that we in our daily activity are evidently superior to the human beings in general, with the exceptions mentioned before. But I would like to ask, in the real life, in the present circumstances in the cities around the entire world, what can be practically done for us, the bicycles?

— How other sister said well before, we are not at home anywhere, neither in the street with cars nor on the sidewalk with the pedestrians because with our speed of travelling, which is very good in cities, we do not have any space for our community of bicycles and we cannot have common interests with any other community which moves, be it motorized or pedestrian. We travel four or five times or even seven times faster than the pedestrians but in no way we can compete with cars in their legal speed limits in the city streets.

A brief pause followed and the bicycle continued her idea sad enough by its realism.

— In these conditions it is clear that the cars represent a permanent danger for us and we represent a nuisance for cars and pedestrians, a frequent danger or at least an annoyance for the pedestrians if we join them or meet them in any place. This is the reality, our bad fate. Listening to all what other sisters had said here, I don't know what can be done differently than to live with this reality and taking all the precautions for avoiding or reducing the chance of an accident.

Followed other short pause with the audience very silent, during which the speaker looked far—off in time and far away in distance and it seemed without anything good to see, only a gloomy future. Later, the same bicycle continued:

— It is very, very sad because of this bad luck and I myself become sad when I think about it but what can we do? This is what it is! Well, it seems that we talked enough about our situation and it is the time to go home.

The presentation of the concept of the Bicycle Expressway System by the bicycle from Morelia.

The tiredness and the disappointment after this prolonged discussion with sad results, offered at that moment a very adequate condition for the suggestion of going home and the bicycles prepared themselves for leaving, when suddenly, the voice of a bicycle was heard in a manner which demanded attention. That bicycle, probably a stranger to the city, was there totally silent from the beginning of the discussion.

— Sisters bicycles, she said, I would like to ask all of you if you could listen to me for a while. I listened very carefully to all the bicycles, which have spoken before. I am from Morelia and I have some good news for all of you.

— From where? was the immediate question by some bicycles.

— From Morelia, was the response of the speaker.

— From Morelia? repeated astonished in a choir more than ten bicycles. I never heard about this city, said one of them.

— Neither have I, said other one.

— But if you say that you are from Morelia, I can believe that such a city exists. However, I don't think that there are many bicycles there. Anyway, I think that at least some of us would like to hear what you intend to say from your city of Morelia, was the invitation of a bicycle that two minutes before didn't know anything about the existence of Morelia.

— The city of Morelia, of Mexico, started the Morelian bicycle following the invitation to talk, is a very old city, with many narrow streets, historical monuments, with a pleasant climate and more than a million inhabitants but not well known in other countries, and for bicycles possibly that it is not known at all even in Mexico. The life there for us, the few bicycles that travel in the city is terrible, in permanent danger because of the motorized traffic extremely heavy, lots of noise and very polluted air. It is really difficult to breath and hear. There are many mini-buses called "colectivos" which in reality are cans of sardines for people and the fare is very high and raising. By all means, it is not recommended to travel by bicycle in this city, which has also big differences in elevation between its various parts. And there are rainy months also. And all this is combined for making life for us, the poor bicycles, almost impossible.

The words of this bicycle were received with much interest and with a feeling of sadness and compassion, in spite of the fact that there are many similar cases well known in many parts of the world. After a few moments, a bicycle interrupted the silence.

— Well, in this case, about what good news for us, the bicycles, did you talk?

— There will be built a fatherland for bicycles.

— A what? asked a bicycle who sincerely thought that didn't hear well.

— A fatherland for bicycles as doesn't exist anywhere in the world, repeated untroubled the Morelian bicycle.

— Listen to me, our friend from Morelia, replied a bicycle, which due to her age and her interesting ideas expressed during the discussion, caught the attention of other bicycles, we all are tired after a day of much traffic on the road and of discussions here, but, if you want to tell us a joke for relaxation from the little known city of Morelia, so be it, we are ready to listen to you. True? she said looking at the other bicycles.

— Yes, yes, yes, was the immediate response by a choir of bicycles, a little bored and ready to have a little of a good time.

— If you expect a joke, I must tell you that you will be disappointed. What I am saying, may be incredible, but it is the pure truth.

A silence what could be a mixture of confusion and real interest, landed over the entire convention of bicycles. It was clear that the Morelian bicycle was received with seriousness and none of the very many bicycles wanted to interrupt the silence.

The Morelian started to talk in a manner that excluded immediately whatever interpretation of joke.

— At present there is a well-advanced plan for building in Morelia a system of expressways only for bicycles, that means a network, which will cover the entire city, with a distance of about one kilometer between the expressways. All the expressways will be elevated at a minimum of five meters above the level of the street, will be covered for protection against the unfavorable weather and will be accessible by escalators to avoid the difficulty of pedaling uphill placed in numerous points of the city. For the same reason, escalators will be installed inside the system in places where are differences in elevation. Consequently, all the expressways are horizontal or with descending slope. All the motorized and pedestrian traffic is left in the streets below and only the bicycles circulate within the system. There are no intersections at the same level between expressways going in different directions. They will be interconnected by ramps for descending and escalators for going up. In these conditions, signs or lights for stopping are not necessary and a non-stop trip will be possible, the bicycles being able to reach their maximal safe speed. There is always a one-way direction for circulation, different levels for opposite directions or a fence between the two directions. In these conditions, traffic accidents within the system of bicycle expressways will be practically impossible to happen. Moreover, in case of a flat tire or other reasons for which one of us cannot function, there is an emergency lane in each direction for each expressway. Also, there is permanent supervision by television cameras and for whatever unpredictable cases there are telephones for emergencies. In many points of the bicycle expressways system, specially in places of general interest as commercial centers, movie theatres, museums, libraries, congested zones with much traffic in the street and other places of interest, there are parking and service stations (PSS). These stations are platforms also covered, at a second level that can be reached directly from the expressway, by escalators. Here there is parking for hundreds and hundreds of bicycles, a restaurant with fast service for hundreds of cyclists, a place for resting or for admiring the landscape, telephones, washrooms, stands where one can buy fruits, vegetables and food to take out and repair shops for us. It is possible to park the bicycle in the PSS and to go out by elevator in the street. Coming back, the cyclist takes his bicycle and goes down by a ramp directly in the expressway, to continue his trip. With these PSS is possible to park hundreds, and if necessary thousands of bicycles, in the most congested areas of the city, where not even one car can be parked.

— With this system in operation, continued the Morelian in absolute silence of the audience, it will be necessary for us to circulate in streets with mixed traffic only for a few hundred meters before entering and after exiting from the system, up to home or other destination and only in secondary streets with much less traffic.

— My sisters, continued the Morelian, well aware of the tremendous effect of her words, conceived in this way, the bicycle expressways system will be the safest, the cheapest, the healthiest and the fastest and most convenient mode of urban transportation for the great majority of residents. The immediate result of the implementation of the system will be a dramatic reduction in the number of traffic accidents, of the noise and air pollution and a great saving of energy and money. With these savings, the cost of the system can be recuperated in a few years.

— My friends, concluded the Morelian, this is the story and the news that I wanted to share with you. I don't know exactly when the system will be built but I hope that soon enough. Then I invite all of you to pedal to Morelia for experimenting with your own wheels this marvelous system, the best dream, I am sure about this, of all the bicycles of this world.

The Morelian finished talking but for a while the audience continued to be silent as transported to the future by such marvelous dream as the very system the bicycle from Morelia talked about with such a precision and confidence.

The enormous difference between the quality of the present everyday life for bicycles and the quality of life presented by the visitor from Morelia generated, a few moments later, an enthusiasm little common for the very silent nature of the bicycles. Finally, a very insisting voice addressed the Morelian:

— Ah, our dear from Morelia, tell us please, how all this happened? Is this a miracle? And why in Morelia? Why all this occurred exactly in Morelia, where as you explained, there are few bicycles and the conditions of life for bicycles are so miserable? asked a very young bicycle which seemed to have no more that one thousand kilometers of age, but very intelligent for this short life distance.

— And other question, she continued, how this incredible and magnificent achievement can be connected with the talk we had here before about the very low quality of the human beings, who for sure will be the ones to build the system you talked about?

No question could have been more interesting because a roar of approval signaled that other bicycles were very much preoccupied by the same issues. A total silence, so real that almost could be touched with the pedal, was established when the Morelian started talking.

— I prefer to start with my answer to the second question, because in this way it will be easier to respond to the first question.

— Well, continued the Morelian, after a short pause, it would be the greatest error to put all human beings in the same basket. Among them and their level of intelligence there is an enormous variety and a distance comparable with the distance from our planet to the sun. It is necessary to understand that truly the great majority of human beings belong to an inferior species, and each day there are many proofs and examples of this, anywhere in the world. But there is also, how it was mentioned before here, a minority of them who are beings extremely intelligent, they are the visionaries who move ahead the science, the technology and well-being of the society, and in direct connection with this, the well-being of us, the bicycles. This minority, without any doubt, is our only and very great hope and support. Regarding the first question, about Morelia, well, this is a very interesting story in itself. Truly it seems to be a miracle, but miracles do not exist. I can say that was a very favorable coincidence combined with inspiration, well, and good luck if you want . . . .

— Whose inspiration?, jumped from her place the same bicycle with a curiosity characteristic for her youth.

— Listen to me please, I didn't finish talking, and I will tell you exactly this, responded in a soft manner the bicycle from Morelia, a little flattered by this unexpected interest from all the bicycles. And she continued her story.

— In the last month of the last year came to visit Morelia and some friends from there, a civil engineer and amateur cyclist, the author and promoter of the bicycle expressway system concept. He was very impressed by the terrible situation of the urban transportation and by the air and noise pollution in the streets of Morelia, by the bad luck of the city residents living day after day in those conditions without any possibility or hope for improvement.

By a lucky coincidence of circumstances, as I mentioned before, he met and got involved with a group of engineers, businessmen and politicians, some of them friends of his friends, which understood immediately the importance and the great advantages of the proposed system. In a very short time, without debate, an unanimous consensus was reached that this system will be excellent, of very much use for Morelia and they supported him seriously in the very difficult task of getting the approval of the authorities and the acceptance of the investors.

The promotion of the concept in Morelia was not in the plans of the engineer before going there. This was a surprise for himself and he decided to use this opportunity. He stayed in Morelia much more time than initially anticipated, dedicating it to this purpose. Based on the maps that he bought in the local shops and on his own observations during the many trips in the city, he prepared a plan in due detail for the bicycle expressway system proposed for Morelia. Working until late at night and with the help of his dictionary, he prepared a documentation including calculations, to demonstrate the economic efficiency of the proposed project. With this material he could explain in a very clear and convincing manner the proposed system during the presentations and official meetings with the municipal and governmental authorities, as with the President of Municipality of Morelia, The Secretary of the Government of the State, engineers, planners and clerks involved. The basic idea of the concept generated much interest and discussions and at the end an agreement in principle was achieved. However, some financial and formality problems according to the local bureaucracy remained to be solved later. As the engineer couldn't stay longer in Morelia, it was decided that the engineer from Morelia and his company will continue to be in touch with the authorities and also with the engineer, author of the concept. Let's hope that now the road is open and that the construction of the system will move ahead without problems. This is the explanation for the apparent "miracle" for the bicycles of Morelia, finished talking the Morelian.

— Now all is clear and I am very happy for you and for our sisters from Morelia, exclaimed a robust bicycle which was far from the speaker. This is to say that during the reunion, the audience of bicycles increased considerably.

— I am happy not only for you and the Morelian sisters but also for the very many other sisters from other cities suffering so much now, because I am absolutely sure that if the system of expressways for us is implemented in Morelia, in short time, this marvelous system will be copied and realized in numerous, and finally, in all cities presently with traffic congestion and air pollution problems and without doubt in my city also. I am from Brazil, from Rio de Janeiro, and now there only the crazy ones and the heroes travel by bicycle in the streets; in what I am concerned, I don't know exactly where is the demarcation line between these two categories.

— A question, please, it was heard the voice of a bicycle who, judging by her appearance, paying much attention to the details, one can assume that she is a student of precise science.

— I am listening to you, exclaimed the Morelian.

— It is a detail, but for my own curiosity, you said that the engineer helped himself with a dictionary for preparing the documentation in Morelia, true?

— True.

— But why? In Morelia, which is part of Mexico as you say, the human beings speak Spanish; the engineer doesn't speak the language? From where is he?

— It is a detail what you are asking, responded the Morelian, but I think that it is a significant detail and it is my pleasure to satisfy your curiosity and probably of others too. He learned Spanish by himself and speaks the language well enough but he is not perfect at this and he knows it. He is from Canada. He went there from Europe, many years ago.

— Many thanks, my friend.

— You are welcome.

— Canada? What and where is Canada? I heard about Europe but nothing about Canada, intervened in the discussion a very young bicycle, probably from a remote place where there are not many possibilities to get information, specially at her distance of life of no more than five or six hundred kilometers.

The Morelian bicycle smiled and continued:

— Canada is a very large country in North America, which is considered rich and developed, with many natural resources, clean, with many cars and with many bicycles also. Unfortunately, our Canadian sisters have the same bad luck as we have here, few of them circulate in the streets jointly with the motorized vehicles and in those cases always with a great risk.

— And why then this engineer from Canada doesn't build bicycle expressways in Canada first?

— Ehe, what a valuable question! exclaimed suddenly a modern and elegant bicycle with twelve speeds, not willing to loose the occasion of being the first one in answering this question. For sure, she was waiting for it and caught it as a lioness catches its prey.

— The answer to your question is nothing more that other proof of the abysmal inferiority of the intellect of the human beings, at least in comparison with us, the bicycles. Due to this inferiority and intellectual deficiency, they do totally absurd things, things against their very basic own interests, in doesn't matter what part of the world. Let me please, explain to you why the proposed bicycle expressway system was not constructed first in Canada from where the engineer innovator is, as it seems absolutely normal and reasonable. I am myself from Canada and know very well the situation there.

The interest of the bicycles present at this reunion raised again to a peak and the attention of all, concentrated on the Canadian bicycle.

— There is much to talk about this, continued the Canadian but I will make this story as short as possible. Listen carefully in order to understand well what happens to us in this country, which the human beings consider to be very developed. Well, because these human beings in this country as in other countries also, cannot govern themselves they have a procedure called "voting" or "elections" which happens every four years when they vote, what means that they choose some of them called "politicians" to think and take decisions for them and solve their problems. These politicians are grouped in organizations called "parties". Well, now look what happens. Because there is a very big competition between the politicians and between political parties, to be elected they promise to everybody the most wonderful things. Immediately after the elections, the politicians which must solve the problems of the human beings which elected them a little before, as improving the economy, the standard of living, to reduce the crime, the unemployment, the pollution of the environment, the congestion of urban traffic and many others, these politicians elected yesterday, today they forget completely these tasks and concentrate to enjoy their own advantages and to solve their own problems and those of their relatives and friends.

What the bicycles think about the social organization of the human beings.

No one of them knows anything about the economy of the country, they don't have any control over the economic and social processes and developments, but all of them pretend and lie in such a way that the mass of human beings believes them. There are frequent cases of robbery at high level as fraud and bribery, and when they are discovered, there always are ways to avoid the punishment following the principle that hands wash each other. For this reason, very many deplorable cases and situations do not change or they become worse.

— All this is so true! and I ask myself how could be otherwise when the economy, presently so complicated is managed not by specialists, experts in the respective field which should be at the top of the pyramid, but by politicians nominated "ministers" which are in very many cases illiterate in the respective compartment and these ministers have the power of final decision, the last word. So for instance, I remember that years ago, a politician was nominated Minister of Agriculture in the Federal Government of Canada, himself being a lawyer. After a few years in this position, in which at least he could learn something about agriculture, he was nominated Minister of Health. What could he know in health matters better than so many specialists with tens of years of experience in medicine and health, he as a lawyer with experience not in agriculture but only as Minister of Agriculture? And the joke, which is not a joke, doesn't stop here. After another few years, for some political reason within the Government, the same lawyer was nominated, not more and no less than Minister of National Defense. It frightens me the idea of what would happen if next day the country was attacked and the minister should take decisions of supreme importance to save the fatherland! And this case is not unique; there are many similar examples.

The same bicycle continued:
— The social organization of these creatures is so stupid that during the four years until the next elections, nobody can do anything to these elected politicians. This period of time is enough for the human beings to forget totally that exactly the same situation, which they don't like today, occurred in the last period with the opposition party, which they rejected in the previous elections. Forgetting the past they will elect the same rejected party again instead of the present ruling party. But not to be concerned about their bad luck, they will be reelected again in the next elections for the same cause: the human stupidity. And this play is repeated and repeated again without stopping since the first elections more than a century ago. Meanwhile, in all this time, with all the speeches and political actions, elections, voting, changes of governments and of ministers, programs and promises, no one, I repeat, no one politician or political party, it means no one human being was capable to solve gradually or in a radical manner, the grave problems of the human beings in this society of theirs which is entitled democratic, to eradicate the poverty, the unemployment, the drugs, the crime and the robbery which occur each day in so many places.

After several moments of reflection and uninterrupted silence, the Canadian bicycle continued:
— Can you imagine that some times, when the car traffic in the street is so dangerous that my cyclist decides to pedal me on the sidewalk where many times are only few pedestrians, he should pay attention not only to these few pedestrians but also to the human beings homeless, sleeping on the sidewalk. They are not drunk, no, simply they do not have a house, do not have a place where to sleep, and this happens also in the main streets, at the base of the

very rich houses or buildings where other human beings have more bedrooms than they can use.

— But how is this possible? asked a very intrigued bicycle, when the same persons were children and were at school, they lived in a house or in an apartment. What happened so that suddenly they don't have anything and must sleep in the street? I don't understand, how this can be explained?

— It can be explained very simply and you will understand. In the human beings society, as it is organized, the essential element, vital, is money; if you don't have money, you don't have anything including a house or apartment. To obtain money, it is necessary to work, usually as employed by a business owner. In their social organization, the human beings have the right to vote every four years but don't have the right to work. This essential condition for everyday life depends totally on the relations with your employer, of the will, desire or mood of this employer, of the situation in the market in a chaotic economy and on other circumstances which do not depend of the poor employed. So, he can be laid off, lose his work at any time, sometimes with a two weeks or a month notice. Since that moment there is no more salary but the rent for his house, apartment or even room must be paid. It is good if the respective previously employed has some reserve of money, let's assume for several more months, that is too much for many of them. What happens after the money is finished? He gets a notification from the owner of the house or apartment with a grace period how it is said, for another month after which follows the forced eviction from his place. The situation turns desperate, and if there isn't a friend or a relative to help, the only alternative is the street.

This is a disaster but not a natural disaster as an earthquake, which cannot be prevented or fought with, is a social disaster specific to this inferior species caused by the same organization of the society of the human beings where the security for the day of tomorrow is only a dream for the great, great majority. The reality is the law of the jungle.

And so the human beings homeless sleep there in the street, with the noise of cars, some of them luxurious, passing at great speed, driven by other human beings rushing to go to their spacious houses, or at least simply houses where one can sleep in a bed, paying no attention and many times not seeing or not willing to know about the very existence of those other poor human beings. Now you understand why there are thousands and thousands of human beings sleeping in the street?

— Yes, I understand very well and it is extremely sad that such a situation is real.

— And all this occurs for so many years that can be considered a permanent situation, normal or acceptable, in front of the eyes of the authorities controlled directly by the politicians elected by the human beings. And what makes the situation more sad and repugnant is that instead of protesting to the politicians against this humiliating reality for the society, many of the human beings in better economic situation come with arrogant and senseless explanations trying to justify the situation to be at peace with themselves, accusing not the politicians but the poor ones sleeping in the street as lazy who do not want to work or do not look enough for work, as drug addicts, drunken and beings without willpower.

With their narrow minds they do not understand that those human beings became desperate, being the victims of the society that function in a grotesque manner.

And to complete the general impression about the way how the human beings are organized in their society, think about that there are millions of human beings unemployed, who cannot find work, for instance for building houses and other many things so much necessary, and the social and political organization of the human beings cannot do anything for changing the situation and avoiding in a very simple way the human poverty and degradation.

— But when there is a need on one hand and the necessary work force available on the other hand, the intelligence of a chicken or a goat will be enough for putting the two together and solving the problem! interrupted a bicycle belonging to the large group for which the elementary and invincible logic is the normal mode of thinking.

— Evidently it is so, responded the Canadian, but the human beings in their biological evolution didn't reach yet that level. In our superior bicycle mentality, if we were human beings we would not accept in our society, doesn't matter in what community and circumstances, not even one single member homeless and unemployed. I want to say that even one single such case in an entire nation or country of hundreds of millions, will be too much and unacceptable. The society has the obligation to create the necessary conditions for avoiding by all means such even one single case, how the mothers and the fathers are preoccupied for their children. But this would happen if we, the bicycles, were human beings or at least responsible for them.

— It is very impressing what you are saying, intervened a bicycle of a conservative model with only three speeds but with the appearance of an experienced traveller with many kilometers of age, I am from England and I travelled a lot in almost all countries of Europe and I can say that, with the respective variations, the situation is similar, even in the richest countries of Europe.

— If you want to see of what are capable the human beings in creating and perpetuating their own misery, please visit India and other countries of Asia, added a bicycle traveller from those places.

— I am from the United States of America, a country considered very rich but in spite of this, I can confirm that there are millions of cases of the situation presented here by you, our sister from Canada. Meanwhile, I would like to ask you why you tell us all this, why you are so interested in the fate of these human creatures?

— I said all this, answered the Canadian, because it has a direct connection with us, the bicycles. Understanding the situation of the human beings, which depends so much of the decisions of their politicians and how these politicians behave with their own human beings, we will understand better our bad luck, which depends also of these politicians. They, the politicians, always travel in big cars and never on bicycles, and because of this they are not interested in the existing conditions in the streets for us and support the construction of new highways for cars but do not pay any attention to this marvelous project for bicycle expressways. More than this, they are hypocrites. To show that they do something for bicycles too, they nominated some very young clerks in a committee paid by the municipality, to represent the interests of the cyclists of the city. So, for instance, in Toronto, the largest city in Canada with two and a half million inhabitants, according to the statistics, there are about one million bicycles but with few cyclists in the street using the bicycle for transporting themselves in the city in a regular manner because of the omnipresent danger and the inconvenience of travelling by bicycle of what we were talking here before.

The story about what happened at the Toronto City Cycling Committee and the help of the ministries.

So, the great majority of bicycles are little used and only for travelling on Sundays in parks or short occasional rides in the streets. At the same time, very many of the residents are potential utilitarian cyclists who would become active cyclists immediately after the adequate conditions for us are created.

These youngsters of the group named "City Cycling Committee" who must represent the major interests of the cyclists, are not elected and controlled by the cyclists of the city but nominated by the bureaucratic administration of the municipality and how we will see immediately, they proved that they represent only themselves and not the city cyclists and their interests. These youngsters do not understand anything about the real problems and needs of the cyclists and do nothing really necessary for the promotion of the mass utilitarian cycling. The limit of the imagination of these bureaucratic clerks is the planning of separating lines with white paint on the asphalt, which gives only a false sense of security as it was mentioned very well here by other sisters. And this was done only in very few of the existing streets.

— I am from the city of Toronto also, intervened in the discussion other Canadian bicycle, and I can tell you with specific examples, what stupid and ineffective is this policy of white lines. When you have the occasion to be in Toronto, you will be able to verify it. And the same bicycle continued:

— It was decided to introduce in one of the main city streets named "College" a separate lane for us, immediately close to the sidewalk. To do this, the parking spaces for cars existing in the same place, must be cancelled. After the scandal with the automobilists and the shop owners in front of these parking spaces who were losing clients who couldn't park there anymore, the parking places were restored and the bicycle lanes removed. To avoid the same situation in the future, on other street called "Beverley" close to College Street, the human creatures of that cycling committee installed the lane, in their opinion for security, exactly between the space reserved for car parking next to the sidewalk and the lane for the cars in traffic. In this way, the cyclist using this "secure" lane could be most probably the victim of an accident when the passengers of the parked cars open the door or when to avoid this, the cyclist gets out of this very narrow lane and moves a little to the left. In this case, he will enter the lane for cars immediately at the left of the lane for bicycles, where the cars travel in full legal speed or more. It is clear that in this situation there is danger of a fatal accident for the cyclist and for our poor sister involved in such an accident.

— Thanks for your information so relevant, commented the first Canadian, and there are many other examples with similar conclusions showing the value of the activity of that official committee and what we can expect from the members of that committee which, as was said before, does not represent anybody except itself. However, being an official committee, part of the administration of the municipality, the Canadian engineer contacted it proposing his concept for improving in a radical manner the cycling conditions in the city. A presentation of the concept and of the plan proposed for the city of Toronto was agreed upon in one of the committee meetings, two months later. The intention of the engineer was to obtain the approval of the committee as a first step in the direction of project implementation.

— And what happened? Why the project was not built immediately after the approval by that cycling committee? asked a young bicycle with little patience for the bureaucracy and for what happens in the real life between an idea and its realization in practice.

— But how do you know that the project was approved by the committee? responded the Canadian with other question.

— Couldn't be other way, although the members of the committee were stupid as you say, still it is a cycling committee and I don't think that they were so stupid to not approve such a project which supports cycling more than whatever other action of the committee. For this, I asked the question.

— I understand perfectly your logic but it seems to me that you will feel the same consternation that I felt when you find out the reality. And after a short pause she continued:

— If in that committee were we, the bicycles, the result of the meeting would be for sure the beginning of a concentrated action, powerful and very fast for supporting the brilliant proposal of that visionary engineer, such a valued friend of ours. Together with him we would fight until we convince the authorities to participate in this grandiose project and to construct it as rapidly and as soon as possible. As representatives of the cycling interests, of all other bicycles in the city, this proposal would be an emergency program Number One and for sure we would pay all the attention to the presentation made by the engineer. This scenario would be the reality of that meeting if, as I said before, the decision would be in the power of our wheels. Unfortunately, the decision of which we are talking about was not in our wheels but in the hands of them, the human beings which proved so many times to be nothing else than imbecile creatures.

Just imagine please, what happened in that committee meeting. It is very interesting and important that all the bicycles know it. One day in the future, this event will be well related in the history of the cycling development and everybody knows that without us there is not cycling.

The interest of the audience of bicycles was again raised to a peak.

— Well, continued the Canadian, in the agenda of the meeting were programmed for the discussion of the committee some problems of minor and local importance which, we must say, in fact reflects exactly not only the real activity of the committee but also its maximal capacity of thinking.
No one of the problems or subjects discussed could compare with the importance of the project presented by the engineer. But if it is possible to imagine, each of these problems were discussed during an hour or more; for one of them, they wasted almost two hours but for the presentation of the bicycle expressway concept, only half an hour was assigned, twenty minutes for the presentation and ten minutes for questions. All was nothing more than a bureaucratic formality to be able to report that attention was paid to this issue too. It was a parody and nothing else, probably without bad intention but generated by the lack of capacity of the members of the committee to understand the major and essential importance of the project for the immediate future of cycling and the difference between items of minor importance and those evidently essential. To exemplify this, here are some of the comments made during that meeting and after,

in the letter sent to the engineer by which he was informed that the committee analyzed but did not approved the proposed concept for the city of Toronto.

The voice of the Canadian bicycle and the general tone of her words gave the sure impression not only that she is very well informed about what happened at the meeting at the Toronto City Cycling Committee but also that she knew well the hard conditions of life for bicycles in the country, in Canada, and that she was very compassionate about it. It is a great probability that this reunion of bicycles represents her first occasion to talk about her strong grievance to an audience which understands and is sensitive to it. There is no doubt that she was very decided not to miss this occasion but to use it in full. It can be said that this was a very fortunate coincidence because the interest of all bicycles to listen to her story was obvious and at the same time a welcomed and well-deserved reward for the Canadian bicycle. After a few seconds break, she continued talking with the conviction of an expert lawyer dedicated to defend a public cause of major importance.

— A member of the committee declared that he doesn't agree with the proposal for the bicycle expressways because in the expressways, being elevated above the street level, covered and always with one way for the bicycle traffic, the cyclists cannot change the direction of their movement according to their own impulse.

— I don't understand, interrupted a bicycle, what he wanted to say by changing the direction according to his impulse?

— Sure that you don't understand, because you are a bicycle and he is only a human being, and as this was not bad enough, he is also a member of the cycling committee of the municipality of Toronto. I didn't understand initially either and when I did, I couldn't believe the explanation, but everything is true, there is an official document about this, it is written very clearly in the letter that I mentioned before.

— Unbelievable, exclaimed the same bicycle. And what the engineer answered?

— He didn't have time to answer because immediately other member of the committee jumped to express its rejection, this time because the difference in temperature inside and outside of the system, for which cause he said, probably concentrating all the strength of his intelligence, the cyclists will have to change their clothes when entering and exiting the system.

Before the engineer could say one word, other creature of the committee, a youngster with appearance of a vagabond, presented his valuable intellectual contribution as an enemy of the bicycles saying rapidly in a few words that the proposed system is very expensive and because of this he doesn't agree. The engineer asked him immediately if he had the opportunity to make any economic calculations and if he compared the cost for the bicycle expressways with the cost of expressways for cars, the highways. "No, but this is my opinion" he answered.

When the engineer started to demonstrate the invalidity of the presented arguments by the members of the committee, the moderator of the meeting interrupted him and stopped his further explanation with the excuse that the available time for presenting his proposal is finished. Immediately after, the committee passed at the following point of the agenda, dedicated to the problem of improving the conditions for the bicycle traffic at a specific intersection in the city, by increasing the radius of the curve at the corner. The members of the committee discussed with much preoccupation during more than an hour this important issue.

A sad silence, if it is possible to say so, reflecting the consternation of all the bicycles, occurred. For sure one could win a bet that all of them were thinking in what incapable and directly enemy hands, although without a premeditated intention, but judging by the result of the action, it is now the fate of the sisters of Toronto. It was also clear that the damage caused by the human creatures of the cycling committee of Toronto was not limited at the quality of life for the bicycles of Toronto because a triumph, a success there would mean a similar triumph, a success shortly after, for the sisters of many other cities in the entire world; and opposite, killing or postponing such a success in Toronto means the same for the fate of such a good project in many other cities.

Without any doubt, it was very difficult for the sane mentality of bicycles to understand how was possible to concentrate such a great foolishness in such a short time, in just a few minutes reserved for comments and questions. This was by all means, a national record, at least, established by that cycling committee. The association with the word "cycling" is nothing less than a grave insult for the very notion of cycling, when associated with the activity and the decisions of that committee.

Together with the sadness for the fate of the project promoted by the engineer, was the feeling of compassion for him personally, for his fight for a great, logical cause and, without doubt, for his frustration. A bicycle with many travelled kilometers, with orderly appearance, expressed this mixed feeling. She asked:

— And what happened at the end with the concept, with the engineer and his marvelous idea, everything was lost after that infamous meeting?

— Ah my friend, you are rushing, responded the Canadian, the end wasn't so close, there are many things that occurred after that meeting that you named very appropriately, infamous. If it was an end, this was the end of the prestige and importance of the committee for the engineer and he decided to respond with a letter, in detail, to all points, and to continue the promotion of the concept, simply forgetting and avoiding the committee which, in a fraudulent manner entitled itself as cyclist.

— Bravo! Bravo! Bravo! exclaimed suddenly a choir of bicycles.

— Ole! Ole! got enthusiastic others, a little more bellicose.

It seems that the related intention of the engineer to continue the promotion of his concept even without the support of the committee, what should be so normal and expected, was a very welcomed tonic for the moral of many bicycles. Many, but not all, because not few of them had the moral always up and even combative. One of these said with self-confidence:

— However, I would like to come back to what was said here by our Canadian sister about the reason for rejection of the proposed concept, by that member of the committee who wanted to have the possibility to change the direction of his movement following his impulse. My question for our Canadian sister is if there isn't there an exaggeration or a misinterpretation of the affirmation, and if all is correct, may be that was the personal opinion of that committee member, but was not the official and final position of the committee.

— I can appreciate the preoccupation of our sister for the truth and authenticity, but unfortunately, everything is true and the position of the committee was very clearly presented, exactly so, in the official letter of the committee received by the engineer, everything can be verified.

— In this case, continued the same bicycle, how one with clear mind can imagine that it is possible to change the direction of his movement in a public road in the existing traffic conditions well known to everybody, in an instant manner, or how said that committee member, following his own impulse? Would he have the boldness to do this when he travels by bicycle in a street with traffic? Or when he drives a car in the highway? What will he do in such a situation if he would like to change the direction? If he is not absolutely crazy, he will go up to the first secure place, or exit from the highway and only then he will change the direction. Moreover, if he travels in a bus, train or plane, can he change his direction immediately, whenever he wants, or must travel up to the first station or stop? Why then he puts such conditions evidently impossible for the system of bicycle expressways? Is there an intention to sabotage a plan so valuable for improving the conditions for cycling? In this case for what reason? Or it is a case of mental deficiency, so common to human beings, especially when facing major problems or visionary solutions and decisions?

— I think that he qualifies perfectly in this category, intervened a bicycle very close to the speaker.

— There is no doubt that this is his case, added other bicycle, but I would like to know what the engineer responded in his letter to the cycling committee about this point.

— Exactly as the comment of the sister talking before you.

— What a coincidence! Exclaimed the same bicycle.

— It is not a coincidence, responded again the Canadian bicycle, it is the logic, the crushing logic, which is the nature of thinking of all of us, the bicycles, and fortunately of some rare human beings as our engineer.

— My sisters, got involved in the discussion a very robust bicycle, look at me, I am in very good shape but I am not so young, just imagine, I lived more than one hundred thousand kilometers and I travelled in many places including Toronto and other cities in Canada. For this reason I would like to comment about the opinion expressed by the second committee member who said that the cyclists would need to change their clothes every time they enter or exit the bicycle expressways, because of the difference in temperature. Well, I can say that in all my life, as I said, of more than one hundred thousand kilometers, in hot and cold countries, I didn't hear a bigger foolishness than this, excepting the opinion of the first member of the committee, that with the change of direction following the impulse.

A wave of laughter propagated in the mass of bicycles from its center in all directions up to the most remote bicycles.

— When I was in Toronto for the first time, in the summer, she continued, in very hot days, and after that in winter, when there is very cold, sometimes in our trips my cyclist decided to take the subway to avoid the dangerous traffic congestion, specially when is dark. There the bicycles are allowed to use the subway out of peak hours. What is good in those trains is that in the hot period there is air-conditioned and during the winter when there is a terrible cold outside, the temperature inside is as in your house. The same happens with the buses. Sometimes the difference in temperature between outside and inside is of forty degrees. My cyclist was in good shape and in many days hot or cold, we used the streets in combination with the subway. In none of these occasions I have seen anybody changing the clothes when taking the bus or when entering or exiting the subway. In the bicycle expressways, which will not have air-conditioned because is not necessary; the difference of temperature between interior and exterior will be much reduced. Why then that second member of the committee assumes that only the cyclists using the proposed system must change their clothes and doesn't ask himself why other millions of passengers don't do the same thing in conditions more unfavorable from point of view of the difference in temperature?

— For the same reasons as the first committee member, the same category of poor mind and being a member of the same committee, jumped with the answer a bicycle close to the speaker.

— Dear friend, said the bicycle which visited Toronto addressing the Canadian bicycle, may I assume that my opinion about the words of the second committee member is not much different from the response of the engineer in his letter to the committee?

— You can be sure, not only assume, that the same response was written in that letter.

— And I know, it is not a coincidence but the same invincible logic which reflects the reality.

— Exactly so, answered the Canadian.

— How interesting, observed a bicycle parked very close, at a pedal distance of the speaking bicycle, two sources of observation, interpretation and thinking so different, the engineer and us, the bicycles, and the same conclusion. This make me feel even more confident, I have the feeling that we are not alone in our aspiration for a better life. I am delighted.

— We also are, exclaimed in unison the bicycles of an entire group, and we have very good reasons for this.

— Our friend and sister from Canada, started to talk other bicycle from the same group, a light bicycle of a nice green color as the grass in the spring, and known as a speaker for that group, as a representative of our numerous group of bicycles, I would like to ask you if it will be too much to suggest that you continue to tell us what happened after that meeting at the Toronto Cycling Committee. It is such an interesting story and you know a lot! Please, if it is not difficult for you to tell us what else occurred, our group is very interested to listen to you.

— Oye! Oye! Exclaimed some bicycles parked in various places in the same moment when the speaking bicycle finished, and addressing her, one of these bicycles said, protesting:

— Well, do you think that only the bicycles from your group are interested to listen the continuation of the story? And we who are not in your group? We also want to know everything about this project. It is too bad that we cannot help for its implementation but at least all of us have the desire to know what happened and what is going on with the promotion of this marvelous and very necessary concept. We are bicycles and not human beings, got a little nervous the bicycle.

— Ah, dear friend, I didn't want to offend you, you know that, I could talk only on behalf of our group and not on behalf of all who are here, I would be very happy if all of us are interested in this story.

— Very well, peace and friendship, replied smiling the other one.

The tumultuous choir of approval that followed this conversation was undoubtedly a vote of confidence for the Canadian bicycle to continue her story. Therefore, she started talking without delay and without showing her profound satisfaction for the so high interest of the audience.

— Dear sisters, do you know what is the difference between genius and stupidity?

This question took the audience unprepared and the response was a roar of confusion, not because the bicycles couldn't give various correct answers but because they had the feeling that the Canadian expected a special response. After several seconds, to end the confusion, the Canadian bicycle continued:
— Well, the main difference between genius and stupidity is that the genius has limits.

A general laughter acclaimed the superiority of the stupidity over the genius in what concerns the limits.

— This saying or proverb, she continued, is reflected very well in the history of the promotion of the concept for the bicycle expressways. If anyone of you thinks that the stupidity in this case was limited to those members of cycling committee who spoke at that meeting, then she is too optimistic. The letter expressing the official position of the Toronto City Cycling Committee is full of foolishness, including that mentioned at the committee meeting.
After the engineer found out that there was no hope in the committee for the support of his concept, he contacted the municipal authorities, the ministries of the province of Ontario of which Toronto is the capital, the Ministry of Transportation, the Ministry of Energy, the Ministry of Environment, the Ministry of Health, the Ministry of Sports and Recreation and the Ministry of Industry and Commerce. The engineer solicited financial support for the preparation of a feasibility study and the governmental support for the promotion of the concept up to the approval and the implementation of the project.

— And what happened with those ministries? asked a bicycle who didn't have the patience to wait until the end of what the Canadian was saying.

— Happened exactly nothing. Nothing, except some meetings, an exchange of letters in which each minister or clerk in a high position of the respective ministry, expressed the opinion that, although the proposed concept is very good, original, innovative, and other positive things, it is necessary that other ministry takes the initiative to organize the inter-ministerial support and then the respective ministry will consider its participation. It was recommended that would be better if the Ministry of Transportation of the Province of Ontario was the leader of this action.

The story about how the concept of the Bicycle Expressway Systems was born and developed.

When the engineer contacted the Ministry of Transportation, the response was that the concept has an undisputable merit but the Ministry doesn't have the money for such a large project, not even for a feasibility study. The engineer argued that a large amount of money is wasted each year, each month and each day for the existing urban transportation and that this occurs exactly because the bicycle expressway system is not built. Such a system could save all this money and with this saving, the cost of the system will be recovered in a few years. Moreover, he added, with the system in operation, thousands and thousands of traffic accidents will be avoided, many of them fatal, many others ending up in life invalidity, which in addition of being a painful human tragedy, cost a lot of money.

When the engineer realized that by talking to a wall he could obtain better results than with these human beings, he tried to obtain a meeting with the Minister of Transportation himself. Although the engineer talked before with other ministers, this minister excused himself, communicating to him that due to his very busy schedule the meeting was not possible at this time, what translating from diplomatic language in current language, means never. In a letter signed by the minister he assured him in the same diplomatic language, that the Ministry will analyze the proposal in connection with other important aspects as the security, environment, tourism and economy and that soon the results of this analysis will be communicated. Translating in the real language, it signifies that the minister will never do anything for this unique project.

— Excuse me please, interrupted a very young bicycle, I don't understand well what do you mean by the diplomatic language, is it a language as the English, French or Spanish, which the human beings speak? I know that they cannot communicate and understand each other in a unique language as we, the bicycles can understand each other in our single language for bicycles from all parts of the world, because a bicycle is fundamentally a bicycle in all countries and places in the world. I know also that for instance in Mexico the human beings speak Spanish but in Toronto they speak English. Is the diplomatic another language spoken there also?

The Canadian couldn't hide a smile very close from an explosive laughter, which she forced to stop. When she could control herself, she answered:

— My dear, your innocent question amused me a lot. Let me explain to you. You think as a true bicycle with such a healthy mentality but it is obvious that due to your youth, you didn't have the occasion to be in touch with many human beings, especially with politicians and others, which are in charge of the society of the human beings. The reality is that we depend for our basic needs of the human beings and they, because of their stupidity, depend totally on these leaders of the political and economic life, which very frequently use, as I said, the diplomatic language.

— This is true, at least in what concerns me, I live in the countryside and my cyclist is a farmer with little relations with others. He is always very direct and clear in what he says and he speaks with his family and others only in English. But what is the diplomatic language? rushed the young one.

— I will respond to your question immediately but before this I would like to make a short digression about the languages of the human beings. Just look, we are in this world much less than two centuries, practically for approximately one century. Our modern history since when we imposed ourselves in the world as such a valuable mode of transportation, can be counted in a few decades. In this short time we achieved such a high level of development that can be said without exaggeration, that we are close to perfection, it will be extremely difficult to invent or to find a real improvement for the modern bicycle. There are a number of sizes and models, which are strictly functional, and we do not need each year other model, how the human beings do uselessly with their cars, and this is done by those who sell the cars to grab more money from those who buy them.

All the bicycles were listening with much attention and she continued:
— Our way of living, functioning and communicating among us is based on harmony, truth, sincerity, and reciprocal respect. In our bicycle communities, in whatever place of the world, we live in peace and tranquility, in a happy manner in our relationship with other bicycles, never do anything bad to any other of us, neither to the environment, neither to animals, neither to this species very inferior to us, the human beings, neither to our direct enemies, the cars. We never take anything from other bicycle, never, in all our history was a single case when a bicycle robbed or killed other bicycle. Not only that we do not have any interest in such an action but because of our high morality, simply we cannot even think about this neither to understand such a way of thinking. We do not have religion to separate us in different or enemy groups as happens so often with the human beings. Also, we do not have different countries

for different groups of us to divide us with national and nationalistic feelings, how only the human beings have. When a bicycle says that she is English, French, Russian or Canadian, she simply means that the human beings from that place or territory call themselves English, French, Russians or Canadians, respectively.

For all these reasons, always when we talk among us, even if sometimes there is a difference in opinions, we never lie, we always speak in a direct manner, truthfully, without the necessity or the intention to hide what we intend to say. For the same reasons, we use our unique language, which any other bicycle in the world understands without translation and without interpretation that could be different of what we want or we do not want to say when we talk.

Looking around and being sure that all the bicycles listen to her with much interest, the Canadian continued:

— Now, we come back to the human beings, with their politicians, antagonistic interests, internal fights for the domination of ones over the others. Very many times this fight degenerates in bloody actions, individual, local or with mass character, worse than between the most ferocious animals known. Many other times the domination or the fights for the personal interests, for instance for maintaining the political or administrative position, takes place without an open fight but by diverting the attention of the human beings involved in the dispute. And this is done by using the language named diplomatic. It is not a language but a way, a manner of talking without saying anything or by hiding with nice words, the reality or the real intentions. It is called diplomatic language because it is used frequently by the diplomats, it means official representatives of one country in another country. Many times when the human beings from one country are preparing themselves for war against the human beings of other country, the first ones send their diplomats to assure the other ones about their peaceful intentions.

— Now I understand perfectly what you wanted to say, many thanks for your explanation so clear and detailed, said the young bicycle.

— In our case, continued the Canadian, with the promotion of the bicycle expressway concept, the ministers and other clerks in high positions, have also other tactics for doing nothing and wasting the time. This tactics much used in many many occasions is to delegate to a subordinate to take the decisions. The subordinate, in many cases the deputy minister, copies the example of his boss and passes the problem to his subordinate, a general director or a director of a department. That director, as the other ones above or below him, doesn't understand the problem and doesn't have the time to examine it being busy with a multitude of minor problems passes it to his own subordinate, probably a chief of a group of two, three or several clerks. Following the same procedure, the letter from the engineer and the attached documentation sent to the minister, which is supposed to have the competence and the decision power for such a large and important project, goes down the administrative ladder to be analyzed by the last available clerk in the hierarchy of the ministry, regardless if this one has the vision and necessary understanding for the magnitude of the matter. As he is stupid enough for solving the problem passed to him which is now in his hands, but not so stupid to recognize this to his boss, he keeps the documentation in his office for a while to give the impression that it is studied with proper attention, and at the end he writes his recommendation which will end up being the conclusion of the Ministry, in an official form. Here he had the choice of two alternatives. The first alternative was to try to understand well the proposed concept, supporting it and recommending to go ahead with the project. But in this alternative he would have to take a decision without way back, to participate in the responsibility for a giant project, involving enormous investments, to take the risk, as the engineer author of the concept, to fight against the inertia in thinking of many others, and what is the most important, of his own bosses. He should demonstrate to all those, and possibly to his minister, the value and the validity of the project, because he knows very well that all the bosses including the minister, rely one on another and he is at the base. How much work! How much responsibility! The peacefulness of today in his office will disappear and the salary will be the same, most probably. In the second alternative, it will be necessary to compose a response of one or no more of two pages, courteously passing the problem to the future, or at least, to other authorities. If necessary, always is possible to invoke some conservative reasons connected with the novelty of the idea, also with the financial difficulties always available, avoiding a formal confrontation. And, he thinks, if some of his bosses would like to change the decision, very well, that boss will take the responsibility.

Unfortunately, everything occurred according to the second alternative and no one intermediate boss up to the minister changed anything in order to help with the promotion of the project. The minister signed the letter, probably without reading it, and sent it to the engineer. And this was the contribution of the ministry for a project, which could change and improve in a radical manner the urban transportation, saving many lives and material resources. This is the typical case for all the interested ministries or which should be interested in this concept, which were contacted by the engineer.

— But, protested a bicycle very indignant by the manner in which projects so important are treated in those organizations of the human beings called ministries, why the ministers of those important ministries, which are supposed to be leaders and visionaries, don't take such an important issue in their own hands in order to avoid to judge with the heads of their subordinates?

— Because what is supposed to be doesn't occur. This situation is another proof of the intellectual incapacity of the great majority of human beings, independently of their position in their society. It is obvious that this project represents a task for which they are not capable. They don't have vision or the capacity to understand the importance of all the problems to be solved by the proposed concept and they are not at the level of their responsibility simply because they can't. There is no other credible explanation.

— And the same thing happened with all ministries assumed to be interested in this project? asked the junior bicycle.

— The same, with some local variations. There are conclusive examples to demonstrate this. So, in his relations with the Ministry of Transportation, the engineer contacted initially and had discussions with officials much below the top of the ministerial pyramid and had an exchange of letters with some of them. Well, after a while, when the engineer received the letter with the response from the very top of the pyramid, he noticed that some entire phrases were the same as in the letter received before, from the official at a much lower level. What does that mean?

— It is obvious that the one seated at the top used not only the opinion of that seated at the base but his words also. It is possible also that the official from the base even prepared the letter signed by the minister, and in order not to waste much time, simply copied some phrases from his previous correspondence, expressed without delay her judgment a bicycle with inclination for detective cases, and the same continued with her verdict:

— Well, it could be a coincidence, but the possibility for such an alternative is so low, that I don't believe that this is the case. Our Canadian sister is right.

— This is one case. Other case, which proves an incredible superficiality of the treatment at the level of minister and of deputy minister, refers to the Ministry of Health of the Province of Ontario. The engineer sent a two pages letter explaining briefly but in a very clear manner, the advantages of the proposed concept for the health of the population, for the perspective of dramatic reduction in the number of traffic accidents, and in direct connection with this aspect, the significant amount of money saved by the Ministry and which will be available for the public health. For these reasons, underlined the engineer, the Ministry of Health should be very interested in the implementation of the proposed bicycle expressway system concept, and therefore it will be very good, even for the specific interest of the ministry, to join other interested ministries, for the faster and more efficient promotion of the concept.

— Was this request of the engineer clear enough and well justified? asked the Canadian bicycle.

— Very clear and very well justified, was the response of a choir of several tens of bicycles.

— Well, and what do you think was the response of the Deputy Minister in the letter to the engineer?

— We want to know, was the immediate answer of other bicycles.

— He gave to the engineer the very precious information that the Ministry of Health deals with the problems of health and the Ministry of Transportation deals with the roads and for this reason the letter of the engineer was sent to the Deputy Minister of Transportation. The very short response letter ended with thanks to the engineer for presenting the issue to the Ministry of Health.

The strong sound of the bell of a far parked bicycle signaled her impatience to speak.

— I think that if the story with this Ministry of Health is not a joke, then it is clear that the signatory of the letter on behalf of the ministry is nothing less than an idiot.

— With one objection, added other bicycle, may be that he or she is only illiterate and couldn't read the letter sent by the engineer to the Minister.

— In such a case, intervened the Canadian bicycle, would be an illiterate of a special category because the letter was signed by a lady with the title of Doctor in Philosophy and Executive Director. Moreover, she mentioned in her letter that she received the task to respond to the engineer directly on behalf of the Minister of Health. And I can confirm that is not a joke, the letter exists, it can be verified.

— What an interesting story, commented amused, other bicycle.

— In this case, continued the same, the situation complicates with other alternatives, as follows:

— the first alternative: the lady Minister of Health is also illiterate and couldn't read the letter of the engineer. To solve her problem, she passed the letter to her subordinate, the lady Executive Director and Doctor in Philosophy, obviously without any indication because she didn't know what the letter from the engineer was about.

— the second alternative: the lady Minister is not illiterate, she could read the letter but didn't because, and here are some sub-alternatives, was lazy, at least in that day, or is not used to read her correspondence, or always she solves the problems using the heads of her subordinates, in this case a lady subordinate.

— the third alternative: the lady Minister read the letter but didn't understand a thing and therefore didn't know which indications were appropriate.

— the forth alternative: the lady Minister read the letter, understood it well, and gave the adequate indications to her subordinate, Executive Director and Doctor in Philosophy, but she, the Executive Director didn't understand anything what her Minister was talking about and passed the problem to the Ministry of Transportation, to the other lady there, the Deputy Minister.

— the fifth alternative: the lady Minister of Health is not very preoccupied with the public health, doesn't have the necessary vision for such an innovative concept and moreover, doesn't understand the direct interest of her ministry in the promotion of this project. In other words, this case is a clear proof that a human being, although being nominated minister and charged with the respective responsibilities, is not able to take, in very many situations, intelligent decisions, simply because her level of intelligence is very low. The same explanation is applicable also to her subordinate who in order to give the impression of activity when she didn't want to do anything, used the diplomatic language of which we spoke before.

— Although all the presented alternatives in such a precise and gracious manner by our friend are possible, it seems to me that the last one, the fifth alternative is more probable, expressed her opinion other participant in the discussion.

— I can imagine how surprised was the engineer when he received the letter with this response, a model of human stupidity, completed the young one.

— He responded to that letter with sarcasm, directly to the lady Minister, explaining again the purpose and the content of his first letter, adding a copy of the response received from her subordinate and suggesting to the Minister to re-examine her position, make it clear the Canadian bicycle.

— And what was the result of this second letter?

— A total silence, said the Canadian.

— What a pity! What a shame! commented with indignation a neighbor bicycle, just look if the Minister of Health would be in charge of other ministries also, or would be responsible for vital problems of the country, of any country, what disasters we could expect.

— Don't worry, the situation in almost all countries is not very far from such an end. And in what concerns the project for the expressways for us, the other ministries which were essential for the project, contacted by the engineer, put themselves in the same category, in some place between the stupidity and the indifference of the Ministry of Transportation and the idiocy of the Ministry of Health.

— Tell us please, what happened at other ministries, insisted a bicycle from the audience, with the general approval of other bicycles.

— Well, in the Ministry of Environment, which should be profoundly interested in this project, at least for its own benefit, the procedure from the Ministry of Transportation was repeated but in a worse manner. The letter and the documentation sent by the engineer to the Minister were automatically passed to the Deputy Minister, and as he was in vacation, the material was sent to the deputy of the deputy, or to the deputy of the Deputy Minister, a general director. Without thinking much this deputy of deputy sent the documentation to a director, probably his deputy. Naturally, the director passed the problem to the other director and this director passed it to a subordinate, who, how it was proven two weeks later, understood the documentation less than a baby would understand, prepared a response so stupid that could serve as a recommendation to be adopted in the famous cycling committee of the city.

Naturally and automatically also, the letter with the respective observations did a vertical trip in opposite direction, it was signed without problems by the general director and sent to the engineer.

— I can imagine the disappointment of the engineer, commented with sadness in her voice a bicycle.
— For sure that the engineer was not happy with this answer, but as a veteran soldier in the fight with all the categories of stupid, bureaucrats and idiots, he didn't waste his time and sent to the director general a detailed complaint against the author of the response, suggesting that he should be replaced with other person better qualified to analyze the documentation and to respond to his letter.
— Very well, I like this decisive action of the engineer independently of the response of the ministry, commented with indignation a bicycle.
— If the engineer acted in this hard manner, I assume that he was very disturbed by something very inadequate contained in the response received from that clerk. Can you give as some details about this?
— Certainly, why not? responded the Canadian. The engineer sent his initial letter to the ministry with the very clear purpose to solicit financial help for a feasibility study in which to analyze all pertinent problems as the civil engineering, the transportation, costs and economic efficiency and many other aspects.

In his response letter to the engineer, the director general didn't make any personal comment, he only said in exactly two lines and one word that a letter with the observations of one of his subalterns is attached. That letter, full of irresponsible affirmations, an example of incompetence and stupidity, was addressed and sent, to the astonishment of the engineer, directly to an organization of the Federal Government of Canada, which tried to help with the promotion of the concept and its first stage: the feasibility study. This letter was signed only by that inept clerk before contacting the engineer in order to clarify the issues. A copy of that letter was sent also to the Ministry of Transportation.

— So, in this manner the two important organizations were completely misinformed by that clerk, without the knowledge of the engineer, observed immediately a bicycle.

— Exactly.

— But it would be so simple, logic, rational for the clerk in charge with the issue, to contact and ask the engineer, for his own information and only after that, if necessary, to send his letters to other organizations, true?

— It is true but is obvious that the clerk was neither logic nor rational.

— Very well, agreed that the incompetence of the clerk was obvious, but where was the elementary internal discipline of the ministry? The response to a letter must be sent to the initial sender and not to a third part without the agreement, even without the knowledge of the sender, in this case the engineer.

— By all means, this case proofs that the human beings of that ministry were not familiar with such an elementary discipline. But, what did the engineer in those circumstances?

— To counteract this malicious action, the engineer was obligated to contact the persons to whom the letter of the clerk was sent and to explain the situation and the incompetence of the author of that letter. At the end everything was correctly understood, but nonetheless it was a very embarrassing situation that could have been avoided.

— Now I would like to answer to the previous question of one of our sisters about the content of the letter, I would say about the foolishness included in the letter signed by the clerk and sent without the supervision or approval of his superiors.

— Very well, we are listening to you, this foolishness is very interesting for us for having fun, the only source for this are the human beings, we, the bicycles, are not capable for such a thing.

— And in what is concerned the supervision by the superiors to check the letter send by the clerk, it seems that doesn't make any difference, added other bicycle, they don't change anything even if they read the letter, because they don't understand anything, they are superiors only by their position in the hierarchy of the ministry. This was proved in the cases of other ministries and also in the case of the Ministry of Environment itself, in which the contribution of the director general was limited to those two lines and one word to inform the engineer that the comment and the evaluation of the concept was in the attached letter signed by his subaltern.

— Probably that to pass the issue to his subaltern was the limit of his capacity and competence.

— Not probably but for sure, completed the Canadian. This was also the conclusion of the engineer after a meeting with the Director General, following the story with the letters. And now I will tell you what the clerk understood about the expressways for us, which was approved without knowing, by the Director General.

— We are listening with much curiosity, said some bicycles.

— The clerk started his letter with his precious advice that before constructing the proposed system, it is necessary to prepare a technical-economic analysis and a feasibility study. Although this is an obvious truth, the clerk didn't know that the technical-economic analysis is an integral part of the feasibility study. After other banalities, he continued saying that the feasibility study should be paid by the interested parties. What an extraordinary discovery! He discovered also that the cost of the construction will be recuperated not initially but after a while; this truth is elementary for everybody and didn't require an official response. And now comes the most interesting part, his personal contribution, saying without explaining that the Ministry of Environment is not interested in this project and that the cyclists will be afraid to use the expressways because they will be elevated above the level of the street and that the pillars sustaining the expressways, pillars built not in the street space but on the sidewalks, will cause accidents because the cars will hit them, and that in winter the expressways will be impracticable because the bicycles will bring snow inside.

— What an idiot! got nervous some bicycles at the same time, doesn't he know that a tremendous number of cars, trains, trucks and bicycles travel every day on very many bridges everywhere in the world, many times elevated at a height much bigger than the height proposed for the bicycle expressways?

— And for what reason he assumes, intervened other bicycle, that the cars will hit only the pillars belonging to the expressways but not the pillars for electric light or the pillars for telephone cables located exactly in the same line on the sidewalks?

— And how does he imagine that the expressways will be impracticable during the winter due to the snow carried inside by the bicycles?

— How much snow can a bicycle carry? How much snow can be put on a bicycle intentionally? And how much of the snow that falls remains on a bicycle in natural conditions during the few minutes of travelling in the street between the house and the closest entrance to the expressway system? And what happens with the snow transported by the pedestrians, who enter a bus or the subway? It is clear that his imagination is very sick.

— And how could he say, argued other bicycle, that the ministry that deals with the environment, which gets worse every day due to the terrible air pollution, is not interested in a project that will reduce in a radical way the air pollution? The clerk of the ministry in charge with the protection and the improvement of the environment, doesn't know that we are absolutely silent in the street and that we don't pollute anything?

— And what responded the engineer to all these false accusations?

— Exactly what you just heard here, responded the Canadian. In a detailed letter of three pages he demonstrated to the Director General the ineptitude of the clerk's judgment and asked for the review of the initial decision.

— Well, and what was the result?

— The result was that during a direct discussion, the director general defended the position of his subaltern without saying anything that is worth to listen to. This director general demonstrated well what is the general value of the intelligence of the human beings.

— How sad for our fate and also for all the efforts of the engineer! commented other bicycle. But it seems to me that you said that the engineer contacted also other ministries and authorities, true?

— True, responded the Canadian and continued:

— Our engineer is a fighter, a combatant, well equipped with all the necessary knowledge for his concept and well informed about the reality of life in all the aspects related to this project. Also he has a rich experience of contacts and discussions with all kinds of people, from very limited and completely stupid bureaucrats to visionaries and people of top level and great intellectual capacity. He was in direct, personal contact with ministers, scientists, highly qualified engineers, clerks and officials in high positions and responsibilities, bankers and top businessmen and investors, politicians of all kind, liars and honest, in various countries including naturally Canada, and so he is not impressed or disarmed by a bureaucrat without the capacity to understand the so valuable advantages of this concept.

I would like to mention in this regard his participation in events as national and international conferences where he was invited to present his concept and the support received in official letters from prominent personalities, articles in main newspapers and technical publications about his concept, in Canada and in other countries and also the speech dedicated entirely to this concept in the Federal Parliament of Canada, on May 7th, 1992. The speech was delivered by a very well known and respected member of the Parliament, one of the few honest politicians with such a valuable and necessary vision for the promotion of the concept. He was of much help also in other occasions. In his speech he explained the necessity of governmental support for this concept and asked for its implementation in Canada without delay.

— It was a talk about us, the bicycles and about this visionary concept in the Federal Parliament of such a large and developed country as Canada? This is a very important and significant event! Intervened immediately and with enthusiasm a bicycle, really deeply moved. And she continued:

— And this is a proof that although such a great majority of human beings think and behave in such a stupid manner, there are human beings which are very intelligent, are visionaries as our engineer and so brave politicians by publicly supporting from such a high level this concept, which is so valuable to us also.

— Very well said. I would like to underline that these human beings are the exceptions, the most valuable ones, and that our engineer is very selective and concentrate his promotional action getting involved only with people of this category. He knows very well that with others it is a waste of time, but those, the others, obligate him many times to waste a precious time without the possibility to avoid this, because many of them have official positions and it is necessary to deal with them for the promotion of the concept. You have heard about the results of the discussions in these cases

— I would like to know more about the activity of our engineer in the promotion of the concept. You, our Canadian sister, know much about this, can you share with us what you know?

— With great pleasure, responded the Canadian, if I may, I will talk briefly about the circumstances in which he started with the idea, developed it later into a complex concept with a solid engineering fundament and economically sustainable. Among other very interesting aspects, it is also an example of long time perseverance, for many years, non-stop.

— Oh, sister, many thanks, all of us are ready to listen.

— Well, began the Canadian bicycle, he is in chronological order, an enthusiast cyclist, an engineer and a resident of Toronto in Canada. He emigrated from Romania to Toronto in 1976 and shortly after was employed as a project engineer in an engineering design company. From the beginning of his life in this new world for him, so different from the one in his country, he noticed, among other things, a very common aspect in Bucharest, his city in Romania, and Toronto in Canada: the urban transportation problem, with the traffic congestion, air pollution, noise in the street, traffic accidents, the very high cost and a tremendous waste of valuable time for millions of residents. This happens specially but not only, in the peak hours. The engineer thought that the bicycle could be of much use for improving in a radical manner the present situation, but the danger of going by bicycle in the streets jointly with the motorized traffic, is the same in Toronto and in Bucharest. He knew that by his own experience because he traveled a lot by bicycle there. He left there two bicycles, one for daily use and a sportive one.

He much desired to explore his new city with its nice parks, also by bicycle and the first thing which entered the apartment he rented, was a bicycle. This happened as follows: in the same day in which he got the apartment, which was unfurnished, he went by bus to a shop to buy the object of first priority, a bed. During the trip, looking out of the window, he saw a bicycle shop. The curiosity and the nostalgia pushed him out of the bus at the first stop and he went to the shop to see what kind of bicycles were there thinking that buying the bed five or ten minutes later doesn't make any difference. The result of this short visit was that he returned to his empty apartment on a very nice bicycle. That night he slept on the floor and the bed was bought next day. After that, he was travelling by bicycle frequently, in the streets around his home, in the parks and also in the very congested avenues, where much attention was required.

— What a nice inspiration! exclaimed a bicycle, continue, please.

— So, in one of those days, after work, he was in a very nice park in an island on the Lake Ontario, at the lower part of the city. Coming back, to reach his apartment, in the central part of the city, he must pedal uphill for a large distance in a street with intensive motorized traffic, and, to make things worse, it started raining. So, our engineer-cyclist had to fight with the three most powerful enemies of the bicycle: uphill slope, motorized traffic and rain, in joint action. He was thinking that could be worse when it becomes dark. He arrived at his apartment a little tired, luckily nothing worse happened.

His cycling experience and engineering spirit drove him to an idea little common, to change the existing situation in the street in a radical manner, to protect the cyclists and their bicycles, by separating them totally from the motorized traffic and pedestrians. How? By creating ways for bicycles only, above the existing streets. Later, this idea developed rapidly in his mind with other inspiration due to his very analytical thinking and to the engineering habit and practice to solve problems. Well, he thought, by building a way only for bicycles totally separated and inaccessible for the motorized vehicles, the most powerful and dangerous enemy, the danger of traffic accidents, is eliminated, but what we do with the rain and the wind? We will cover the entire way for the bicycles with a transparent, sun reflecting material. This is good, he was thinking, other enemy is eliminated. The remaining enemy, the natural topography of the city, the significant differences in elevation between many points of the city, seemed to be unapproachable, but not in the fight with the engineering. For our engineer, looking for a solution means finding it, and he found it. Being a cyclist himself, he didn't need explanations from outside for the problems and the difficulties for the cyclists. This solution will be a little more costly but by all means it pays off. It will transform all the uphill streets in horizontal ones, not less than that!

How? With the help of escalators installed in the points where the slope starts. So, the third enemy was also neutralized. Afterwards, additional improvements completed the initial idea. The intersections of the bicycle ways at the same level were eliminated and so the traffic lights not necessary anymore, were also eliminated. Now the ways for bicycles will intersect at different levels and the necessity to stop at each intersection with the respective waste of time also disappeared and by this, the ways for bicycles are transformed in bicycle expressways in which it is possible to travel non-stop and without danger, long distances with all the convenience.

The idea created a passion in him and detailed calculations and drawings were prepared. Finally, when the engineer was convinced that the concept is efficient, sustainable and of much help for the urban transportation, he asked himself: the idea is very good, but what is its use if I keep it only for myself? His intention was to put it in practice, to build a network or a system of bicycle expressways in whatever large city in the world, preferably Toronto, and afterwards in other cities.

— This is the history of the birth of the concept of Bicycle Expressways. If you so desire, I can continue with the history of promotion of the concept in Canada and other countries.

A roar of approval was the clear response of the entire audience of bicycles and the Canadian continued:
— In parallel with his work in the engineering company, our engineer started to make his idea public, beginning with contacting the cyclist organizations in Toronto and Montreal, in Canada; the idea was published in the magazines edited by these organizations.

Continuation of the promotion of the concept.

In June 1981 the first important success occurred, an ample article was published in "The Toronto Star", a prestigious daily newspaper and one of the most important in Canada. In March 1982 another article with a very positive comment was published, this time in French, in the main daily newspaper of Montreal, "La Presse". In the same month he was invited to present his concept at the Congress of the cyclist organization of Montreal "Le Monde a Biciclette". He speaks French too and his presentation was in French, to be better understood, because in Montreal the main spoken language is French. In the same year, in October, following the first invitation from outside Canada, he presented his concept at the International Conference in Colorado Springs, in the state of Colorado, U.S.A. In the first day of the Conference, a very favorable article by a famous American writer and editor appeared in the daily newspaper "Philadelphia Enquirer" which was of much help for the presentation of the concept at the Conference. The same article was published afterwards in more than one hundred newspapers in all parts of U.S.A.

— I think that this was a very interesting debut for his following promotional activity of the concept in the international arena. I am interested to know, what was the result of this unexpected and very good publicity in the press?
— The response was, true, unexpectedly good and promising. After the publication of this article, the engineer received hundreds and hundreds of letters from all parts of the United States and also from Tokyo, Japan, from where a company for scientific research was very interested in the concept and willing to collaborate for the implementation of a system of bicycle expressways in Tokyo, a very large city, the capital of Japan and in other cities of Japan and Asia. Other organizations and private persons expressed their interest in the concept and asked for more information about this issue. Among

the many other interested organizations I would like to mention the Municipality of Honolulu, the capital of Hawaii and the administration preparing the International Exhibition for Transport in Vancouver, Canada.

In June 1992 he was invited to present his concept at the United Nations Conference on Environment & Development, in Rio de Janeiro, Brazil. His contribution was well appreciated and he received a letter from the Institute of Technology expressing the interest in his concept for the city of Rio de Janeiro. The General Secretary of the Conference, a high level visionary, understood perfectly the great potential advantages of the bicycle expressway system for the cities of the entire world and after the Conference he was of great help for the promotion of the concept.

In 1994 the engineer received a letter of support for the concept from Prince Charles of the royal family of England, a known activist for the improvement of the environment. In the same year, after detailed discussions with representatives of the Government of Jamaica he received an official letter of support for the concept with the mentioned possibility of its implementation in Kingston, the capital of Jamaica; the letter was signed by the Permanent Secretary of the Government.

— What was the practical result of all these very positive responses?, asked a bicycle which doesn't take the nice words as an absolute value if not followed by the respective actions.
— Your question so direct, short and clear makes a lot of sense, but the answer, in order to be also clear and objective, cannot be short. This question is very important and I will take all the necessary time to give the adequate response. But before answering, I would like to say that I can guess that you asked me only the first part of the complete question that you have in mind. The second part, which is also very reasonable, is why an appropriate and immediate action

for the implementation of the concept, which received such a large support, was not the normal response to all this publicity so positive? True?

— Simply you amaze me. This is exactly what I had in my mind, I didn't ask it because I hoped that the answer to the first part of my question would include the answer to the second part.

— Very well, now I will explain why this expectation so logical didn't occur, and how great, gigantic, is the distance in the world of the human beings between a very good idea and its practical realization. In the great majority of cases, almost without exception, the good, innovative ideas belong to a minority, very intelligent but without political or economic power, and those in charge with the economy and who have the governmental power are not open to the good, innovative ideas of the intelligent minority. To implement these good ideas, almost always there is a ferocious fight, which consumes very much energy and time, and how it is said that time is money, the lost time for the promotion translates into a great loss of material resources. In this direction there are many examples in the history of the development of the technology and of great projects, I will mention only four of them.

The first example refers to the installation of the underwater cable for communication between Europe and America, more than a century ago. When this necessity was more pressing every day, twelve years had passed until the project was approved.

The second example. When the inventor of the telephone, Graham Bell, built a valid telephone model and wanted to expand his invention on a large scale, even some of his friends told him that this invention doesn't have practical value and that it is only like a toy to communicate from one room to another in the same house. Years passed until the value of the invention was recognized and the telephone entered the commercial market. Can you imagine how would be the today's world without telephone?

The third example was noticed by our engineer when, after passing in his car on the very famous bridge "The Golden Gate", in San Francisco, California, he stopped to visit a small museum close to the northern end of the bridge. There he found literature about this great project and also a small monument dedicated to this construction and to the author of the concept, the engineer Joseph Strauss. The San Francisco bay with a width of one and a half kilometers caused enormous difficulties for the transportation between the north and south parts of the city. There were only two alternatives: to travel a long distance around the bay or the other alternative, to use the ferry for transportation, which has substantial difficulties in connection with the high tide and the strong waves and because of this, frequently the passage by sea was not possible. This situation continued for many years without any possibility of change. A bridge would be an ideal solution, but this alternative was considered impossible because of the great width of the bay and the impossibility to build intermediate pillars. The water being too deep in the bay, the tide being too high and the strong waves, eliminated the possibility even to think about intermediate pillars. So, the idea of a bridge across the bay remained only a dream. A dream until one day when the visionary and innovative engineer Joseph Strauss was inspired by the genial idea to build the bridge without intermediate pillars with one single opening for the entire distance of almost one and a half kilometers. When the engineer started the promotion of his concept, looking for investors, this was considered no more than foolishness. The engineer persevered and fifteen years later he met a visionary financier, A.P. Giannini, the founder of the Bank of America, who being convinced by the feasibility and the great commercial opportunity of the bridge, decided to invest the necessary money in the project. The construction lasted three years and in 1936 the impressive bridge, the largest in the world, was open for traffic. This bridge, a marvel of engineering, even today is the pride not only of the city of San Francisco or of the State of California but also of the entire country, the United States of America. Now nobody can think about the city of San Francisco without thinking about the bridge. And it was a time when nobody wanted to hear about this bridge; how things change! I think and I have the hope that something similar will happen with the concept of our engineer!

Other example also significant refers to a special astronomic observatory conceived and proposed by a scientist astronomer, of much use for the very precise astronomic observations, which was built forty years later. Forty years!

There are also ideas, projects, proposals of technical, economic and social nature extremely important for the well-being of the society of the human beings, as the solution for the homeless people, unemployment, free medicare for everybody; in the United States at least a quarter of the population is in deadly danger if people get sick and cannot pay the astronomic cost required by the private doctors and hospitals. These issues are discussed and discussed for decades without any result because of the adverse interests of those who control the society.

All this means that a good idea doesn't include automatically the guarantee that it will be realized or that it will be realized without delay. This is the way the human beings operate. Remember, they are not bicycles with clear mind for solving problems of prime importance for themselves, they think and act as primitives, without accepting that they are primitives.

Now, coming back to the result of the very positive publicity for the concept, we can say that certainly this publicity is of much use, is as part of the foundation for the future edifice of this concept. We must have lots of patience and perseverance; there is no other way out. The human beings do not solve their problems, and if they do, this process is not direct and fast as a ray of light, but moves as a caterpillar in a labyrinth. We can choose, to sustain the fight for the concept, with all the attached complications, it means entering the labyrinth with a possibility to exit at the other end as a winner, or the other alternative, to avoid all this work and nuisance of entering the labyrinth but in this case without any chance to win. Our engineer chose the first alternative, the fight. Now is everything clear?

— Very clear, many thanks, the response is complete.

— And I would like to add that all this tremendous activity of incessant promotion, with very positive and realistic articles in the main publications, with interviews with the main and national networks of television and radio, with presentations at prestigious International Conferences and Seminars, by direct contacts with businessmen and politicians, has created a very solid base for a positive reception by those who at the end, make the decisions. One cannot compare the today's reputation status of the concept, after all this promotional activity with the situation of almost unknown at the beginning of the promotion. This is not to say that there is a guarantee of success, never forget that in this action we don't deal with one of us, the bicycles, but with human creatures, so many times unpredictable. However, in the present situation, the chances of success are much better. This is the main positive result. Is it clearer now?

— Ah, yes, everything is very well explained and understood, many thanks.

Other aspects of the society of the human beings in the interpretation of the bicycles.

The human beings live in this world for more than ten thousand years of well-known history and many thousands before. The question that demands an answer is: in comparison with us and with our short history of no very much more of one single century, how close are the human beings to the perfection or to that superior model represented by some prominent human beings in their masterpieces of literature, philosophy, theatre, movies, painting, about their development during those thousands of years? Doesn't matter if the representations as superior beings are made by arrogant people enchanted with their own species or by idealists, dreamers who take their desires as a reality.

— I think that it is not possible to talk about a unique aspect of development or level of human beings society, intervened a bicycle connected through her cyclist with circles of social sciences. My cyclist, she continued, is university professor specialized in the history of the development of human societies in various countries and I had the occasion to listen to many of his discussions with his friends and colleagues. According to him, and I think he is right, there are two main spheres of human beings' activity and their achievements. One is the sphere of technical activity and other sphere refers to all other aspects and activities.

— This is exactly so, and I want to explain this in more detail because it is very important for us, for the fate of all bicycles.

— Excuse me for interrupting you.

— Don't mind, it is my pleasure to hear the confirmation from a respectable source for what I intend to say in continuation.

— Very well, thanks, we are listening to you.

— Talking about the sphere of technical activity of the human beings during those thousands of years of their existence, occurred a tremendous development of the technology and of the mass production of material things, because this activity was and always is based on the progress of the spirit of engineering, of innovation and science. This spirit or thinking always goes forwards and up with variable intensity in various places and historical epochs, but always forwards and never backwards or downwards. Those human beings who participated in the development of the technology have the undisputable merit of moving ahead the society of human beings from the level of primitive stone tools up to the electronic, nuclear and inter-spatial technology. Just look please, some thousands of years ago the most sophisticated instrument that the human beings had, was a very rudimentary hammer made of stone. Today they are surrounded by a multitude of fascinating articles as color television sets, telephones, giant planes, transatlantic ships and also by millions of modern cars which we must recognize, represent a marvel of engineering, even if in the present situation they are our most dangerous enemies.

— They, the technicians and the visionaries of those times are the spiritual ancestors of the modern science and technology and also of our engineer, intervened a bicycle transported in the far past of the human beings history by the convincing words of the speaking bicycle, but without forgetting the present.

— Very clearly so, was the immediate response of the other bicycle. After a few seconds, required probably for transporting herself also from that past to the present with a speed of thousands of years per second, she continued:

— My darlings, I would enjoy very much if it were possible to talk about other sphere of human beings' activity in the same way that we talk about the sphere of their technical activities. Unfortunately, this is not possible because, this sphere containing so many other aspects and activities of them, offers results diametrically opposed to the sphere of their technical activities. What is the rule in the first sphere is only a very rare exception in the second sphere which gives the undisputable proof of their nature not only primitive, but also very inferior to all other animal species. Moreover, in many cases, this nature of them is directly diabolic.

— I don't understand well what you want to say, said a bicycle which listened with much attention to all the discussion, how is possible to demonstrate the inferiority of the human beings, even considering the bad sphere of their activities, which by all means requires some level of intelligence, if to compare for instance, with a caterpillar, or with a crocodile or with a monkey?

— We want to ask you the same, added in one voice a group of other bicycles.

— The question is very reasonable and I am glad to answer to it because this will help to clarify better the situation. Well, let me ask you, if to compare the transport capacity of a small car only for the driver and three passengers, with a big bus for the driver and fifty passengers, which is superior and which is inferior, talking only about the use of transporting more passengers?

— It is obvious that the bus is superior, any child could say it, was the immediate and little irritated answer, probably because of the simplicity of the question.

— Very well, but if the car works in normal conditions and can carry all the three passengers and the bus, because of some defect, cannot carry more than two passengers, in this case, which is superior and which is inferior?

— Well, in this case the bus is the inferior.

— Even if the bus is so big and has the nominal capacity of fifty passengers?

— What is the use of the size and nominal capacity if the real use doesn't correspond to its nominal capacity?

— Correct. One question more and after that I will explain the purpose of my questions. Now, if nothing changes for the car and the bus can transport five passengers, which is the superior and which is the inferior?

A moment of silence followed and nobody was in a hurry with a very eloquent answer as little before. Finally, the first bicycle participating in this verbal duel, expressed her opinion:

— The problem is a little more complicated in these conditions because on one hand, is true, the bus transporting five passengers is superior only because five is more than three. But this would be a very rudimentary judgment. We must consider also the efficiency of each of the two vehicles. The small car transporting only three passengers, works at its maximal capacity, it means with hundred percent efficiency. The big bus transporting five passengers, almost double than the car but ten times less than its nominal capacity of fifty passengers, works with a efficiency of no more than ten percent and from this major point of view, the bus is the inferior, without any doubt. Everything is relative. The achievement must be related to the capacity, to the cost, to the expectation and also to the pretension. But the last one refers not to vehicles, only to the human beings, which pretend so many times to be what they are not.

— Very well said, your conclusion is my most important argument, responded the Canadian. Now, relating to the human beings, with their pretensions of intelligent, advanced and developed beings, we will analyze their real achievements in this period of more than ten thousand years of evolution from the animal stage or primitive beings, besides the technical sphere about which we talked before.

— It is very interesting to listen to you, said a bicycle.

— For us also, completed others.

— Well, began the Canadian bicycle, we will see what happened in this period of so many thousands of years in some vital directions and areas for the human beings. But before anything, many thanks for your interest in this discussion. Also, I didn't forget about the caterpillar, the crocodile and the monkey, the characters from our friend's question, to which I will respond now. Coming back to the previous question about the comparison between the intelligence and the behavior of the human beings, even those who make bad things and the intelligence and the behavior of the beings from the animal kingdom as the caterpillars, crocodiles and monkeys, we must say that these human beings are in an inferior position. In the example with the comparison between the bus and the small car, these human beings represent the bus with two passengers even if its maximal capacity is of fifty passengers, it is to say that in their achievements they are much below their possibilities, while the achievements of the caterpillars, crocodiles and monkeys are at their maximal capacity. In what concerns the behavior, these animals lead by their instinct behave in a better manner. The vital, all-powerful objective of these animals is to survive by using the natural conditions to satisfy the vital needs and nothing more, without criminal or crazy actions that so frequently happen in the human beings' society. Even the crocodiles, considered ferocious animals, do not kill other crocodiles, only individuals from other species and only for food, for surviving and nothing else. It is well known of what cruelty without any justification are capable many human beings. For this the comparison with these animals is not favorable to the human beings.

Now, let me discuss initially an important problem but minor compared with others much more severe, I am talking about the communication problem among the human beings themselves, started her explanation the Canadian. We, the bicycles from the entire world, doesn't matter from what place or country, are of the same physical constitution, we function in the same manner and from the beginning of our short history we speak the same language between us although we understand the languages of the human beings. They, after more than ten thousand years speak hundreds of languages and dialects totally different and they couldn't come in ten thousand years to a common language for all of them. And as we do, they have also the same physical and biological constitution as human beings, for all of them regardless in what part of the world they live and all of them function in the same way. This multitude of languages and dialects not only creates a great difficulty for communication and a barrier between various nations and groups but also represents a permanent source of hostile actions, of isolation, which contribute many times to initiate bloody fights and wars between those nations and groups. Moreover, even in conditions of peace and collaboration, there is a very costly army of translators and offices to make possible whatever collaboration, translators which would be totally useless if one single language would exist. And what a waste of precious time for millions of them, who instead of producing useful things or giving necessary services, all their lives don't do anything else than translating. And some of these languages are so difficult and irrational, that the human beings speaking them, and there are many hundreds of millions of them, must waste years of their life for learning the basics of the language.

— It wasn't any visionary, as in the sphere of technical activity, trying to change the situation? asked a bicycle impressed by the bad luck of those human beings.

— Yes, surely were, but they were crushed by the giant wave of human stupidity and consequently nothing changed and it seems that doesn't exist any hope in this direction for the foreseeable future.

— There is lots of sense in what you are saying, got involved in the discussion other bicycle, I understand this very well because my cyclist is a translator of books, business letters and other documents and I can say that there is much work for a good translation, sometimes is more difficult and more work to translate a document than to compose it. Indeed, it would be much easier to live in this world of human beings without these language barriers. If anyone has doubt about it just imagine for a minute what would happen if suddenly, in a nation or whatever community, the human beings were not able anymore to communicate in the same language, but in ten different ones, or in five, or only in two. It would be a terrible confusion and difficulty, true? Well, thinking in the opposite direction, we will understand how much easier will be the contacts among them if the language differences between two, five or ten communities or nations would disappear.

— This is very clear for all of us, and maybe for some of them, but the immense majority of human beings cannot change the situation as they couldn't change it during the ten thousand passed years, and this is without any doubt a clear proof of collective stupidity and not of intelligence, a proof of inferiority in face of an obvious necessity, and this is exactly what our Canadian sister wants to demonstrate.

— Thanks for your conclusion so precise, responded the Canadian. I think that this point is very clear and now I would like to talk about other aspect, which proofs the inferiority of the human beings, this time in what concerns their social organization. This aspect is much more important than the one of language and consequently the proof of their inferiority is respectively stronger, in addition to the first proof, because if with a multitude of languages instead of one still it is possible to live, although not so comfortably, it is possible to manage without catastrophes or terrible personal difficulties, their social organization provokes exactly this, in millions of isolated cases and also for entire categories and enormous groups of them. And this situation is of permanent character, not due to natural causes or insurmountable conditions but only and totally due to their incapacity to reason, to think and organize themselves better, at least at the level of many communities of the animal world, to which the human beings consider themselves being so superior. This pretension is even a sign of mental disability because they are not capable at least to copy or to imitate what is good in the societies of the animal kingdom for their social organization, they limit themselves to solutions totally unacceptable for intelligent beings. Talking about their social organization in time, the result is not positive, by the contrary, many times is a proof of backward movement in comparison with the life of hundreds or thousands of years before. And there are so many aspects in their life in which this is a very sad reality that is somehow difficult to choose of which to talk first. And thinking for a short while, she continued:

— Well, I will start, not necessarily in order of importance, with the major aspect of their housing, the way that they live today in their cities and how they lived before. Nobody can deny the great difference in quality between the houses in which the human beings lived thousand of years ago, and even one or two centuries ago, without electricity, without running water, without sewage, without central or automatic heating, without air conditioning, in urban areas with narrow streets with little fresh air or natural light, ugly and uncomfortable, and the multitude of modern houses and other buildings of today with all the conveniences as everybody knows. In those times only in the royal palaces and in the palaces of the very rich the conditions of living were better. Today, due to the inventive spirit and the very valuable work of the technicians, the engineers and scientists, the modern housing became possible, and not only that, due to the modern, very advanced methods of construction, it became possible to build the modern houses and apartments, in mass production, very fast, with the real and obvious possibility to ensure the living in this modern housing for all human beings of this world, I repeat, for all without exception.

— Excuse me please, rushed into the discussion a robust bicycle, adapted to carry not only her cyclist but also some load, what you are saying my friend, modern housing for all, may be you intend to talk about a desire, about a dream. I am from Bangkok, a large city, the capital of a tropical country named Thailand. Go there to see how the human beings live, the great majority of them, in what poor and unhealthy conditions. Take a trip in a boat for tourists to that part of the city with houses built on wooden pillars in a network of canals with dark, dirty water. The human beings live there in primitive conditions, use the same canals for sewage and for bathing, an incredible poverty, without any possibility to get out from there, and you talk about modern houses for all. There is, sure, a very nice royal palace and big and clean houses for the few rich, but what can be said about the houses I am talking about? Excuse me, but your story is very far from reality, at least in my country.

— For what to excuse you, my friend? asked immediately the other bicycle, for what fault? If you have a fault, but I don't think that it is a fault, is that you were a little bit in a hurry. In fact, you said as cannot be said better, precisely what I wanted to say in the following minutes. That what I said is the pure truth, today there is the real possibility to built modern and comfortable houses for everybody, I repeat, this possibility exists!

— I agree with this.

— What you said about the miserable existing conditions is pure truth also.

And this is the obvious demonstration of the stupidity and inferiority of the human beings in charge not with the development of the technology but in charge with the administration and the well-being of the human beings. With all their pretensions of intelligence and progress, simply they are not capable to solve problems for which there is not other difficulty for solving them, than their own stupidity.

— Do you remember the example with the small car and the big bus?

— Sure, I remember.

— Well, if comparing the small car which can carry only three passengers with the society of human beings of those times far in the past with primitive technology and limited capacity, and comparing the big bus with the nominal capacity of fifty passengers but which transports only five, with the society of human beings of today, with the very modern technology and tremendous production capacity but which do not produce what is necessary, we get the general picture of stagnation, and what is worse, of regression of the intelligence of the human beings, in spite of the appearance of progress. The progress is only technological. The efficiency of using it in a reasonable manner for their own well-being, which would justify the very progress of the technology, is totally other matter.

The poverty of the past times was justified by the lack of resources and not by the default of utilizing the existing resources. The poverty of the present time is not justified by the lack of resources but only by the default of utilizing them, and this is the default of the intelligence or the regression of the human beings intelligence, by comparing the present circumstances with the circumstances of many centuries and thousands of years ago.

— This is to say that when a man and his child are suffering from hunger because there is nothing to eat, it is sad, but it can be understood and there is no reason to accuse him. But if the same happens when there is plenty of food around, the same man is an idiot or a criminal if we think about his child, said a bicycle.

— True, a very good example clarifying well what I said, responded the Canadian.

— Everything is very clear, intervened other bicycle, but I would like to know the magnitude of the problem, in this case the inadequate dwellings in the world are isolated cases, or only in some very poor countries, or is a more general case?

— It is an undeniable reality that today there are many modern houses occupied by a significant greater number of human beings simply because before this number was very reduced due to the prohibitive cost for the mass of employees. Due to the modern technology, the cost of these houses and apartments is lower and for this, a greater number of workers and clerks can allow themselves to rent and even buy at credit an apartment or a modest house but in good condition with modern facilities. Unfortunately, this applies only in countries called "developed" in Europe and North America, and there not always. In other continents modern houses for workers are very rare cases. However, all of you will be surprised to know what a high percentage of the world population lives in conditions that varies between very modest, less than modest and directly miserable. This percentage reflects not only the majority, that in statistics represents fifty one percent, but the great majority of human beings living on this planet. This is translated in numbers involving not millions but billions of human beings. And this is a well-known reality, and occurs in the time of practically unlimited possibilities for the existing technology to solve rapidly this problem so important. This is the result of human beings in action and this action reflects exactly their level of intelligence. And this is talking about the conditions of their housing. Unfortunately, there are other areas of their life where the results are even worse. It is very sad that our situation depends so much of these creatures.

The silence that followed was caused by the profound impression produced by the words of the Canadian bicycle. After a while, a bicycle with an appearance far from being luxurious, interrupted the silence:

— I am from Asia and I travelled a lot in the most populated countries of this continent. I can confirm everything that our sister just finished saying. A huge number of human beings live in deplorable conditions, so far from the modern houses about which you spoke, as from here to the moon. And the poverty of these human beings affects directly our health, which depends on the maintenance for us. If the human beings are poor, so is our health and well-being. Very many human beings, the immense majority of them want and can work with the highest productivity but their social system doesn't create work for all and those who have work today, never know what will happen to their work tomorrow, they don't have any security neither the right to permanent work. And in their stupidity and collective limitation in thinking, they don't know how to change the existing system.

— The same story is a daily reality in Africa. I am from Nigeria, a country very rich in material resources but very poor in what concerns the standard of living of almost all the population, and certainly this low standard of living includes the low level of housing. In many places the human beings live in directly primitive conditions, as thousands of years ago, without any hope of change for better.

— I have a very important observation about the difference between the poor and unhealthy houses from before and from today in the poor countries and the modern houses in the countries named developed. I am from the United States of America and I know very well the housing situation in this country, which is considered by all as very rich. All who do not know or do not want to know the reality.

— And what is the additional difference between a very poor small house, even primitive, and a modern house, more than what it was said in our discussions here?

— A very great difference.

— A difference in what?

— In the security and peace of mind. And this is an additional proof of the inferiority and the regression of the intelligence of the human beings.

— I assume that you will explain to us in more detail what you want to say.

— Certainly. In the primitive times, and today in the tribes of the jungle and in the ghettos in the very poor countries, the houses weren't and are not commercial objects, they are not for sale or for rent. Usually the occupants of these dwellings build them for themselves, and even being so uncomfortable, they are their property and the inhabitants are not in danger of losing them, about this they have peace of mind and they can concentrate in solving other problems for living. In what concerns the modern houses in the countries called "developed" these houses do not have only electricity, running water, heating, telephone and other conveniences, but also a bomb, which in some unforeseen circumstances, may explode.

— A bomb? Of what bombs are you talking about? Who puts them?

— They are bombs which do not destroy the house, by no means, only they push the inhabitants out of the house without the possibility of return. In fact, there are two bombs in each house or apartment rented or bought on credit. The first bomb is put by the employer of the inhabitant. The second bomb is put by the owner of the house or apartment. The first bomb has a timing device which, when the time is right, all what it does is to detonate the second bomb, which doesn't explode immediately, but also with a timing device, it may be one month later, but explodes for sure and the inhabitant with all his things is thrown out of the house. If he cannot find immediately other solution, his new dwelling will be the street or a park.

Not always these bombs explode. In many cases they don't explode the entire life, but they may explode. The timing device works non-stop and never gets out of order. It destroys the peace of mind and creates a permanent feeling of anxiety and uncertainty and sometimes depression for the inhabitants. Do you want to know the aspect of these bombs and how they function?

— We are very curious, we are listening.

— The first bomb, the product of the intelligence less than primitive of the human beings, has the shape of a letter signed by the employer of the inhabitant of the house, in which it is said in a dry manner or with crocodile tears, that due to some unfavorable circumstances, the employment cannot continue and that this is a notice that in two weeks, or a little less or a little more, the employment is terminated. This is to say certainly that after that date there is no more salary. Without salary and without savings, the rent or the mortgage cannot be paid. Then the second bomb explodes. This bomb has the shape of a very polite letter from the owner of the house or from the Bank if there is a mortgage, in which the inhabitant is reminded that the rent or the mortgage was not paid. A grace period is given to the inhabitant, let's say a month; after this time, by an order of the Court of Justice the inhabitant must leave the house or the apartment.

Can you imagine the situation of the poor inhabitant which yesterday was an employee, with salary, with house, possibly with a happy life, a human being with dignity, and today is nobody, because in the society of human beings with their social organization directly imbecile, if you don't have money you are nobody and cannot be sure at least about your home even a very modest one. In the primitive society this was not a problem. In the today's society called civilized, advanced or something similar, this is a problem and a big one.
— Then which society is more primitive, that one from yesterday or this one from today?
— The response is very clear, answered the American bicycle, we talk here without any exaggeration about a typical case of degeneration of the intelligence of the human beings in long range. To make this even clearer, I will present the following three situations:

A. In this society (we will name it A), the dwellings are totally simple, as huts for basic protection against the weather, nothing else, without technology. These dwelling were the reality in some stages of the life of the human beings, thousands of years ago, and is the reality even today in some parts of the world. For our demonstration, this is an alternative for an inhabitant. This hut or very simple dwelling is his and nobody can evict him from his little house. If he loses his job, at least he has where to sleep without problems.

B. In this society (we will name it B), the dwellings are very modern, with all the conveniences of the modern technology. This is the general case of the modern society of the human beings. For our demonstration, this is other alternative for the same inhabitant. A modern dwelling, with electricity, running water, heating, television, telephone, all. With one single condition. The dwelling is not his and he could be obligated to get out at any time, with a notice of two weeks or a month. In default of other solution, the alternative is the street.

Question: what will choose one who needs a place to stay, the alternative A or the alternative B? There are two big differences between the alternatives A and B. In the alternative A, the little, very simple house doesn't have the modern technology but neither the bomb with the timing device about which we talked before. In the alternative B, the house has all the modern technology but also the bomb with the timing device.

— The response to your question, says a bicycle, is a strong dilemma, the dilemma between security and convenience. The reality of today's life shows that the immense majority of the population, if it could choose, will choose the alternative with the technology taking the risk with the bomb.

— This is true, responded the American bicycle, but as you say well, even if it was possible to choose, in the alternative A, in the primitive society, the space belonged to all or to the first occupant. Today there is not anymore free space where one could build his very simple, little house, everything is private or governmental property. The alternative B, which is the reality of today, is a terrible mixture of high technical intelligence of engineers and of the highest peak of stupidity of the human beings in their activity of administrating the society. There is a tremendous technical progress and a disastrous administrative regression.

— Now, continued the American, there is a third alternative, the alternative C. In this alternative, all the dwellings are very modern, with all the technology but without bombs. It is to say that each member of the society when reaches the maturity age receives from the society a very modern dwelling and the opportunity to work. Both are his fundamental rights as a human being. In no circumstance he may lose his house or his work. If for whatsoever objective reason his work is not necessary anymore, the society has the obligation to secure other work or the retraining for other work, without the danger to lose the place where he lives. All the unhealthy houses or of low quality are destroyed and replaced with modern buildings in an adequate urban scenario, for all members of the society, for all of them, which in exchange will contribute with their well organized work to make this alternative possible. Is this alternative better?

— Certainly it is better but you talk about a very nice dream. Such an alternative doesn't exist.

— It is true that doesn't exist but it is perfectly possible, is more than a dream, is a realistic concept, sustainable, which can be realized in very short time.

— And why it is not realized, at least in your country, which is so rich in resources?

— Very simply, because in many aspects of life, the United States is a jungle with high technology and very rich in material resources but for the human beings it is still the jungle with its own law. The powerful of the jungle do not have any interest to change anything and on the other hand there is the collective stupidity of the entire society of human beings. This mass abandons itself to the will of its political and economic leaders without protesting or inefficiently protesting, it behaves generally as a herd of cows in its way to the abattoir. There is not much hope that this situation will change in the foreseeable future.

The very sad words of the American bicycle in their naked realism, touched a very sensitive cord in all bicycles and there was a period of silence until other bicycle interrupted it.

— The previous speakers related the situation, which is the same also in our continent. I talk about South America, an immense continent as the North America but very poor for the great majority of inhabitants in spite of the not less immense natural richness and possibilities for development. I am from Lima, the capital of Peru, a country with an ancient culture, with a very varied geography and nature, extremely rich and interesting including majestic mountains, the famous Andes, some of the highest mountains in the world, the giant Amazon jungle, the Amazon, the largest river in the world, the unique Altiplano, which signifies a vast field at a height of more than fourteen thousand feet, where is in operation a very old railway, the world highest railway. There are also beautiful lakes as the famous Lake Titicaca at a very high altitude in the interior of the country, and the long coast of the Pacific Ocean, but my friends, excuse me, I got lost describing the country instead of talking about us, the bicycles, in connection with the problem discussed here . . . .

— Continue please, it is so interesting what you are saying, responded at the same time some bicycles expressing without doubt the opinion of all others.

— I can imagine the beautiful places of which you are talking about, completed other bicycle, I hope that one day I will have the occasion to visit them, at least the city of Lima.

— Many thanks to all of you, continued the Peruvian bicycle. Lima could be a very nice city, has large and long avenues, flat, the entire city is basically flat with surrounding hills. There are some historical monuments and nice houses but the great majority of them are old, ugly and unhealthy. The poorest had built ghettos or "favelas" how they are called in Brazil, which represent a shame for the city and for those who have the power to eradicate them and don't do it. But this is only a part of the very great problem of the social organization of the human beings in all parts of the world, about what other sisters talked here. The circulation in the city, with intense motorized traffic, is very difficult and the high level of the air pollution makes life in the city not very pleasant. For the same reason, the life for us, the bicycles, is also difficult and dangerous. What a marvelous solution would be the construction of the system proposed by our engineer, the conditions, including the climate are so favorable! Maybe, one day in the future . . . .

The Peruvian bicycle didn't finish her sentence but all the bicycles understood what she wanted to say. The words about this marvelous dream provoked the immediate intervention of the Canadian bicycle.

— This dream so nice was also the dream of our engineer. He visited Lima three times; the first two times, in connection with a hiking trip, difficult but extremely interesting in the high mountains of the Andes with a sportive group, including the visit to the famous Inca city Machu Pichu on the mountain of the same name and an extraordinary adventure with inflatable boats on the Urubamba river. Our engineer is not only a dedicated engineer but also a good sportsman and explorer at the same time. After this ascension on the mountains with the group, he continued his adventure by himself for almost two weeks in the Amazon jungle, accompanied only by a local guide. This was a unique experience that cannot be compared with any other trip or tour organized by the tourist agencies. A totally different world which doesn't have anything in common with the civilization to which we are so accustomed, a cruel and magnificent world at the same time where the supreme law that counts is the law of force, which is the law of the jungle where the death for some means life for others and the life for some requires the death of others. At each step you have to be extremely careful and learn very rapidly the dangers, the signals of the dangers and how to avoid and fight them, when possible. The fight for existence, for surviving, is the reality of each day, of each hour, of each second. There are no excuses and no forgiveness or compassion.

The nature is grandiose, everything is green and full of life, day or night. During the night there is an incessant choir of birds and other sounds which advise you not to get out from your hut. It is very interesting to observe things which cannot be seen in any botanical garden or zoological park, with much to learn. The help of the guide was of enormous value for the engineer. He remembers some experiences in this short time spent in the jungle. If you are interested, I can tell them to you.

— Extremely interested, we will never visit those places, continue please immediately was the categorical answer.

— Well, some of the cases that the engineer remembers, not necessarily in chronological order, are as follows.

The promotion of the concept in South America: Peru, Uruguay, Argentina. The adventure in the Amazon jungle.

One morning, on a path in the jungle the engineer noticed something like half of a football balloon of black color which moved very slowly from one side to another of the path. When he came close, he saw clearly that this was a community of totally black worms which moved together in a very strange manner: the worms from behind were climbing over the community of worms and were moving until reaching the base in the frontal part. At the same time, other worms from behind were doing the same thing, climbing from behind and descending in front, at the ground level. This movement is similar with the movement of the chain around the wheels of a tank. Why they move in this manner? Nobody knows but this is a reality of the jungle. Other reality, and a very dangerous one, was a tree branch of gray color and two or three centimeters in diameter, across of a path. Walking forward in his way, the engineer almost stepped on the branch but the guide stop him immediately. What the engineer didn't notice was that at the extremity of the immobile branch across the path was a portion of about ten centimeters in vertical position with a small head at the end moving very slowly. This was not a tree branch, it looked like, but was a venomous snake extremely dangerous. If touched, it could jump in a fraction of a second and bite; if the bite is not treated in less than two hours, the case could be fatal. The engineer was at three days distance from civilization.

Other time, walking on the path which was less than one meter wide, the guide who was walking in front of the engineer, suddenly got out of the path for a short detour signaling to the engineer to do the same. What happened? Across the path was a very fine spider's web, very difficult to notice. If touched, in less than a second a spider big like a fist will touch the skin to give a fatal bite.

Other day, hot enough, during a trip by boat on a very nice and quiet lake, the engineer wanted to swim a little in the clean and warm water. The boatman told him that is no danger and he entered the water. Fortunately he swam very close to the boat; a minute later he couldn't believe what he was seeing, at no more than fifty meters a big crocodile head appeared at the water surface. The engineer was amazed by the speed with which he returned to the boat and jumped into it, at the price of a small bruise. The boatman was more frightened than the engineer and the engineer didn't tell him anything. The next day he was by boat on other lake, also very nice, clean and peaceful, this time without any desire to swim, not even for a million dollars, in spite of the very hot day. This decision was very well justified, the boatman of this boat told him that in this lake there are boa snakes of fifteen or twenty meters which suffocate the victims under the water before eating them.

In the night before leaving the jungle, a nocturnal excursion by motorboat was organized on a nearby river to watch the crocodiles waiting for their catch. When arriving there, an absolute silence was required. After a while, all that could be seen was the crocodiles eyes. This was another interesting experience, but nothing can be compared with the feeling of relief after the return to the Maldonado small airport and from there to Lima.

After this very valuable experience about the life in the jungle, the engineer was thinking that the human beings have learned and copied much in their behavior, from the cruel life of the jungle. There are many situations in their society when the human beings live in similar conditions with the life without protection, as animals in the jungle.

At the end of this unforgettable exploration, the engineer visited for the second time the city of Lima before returning to Canada. The existing situation in Lima, which is exactly as you described it, inspired him to think about a system of bicycle expressways, that in the very favorable conditions of climate and topography, with the flat surface of the city and on the other hand with the intensive motorized traffic, the improvement of the urban transportation with the help of this system for bicycles will surely be a very welcomed solution.

With the decision to try to put in practice his idea, during his third visit to Lima, which was the starting point of a longer trip in several countries of South America, Peru, Brazil, Uruguay, Paraguay, Argentina and Chile, the engineer contacted the municipal authorities of Lima and the cyclist organization of the city. The idea was well received, at least apparently, discussions and contacts continued for a while in the city and after his departure from Lima but at the end our engineer understood that all this was only an exterior appearance without a serious intention from the local bureaucracy. He contacted also the World Bank to investigate the possibility of investment, but without a real interest and commitment from the authorities of Lima, nothing could be done. Years later, at the International Conference in Perth, Australia, where the engineer was invited to present his concept, he met with the representative of the cyclist organization of Lima and with the representative of the World Bank with whom he discussed before. They told him that with the help of the World Bank of three million dollars a bicycle path will be built in Lima at the street level, to improve the urban transportation. Two years later, the engineer read in a publication that this path was built but that the real result was totally different from the official fanfare. The path, very narrow, was built not in a place of major interest for the bicycle traffic but using an abandoned railway in a very lateral part of the city. The bicycle traffic was insignificant and in short time the path space was used also by the local vendors and so, practically everything ended with the waste of three millions of dollars. What an astronomic difference between this path and the project of the engineer! Poor human beings of Lima!

In his trip in South America, being in Montevideo, the capital of Uruguay, the realist-dreamer engineer wanted to use the opportunity, and contacted the municipal authorities of the city. For that city as for many others, the implementation of the proposed system would be a bonanza, but after the amiable discussion with the representative of city authority, the conclusion of the engineer was that this time he was more of a dreamer than a realist. The same thing was repeated in Buenos Aires, the capital of Argentina, where after discussions with the pertinent authorities, he came to the same conclusion: the bureaucracy, the lack of interest for the well-being of the society, the lack of intellectual capacity of those human beings to understand well the meaning of the proposed concept, represent in so many cases a terrible barrier on the way of the progress and the change for the better.

The only positive result of the meetings in Buenos Aires was that he received a copy of a magazine of October 1990 with the photography on the cover of the President of Argentina, Carlos Menem on bicycle, during a bicycle rally for the promotion of the utilitarian use of the bicycles. The photo is a significant proof of the good intention, which in that case also was only a good intention.

— Excuse me for interrupting such an interesting presentation about Lima but I was thinking that my information about the promotion of the proposed system of expressways for us would be of interest.

— Truly, it was of very much interest, thanks. The pause that followed proved that the bicycles were yet thinking about what the Canadian bicycle just said.

— My sisters, interrupted the silence other bicycle, I remember with much pleasure my visit to Peru, especially in the mountainous area around an old city called Cuzco. All that our Peruvian sister told us is exactly so, but I would like to relate in a few words other aspect of this country that impressed me very much, its popular music. My cyclist is from Europe and since he was a youngster and had the occasion to listen to some Peruvian songs so melodious as for instance "El condor pasa" and the so nice songs sang by the unforgettable and famous Peruvian singer Ima Sumac, with her unique voice with an incredible range of musical notes, he never missed the opportunity to listen to them again when it was possible. A very good opportunity appeared during our stay in Cuzco. There are there some places called "penas" where you can have a very tasty dinner and at the same time listen to some groups of local singers, very talented which performed a great variety of popular songs. Every evening until late by night, we were listening in various penas the respective programs until the end, my cyclist inside and me waiting in front of the pena from where I could hear everything very well. I liked enormously the songs interpreted with an instrument similar to a flute, which is called "chimpoia". The melodies are so profound, powerful and very sad, reflecting, it seemed to me, the magnificence of the omnipresent mountains and the very sad fate of the people.

— I am very moved by your story, commented the bicycle from Morelia, which a few hours before was the great sensation of the reunion, I know very well these songs and I can inform you that our engineer in his marvelous proposal for the system of bicycle expressways has the intention not less unique and not les marvelous, to combine the convenience and the security to travel in the expressways with the pleasure of listening to beautiful melodies of various kinds and countries, in different sections of the system of expressways. In one or more of these sections will be transmitted softly by the audio system, the same songs about which you just talked, said the Morelian addressing to the bicycle speaking before her.

— What a marvelous idea, really, exclaimed a neighbour bicycle.

— Yes, it is very nice and very intelligent, what a contradiction and what a difference if compared with the stupidity of others, of the great majority of human beings of which we are talking now, exclaimed a bicycle with much conviction.

— My sisters from three large continents, Asia, Africa and South America where the poverty of the human beings living there is more obvious, told us about the very inadequate conditions of housing in spite of the existing possibilities to improve the situation. This is considered as an unmistakable proof of the general mental insufficiency of the human beings who live in these continents belonging to the third world following the classification adopted by the human beings from the remaining three continents, Europe, North America and Australia which are considered more advanced and richer. And the human beings of these continents consider themselves superior in their intelligence to those from other continents. There is here a contradiction, which disputes the veracity of this assumption, at least in what concerns the housing problem.

I am from France, one of the richest countries of Europe and I live in Paris, the capital of the country, named by some also "the City Light" due to its high cultural level. Without any doubt, the level of economy of France, as of the other countries of Europe also, is significantly higher than the one in the countries of the third world but the conditions of living in cities are in many cases deplorable. For instance, my city, Paris, the "city light" is in its great majority a very old city, with many narrow and winding streets, with old, ugly and uncomfortable houses with little light and space. More than this, the cost of housing is very high. To buy or to rent a house or an apartment is very expensive, but to buy or to rent a modern house or apartment in a central place or at least acceptable, is a luxury that few can afford. To pay for this, the great majority of human beings must work all their lives leaving very little for other necessities.

— But where is the high economic level, asked without delay a bicycle, how is the work productivity of those human beings?

— The industry is well developed and the productivity of work very high, responded the French, but the general organization of their society is very bad and in this consists the proof of their foolishness. The cost of building a modern apartment with the existing technology is very low but the selling price is very high. There is no economic justification for this. Everything is based on the collective foolishness of the mass of human beings who are the buyers and on the greed of the grand owners that build them for selling or renting with a great benefit,

— But aren't there limits, which could be imposed for the magnitude of these benefits and with the difference, to lower the selling price?

— No, there are no legal limits because the owners make the laws and impose them. Not by themselves, they don't have time for this, they are too busy to grab more and more money and to enjoy their luxurious life. To impose their will, they use the politicians and the government.

— One moment please, but the government is elected by the people, what means by the mass of human beings which are in their great majority those who rent or buy the dwellings, true?

— Nothing can be truer. But an integral part of the same truth, which you don't know yet because you are very young, is that the government elected by the people is the loyal servant of the owners. It is true that the government serves the people also, but only in small things, which do not offend the owners. The benefits of these do not have legal limits, only the employees salaries are very limited in very many cases to the basic necessities for a very modest life. There are many disputes and strikes for a low percentage increase at the base of the social pyramid but at the top, the personal benefits can be millions, tens of millions or hundreds of millions per year.

— I simply ask myself, just for curiosity sake, why these millionaires always grab more and more money, which never is enough. Really what is the rational use of so much money? How much one can eat? How many clothes can change these creatures? In how many beds they can sleep? Even the luxury has its limits. What is the reason for all this?

— Who told you that they have any reason? Not one millimeter, not one milligram. This is among other things a psychological disease combined with arrogance and the desire to show off until a state of dementia.

— Listening to your comment and questions about the limitless appetite of the millionaires and multi-millionaires, I remember the comparison made by our engineer between those you just finished talking about and the lions of the African jungle. Many years before, he was in Nigeria to negotiate a project for the company for which he was working at that time. He took several days of vacation to visit a reserve in the neighbouring country, Kenya, where all the wild animals live in total freedom in their natural environment and the visitors travel in mobile cages, well protected by metal bars. In a place, a group of lions were observing a large group of zebras, which were approaching. Suddenly a lion jumped from his place and attacking the group of zebras, killed one and started eating it. After a while, when its hunger was satisfied, it returned to its group and everything went back to the peaceful situation as before with the zebras in the close vicinity. The lion could easily kill ten zebras or more but one was enough for him, its instinct stopped the lion from killing uselessly other zebras. The engineer reflected that if instead of that lion with the natural instinct was there a human being millionaire, with his reasoning of superior being, he would have killed not ten but all zebras, without no practical use for him.

— What an adequate comparison, commented the bicycle which talked before about millionaires.

— But why all this immorality is permitted, when there are so many necessities around us, children without enough food, homeless people and so much chronic unemployment, just to mention a few. It is said that we live in a democratic society; is this the democracy in a developed country with parliament, deputies and all the respective bureaucracy?

— Oh no, my dear, all this is a circus well staged, democracy is an empty word without any meaning, only to be consumed by the naives or people with infantile mentality.

— But those human beings in this modern society who live at the border of poverty do not rebel against this situation when other human beings have so many millions that they don't know what to do with so much money?

— By no means.

— You want to say that they consider this situation normal?

— Not only that they consider it normal and do not think to rebel or accuse, but also by the contrary, they consider them as heroes and dream to be one day like them. This is the mentality of the human beings, at least of the immense majority of them in countries called developed and also in the countries of the third world. And this mentality is maintained every day by the leaders of the society with an intensive propaganda trying to convince the poor that each of them can be rich, when in reality this is only an illusion, for diverting the attention of these poor from the real cause of their poverty and so to avoid or prevent potential conflicts. For this purpose, the irrational, the hope for a miracle, is also used. An example for this is the lottery, which is a very successful business. The real probability to gain a million is extremely remote, one in several millions, considering also the profits for the organizers, but the very powerful propaganda never talks about this, always shows how the new rich enjoy their money won at the lottery. And the short minds think that this possibility is just around the corner and buy lottery tickets with the little money they have. In many cases this becomes a habit and from here there is a short distance to the addiction. This habit and addiction is a very solid fundament for other similar industry, the casinos, which produce very big profits for the owners together with many significant loses of money that sometimes end up in personal disasters and for the respective families and also in suicides.

— I want to mention other factor of essential importance in the society of human beings of the United States and other countries also called developed, because of which the situation for them will not improve, intervened the American bicycle, at least for the future about which we can think without dreaming.

— What is that factor? asked a bicycle without patience but very curious.

— It is the very powerful individualism, which characterizes the human beings society of these countries. A collective and solidarity spirit is very rare, everyone is for himself or in the best case for his family or the very immediate professional community with which he has direct material interests. For this, all actions of protest to increase the salary for instance, are reduced to the closest affiliation. So, if there is a nurses strike in hospitals, the other employees do not join the strike, only the nurses, and not necessarily of all the country but most probably in the local or regional area. If there is a strike in an industry, the workers from other industries do not participate because they do not have in this action an immediate interest. This does not represent a great or immediate danger for the rich owners of the industry and the political leaders of the country and they solve the problem by negotiations losing very little without endangering the very base of their power. For this, the present situation of the human beings continue as it was yesterday and tomorrow will be as it is today.

— How bad and how sad, commented a bicycle.

— And this is not all and not the worse, intervened again the French bicycle. I agree completely with what the American sister said.

— If what she said and what you described earlier is not bad enough, what can be worse? asked without wasting time the same bicycle.

— Coming back now to the so important problem of housing, the worse is that in spite of the material and technological possibilities to built houses for all human beings in the society, there are homeless people in France also, without a little place to live no matter how modest.

— And where they sleep?

— In the streets, in parks, under the bridges and in other places of the same level of comfort and human dignity.

— Unbelievable, but why don't they buy or rent a very modest place to live?

— Because they don't have any money.

— What do you want to say, they work for free?

— No, they don't work.

— Why they don't work? Don't they want to work? Why in this case other human beings, their community, don't obligate them to work to save their dignity and to solve this very scandalous and disgraceful social problem?

— There is not even a single case of which you are talking about. They don't work simply because there is no work and nobody is preoccupied of the fate and well-being of these brothers of them, other human beings. They could create work, very easily, but they don't do it.

— In this case, I have a solution, they can build houses for themselves, because if they don't work, they have enough time.

— Your solution is not applicable in this case, would be applicable if the human beings could think at a superior level as we, the bicycles do, in which case the problem would not be a problem, but they are only human beings, not bicycles.

— Why is not applicable? insisted the bicycle.

— Is not applicable because there is no free space where to built, everything is private property or owned by government. It is possible to buy land if one has money but it is not given for free only because one is poor, and those human beings don't have money.

— In this situation, said the same bicycle that didn't want to give up, they could build a little house outside of town, in the field or in the forest.

— This alternative is not possible either. The field is private property for agriculture, and building houses and living in the forest is not permitted because it belongs to some person, private organization or to the government.

— But the animals live in the forest, they have their places where they sleep in a comfortable manner for them and the birds build their nests in the trees, which are their houses, without the need to ask for permission neither from the human beings nor from other birds. Why the human beings cannot do the same?

— Very good question, and the answer is the greatest difference between the intellectual level of the human beings and that of the birds. When the human beings will arrive at the same level of intelligence as of the animals and birds and due to this, they will behave among themselves as the animals and birds of the same species, then, the problem could be solved as you say. But not before.

The discussion continued with the same interest. To each question there was an answer and to each answer there was other question and that made the discussion very lively and interesting. So, here comes the next question:

— I am not from Europe and I didn't have the occasion to visit it, but I heard a lot about the high economic level there. In connection with this information, I would like to know what is the magnitude of the situation described here in such eloquent manner, they are very isolated cases or more than that? asked a bicycle very careful in double checking the information before believing it.

— Unfortunately, they are not isolated cases, was the answer, there are very many such cases, with enough variables in what concerns the level of lack of correspondence to the existing possibilities. We don't talk here about statistics, about percentage, we talk about the level of intelligence or of stupidity of the human beings, how you like to put it, and for this, a single case is enough to prove how low is this level of intelligence or respectively, how high is the level of their stupidity. Poor creatures, they cannot escape from the only one but powerful, implacable question: why is the existence of that only one, unique case allowed, if there is the possibility to eliminate it, to solve the problem. The impossibility to answer in a satisfactory, logical manner, is the accusation. The accusation says that this situation, even in one single case, is the proof of incapacity, of inferiority of the human beings. The default to justify, to respond in a logical manner to this question, transforms automatically the accusation in verdict. If there is not only one case, but there are a thousand cases, the problem is amplified one thousand times, if there are a million cases, the problem amplifies one million times, but the verdict mentioned before is justified by one single case.

— It is as the difference between a criminal who killed one single person and a criminal who killed one thousand people. Both deserve the death penalty. Only the amplitude of the crime is different, completed a bicycle, which much liked to clarify the explanations with adequate examples.

— Exactly, completed other bicycle, and for being even clearer, the death penalty for a criminal who killed one thousand people doesn't mean that a criminal who killed only one person has the right to a punishment thousand times lighter, as an admonition only.

— Or if a thief steals from a person the only dollar that person has, deserves the same punishment like other thief who steals from a person all the money he has. The guilt is the same, the stolen quantity and value is a detail.

— Everything is very clear, totally clear, added a bicycle which didn't talk before, and the fact that the practical possibility to solve the problems is higher in the European countries in comparison with other poorer countries doesn't diminish the guilt, but by contrary, adds other accusation, of lack of efficiency, as in that very good example with the bus of large capacity which transports only five passengers instead of fifty, compared with the small car which transports three passengers what represents its maximal capacity. That bus is not efficient because doesn't utilize the existing possibilities.

— Is like comparing for instance, a man who doesn't have and cannot build a house and for this he sleeps outside, with a man who can build a house but he doesn't build it and sleeps outside in the cold, or worse, has built the house but without explanation, sleeps outside in the cold. In this case we talk not only about low efficiency but also about imbecility, completed the bicycle specialized in giving clarifying examples, and getting involved in this competition or better said open forum for the best examples, other bicycle gave hers:

— I think that closer to the reality about which we are talking and in connection with the same example with the house which is not used, is the case of a man who has built a large house in which he and part of his family sleep very comfortably and there is more room inside but other part of his family sleeps outside in the cold because doesn't have access to the house, without any logical reason.

— In this case we must add to the lack of efficiency and imbecility, also the extreme selfishness and cruelty. I think that this completes very well the other examples and reflects well what is going on presently in Europe.

— Well, this demonstrates that the rich Europe is not so rich, at least with regard to the housing. I am from a less fortunate continent where homeless human beings or living in deplorable conditions are very common cases. I didn't know until our discussion that there are human beings living in precarious houses or without any, in Europe also. I wonder what is the situation in the rich countries, or developed how they are called also, of the North American continent, the United

States and Canada where so many people from around the world dream to emigrate to live in better conditions.

— I don't know who could answer better your question, intervened a sportive bicycle, I am from the United States and I traveled extensively in many places of this very large country, in many of the main cities. With a sportive group, I traveled across the United States from one ocean to the other and I can say that I know very well what is going on in the country. I agree completely with what our American sister who talked a little earlier in a realist and objective manner said.

— Well, and what is your impression about the housing conditions of the human beings of that country? asked a bicycle very curious to get news directly from the source. Are there also ugly, unhealthy houses or below the level of modern house building technology? There are also human beings sleeping in the street, or at least in a country so rich in resources and possibilities as the United States, everything is at the same superior level as its technology?

— All what you were talking about can be counted in millions, was the answer of the American bicycle.

— What do you want to say?

— I want to say exactly this, that there are millions of modern houses, very nice, at the superior level of the modern technology for building houses and apartments, very comfortable and elegant equipped with all modern appliances for the kitchens and washrooms, heating, light and running water, also with swimming pools with water temperature controlled automatically. Individual houses and apartments in high-rise building with all these conveniences are built very rapidly, with great efficiency and a very low production cost due to the high work productivity which is the direct result of the ingenuity of the engineers.

— Finally, a place in this world where everything is very good, exclaimed a young bicycle, enchanted by the description of the North-American bicycle.

— I didn't finish talking, cut short without courtesy the American bicycle. I didn't finish to count the millions. There are also millions of old, very ugly houses, and specially in big cities as New York, Chicago, Detroit, entire buildings of abandoned apartments, the preferred places for the thieves, drug dealers and all sort of criminals. To walk in these parts of the city during the day and especially after dark, represents a great danger for your life. A flagrant example of this kind of achievement of the intelligence of human beings of the United States is called Harlem, in the center of New York and close to the very elegant commercial and financial center, in the famous Manhattan Island. There is an unimaginable difference between these two places and it can be said without reserve that Harlem is a shame for the city and for the United States also, a shame for any civilized society.

— And why they don't use the existing modern technology to demolish these ugly, old and unhealthy houses and build modern buildings, transforming the existing situation into a happy alternative? asked with good reasoning a bicycle with a passion for logic and good intentions.

— You can direct this very reasonable question straight to the human beings. For sure, it will be an embarrassing question for them. But it will be much more embarrassing, not to say more, when I will finish to talk about the other millions about which I intend to talk, responded the American bicycle.

— You talked about millions of nice and modern houses, of millions of old, ugly and uncomfortable houses, if I am not mistaken, I think that you want to talk about millions of average houses, true?

— You are right but only partially.

— What do you mean?

— It is true that there are millions and millions of average houses, which are neither nice and modern nor miserable, but surely much below the level of existing technology and possibilities and this is the situation in fact that anyone can verify, and at the same time an accusation, the proof, or better to say, one of the proofs, of the low efficiency of the modern human beings in administering their own society and consequently, one of the proofs of their low capacity of thinking at the pretended level. But not these are the millions that make the housing situation even worse.

— What can be worse?

— What can be worse? repeated the question the American bicycle. Worse is when there are in so many cities of the United States millions of human beings for which the house is the ghetto or the street. In the rich America as in the rich Europe and how our sisters from other continents related here, there are millions of human beings who simply do not have a place where to sleep and relax, even a small dwelling of a single room. More than this, they don't have even the hope to have such a place. I remember that many years ago, a main television network presented a documentary realized with the help of an organization of American women, about the sad fate of the homeless and depressed women in the city of New York. According to that documentary that could very well be incomplete, at that time existed six thousand women, many of them old, who had only a bag or a purse as all their belongings and slept in the streets of the great and famous city of New York. What a shame! All this due to the immense human stupidity! I don't know what can be more stupid than not to build houses when they are needed and the possibility for this exists, and what can be more inefficient than to waste so many resources and not to modernize your houses when this is very necessary and perfectly possible, I want to say to modernize the existing cities, rebuilding them in a rational manner.

— I know what can be more stupid, intervened suddenly a bicycle until that moment, silent. I am from Warsaw, the capital of Poland. As in many other cities of this country, which in their great majority are very old and uncomfortable for living, there is in Warsaw an area of the city named Staroe Miasto, what means the old place, with ugly houses and narrow and winding streets. During the Second World War, almost the entire city, including Staroe Miasto, was completely destroyed.

— A sad and unfortunate page of history, but at the same time a good occasion to rebuilt the houses and the city in a modern manner, interrupted a bicycle.

— This is exactly what I want to say, continued the bicycle from Warsaw, but what do you think the human beings did there, at least in this part of the city that I know well?

— I want to believe that it was rebuilt in a totally modern manner, as our friend who talked before me, said.

— All would occur exactly in this intelligent manner with one single condition, responded the Polish bicycle.

— What condition? wondered the other bicycle.

— The condition is that those human beings were bicycles or at least were thinking as we do. And as this was not the case, but unfortunately they were only human beings, they reconstructed the houses and the narrow streets, everything exactly as it was before, in accordance with the old pictures.

— Unbelievable, exclaimed a bicycle, very surprised.

— Unbelievable for me also, responded the Polish bicycle, but this is the reality that now is already history. Well, I demonstrated what can be worse than not modernizing the houses in normal conditions, it is to say, worse is to repeat the error.

— In this case we must review the well known Latin proverb that says, "erare es humanum, perseverar es diabolicum" what means "to mistake is human, to persevere in the mistake is diabolic". Now we must say: "to make a mistake is human, to persevere in the mistake is more human".

— Very well, very well, said the Polish bicycle accompanied by a general laughter of the audience.

After the laughter about the relationship between the human beings and their own errors calmed down, the discussion including the developed countries continued with the question of a very young bicycle.

— I heard in this discussion many interesting and new things for me about what really a developed country is. I didn't have the opportunity to travel out of my city and my information about this issue until now was that a developed country is a rich country. The sisters talking here have given me a very different image about what may happen in the countries called developed. Then, I would like to know how can we define the notion of a developed country. Can anyone of you explain to me?

— Why not? with great pleasure, responded immediately a bicycle. I am myself from a country with this title of developed and I traveled much in other countries with the same title because my cyclist worked in a tourist organization for long distance trips by bicycle. I am telling you this because we have many tourists from other countries and their impression on the visited countries is based not only on what they see but also on what they can understand. Some have only a superficial impression about the country, others think more profoundly. For this I am asking you, do you want a more general response, or a definition in depth which will give a realistic image about what means the notion of developed country with its multiple aspects?

— Without any doubt, I want a complete image.

— Well, I will start with the general aspect that all tourists and visitors can see and understand and after I will talk about other specific aspects which cannot be seen in the street by everybody. So, some consider that a developed country is a rich country with high national income compared with a poor country of the third world. And this is all. Point. This is true but this information is misleading and far from the complete reality of life in the country. Without giving names for not offending anyone, if someone takes a walk in a city of a developed country and a walk in a city of a poor country, of the third world, obvious differences appear immediately, in the quality of public transportation, general aspect of the city, number and quality of cars, the level of hygiene, the quality of services and other positive aspects. These are undeniable positive aspects. If this were all, it would be wonderful. But this is not all, there are also very negative aspects, some extremely negative, which put in shade all the positive achievements and aspects. Some of these negative aspects do not exist in the poor countries, other exist there also, but by no means this could be an excuse for their existence in the developed countries which have much greater possibilities.

I will concentrate only on some of these negative aspects, the most important ones, some of which that cannot be seen in the street and the visitors with a superficial judgment simply think that they don't exist. I will describe them following my inspiration, not necessarily in order of their importance.

So, a major characteristic for the developed countries is the volume of waste.

— Waste of what?
— Waste of everything, of material resources, of natural resources, of social time, of money, and what is the most important, of peace of mind and of hope. There is a very long list of what is wasted, I will give only some examples.

What the bicycles think about the developed countries.

The water, such a precious natural product, vital and limited, is wasted without scruples. When a human being takes a shower, or washes his hands or something else, for each liter of water necessary to be consumed, ten or twenty liters are wasted. He doesn't have any idea about how difficult it is and how many problems must be solved to bring the water from the river, mountains, lakes or underground reserves, to treat it in special stations and to deliver it to him with maximal convenience. In the third world the value of the water is well appreciated because in very many cases the water is transported on one's back, from the river or other source for a distance of a few kilometers, and the treated water is an expensive and rare luxury. For this, it is consumed in very limited quantities, strictly how much is necessary and many times less than this. In this same world where so much water is wasted, there are places where the population, as the Aborigines in Australia, use the water only for drinking, using the water for washing is considered a waste.

Much food is wasted. In the United States, more than in other developed countries, between a quarter and a third part of the population, including children, suffers from obesity. Lots of unhealthy food is sold for more commercial benefit. Electricity is wasted also, in cities one can see office high-rise buildings in which the light is on during the entire night. A lot of electricity is wasted in houses and apartments and especially for useless commercial advertising. An immense amount of gasoline is wasted because of the irrational urban transportation and of the abuse in the use of private cars. The bicycles, especially with the concept of our engineer, could save a great part of this gasoline, which is also a limited natural resource. With the rational use of bicycles, a car could serve two or three times longer, to reduce the trouble of driving in the very congested traffic and to save a valuable time.

An enormous amount of social time is wasted in an also enormous bureaucratic apparatus extended very much more than it is really necessary. This wasted time and money could be used in a rational manner to solve the urgent problems of the society.

An enormous amount of time and money is wasted for the promotion of fashion and for the cosmetic industry which is greatly a joke and a speculation for the naïve buyers, better to say for the "she" buyers, which automatically become naïve and an easy prey when the issue is the fashion or the cosmetics.

A waste without limits and without decency or shame is the all powerful commercial advertising which cost the society galore of money, other immense amount of wasted time, an incessant nuisance everywhere, including the television programs, newspapers and magazines and also the private mail and phone lines. The total and global result for the entire nation is a huge zero in addition to the cost of wasted time and materials. This is exactly so, because with advertising or without any of it, the buying capacity of all the buyers, as part of the national revenue, is the same and they spend the same amount of money, not a cent more, with all the commercial advertising and propaganda in comparison with a situation without anything of this. All the difference is between different vendors, owners of small shops and large companies, what one gains due to advertising, other loses but per total, the value of all sold merchandise to the entire nation, let's say in a year, is exactly the same. In other words, in the same society, using the advertising, which in principle is lying and exaggerating, and on the other hand the stupidity and credulity of the buyers, some vendors become millionaires and many others lose their business and become poor. It is a kind of jungle with aspect of civilization. But, what is sure, is that the commercial advertising is not for free, independently of its effect, is paid integrally by the buyers, evidently without their knowledge.

A waste of material and natural resources directly scandalous is with the press. Instead of being a source of information, pleasant to read and useful at the same time, the newspapers and other publications are transformed into a pile of advertising with little left interesting to read. So for instance, if you buy the Saturday "Toronto Star" newspaper in Canada, or other main newspaper, with its more than two hundred pages, at first this is a heavy task to carry it, secondly, it is an annoying and precious time consuming task to travel through and search these two hundred pages looking for something interesting to read avoiding the avalanche of commercial advertising, some of them with one single word on a whole page, which requires lots of imagination to guess what is the meaning. From all these two hundred pages, the great majority of those who buy the newspaper are interested in no more than four or five pages; the rest, including entire sections dedicated to the selling of cars, houses, fashion items, sports, goes to the garbage. And all this is published in about seven hundred thousand copies each Saturday and about half a million copies in other days of the week.

— Excuse me for the interruption, intervened suddenly a bicycle, but I want to correct something important. We don't talk here of two hundred pages in the Saturday newspaper.

— I said about two hundred, probably more, but I am not sure.

— You can be sure. Not longer than last week, I was thinking about the same issue, the waste of printed paper which is not read, and for curiosity sake I looked in the Saturday newspaper that my cyclist bought to read an editorial article in which he was interested. The rest was thrown in the garbage. I counted the total number of pages. Do you want to know how many were?

— More than two hundred?

— Two hundred seventy four and moreover a magazine of eighty pages with the size of half of a newspaper page which if converted, is equal to forty newspaper pages, or a total of three hundred fourteen pages of newspaper plus other separate pieces of advertisement which are distributed jointly with the newspaper. Three hundred fourteen pages to read in one day! Because the following day comes other newspaper with other pile of pages! How many are interested in so much information or have the time for this? I am sure that nobody.

— Many thanks for your precise information, it is very important.

— Just look how many trees are cut, are transported and transformed in paper and after that in newspapers and magazines, an entire forest each day. What for?

— To be thrown directly to the garbage. What a waste of material resources, of money, of work and time in these developed countries! Where is the development?

— I have an idea for reducing this waste in a significant way, intervened a bicycle with good ideas.

— Tell us please, it is very important to find a solution to stop or at least reduce this enormous waste.

— I propose to cut the trees in the forest and to destroy them directly there or burn them outside of the forest, to avoid a fire.

— I don't understand you, said without delay other bicycle, what is achieved with this action?

— How you don't understand? Don't you realize that a great saving is achieved by avoiding the transportation of the trees, the production of paper, the publication of all these useless pages, all the time and money involved in this waste?

— Well, and what those who buy the newspaper get?

— They get the four or six pages of general interest plus a list of specialized publications for those interested in shopping and other issues, which can be bought or ordered in addition and separately from the newspaper. In this way, the entire adequate information is directed to the very reduced minority really interested in that specific information as car selling, house selling, fashion, sports and other subjects, instead of creating a flooding with useless literature for millions of innocent victims.

The complete newspaper is produced presently, let's say in a million copies, including the information and advertising about the selling of cars and houses; we will refer now only to these two items. I have a question: how many from that million which buy the newspaper with the complete information and the respective advertising and propaganda about the car sale, really want and buy a car in that day or following the information and advertising included in the newspaper? Maybe one hundred, or one thousand, but not a million and no half or a quarter of a million, or one hundred thousand. The same is true for those who want to by a house or an apartment. Why then, waste all this information thousands of times more than it is necessary? And other question: who pays for this million of copies with the information and advertising about cars, houses, or about other things for which the advertisement is made in the newspaper? Not the buyers of the newspaper. A dollar and a half, which is the price of a Saturday newspaper, cannot pay for more than three hundred printed pages with all the advertising. This can pay only for a few pages of general information. All the difference of a multitude of millions is paid by the vendors of cars, houses and of other items for which the advertising is published in the newspaper. This cost including the cost of advertising is transferred immediately and directly to the buyers of those articles. So, if a car is sold for thirty thousand dollars, a significant percentage of this price, many thousands of dollars represent the cost of the advertising. If the cost of advertising, which depends, also of the number of newspapers and magazines in which it is published, is reduced, the cost of the respective merchandise, car, house or else, is also reduced.

— There is lots of sense in what you are saying, everything is very rational, except a thing that gives me a great concern.
— What thing concerns you?
— You said at the beginning of your intervention that you propose to destroy the trees directly in the forest or burn them outside. This seems to me a totally crazy idea and here among us we wondered if you got crazy or worse, if you got sick with the mentality of the human beings. Can you explain to us in a rational manner what is the use of destroying the trees in the forest by burning them or in other way?

The interlocutor couldn't hide a very ironic smile, which didn't pass unnoticed by other bicycles. This smile increased the curiosity for the expected answer.

— It seems to me that all of you agree with the second part of my proposal, with the saving of the paper and other advantages by reducing the number of pages, true?

— True.

— And who will realize this project of massive savings, we the bicycles or the human beings?

— What a question! Certainly they.

— And do you think that if the human beings can waste ten million, they will save them by an intelligent organization of the action? They will waste everything, as they are doing today. I was thinking that by giving them the possibility to waste only part of the value, in this case the trees, they would agree to save the rest. What I am saying is only a proposal, not for us, the bicycles, but for them, the human beings, but I don't think that they will accept it, they prefer to waste all. This example with the press is significant for the daily life in the countries, which are called developed.

When the bicycles understood finally that the proposal of the speaking bicycle was an ironic joke about the stupidity of the human beings and that she, a sister of all other bicycles, was not crazy, one of them said:

— You can be an actress in the theatre for the role of a bicycle with the sick mind of a human being.

A wave of very healthy laughter finished the discussion about the waste in the press in the developed countries.

— Other major characteristic of the countries called developed, is what can be seen by everybody in the street and that what cannot be seen, said a new participant in the discussion. What can be seen, is the multitude of cars of many models which are changed uselessly each year, and this is a tremendous waste in itself, the elegant and expensive shops, the beggars and homeless people which sleep in the same streets where the elegant shops are. A society, a country which cannot find an immediate solution to return the dignity to these poor which must beg in the street in order to eat, and don't have a home, is a developed country specially in stupidity and cruelty.

— The other characteristic of the countries called developed, what cannot be seen in the streets with vibrant life, with luxury cars and expensive boutiques, are the desperate unemployed which cannot find work for months or for years, and when they find work, never know for how long, said the same bicycle. The permanent insecurity for the day of tomorrow and the anxiety generated for themselves and for their families, cannot be seen in the street, but exist.

Not a single case of unemployment can be justified, but there are millions of cases in the countries which are not poor, are "developed". The unemployment is a chronic sickness, stinky, in these countries and the epicenter of this horrible disease is in the brain of the human beings, of those who are responsible for the present organization of the society and of the mass of other human beings who accept passively this situation and those responsible for it. In various countries and in various periods the number of unemployed varies officially between five and twelve percent of the population, this percentage in reality is usually higher, and in the periods of economic crises, which is another characteristic of the developed countries, this percentage can jump at twenty or more. The officials of these countries talk little about this, they take the position of innocent, of spectators that came from other planet, watching a natural phenomenon and not as directly responsible of the disaster, and for sure they don't do anything to eliminate this social shame. This is the waste of the hope and peace of mind not only for the unemployed of today but also for all others, which can be the unemployed of tomorrow. But the country is called "developed"

— What a sad and true reality! exclaimed a bicycle much impressed by the story describing so well this specific characteristic of the developed countries. And I am afraid by the idea that this is not the last unpleasant aspect, she continued.

— This is precisely so. My age is of more than one hundred thousand kilometers and I know very well the life in the United States and in other countries with the name of developed from Europe and I would like to share with you other characteristic specific and very painful for the countries which I cannot call developed without a grimace. It is the manner in which one dies.

— How one dies? asked amazed a very young bicycle from a small quiet place. I don't know what could be the difference between various countries for this very sad but natural phenomenon.

— There is a great difference, the human beings life is not totally happy in no one country, developed or not, but in the poor countries the death by natural causes is the case with the major frequency and there are much less causes which provoke the violent, terrible death, as occurs so often in the countries that some call developed. So, in many countries, the firearms for personal use are forbidden by law with very severe punishments. In the United States, to buy a fire arm is not a problem; because of this, there are many crimes and this represent a permanent danger. Children are killed, are kidnapped, raped and afterwards their bodies are found. There is also other way of dying, of a new American style, by being shot in a plaza or gas station by a sniper well hidden in his car. It is true that until now there weren't many such cases, but only a few isolated cases are enough to terrorize an entire country, especially when this kind of crimes is very difficult to control or to prevent.

— I am from the United States and I want to confirm all that our sister said and to add other possibility to die in this country so developed, this time for pupils in the school. There were some cases in which pupils killed with firearms their colleagues and nobody knows how this can be prevented in the future.

— Everything is possible due to the ease to obtain firearms and to the general fault of civic education of the population starting with the children and to the opposition to the legal prohibition of firearms, I didn't hear of similar cases in poor countries.

— In the primitive society, intervened other bicycle, at tribe level, this is an unimaginable situation. For this, here comes the same question: what society is more and really primitive and what is the value of the title of developed country when so many terrible things happen? Where is the high education well controlled by intelligent beings that could prevent these terrible phenomena?

— It is obvious that there isn't proper high education, there is only the education directly criminal at the national level by movies and television programs stimulating the criminal activities of all kind and giving new ideas and suggestions about violence, how to kill, to destroy, to rob and to escape. This criminal education extremely dangerous, specially for children and youngsters, is available twenty four hours every day, by television, movies, internet, newspapers, magazines, books and other publications. Over all this activity which should be cultural, nobody has any control, and less of all the authorities, in the name of the freedom of expression, if it is possible to imagine a greater idiocy.

— It is very sad that in addition to all that was said there is another aspect, which cannot escape our attention when we talk about developed countries. This is the massive use of drugs which besides the multiple mental and physical diseases, causes many crimes and traffic accidents which represents other way of dying much more specific for the developed countries that for poor countries. In normal conditions traffic accidents should not happen. There are very careful drivers, who didn't have any accident for decades. This should and it is possible to be the general case for all willing to have the right to drive a vehicle. Due to the stupidity and irresponsibility of many human beings, who drive when they are under the influence of alcohol or drugs, or drive when are very tired, they cause accidents frequently fatal. This danger is today increased by the habit to talk by cellular phone when driving, other achievement of developed countries.

— I have a basic explanation for the lack of discipline and violation of the law, which among other negative results, provoke frequently many accidents and abuses in these developed countries, very developed in these activities.

— We are listening to you.

— The entire juridical system is corrupt, with laws created not for protecting the victims of fraud and abuse but for protecting the thieves, criminals and the authors of frauds and abuses with very light penalties for grave crimes and abuses. The incredible bureaucracy and the lack of elementary logic or at least, the lack of common sense, protect those which abuse their position and leave practically without defense the honest and those who cannot afford to hire or better said to buy, a lawyer, it means, most of the times a robber.

The existing juridical system is very bad and causes more problems than it solves, in relatively minor and also in major cases, and this produces a great damage to the society.

An example of a typical case relatively minor for the society but major for the involved person, is when is necessary to repair the heating installation in your house. What is the normal procedure? To call a specialized technician, to explain the problem, to reach an agreement about the price, to pay a part of the total cost, the technician does the repair, to pay the remaining cost and this should be the end of the history. But what happens when the repair was not of good quality and the heating system doesn't work? Call the technician to make the necessary corrections to his initial repair already paid for, but he doesn't come, the call is repeated and a message is left but he doesn't come and doesn't answer to the messages. At the end, the owner of the house understands that after the technician received all the money for the repair, he doesn't want to do anything to fulfill his contractual obligations. In this case there are two options or possibilities. The first, which seems more reasonable and normal, is to take the case to the court of justice. But with the existing legal procedure this can take a year or more, this is the reality, and the heating is necessary immediately. To use the service of a lawyer, the cost will be too high. The second option is to forget completely about your rights and the legal procedure, to contact other specialist and start everything again hoping that this time everything will work well. This example is a real case from Toronto, Canada. If the owner of the house wants to be a Don Quixote fighting with wind mills or with the legal system for these cases, what is exactly the same thing, he can choose the first alternative. If he is a rational and realist being, will choose the second alternative. But this second alternative has its own traps which in the legal system in force, represents risks not less than in the first alternative, starting with the first visit of the first new technician. This visit costs between sixty and one hundred dollars only for seeing what is the problem. If he says that he cannot do the repair, the visit should be paid anyway. He can recommend other technician who also should be paid for his visit without the obligation to make the repair. He can recommend a very costly solution. To check the validity of this solution with other technician, the explanation by phone is not accepted, he wants to come and see, this is before anything else, one hundred dollars in his pocket, again without any obligation. He can say very well that the solution recommended by the previous technician is not good and with sophisticated explanations recommends other solution. This play can be repeated many times.

The owner of the house is a lady who worked many years to buy this house which was not new, and worked as a bee in all kind of repairs and maintenance with the dedication and precision which could make a mathematician very envious. In spite of being a University graduate, she did many difficult physical tasks, sometimes dirty, with which many men couldn't compete and she understands many technical things much better than many men which are considered having the supremacy in the technical field. She knows very well the value of the money for which she worked with honor and dedication and the value of time. But she cannot solve all the heating problems in a house and for this she needs, as is normal, the help of specialized technicians. But these technicians, who are very well paid, try to take advantage of their technical knowledge and speculate without scruples knowing that they cannot be controlled and behave with defiance for the time and patience of his client, which for them has no value. The lady owner of the house must wait four hours or more to receive the visit of the Prime Minister technician of heating, not being sure that at the end he will come.

— And this abusive attitude cannot be reported? asked a bicycle very impressed by this story.

— No, there is nowhere to get a prompt action. There is an official governmental office called Consumers Services Bureau and also a public service office named "Better Business Bureau" which are not efficient in solving the problems connected with the incompetence and the speculative attitude of these technicians.

— I can imagine the frustration and nervous tension of that lady, added other bicycle much intrigued by the very existence of this situation in a civilized country.

— I know very well this case, continued the first speaker, and I can tell you that I am very sorry for this lady and this savage treatment, without exaggeration. It is the jungle with a civilized façade. I hope that finally the lady with her qualities and much good luck will solve her problem, even in this human jungle.

— In order to create the real façade, absolutely correct, of jungle, I propose that those technicians should come to their visit, almost naked, with ostrich feathers on the head, with painted bodies and jumping at the rhythm of tam-tam produced with their drums by other members of their tribe of speculators, said a bicycle, to give a comical note to this very depressing situation.

The proposal was received without delay with a wave of laughter, marking the approval of the audience. Afterwards, the first speaker continued her idea.

— The question which is imposed, at least for a developed country, is: why a legal organization is not created to replace all the existing parasite bureaucracy, a legal organization with juridical and executive power including the police, with immediate action, it means in the same day or not later than next day, obligating the respective technician to solve the problem without any delay and to pay a fine that he will not forget in years, and with immediate perspective of jail if he doesn't comply with the decision. With this approach, this technician will understand very well that his work, the time, the rights and the peace of mind of his clients are not a joke.

By publishing this case in a well visible place in the press, in the television and radio news, the repetition of such a case will be for sure a rare event, because where there isn't consciousness and honor, the fear and the punishment are the most efficient ways to treat the human beings. This service must be free for the claimant as his right as a citizen of the country, all the cost being paid by the culprit. It is very clear that this policy of protection of the consumers of goods and services is not limited to the repair of the heating systems but must cover all the services for the population. This method to solve the problems can be perfectly accomplished by an intelligent administration, for a stupid one, this is an impossible task and for this reason, with the present administration these problems are not solved, even if the country is called developed.

What the bicycles think about the judicial system of the society of human beings and of the related aspects.

The inefficiency of the juridical system in all the cases of anti-social behavior, crimes, robbery, harassment, kidnapping, has a very grave and permanent effect on the society. The purpose of the punishment is to punish the culprits for their actions and to be a deterrent for preventing similar actions by the same or by others in the future. The punishment used at present by the juridical system, including prison of developed country type, at least how they are in the United States and Canada, where the prisons are more like resting houses with all the conveniences about which the honest poor can only dream, is not a punishment and cannot scare the candidates to the infractions. At the same time, this legal procedure with its mild punishments is very cynical, at least, for the victims of the atrocities committed by the convicts. From this point of view, the poor countries of the third world with tough conditions for the incarcerated criminals and thieves, are more developed. Being good with the bad ones is to be bad with the good ones.

— This is hundred percent true, commented immediately other bicycle. A civilized society in a country really developed must treat the anti-social behavior which provokes death, theft, fraud, it is to say physical and psychological pain, exactly how are treated the microbes of cholera, with the only efficient remedy, the eradication without any pity.

— I totally agree with you! exclaimed with enthusiasm her neighbour, but at the same time with the eradication of existing cases it is very wise to think about the prevention of potential cases in the future. For the science it is clear that the cause which provokes all these horrible actions about which we were talking here, is a mental disease exclusive to the human beings. No other species of the animal kingdom is in danger to acquire this disease because they are very well protected by their very powerful instincts. The human beings brain, which commands and controls their actions, is very much influenced by exterior factors of material and psychological character up to a level that can be extremely negative, not known to all other animals. However, this disease can be prevented, and what is interesting, very much easier than can be cured.

Unfortunately, to cure is not possible in all cases. My cyclist is a psychiatrist and knows very well how dangerous the human brain can be when it gets sick with a mental disorder. Sometimes he discuses these problems on the terrace of his house with his friends, doctors also, some of them cyclists, and from my place I can listen to everything, and it is very interesting. I remember that once one of these friends said that the human brain is like a recording tape, and as a real tape, what is recorded, that will play and at least this is the base for the intellectual formation and ulterior behavior. For this reason, the correct education is so important not only for the respective individual but for the society also.

— And the value of the prevention cannot be overestimated. A well-organized and complete prevention action in the daily life of the society, with all the seriousness and carefulness of a surgical operation, can prevent almost totally the terrible effects of this sickness. If, in spite of all this preventive and very careful action, still there are members of the society which are refractory and persistent in their destructive impulses, the unique solution for the protection of the society is their total isolation for long term or permanently, or much better, their physical destruction with all the publicity and propaganda very necessary to teach all others what will happen to them also if they committed the same errors which will be fatal for them.

— It seems that this theory has a solid logical fundament, and very probably will be efficient. However, I would like to know which are the preventive actions, which by all means are of paramount importance.

— I had the intention to talk about this later, but because your very welcome question I will clarify this fundamental issue just now. The preventive action has two parts equally essential. The first one is of material nature and the second of psychological nature.

The action of material nature is the total and complete elimination of poverty in all its existing aspects. This is perfectly possible and must be compulsory in a society, which wants to be developed. This includes the definitive elimination of the unemployment, which means to ensure adequate and permanent work for everybody from the day the education is finished until retirement and after that if the respective member of the society can and desires to work. Ensure excellent and permanent condition of housing, transportation and health for all and all other conditions for a decent and civilized life. Ensuring these conditions, means destroying without any doubt the material base and the incentive for the appearance of robbery, fraud and crime usually associated.

— Today this seems nothing less than a marvelous dream, but I am convinced that it can be realized very easily and I know how. Simply for curiosity, to verify my own opinion, I would like to know yours. Some human beings say for instance that the unemployment problem is impossible to be solved and that always will be unemployment and if it could be reduced from ten percent to eight or seven, this would be a great achievement. I think that this is only the official propaganda for maintaining the unemployed as a reserve of cheap labor and to keep all workers and other employees under the pressure of the fear of being unemployed. To say that this problem cannot be solved or that it is not known how, one should be more than stupid, directly idiot for not having the common sense to solve such a simple problem, if there is the power and the will. The leaders of the society have the power but not the will for the reasons mentioned just before. How the unemployment can be liquidated? Very simply. Today, the vacations in the United States and Canada for instance, are for the great majority two or three weeks for an entire year of work. Two weeks represent only ten working days allowed for vacation for a year of difficult work. This is a kind of modern slavery in countries called developed. On the other hand there are millions of human beings who don't do anything the entire year because there is no work for them. Share the work among all members of the society, with longer vacations so much necessary for all and the unemployment will not exist anymore. As simple as this. The time for additional vacation will be paid from the savings of money presently wasted for unemployment and welfare subsidies. In fact, the savings of money will be very much higher than the cost of these subsidies when all work regularly. And how is possible to evaluate in money the peace of mind and the joy of these millions who received permanent work and of their families, and the peace of mind of those employed now who will no longer fear loosing their jobs? And there are also other additional possibilities, very efficient, to terminate the unemployment. This is what I think about this issue.

— I think that you have a photocopy of my opinion or I have one of yours, how you wish, doesn't matter.

— How interesting! We all here have photocopies of the same opinion about this issue, added quickly a bicycle representing a large group of bicycles.

After this reciprocal recognition of common ideas, a bicycle until then silent, intervened with a story about a little known case.

— From what you said it results that the employers are always the bad ones, which are not preoccupied about the fate of the unemployed, which are always the good ones. I want to relate a case in which the opposite is the reality and reflects the human beings nature independently of their social position. This case occurred many years ago in a school in Montreal, Canada. Because of unfavorable economic circumstances, the number of employees must be reduced by ten percent. The director, who was an exception from the rule, a good and intelligent man, didn't want to throw in the street, without work, the ten percent of his employees, innocent of the economic situation. He had an idea that could improve much the situation. He called a meeting of all the employees, presented the unfortunate situation of the school and his obligation to reduce the budget for salaries by ten percent. He proposed to the employees to vote for one of the two alternatives: the first, to reduce the number of employees by ten percent and the second, to keep all the employees, but to reduce the salary for all by ten percent in this difficult period. And what do you think was the decision of almost all the employees?

— Clearly that in the spirit of solidarity and humanitarian feelings, their decision was to keep all the employees, many of them being friends and colleagues, even with a reduction in salary of ten percent.

— No, the almost unanimous decision of the employees was, none of them knowing who will be kept as employee and who will be unemployed, to reduce the number of employees by ten percent and to maintain the full salary for the rest. This was the decision of the employees themselves and so it was implemented

— Incredible and sad, these are the human beings. I don't know if this example is valid for all the employees from all places, but it cannot be ignored. Some times I feel sorry for the employees and also for the unemployed, as victims of the owners, but at the same time it seems to me that if next day the same employees or unemployed by a miracle become the owners, they would do exactly the same things as the owners of today. It is sad but I am afraid that this could be the reality.

— The case related by you is interesting and alarming at the same time and must be treated very seriously. The human beings are as they are and their greed and their desire for money as a first priority are well known. Your example shows once more that the mass of human beings cannot organize themselves in an intelligent manner, they go as a herd of sheep where the leader goes, to the good or to the bad. For this, in their society everything depends on who is the leader. With stupid leaders and without vision, the society, or the herd of human beings, moves in a circle, doesn't advance, as it would be possible with intelligent and visionary leaders. All the rational social organization which a sister said that today is only a dream, would be possible with the only condition "sine qua non", what means undisputable, that the herd of human beings was led by the intelligent and visionary leaders about which I talked. The leaders of the society must be not the politicians of today but the engineers, because the base of the organization of the society must be the science named the social engineering which will solve all the major problems of the today's society and will prevent all the present social, economic and psychological-spiritual disasters.

Your example when the employees voted for the stupid solution, which you said, is an alarm signal but it doesn't mean that the intelligent solution about which we talked before, is not possible. With the control of the mass of human beings in an intelligent manner, such a voting will not be necessary because the unemployment will not be an option. So, the ideas expressed here before, are perfectly valid, don't worry about it.

Well, said the same bicycle, now I want to continue my idea about the necessary conditions for the prevention of the anti-social activities. Only to ensure the material base is not enough, it is not a guarantee for the success of the action. To create this guarantee is necessary the second part, the intense program of permanent education, from two years of age until the end of life. This refers to the complex education, moral, civic, professional and scientific. The religion and the superstition must disappear from the life of a developed country as a very dangerous cerebral infection and as a label of primitivism. At the present, in the countries called developed, there is an entire system of religious education of all denominations, making sick the mind of the human beings from children to youngsters and adults in institutions called "religious schools" and "theological universities". What a direct, shameless insult to the noble title of school and university! These institutions must disappear completely from the territory of a country, which pretends to be "developed", as whatever other institutions where extremely dangerous drugs and narcotics are prepared, sold and distributed. The profession of priest, which is identical with that of thief, crook and criminal for the guilt of poisoning the defenseless brains, especially of the children, must also disappear and the existing priests must be obligated to retrain for a productive manual labor, or to leave the country without delay with the alternative of being expelled.

— But this action will represent the recognition of their power and that the only way of convincing an audience about the truth of an opposite theory, is to eliminate the adversary, which has other opinion.

— This is a very valuable observation but not correct although seems like that. What you are saying is exactly so. With one single difference. The priests are the ones who are doing it, not their opponents. Always and on a grand scale. In all the public presentations and sermons there is never an opponent, it is not permitted to anybody to ask questions or to make comments accordingly with the principle "believe and don't ask" There are many congregations in each place of prayer and also large televised conventions with thousands and thousands of participants. Who speaks there? Only the priest, delivering for hours such an amount of idiocy and stupidity that could bore an atheist up to making him fall asleep in five minutes, but has the hypnotizing effect on the mass of believers which behave and look at the priest as a herd of cows without any sign of intelligent reaction. And the priest talks and talks playing the role of the only expert in everything and of all-powerful fighter in a fight without enemies present there.

In these reunions, the priest, sometimes a well-known evangelist, multimillionaire with the money robbed from the believers, always smiles and gesticulates with absolute confidence based not in what he says but on who are listening to him. He knows that nobody from the thousands of participants can be an opponent, or ask the most timid question. This can be seen also in the sermons of each Sunday morning in some main television channels.

— The most advanced technology at the service to the most advanced idiocy! But the country is called "developed"! was the observation of a bicycle very indignant about this flagrant contradiction.

— This is true, we live in such a strange world! To finish my response I want to say that the priests never address to those who can ask embarrassing questions and put them in doubt. They always choose for their activity victims without defense. For this, we want these parasites of the society, out of the country. Otherwise they will always look for other victims for their activity. If we, the bicycles, were in control of the scientific education of the society of the human beings, we would organize televised conferences with the participation in a free discussion of all the priests, which would like to enter in a dialogue with scientists, engineers, doctors and even with persons without a special qualification but with common sense. I think that no one priest will attend because they know very well that this will be a lost battle, but in this way we invite all the believers who have at least a little of critical spirit, to listen, ask, judge, and may be to revise their opinions about their own belief.

— I have one last question. You said that the priests, among other bad things, are also criminals for the offense of poisoning the mind of children. I agree with this because this is the potential cause of terrorism. Who knows, due to this action of a religious leader of whatever denomination one of today's children can be converted in a terrorist twenty years later. Is very clear that the terrorism is the direct result of the religious fanaticism, which has its roots in the religious education. With this logical relation between cause and effect, a priest or others in similar capacity can be condemned by law as a criminal. Why all of them enjoy all the freedom in total defiance of this logic?

— What an opportune question! The response is that in fact for the demonstrated reason, a priest or a representative of any other religion is a criminal but legally he is not, and cannot be convicted because first is necessary to change the juridical system which at present is itself criminal, at least in this regard. But nevertheless, the country is called developed. Is it clear?

— Now everything is very clear, thanks.

— And in order to be even clearer it is necessary to analyze briefly the reality of prisons in the developed countries. The same bicycle continued with her idea.

— Talking about prisons for those with long terms convictions, for many years or for their entire life, who are beasts which committed terrible things, although there are not crimes which are not terrible, a realist judgment is imposed about the cost of these prisons for the society and how this cost can be justified. The society has the right to know how its money is spent, or wasted, and the prisons cost a lot of money. The question is how this is justified, or is not justified?

I want to make it perfectly clear from the beginning that this judgment is not caused by a selfish thinking, or by greed or indifference for the human life. By the contrary, this judgment is determined with pure objectivity considering all parts involved and with a very necessary mixture of human feelings with the elementary logic. Now let me apply this method of reasoning to a case of a criminal convicted for life in prison for one or more crimes.

The first question: how much this decision of the court costs? Costs lots of money, more than a luxury hotel, every day, considering all the expenses to maintain a prison.

The second question: for whom this money is spent? It is spent for a criminal who killed a totally innocent human being, who lived before a normal life, maybe happy, being a child, a mother, or a father with children, now orphans. Can you imagine the physical and psychological torture of the victim before dying by the hands of the criminal? Doing this, this criminal can be considered a human being with rights? The categorical response is NO! He is not a human being, only has the appearance of a human being but he is a beast, which has one single right: to die, without delay and with a very painful punishment before dying.

The third question: what is the purpose to keep this criminal, this beast, for all his life, or even for twenty years, in a prison with all the facilities of a civilized life, at a high cost which is in fact a big waste? The only purpose that can be seen is to reward the criminal, the beast, for his crime, by ensuring an existence without problems for all his life and with the police protecting his personal security from the enemies he might have outside the prison. The society is not well protected with the criminal in prison. Always there may be a possibility for him to escape, to be released on parole, and for those with a limited time of detention, there is no guarantee that after their release from prison they will not repeat their criminal behaviour, at least for revenge. The thousands of recidivists are a very eloquent testimony. The society will be better protected, and it can be said really protected, by executing these criminals. At the same time a significant saving of money is achieved, money so much necessary for urgent problems. The employees of the prison could change their depressing work, which produces nothing, for an enjoyable job, productive for the society, which will result in an increment of the standard of living for all.

The fourth question: which are the rights of the society and of the victims of the criminals and of their families in what concerns how to proceed with the criminals? None. Nobody asks the society, the victims and their families and friend about this issue. Simply and automatically their money is robbed from their salaries as taxes, for the maintenance of the prisons and of criminals, with all the defiance, arrogance and cynicism possible.

The fifth question: knowing all this I just talked about, how can be explained the present position of the legislation, of the government of a country called developed, in face of this reality which is not less than sinister? Are the legislators guilty? Certainly they are, clearly not directly for the behavior of the criminals and thieves but indirectly they are guilty for the effects of the existing laws with which they justify themselves even if these laws do not make any sense and are contrary to the basic interests of the society. Can you imagine how, according to the existing laws, the fathers of the killed children or the sons of the killed fathers must pay for the maintenance in good conditions of the beast, which killed a dear being of his family? And this relates also to the friends of the victims and to all other human beings with common sense sympathizing with the victims, who think in the same manner.

As soon as the previous speaker finished her last word, a very impatient bicycle to express her opinion, started to talk:

— In connection with the death penalty for the criminals and thieves with which I am completely in agreement for reasons so well demonstrated here, I have a proposal and a question.

— Tell them please.

— My proposal is to increase to the maximum possible the justice where the death penalty is applicable, confiscating everything that the condemned have, to compensate as much as possible the terrible damage done by them to the society.

— You want to say, to recuperate everything what they robbed and all what they have, their personal things and values? I agree that the law should mention this, make it compulsory. They, these criminals and thieves don't deserve anything and nobody should have the right to enjoy the inheritance of a criminal or thief.

— This is very clear, but I am talking about all what they have, not only the material values as money and things.

— This is all. What more?

— Their body with all the organs that could be transplanted and so to save the life of very sick people whom without these transplants will die. The criminals condemned with death penalty will die anyway and there is no reason for not making their death of some use for the society.

— The idea seems to me more than reasonable, is very humanitarian and must be obligatory. Now, what is your question?

— My question is: why this is not the current practice at present, knowing that there is a long waiting list for these organs and so much suffering could be eliminated and so many lives saved?

— Your question makes very much sense but the answer is very simple, the lack of logic and real humanitarian feelings of the human beings which must be responsible of this aspect. At the same time, it seems to me that maybe also the concern for abuse, for the traffic of the organs obtained with the death penalty, but I am sure that this can be avoided and that the enormous gains, real and immediate, cannot be compared with the mentioned risk which is only theoretical and very improbable.

I am firmly of the opinion that the very institution of the prison cannot solve neither prevent or eradicate the phenomena of crime, robbery and anti-social behavior in general. This is demonstrated in an absolute manner by the undeniable reality that both co-exist for many centuries without any sign of success or at least of essential improvement of the situation. I am also of the opinion that although the death penalty is more efficient, the civilized society must and can reach the level when the prison and also the death penalty are not necessary anymore. Not immediately but this is possible and if this is a lock, the key is the education. And the bicycle continued with her very interesting idea:

— An important part of the education is to start with the normal behavior in the society in all directions, cutting first in a radical manner all negative influences. At this chapter, what requires an emergency change is almost all television programs and the movies playing today at movie theatres, the immense majority of which are Hollywood productions. These programs and movies educate all, children, youngsters and adults in the spirit of crime, violence, lack of noble human feelings, or promote the naked stupidity. The programs of cartoons for children are in their great majority horrible, with much violence also and without any intelligent sense. The characters in the cartoons have horrible faces and roles playing in actions from which the children don't have anything good to learn; in the best cases the children get accustomed not to think. Watching these programs and movies for years, produces a damage that could be irreversible to these brains so young and fragile. They have the same effects for adults. There is nothing really what to enjoy, only to watch. The programs and movies with crimes, violence, robbery and other negative aspects in an incessant torrent represents a similar danger with a crime against the society and must be treated as actions directly connected with the roots of crime and robbery.

— Everything is very well and intelligent, but what happens if both actions jointly, the material security and the intensive education, in some cases probably isolated, do not produce the expected results? asked a bicycle which does not accept incomplete actions.

— It must be very clear that only these two basic and peaceful actions are not enough. The civilized society cannot permit the defiance of some, even very few, which can cause with their example of anti-social behavior a great damage to the entire constructive policy. For this is necessary and obligatory an additional action, the uncompromising force and the total change of the present legislation which in fact stimulates the offenses against the law by a system of too mild punishments which do not produce the expected positive results.

— This is true, intervened a very bellicose bicycle, the prisons for long-term detention are not necessary, only the ones for a temporary detention until the cases are clarified. If the suspicion against one accused is not justified, the accused must be released immediately. If the suspicion for a crime or robbery is justified, and especially in obvious cases, the death penalty is more efficient than all the prisons together. This may sound inhuman but firstly is necessary to clarify well who deserves a human treatment, the criminal or the victim? As was demonstrated in many cases, the prison is nothing more than a school where one can learn how to be a better criminal or robber, how to avoid to be caught and how to improve his criminal skills. This is proven by so many cases of repeating an offense in all kind of actions against the law, including crimes and robbery. How can be explained that a delinquent is condemned four or five times? Some of them have an unbelievable number of a dozen of infractions. The explanation is that the prison is not the solution and a thief or criminal doesn't get better for the society, he continues to be a potential thief or criminal, who can always use an opportunity that seems to him without risk. And while in prison, the criminals have all the comfort, running water, hygienic conditions, television, sports programs, food three times a day, clean clothes, cultural programs, visits by family members and friends, the benefit of being released on parole and, as incredible as it can be, the automatic release when the condemned reaches the age of seventy. This was a case published in the Canadian newspapers about a criminal with twelve convictions, which in short time will become a free citizen in spite of all the protests of one of the victims of his own family who is now very scared by this perspective.

— And to add insult to injury, some condemned for multiple crimes, take university courses, write books which are subjects for movies which will produce millions of dollars. So they prepare themselves for a luxurious life enjoying the proceeds of crime, which proves to be the vehicle for this better life. What is all this, justice or joke? This shows without doubt that the entire justice system is bad, as a dirty business involving legislators, judges, lawyers, the entire prison industry, all the immense bureaucracy involved in interminable lawsuits which end up very frequently with a minor punishment for the criminal, without much consideration for the victim. Who knows how many officials in very high positions and possibly even members of the government, are directly interested in preserving the present situation forever.

— This possibility is a probability that could very well be a certainty. How otherway can be explained that such powerful countries like England, France, Canada and the most powerful in the world, the United States, which in the Second World War could defeat in less than six years such a strong enemy, well organized, and which with its armies kept under direct control the entire Europe, as the nazist Germany, and the same countries with all their armed forces much more powerful today than before, with all the force of the police, and of espionage and counter-espionage agencies, during the last more than fifty years after the world war cannot win the war against the car theft for instance? In fact, this war is lost every day. I don't know the exact statistics in France and England and in other countries "developed" in car theft but I know that in the United States and Canada this is an entire industry and daily business with a number simply incredible of stolen cars, after that modified and sold in the same country or exported to third world countries. There are shops specialized in this and an entire underground network which deals with this very profitable business involving tens of thousands of cars each year. Where are the police? All the detectives? The few cars, which are recuperated, are only a joke. It is impossible for such a powerful state with so many adequate resources to win this war? Or simply the leaders don't want to declare such a war because of their hidden interests?

Exactly the same is the case with the war against the drugs. This is other war lost each day also demonstrating the incapacity of the powerful state apparatus, of the police and detective agencies equipped with all necessary resources, to finish definitively with the drugs and with addiction to them. They cannot or do not want. Possibly both. It is simply a lack of common sense and a shame to use the word "developed" to describe a country where the drug dealers are in fact stronger than the police and the state.

— I am convinced that if the police gets the permission from the government, or more than this, if the government orders the police to eradicate the car theft and the drug business taking all the necessary measures, in very short time the car robbery and the drug business will be a thing of the past, of a shameful past. And the car theft is only an example; the same applies to all stolen things.

— Among all other stolen things, as you said, I would like to make a special mention to the massive bicycle theft. I am from Toronto, Canada, a quiet, clean city with civilized appearance, but the official statistics say that Toronto is a city world champion in bicycle theft. This is also a well-organized action and business and practically the police don't do anything to stop and counter-action this criminal activity. They rob us, mistreat us, and sell us in whole and in parts. The thieves, who are street bandits, do not have any scruples. My cyclist and I travel a lot in the city, in parks to relax or in the streets for some interests, but my cyclist never leaves me without supervision when we stop in some place. He never leaves me in public places for long time, although always protects me with two solid chains.

When we go to buy vegetables and fruits at a Chinese shop not very far from the house and he enters the shop only for five minutes, he always ties me with the chain to a tree or metal pillar. With him, I feel completely safe but other cyclists are not so careful and because of this so many of us are stolen.

— It is very sad but very true what you say. I have my ideas but I would like to hear what other sisters think about the ways to cut this theft that occurs each day in Toronto and in very many other places.

There are very simple methods but extremely efficient, but the human beings don't want to use them, got involved again in the discussion the bellicose bicycle. She continued:

These methods are applicable not only to cut the theft of us, the bicycles, but also to cut the theft of cars and of other things.

— And how in your opinion, this theft can be cut?

— Using a very old method but very efficient, cutting the hand which steals, by an open, massive terror which must be legal, against the terror of thieves of any kind. For grave cases and for all the crimes, cutting not only the hands, which are the performers, but also the head, which plans the action.

— But in this case it will be a real massacre.

— Massacre of whom? I think that you agree with me, we don't talk here about a massacre of human beings; this will be a massacre only of thieves and criminals, which will clean the society in an efficient and irreversible manner.

— Yes, I agree with you, and I think that all of us agree with you, but I would like to know, there is other method that could be used with these thieves and criminals?

— Certainly, but I think that will not be so efficient.

— Tell me please, which is this method.

— To give to each thief and criminal a kiss and caress his head telling him at the same time: "many thanks my dear, repeat your actions please, as many times as you want".

A wave of laughter that seemed that couldn't end covered the entire audience. When finally the laughter calmed down, the bellicose bicycle continued her idea:

— Talking about the massacre of thieves and criminals, I want to repeat without reservation that if this is necessary to eradicate the theft and the crime in the society, this price is insignificant, but I can say with scientific precision that a massacre will not be necessary.
— Why?
— Because all the thieves and criminals are neither idealists nor religious fanatics of suicidal category, those are of other kind, more dangerous, with whom it is possible to deal in other way. The thieves and current criminals are selfish and cowards, they don't want to die or to be hurt or maltreated, all what they want is to rob and kill for their own interests without danger for themselves and without punishment.

To avoid the necessity of a massacre, which is not a pleasure for the society, the punishments, as I said, must be done not in secret but with the largest publicity in the newspapers, other publications, television and radio, and also by official announcements. By this, only a few cases of punishment will be enough to cut the desire of very many, if not all, other potential criminals and thieves. The number of cases of fraud, theft and crime after only a few cases of punishment with good publicity will be reduced with the speed of a stone in free fall.
— I have an example to sustain this probability, in fact, two examples.
— Tell them.

— The first one refers to the necessity to isolate those with anti-social behavior in the same way as we proceed with the rotten apples in a box with good apples. What do we do with the bad apples, we leave them in the same box with the good apples hoping that they will take the good example from the good apples and will become themselves good apples? Or we put them in a prison for apples hoping that there they will be reeducated and will become good apples? Or simply we put them in the garbage and so we save the good apples? There is a greater probability for a rotten apple to become a good apple than for a criminal to change his behavior. Why take such a great risk with his power or lack of power, to control himself in the immediate or in the far future? Do they deserve it? Clearly they don't. The undisputable proof for this are the criminals and thieves recidivists. Not only some of them but many of them are recidivists for two, four, five times and more, due to the unlimited stupidity of the human beings, which in spite of the evidence, think that the prison is a miraculous cure. It is better to learn from Mother Nature and her iron rules. And here it comes my second example. How many human beings come close to the edge of an abyss or outside of a balcony? Almost nobody. Why? Because they know that the nature with its law of gravity, doesn't have pity for anybody, neither for an innocent child, if one falls, dies. The human beings know this and don't take the risk. They know also that the nature does not give to anybody fallen in an abyss for instance, the second chance, what is also the possibility to repeat the mistake. And the society doesn't suffer because of the existence of these implacable laws of the nature, simply obeys them and everything is fine. The same will happen if similar laws to those of the nature were adopted for the protection of the society. Everybody will enjoy a peaceful and tranquil life without permanent fear of criminals and thieves, and nobody will care about the death of a criminal or robber, which with his actions, caused his own bad fate, knowing well the involved risk.

— Very well said, and all that you demonstrated so clearly is very logical and rational. However, I am wondering why the same logic is not shared by a category of human beings, which never did anything bad in their life, but are defenders of the criminals and thieves. They are called "activists for the human rights". And they fight, in fact they make the society waste time and resources, to improve the conditions in prisons, for the abolition of the death penalty in the countries where it exists and for not introducing it in the countries where it does not exist, said a bicycle with a fine feeling of observation.

— An effectively very interesting question. The human beings society has a great variety of strange or very curious cases. These "activists" are such a case and they try to defend the human rights for those who are not human. It is not very clear how the head of such an "activist" works. What is clear is that they want to be in two boats at the same time or to have a cake and eat it. They want, or they think that they could be good with the criminals and with their victims. This is simply impossible and in fact they do a great damage to the society. These goodies—goodies, probably without bad intention, or even not conscious of the result of their actions, provoke indirectly, more victims in the society.

— And what can the society do or must do with these creatures?

— I have a solution that surely will cure them, said a bicycle with much practical spirit.

— We are very interested to listen to you.

— These "activists for the human rights" are like those who like the war and the horrors of war when watching them on television or at the movie theatre. But if suddenly they are mobilized and sent in the first line of the real war, this will be a quite different story and the taste for the war will disappear in very short time. They don't know by their own experience the horror of being attacked, or attacked and raped, there are many women also "activists", and how one feels when a thief enters his house during the night. If one day their own son or daughter is killed or wounded by a bandit, it is sure that the "humanitarian" feelings will disappear in the same moment in which this disastrous news reaches them. If this doesn't occur, we talk about a mentally sick or about one with a stony heart.

The solution is to put these "activists" in the situation of the victims or at least of potential victims, leaving them officially and with everybody's knowledge, without police protection. The authorities would confirm publicly that if they are attacked and the culprits caught, they will be treated with much affection and attention for their human rights according to the desires of the "activists". I think that this treatment for no more than one month, in which they will have little sleep and be always scared even by their own shadow, will be a very efficient cure.

— Very good idea, such a situation surely will wake-up these "activists" from their dream about the human quality of these ferocious animals whose rights they are defending.

— By using these mild punishments, intervened in the discussion a bicycle with passion for discipline and security, the legislators are like these "activists" indirectly guilty of all crimes, robberies and other anti-social activities. A mild punishment has the same effect as an insufficient dose of medicine, doesn't cure the sickness, only makes the sick person to feel better for a while; the microbes are not destroyed, they become stronger and attack again. A doctor who prescribes an insufficient dose is in fact guilty for the disease of his patient. If this is repeated, the doctor is not good and a legal action in the court is possible. Other example is with a fireman who extinguishes a fire but not completely, and afterwards the fire revives and continues to provoke damages.

The today's legislators in countries called "developed" behave without responsibility as that doctor or fireman from the examples, and being at the top of the legislative pyramid, nobody punish them. Comparing them with "activists for the human rights" who only can ask for mild punishments, the legislators are more dangerous because they make the laws and take the decisions for milder penalties, with all the respective negative effects.

— The people, the mass of human beings, do not have anything to say?

— As can be seen, always accept all the decisions of their leaders without protesting.

— I have one more question, said the young bicycle. The opinion of the tourists and visitors about the real situation in the developed countries is important but not essential. What are essential, is the opinion and the reaction of the inhabitants, citizen of the developed countries about these unacceptable situations in their own countries. I would like to know this reality also.

— You are very young but your question has a very profound sense. The response is sad enough for the value of the human beings and confirms the low level of this value. The great majority of them are indifferent to what is going on in the society, even if the negative aspects of the reality could affect one day, their own lives. Very many of them simply do not understand the real causes of the existing situation and not only that they don't know how to change it, but also they do not think about changing anything. If they see beggars and other human beings sleeping in the street, they continue walking in their way considering them as part of the environment and no more. They don't mind and never protest. If you ask them directly about the existing situation, they feel bothered in their mental comfort and look for excuses, saying for instance, talking about the beggars and homeless people in the street: "how many of them have you seen? only some, the great majority have houses and also don't beg" or they are "lazy, don't want to work, they are drug addicts, are drinkers, are crazy, don't want to live in a house" and other bad things about them. Only they have all the guilt, the society is innocent like an angel. They think the same about the unemployment: "only ten percent don't have work, but the great majority works. Maybe that the unemployed don't want to work or don't look well for finding work"

So, these indifferent with very short minds wash their hands and feel good. Until the day when they themselves lose their jobs and become desperate for money. Then they wake-up, understand that not everything is good in the society, think about their bad luck, accuse their bosses, but not the economic system of the society, they cannot see so far. And for this the system continues to exist safely and to produce other victims, without stopping. This is the reality about how the human beings think and act, or better said how don't act. It is true that there is also a tiny minority of citizens of these developed countries which understands very well the real causes of bad things that occur in the society as the rule, but they understand at the same time that with the existing mentality of the great majority, nobody can change anything and that the only solution is to live with this reality. Now I think that the definition of what a developed country means, in more than one aspect is clear enough.

— Very clear, I learned a lot, answered the junior bicycle, which initiated all the discussion with her question about the developed countries.

Followed a short pause in which the bicycles reflected with sadness about the much more complex reality than can be seen at the surface and tried to understand well the multiple aspects of this reality. Suddenly a demand to talk was heard.

— Excuse me please, hurried to make public her opinion a bicycle which listened with much attention to this issue of the discussion, I have a very dirty but very adequate example for the situation described here in the developed countries.

— Dirty? Dirty example? asked with curiosity other bicycle. Tell us please, this dirty example.

— Well, it was presented here as an undisputable fact that in the countries called developed, with great material and technological resources, with great wealth for all to enjoy, not only for a minority, there are also cases of misery, of poverty, of homeless people sleeping in the street, without work, desperate. I don't know how many are in this situation and I am not interested. All that I am interested in is that by all means there is at least one single case, which can be solved, and nobody does anything for this.

Now, to understand better the situation, just look at this example. In a very rich, even luxurious restaurant, very elegant and clean, with round tables for ten people, with all the plates, cutlery, tablecloth and napkins brilliantly clean, elegant waiters who carry fresh and tasty food for the guests also very elegant and well dressed waiting very hungry to savor the food; everything is very good with one exception. In the middle of the table there is one single plate that is very dirty, with a very stinky shit. This dirty and stinky plate shouldn't be at the table, by no means, but if for whatever reason it is there, it can be easily removed and clean everything to be as clean as the clean rest of the table but nobody does anything and all continue to eat with this view in front of their eyes and with the stink mixing with the flavor of the tasty food, exactly how in the modern society, rich and developed. Final.
— Your example is dirty indeed, but very adequate for the situation existing in the society of the human beings in the countries called developed.

It seems that to discuss about the stupidity and the mental incapacity of the human beings, about their obvious inferiority to all other species and for sure to themselves, the bicycles, was a great pleasure for all the participants in that reunion and many of them didn't want to lose this unique opportunity to present their opinions and in a very obvious manner, to discharge their anxiety. It was as an International Court of Justice in which the judges were at the same time the witnesses, the public prosecutors, and in some isolated cases, the defendant lawyers. What is very interesting to notice is that all the expressed judgments are just, have sense and are impossible to fight by a sane mind.

The few questions and observations almost comical were due to the youth and to the innocence of the respective bicycles and were explained and clarified without delay and thoroughly by other bicycles with more life experience.

Well, now is already very late at night and the discussion will continue with the same passion, ingenuity and rich participation next day, according to unanimous decision of the bicycles, in the same place, at the same time.

SECOND PART

Comments by the bicycles about the arts of the human beings.

Next day, as it was decided, the second bicycle reunion took place to continue the very interesting discussion about other aspects of the life in society of the human beings, with the totally objective and neutral interpretation pertinent to the bicycles.

The first issue of the discussion was the art and how the stupidity of the human beings is reflected in this field of their activity.
— The stupidity of the human beings is so big, profound and multilateral that we can discuss about this subject with a multitude of interesting examples, a week, a month or even a year, but we don't have this time.

The housing problem, about which we had such a prolonged and ardent discussion, and also very instructive for all of us, represents only one of the multiple aspects of the so irrational life of the human beings. However, there are also other aspects of their unlimited stupidity. There are many of them, but I would like to talk and discuss between us about the most obvious ones. Understanding them well is very important for us due to our dependency of the human beings.

If we cannot change and improve them, at least we must know them very well in order to be better aware of what we can expect from them for us. In what concerns me, I would like to talk and to listen to other opinions about, for instance, the culture, the sports, various consequences of the social organization of the human beings, which affects us a lot, directly or indirectly.

The words of this participant for first time in the discussion were accepted with a roar of approval. And she continued:

I live in a small town but I traveled a lot, I know many places in various countries. My cyclist always takes me with him in his business or vacation trips and so I had the occasion to know about a great diversity of habits and activities connected with the culture, with the way of life of the human beings in many characteristic situations. For sure, there are interesting things, good and easy to understand for a rational mind but, very unfortunately, these are the minority, and what is worse, this minority is reduced with each passing day. The very fact of advancing of the human beings society in this direction with little or no resistance, is a sad but very sure sign of their continuous degradation.

There are so many things about which I would like to talk, that I don't know with which to start. I will do it at random. Well, let's talk about their cultural life, the arts for instance. The ancient Greeks were famous for their nice sculptures, for the accurate and tasteful reproduction of the human body. Two thousand years later, at present, the sculptures that can be seen in museums or exhibited in public places are in the best case, horrible representations, which only can scare a child or make an adult to lose his good mood.
— You say that this is the best case, asked a bicycle, but what can be the worse case?
— The worse case, worse for the very notion of art, is that is not possible to understand anything of what the sculpture represents.

Nobody with his mind functioning normally can understand or describe it. The "work of art" can be a stone, a deformed piece of metal, or a set of such pieces, a concrete block, a piece of wood without a specific shape, a whatever combination of materials of various shapes and sizes, defying the elementary common sense, and which do not mean absolutely anything, in spite of their titles, sometimes very precise. Briefly, this art called "modern" or "abstract" is an insult for the definition of art and for those who enter an art museum to enjoy.

— In other words, today every idiot can be an artist, commented other bicycle,

— Exactly, but these idiots or crazy who produce these abstract "works of art" are not at all idiots or crazy when the issue of money arises. These pieces of garbage cost a pile of money if you want to buy them.

— But who buys them, if they are bought.

— They are bought, other idiots buy them. They themselves do not understand a thing about what these very expensive "sculptures" and "works of art" represent, not because they are idiots but because there is nothing to understand. However, they buy them exactly and solely because their price is so high. In this way they think they can show off in the eyes of others.

— It would be very interesting to know how much costs to produce these "works of art", was the comment of a bicycle which in fact was a question soliciting an answer.

— I don't know exactly, was the answer, but in general the production cost for these objects is close to zero. What is important is the cost for transporting them, and this varies a lot. Some of these objects called "works of art" can be carried in the pocket, like the famous "work" exhibited in an American exhibition and which is nothing more than a piece of eight or ten centimeters of the most ordinary rope fixed on the wall with two nails or bolts. The value of this "work" was established to eight thousand American dollars. This is a real case shown in the well-known American television program "sixty

minutes". On the other hand, there are other "works" which are objects meaning nothing also, but which are of concrete or metal and weight several tons. The cost of transporting them is similar with the cost of transporting the same weight or amount of garbage.
— And why those idiots who don't understand them, buy them paying so much money?
— To show them to other idiots visiting them, friends and businessmen. They don't understand anything either, but are impressed by the price paid and by the cabalistic description made by the artistic mafia which is an integral part of this circus. And no one of those visitors who look at the strange objects named "works of art" has the courage or enough intelligence to declare that all this is not more than a grotesque farce, or at least, that he or she doesn't understand it and that doesn't feel any artistic emotion. Except an insignificant minority, this never occurs. Looking at these "works of art" which are in reality pure garbage, in museums or in the private houses of the owners of these "works", they pretend to understand them, or to be experts, launching courtesies to please their bosses or friends. Without any doubt some of them lie, all others, which sincerely think that they understand the message transmitted by the admired "works", are authentic idiots. This behavior specific only to human beings is one of the undeniable proofs of the really very low level of their intelligence. Talking from the point of view of the artistic sculpture and comparing it with the level of intelligence of the ancient Greeks, of two thousand years ago, this level is obviously going down.
— The same happens with other arts, got involved in the discussion a bicycle, which was clearly in a hurry to express her opinion about this issue.
My cyclist is an amateur painter in his free time. In our trips I had the opportunity to see many paintings of different styles and epochs, very nice paintings of several centuries ago, very impressive paintings, so much alive, painted by famous painters, especially from the nineteenth century and also paintings belonging to the art

called "modern art" of the second half of the twentieth century. In several decades this "modern art" about which spoke before other sister, invaded the artistic and cultural life of the society of human beings and inundated it with an avalanche of works similar in value and in manner of expression with the "works of art" in sculpture. Looking at these "works" which today occupy an enormous space in art museums and private exhibitions, you ask yourself how is possible for human beings who consider themselves rational beings, to substitute the real art of painting which requires so much feeling, talent, capacity of communicating and sense of reality, with some drawings or paintings which do not represent anybody and anything, which are no more than an irrational mixture of lines, curves and colors, which do not have and cannot have any message. These so called "works of modern art" or "surrealist" represent the intellectual disaster of the human beings, a shame for the true culture, an insult for the lovers of painting as a sensible art, involved in an intimate manner with the reality and with the common sense. The surrealist substitute is only a graphic representation of a crazy mind.

— There is so much truth in what you just said, commented other bicycle addressing to the speaker. If one wants, it is possible to give an endless number of examples about this issue.

What is more important is the aspect of evolution of the intellect of the human beings in the direction opposite to the progress. If a visitor from other planet, studying the history of the evolution of the human beings from the primitive stage to the present, discovering the paintings of classical art of the last century and of previous centuries and the works of ""modern" art of the present time, he will relate for sure the paintings of realist, classic style, to the present time, as the result of evolution of the art of the human beings from the Stone Age to which the extra-terrestrial visitor would thing that the "modern art" works belong.

— However, mentioned other bicycle, in spite of all this which is the pure truth, the incomprehensible works of "modern art" are at the same time a shame for the culture and a very good business for those who produce them and those who sell them. If you have the adequate connections, you can make a fortune in a few minutes.

— How

— Very simply. Take a piece of carton, preferably rectangular, the color doesn't matter and neither the size, can be from half of a square meter up to several square meters, draw on this carton for instance, a square of other color, of the same color is also acceptable, and the painting is ready to be exhibited and sold.

— This is all? asked with a tone of disbelief a very young bicycle.

— All. Believe me please, this is all. However, I must mention that depending on the inspiration of the "artist" or "painter" how the producer of the garbage wants to call himself, the square may be not exactly a square, the painting can contain more than a square, can be whatever combination of geometrical and non-geometrical figures, for instance of some circles not very round and a human eye, briefly, an infinity of alternatives.

— But there are not rules and regulations for the painter according to the subject and with the title of the painting? asked the same young one.

— No one rule, absolutely none.

— If I understand well, in this case, if I were a human being, I could take a piece of canvas or carton, throw on it the paint of various colors, dry it, put this piece of carton or canvas in a frame and pretend that I produced a work of art?

— Precisely. With the only comment that you don't have to worry about various colors, with only one color you could obtain the same result. And the frame is not a must either.

— And you say that I could exhibit this work of art of mine and sell it, possibly for a high price?

— Well, up to this point the road is open for all but here you find a barrier. Everything depends on your status. Everybody can produce such "works of art", especially the authentic idiots and including also monkeys in the zoo, but to exhibit and sell them, this is other thing, for this you need relations and a name, a name of an idiot well known and accepted by the artistic mafia of the human beings society. Other comment: if you have a normal mind and live in a circle of very intelligent people and suddenly you start to produce such "works of art", they can consider you crazy. If for instance, you are an engineer and you show to your boss your production as a work of art, there is a great risk to lose your job.

— But if you are mechanic, doctor or lawyer? asked with curiosity the same bicycle.

— If you are a mechanic or a doctor you can lose clients or patients, but if you are a lawyer, you don't have any problem.

— Why? The lawyers have a special position?

— Clearly, because most of them are by definition legal bandits and thieves, and there is a great similarity between a surrealist "artist" of "abstract" or "modern" art, doesn't matter how it is named, trying to present his work as real art, and the work of a lawyer trying, and many times succeeding to demonstrate that one who robbed a million is a honest man and that a criminal is the victim or an innocent. They charge for one hour of their time a pile of money, in many cases the salary of a qualified worker for a week. Trying to clarify the social aspect of this anomaly, the same bicycle asked:

— But if they, the lawyers, are so bad, and I say "if" because I didn't have the occasion to know them or to hear much about them, why the other human beings accept them?

— A very interesting question. The answer is not favorable for the human beings in general because it shows other aspect of their profound stupidity, this time in what concerns their social organization.

Many years before, in other epochs, lawyers didn't exist, the human society could function without them. All legal problems were solved by the good judgment of the human beings in charge with those problems and many times by the common sense of the older members of the community. The law was more simple and easy to understand. Look what happens today. Instead of being the way to obtain justice, the law was transformed in an instrument of speculation rather than of protection. And it was made so complicated that even a graduate cannot understand it. No transaction can be made without lawyers, who take maximal advantage of this situation and make every possible effort to complicate it more. To legalize a contract or a business deal by shaking hands or by a gentlemen agreement is an antiquity, which is not used anymore.

— Talking not about very rare exceptions but about the immense majority, the lawyers are licensed thieves in the society of human beings and today represent an entire category of parasites which do not produce anything and live very well, extremely well, by using an artificially created necessity, exactly as the priests. I am from the United States of America, I don't know what is the situation in other countries, but in the United States there is now an epidemic of lawsuits with the obvious intention to use all the flaws of the laws to get rich very fast. Some of the participants in this game gain, others lose, but the lawyers always gain.

— What an interesting digression, to start with the surrealist art and to arrive at lawyers! commented other bicycle.

— Both have something in common, are representatives of the stupidity and decadence of the society of the human beings, completed a third bicycle.

— True, true, true, pronounced her verdict other bicycle with much conviction. Although this discussion about lawyers is so interesting, I would like to return for a short time to the surrealist or modern art, if we can name it art with this manner of painting, because I have some other questions about this issue.

— We are listening to you.

— I had also the occasion, as our sister who talked before, to see exhibited in different places some surrealist or abstract paintings, which is another name for this activity, I cannot call it art, and I want to confess that my main feeling was of repugnance, I didn't understand anything because there was nothing to understand, but I asked myself, how the human beings, many of them well educated, put themselves voluntarily in such a humiliating situation to accept to exhibit and see in their art museums this garbage and to waste their time listening the sophisticated explanations but without any sense delivered by thieves which pose as artists, art critics and specialists in understanding the painting? My other question is, does it exist or can exist specialists in taste, in what is nice, can we agree with the notion of such specialists?

— I think that such a notion is foolishness, what do you think? responded a bicycle from the audience.

— I think in the same way, answered the first bicycle. In my opinion a work of art is valuable and can be named work of art only when has the capacity to communicate its message without translator, without explanations from outside. And this message cannot be imposed by some, doesn't matter how they call themselves, to everybody else. This truth applies to the art that can be called real or normal and at the same time disqualifies totally the abstract "art". The first condition for evaluating the artistic merit and the value of the message of a work of art is that the message can be understood. Whatever "abstract work of art" doesn't contain any message whatsoever in spite of the very ostentatious titles. However, the promoters of this "art" are trying to convince those who listen to them, about the virtue and value of their products. Is like a bicycle entitled herself a specialist in wheels, would intend to sell to other bicycles square wheels explaining to them how good are these new wheels which, will say, are called "abstract". No one of us will accept such an explanation, but the human beings, in similar cases, accept it without understanding it.

— Not only that they accept paintings and sculptures that they cannot understand, they also use very uncomfortable clothes and shoes up to an irrational level for the only reason: they are told that these things are in fashion.

— There are also in their society some called theatre and movies critics who decide which films are good and which are not, as if others could not or they were considered unable to enjoy and understand the film by themselves, without the opinion of the critic, or it is supposed automatically that the critic is the only one capable to qualify the movies and that the opinion and the taste of others don't have any value.

— It is true what you are saying, gave her opinion a bicycle close to the speaking bicycle, I remember very well the comment of my cyclist to some of his friends; he was at a movie theatre with his brother in an afternoon to see a movie, little known and without the usual propaganda in the newspapers. There were only four or five spectators, what is considered usually not a very good sign for what should start in a few minutes. Contrary to all these expectations, instead of getting bored, my cyclist and his brother had the occasion to see one of most interesting, profound and most memorable movies in many years. In their opinion, that movie deserved a very good comment and advertising. Instead of this, a few days later he read in the main newspaper a commentary little favorable to that movie, surely done by a critic, who thinks that he has the monopoly of the cinematographic culture. By the contrary, in many other occasions, seeing movies with an endless advertising and flattering comments, my cyclist considered that it was a waste of time. The conclusion is that today the culture in their society is no more than a monopolized business with an only gigantic purpose: to grab money, as much as possible, the quality and the consequences of a movie, theatre play or television program, being not important. The purpose is not anymore to educate the public, the society, but to produce according with the demand of the market, it could be said similar with the business of selling cheese or salami. The cultural life is today a commercial market. It is very clear that the demand of a society with low cultural and moral level will be for productions of low quality and this is a vicious circle or a spiral moving the quality of the society downwards, not upwards.

— All that our sisters have said here shows and explains how irrational and stupid are these human beings and there are many other examples to demonstrate this. Nevertheless, I would like to add that I have seen the same North-American television program called "sixty minutes", about which other sister talked before in relation with the surrealist sculptures, in particular with that piece of rope of several centimeters, with a pretended value of eight thousand dollars. Well, I can say that that piece of "art" is very cheap, a bargain in comparison with the "paintings" on carton sheets of approximately one square meter each. The "painting" on these cartons varies from a red square up to two or three squares of the same color or of various colors. The price for these "works of art", . . . well, do you want to know it?

— According with what you just described, the price per piece must be about fifty cents, expressed her valuation a very realist bicycle.

— No doubt, you are talking about the cost of production for these "works of art" including the cost of material and the cost of the necessary time for the "artist" of great qualification, inspiration and talent to paint a red square, but my question was if you want to know the selling price for these very precious cartons.

— Admitting a very generous benefit of one hundred percent, the selling price must be then around one dollar, calculated rapidly with professional precision the same bicycle.

— Excuse me please for the insult, but the catalog price for the cartons with the squares varies between one hundred thousand and two hundred thousand American dollars. At least these were the prices in the catalogue shown from very close in the television set by the lady director of that department of the museum.

— What a dirty trick, exploded with indignation a very combative bicycle.

— And how all this is permitted, why these human beings have heads? With what do they think?

— Some say that they have the heads to show the last fashion hats. Other theory says that the use of the head for the human beings is for protecting their necks against the penetration of the rainwater. And they think with their asses. This is very clear.

— Wait a moment, intervened a bicycle with some suspicion, may be that the televised emission referred to a very small museum, little known and perhaps illegal. Do you know the name of that museum?

— Sure. The museum is "the National Art Gallery" of Washington, the capital of the United States. One of the greatest museums, with spacious, large rooms, and to each of these "paintings" an entire wall was dedicated.

The very precise and eloquent response about this case involving such a prestigious museum provoked a moment of silence and eliminated whatever doubt about the present level of intelligence of the human beings, shown this time in the field of their culture.

A sound of a bell meaning the intention of other bicycle to talk, interrupted the silence.

— I would like to know why, or in name of what, the human beings allow this cultural activity of so low quality.

— They say that in the name of freedom of expression.

— But what is the use of this freedom of expression if it is abused in such a grotesque manner?

— Very good question but it seems that the human beings do not have an answer to it.

— Freedom without discipline and purpose has no value, or worse, it is very dangerous, was the opinion of other bicycle. To what purpose serves the art, which is called surrealist, that cannot be understood and doesn't educate, or the movies with horrible crimes which flood the cultural life of the human beings including their children, in the movie theatres and television? became indignant the same bicycle.

— The answer is very clear. The products of the abstract "art" serve, and serve very well, for the imbecilization if it can be said so, of the mass of human beings. By this, the politicians and the thieves which rule the economy can lead this mass very easily diverting its attention in other direction, away and far from its own interests, at whatever price. And the movies with subjects of crimes and robbery serve the same purpose.

— But these movies generate so much crime and robbery, teach the youngsters of their own society how to rob and kill.

— It doesn't matter to them.

— Nobody takes the responsibility of this situation?

— Nobody. No one government was capable to solve these problems. It seems that the only one responsible of this situation is the very bad nature of the human beings.

— I want to say that, however, in the same circumstances, this freedom of expression is not equal for all the members of the society or for various professions.

— What do you want to say?

— I want to say that a human being working in a factory for instance, or whoever else who doesn't have much money, doesn't have the same freedom of expression as an owner of a newspaper or somebody very rich.

— This is very clear, if it were not like that, the human beings would be very close to the perfection but they are not. How about the professions?

— I want to say and to ask why a surrealist painter or sculptor can allow himself without being afraid of punishment, to produce whatever thing in whatever manner, without obeying any rule and at the end to receive lots of money for his work so insignificant, and on the other hand, my cyclist for instance, who is engineer, as an engineer must design or build exactly what was ordered. Moreover, if he doesn't obey the rules, which are very strict, the punishment could be to lose his job, a considerable fine and also prison. If the task of an engineer is to build a bridge, he cannot say that due to the inspiration in that moment to build a house, he had built a house instead of a bridge. And even designing a bridge according to the given task, he is obligated to respect strictly a multitude of design rules and legal provisions. Why this inequality?

— Without any doubt this inequality is real and is not just. The base and at the same time the explanation for this situation is also real, very simple and logical. What these "artists" are doing, in many cases doesn't matter to anybody and in no way affects the functioning of the society, its safety of existing. When the realist artists produce works of art, which are nice, people admire them, when they are not nice, they don't pay attention to them as in the case of the "works" of the surrealist "artists", or pretend that they like them, but in this case no disaster is possible. With the engineers it is totally other situation, other story. They, the engineers represent the fundamental pillar of the modern society in its activity of each day, of each moment. Without them and their work at level of excellence, the present civilization of the human beings simple cannot exist or survive. For comparison, imagine for a moment a strike of all the artists of a country, let's say for an entire year. What happens with the society? Who dies from hunger? Who suffers from cold? Who cannot use the transport to reach his work? What factory stops the production? Nothing of all this. Everything continues to be exactly in the same way.

Now, just look what happens if all the engineers of the same country go on strike. What happens in this case? An unimaginable disaster, with extremely grave and immediate consequences. Everything stops, everything goes to chaos. The supply of electricity, water and gas stops immediately. In the same second all computers are blocked, electric trains, the telephone communication, the control of the planes, the functioning of the factories, what to say more, stops, you yourselves can imagine what follows. Also, if the engineers don't calculate well or don't build according to the rules, little time after, buildings will fall in the streets and the planes will explode in the sky. As discussed before here, the only real progress in the society of the human beings is the progress of the technology, and this is due to the world corps of engineers. There is nothing to talk about decadence or regression in engineering as is the case in the field of arts, politics or social organization. The engineering always advances and the engineers are responsible of what they are doing and in their work there is no space for the foolishness of which are full the arts and the politics.

— Everything is very clear, many thanks for the response so well documented and convincing. Now I understand very well the great difference between engineers and their responsibility towards the society without which the modern society cannot exist, and the abstract "artists" who don't have any responsibility and the practical necessity of which for the society is exactly zero. However, the manner in which the society of human beings rewards the two categories, is not right: the engineers get many tasks, much responsibility, many rules to follow and little money and recognition while the abstract "artists" get everything inversely, what means no specific tasks, no responsibility whatsoever, no rules to conform with, but much money and publicity.

— I have an idea to wake-up the surrealist or abstract "artists" of all kind to the reality in which they live, expressed suddenly her opinion a bicycle.

— I don't know what you intend to suggest but I am sure that these "artists" are not sensitive to the reality.

— We will make them to be, answered the bicycle with the idea.

— How?

— Very simply but very efficiently, with sure results. How? By creating and obligating them to live themselves in surrealist or abstract conditions. In these conditions they will react for sure and immediately. I have a list of services and products only for them, exclusively abstracts without any possibility to exchange them for real things.

— We are listening with much interest, exclaimed in a choir, the very curious bicycles.

— Well, we will prepare for them a special food, surrealist, for instance fried stones, wood salad with nails, soup of sulphuric acid with little cubic spheres of plastic, grilled rubber foam, and for drinking, gasoline with car oil in bottles with labels of various colors with abstract drawings.

A general laughter contaminated the entire audience, looking like without possibility to stop it soon. After a while, the same bicycle could continue her idea:

— Please, please, let me continue, I didn't finish my idea.

Finally, with great difficulty, the wave of laughter diminished, although explosions of laughter could be heard in various places. A relative silence was established again, solely due to the tremendous curiosity of the audience to hear what other so marvelous things contained the rest of the idea of the speaking bicycle. And she continued enjoying an attention for which many human beings politicians would be very envious.

— These surrealist "artists" eat everyday very well, delicious food of all kind produced by other members of the society. In order to justify this right to eat, the "artists" produce nothing more than surrealist or abstract garbage that cannot be digested by the producers of the real food that can be eaten. The time came to change the roles. Will be interesting to see what happens when these "artists" must eat things of similar use and quality as of those they produce for others. But they not only eat, they live a very complete life using real products to satisfy the needs of their life during which they produce in exchange, abstract garbage. They must also dress, sleep on very comfortable beds in also comfortable houses and travel using real vehicles for which so many engineers and technicians worked involving all their energy and talent.

My idea is to change the way they are treated, providing them with surrealist resources well related with those that they, the great surrealist "artists", produce for the society. Now I will exemplify, but the list will be open for your other suggestions.

In the short pause after these words, a roar of satisfaction was heard, connected with the hope of the bicycles to enjoy themselves more, in such an unexpected way.

— Well, continued the bicycle, to dress them, I suggest to give them metal clothes to be put directly on their naked body. The clothes have many holes for ventilation, especially during the winter. If they want to use intimate clothes, we can prepare them especially for them, from a very strong material as reinforced concrete. The same material can be used for swimsuits, if they want to swim during the summer. Some of these "artists" can help us to create very abstract models of the last fashion. If they want to sleep, they can do this in an abstract manner sleeping in a standing position or, if they want to use the realist position, it means horizontal, as a reward for their very useful work for the society, the same society will give them the possibility to choose between various surrealist models of very sharply pointed stone beds, or wooden beds with nails of several centimeters in vertical position. Finally, to transport themselves to various exhibitions of abstract "art", they could use wooden horses. Also, if they want for their personal use in the city, our community can give them some surrealist bicycles with triangular wheels and frame from rope.

This is all from me. I am sincerely convinced that the proposed program will help a lot to all surrealist "artists" to understand by their own experience, the real value and the use of their "works of art" for the society in which they live. Many thanks to all of you for your attention.

After these final words of the bicycle with such good and original ideas, a new wave of laughter and relaxation, propagated from one side to another, across the audience. When the mood of the bicycles came back to the discussion level, a bicycle commented:

— I think that the idea of our sister describes the unique possibility for the human beings to eliminate from their society this decadent art which can be called also a parasite art.

— This definition of parasite art is excellent, but I don't think that they have the intellectual power to organize themselves to eliminate these parasite "artists" from their society.

— I think that you are right, my friend, and the proof for this is the reality that this decadent "art" and the involved "artists" can co-exist very well in the society, already for many decades, only due to the stupidity of the rest of the human beings.

— My sisters, got involved a sportive bicycle, our discussion about the artistic life of the human beings with its aspects so negative was very instructive and interesting but unfortunately for us who are expecting so much from the human beings, there are many other aspects at least as negatives in other spheres of their activities, as their habits, the sportive life for instance, about which I would like to share my experience with you.

— We are ready to listen to you with much pleasure because we all are sportive by definition, although not all of us are in such a good shape like you.

— A million thanks, my sisters and friends, this is true, we the bicycles, mean in principle, transport, relaxation and sport. I assume that all is clear about our contribution in transportation and relaxation. In what concerns the sportive aspect, I want to say that not everything is good. When the human beings use us for amateur sport, for physical exercise, everything is very well but when they use us for their maniac inclination, the competitive sport, our life and health are in danger. The very notion of competition is a proof of primitivism, of low moral and intelligence and of lack of feeling of purpose in a community, in no way a proof of something good.

Comments by the bicycles about the competitive sports.

The sport means an intensive activity to maintain the physical vigour, and the intensity of the exercise can be regulated on a scientific base to ensure the efficiency of the exercise and by no means requires competing. The competition in sports as in other areas also, creates a tension, which is not healthy, doesn't serve to any positive purpose and can create very grave problems. The initial notion and purpose of competition has the roots in the ancient Greece, with the sportive competitions in Olympus, from where the name of Olympic Games comes, which were honest competitions only for the promotion of the sportive activity. The same notion of competition is used today for a totally different purpose and manner, to sustain an intensive commercial activity involving drugs, violence and manipulations of all kind totally forgetting the ancient honesty. The present sportive competition usually degenerates in very ugly things, reminiscent of the law of jungle. The sport of competition stimulates and promotes the violence between the participants and also between fans, the fight many times bestial, to be the first, the winner. The fight between animals in the jungle is justified by the necessity to survive, is a competition imposed by the cruel laws of nature; this is also the only reason for which the animals fight, kill and sometimes participate in a cruel competition only to survive. The beings of all other species don't have any reserve of resources, no other possibility to survive, don't have technology to protect and assure their life and at least, don't pretend to be civilized, advanced, with high morality and all that the human beings pretend.

— Explain to me please, addressed to the speaker a bicycle with little experience in the hidden activities of the human beings, due to her youth, why in the sportive competition it is so important to be the first, to win the game? Why they cannot play in a friendly manner, without winning or losing?

— Very good and very peaceful question, but the answer is very bellicose. The answer to the first question is the money, the total commercialization of competitive sports. The system is established by the human beings in such a manner that only the participant who wins gets lots of money and all the glory and publicity, all others who lose get the humiliation and nothing else. This principle applies if in the competition there are two participants as in boxing, or very many participants as in races of cars, horses, bicycles, or in marathons. The same principle is applied in individual competitions or in competitions between teams, as football, volleyball or canoe. The greatest foolishness and injustice of this system is that, not sometimes but always, the difference between the winner and the loser is extremely small, very many times infinitesimal, a fraction of a second up to one percent of a second. Practically, from the sportive point of view, there is no difference between the sportive qualities of the first and the second and other participants that arrive to the final point a fraction of a second or even a few seconds later. All are and should be considered excellent sportsmen and winners, all of them. In cases of marathons that last a few hours, the same reasoning makes sense for differences of ten or fifteen minutes. I want to quote the wise words based on personal experience of a champion in the famous cycling competition "Tour de France" about bicycle racing: "There is no reason to participate in such a feat of idiocy. It is a competition of suffering without purpose". Very well said.

— The pure truth, completed the idea other sportive bicycle, is that if the competition was repeated in the same conditions, with the same participants, there is a great probability that the winner will not be anymore the same winner of the first competition, maybe that he will be this time the second, the tenth or the fourteenth. And the fourteenth of the first competition could finish the eighteenth, the second or the first. If the competition was repeated for the third time, the results could be different again for the great majority of participants. Even the highest record of the competition, local or worldwide, can change for a better or a worse one. I would be very curious to compare, if it was possible, the results of a singular competition with the statistics of the same competition repeated let's say, ten or twenty times, and with the percentage for each place gained for each participant in these ten or twenty competitions.

— What a good idea, just and intelligent! exclaimed with enthusiasm the first sportive bicycle. Truly, such a competition repeated in similar conditions and with the same participants, would give a general impression incomparably more veridical and would determine in the same veridical manner the position of each competitor, including the winner, if we want to have one single winner, meaning the first one. But the position of this winner will be based on a scientific statistic and not on the luck of the moment.

— And I am wondering, why really the human beings don't use in their sportive competitions such a brilliant method as the one proposed by our sister, the sportive bicycle?

— Do you want to know why?

— Yes, for sure

— For one single reason, because the human beings don't have the level of intelligence, the depth of thinking of us, the bicycles. For this reason, never in the history of the sports of the human beings, no one of them made such a proposal. And if they get such suggestion from one of them or from outside of their society, I doubt very much that they will adopt it, precisely for the same reason, their great stupidity.

— I want to clarify something very important in order to avoid confusion.

— Confusion? about what?

— Confusion about the very necessity of the competition, in a scientific manner as the idea of our sister or in a stupid one, how it is practiced today. It must be absolutely clear that the competition itself, scientific or not, doesn't have any rational purpose. By the contrary, generates adverse feelings close to the law of the jungle and simply for this it is not necessary and it should not be welcomed in the life of the society. However, only from the theoretical point of view, if for whatever reason independently of the will of the society, the competition is imposed, then, is better to use the scientific approach which is without doubt, better than the stupid one.

— Many thanks, said the sportive bicycle. Now, with your clarification, my idea is complete.

— If who is the winner doesn't matter, we can say that marking the time doesn't matter either? asked a new participant in the discussion.

— The answer is a "no" and a "yes". The "no" is for the winner. All those who participate in the sportive activity are winners; if one arrives at the final point of the respective activity with a second before others we must call him a winner? Winner of what? Of a second? This is simply childish. The "yes" is for the necessity to mark the time, but not for determining who is the winner. The time is important and it is necessary to mark it because below certain speed of action, the respective activity will not be a sportive activity anymore with all the positive consequences for the body but only a recreational activity, of resting, not stimulating. The problem can be solved in a very simple manner. Everything depends on what purpose is given to the sport activity, to the sports in general.

— What do you want to say?

— I want to say that everything depends on the level of intelligence at which the sport is treated. If the level of intelligence is zero, as is today in the competitive sport, the sport is transformed into a brutal activity, into a dirty business involving hundreds of billions of dollars, for the benefit of very few, the manipulators of all the competitions. From their fabulous revenues these manipulators can easily afford to pay very well the winners of the competitions.

— Does anybody know how much do they pay to these winners? They pay them incredible amounts. In the United States for instance, the players of the famous football teams receive many millions of dollars per year if they have an annual contract, and maybe that ten or twenty million dollars are paid to the winner of an international championship of boxing.

— I understand that these amounts of money are very big but I am not from the United States and I would like to know for comparison, which are the average salaries for other professions.

— For employees of various professions including mechanics, engineers, doctors, clerks, the annual salary varies generally between thirty and one hundred thousand dollars and can be more for positions of high responsibility, but no millions.

— And there are salaries less than these?

— Oh my darling, to this sharp question the answer is very, very sad. The salaries that I mentioned are only for a small minority of employees. Very many employees work for a salary of less than twenty thousand dollars per year and very many also for the minimal legal salary which is lower than this. A great number of workers, especially illegal immigrants must accept a miserable salary, below the minimum legal salary. The only other alternative is nothing, no employment.

— How sad, really.

— Sad? Don't rush, please. What is sad for some in the United States or Canada, is only a nice dream for hundreds of millions of workers, I repeat, for hundreds of millions, in other countries of Asia, Africa, South America, where the salary per day is less than the minimum salary per hour in Canada for instance, only five, four, three or less dollars per day. Can you imagine how those human beings live?

— And what happens if one of them gets sick and needs an operation or expensive medication, do they have medical insurance?

— You talk like one just arrived from other planet.

— Then what does he do?

— He has two possibilities.

— Which?

— The first one is if the sick person has good luck and his body has natural resources to get well by itself.

— And the second?

— He dies.

— And what does in this case the company, which has employed him?

— Employs immediately other worker. Without problems. The waiting list is very long.

— What a terrible life like monkeys in the jungle!

— Please don't insult the monkeys, they are not so cruel one to another.

— Well, terrible, let's come back to North America, how much does the President of the United States get?

— His annual salary is about two hundred fifty thousand dollars.

— And then why they pay to a boxer or football player, millions?

— To a boxer they pay to mutilate his adversary in a public place with thousands of spectators as witnesses and to a football player they pay to give a kick well directed to a ball in a special place called stadium in the presence of up to one hundred thousand spectators.

As some bicycles of the audience, many of them very young, were not familiar with the details of the sportive life of the human beings, followed some questions with appearance of naivety, but which in reality contained a large dose of common sense.

— And what do those one hundred thousand spectators in the stadium do?

— Nothing.

— Then why did they go there?

— To watch.

— To watch what?

— Watch how two teams of eleven football players each, vigorous and in very good shape, run all the time for one and a half hours, that is how long the game lasts, passing the ball from one to another trying to get it through a small place named gate, of the adversary team. All the players run until exhaustion.

— And what physical exercise are the spectators doing?

— None, only watch and shout and sometimes become violent, but this doesn't do any good to their health.

— In this case, if the spectators don't perform any sportive activity and they are there only for the enjoyment of the players which receive so much money for their very intense sportive activity, how much they pay to the spectators for their time lost there without participating in the sportive activity?

— Don't pay them anything, my dear, they the spectators pay, and the entrance tickets to the stadium are not cheap.

— What an injustice! Those who don't produce anything in all their life, only exercise in an intensive sport, are paid millions, and the many others who don't do any exercise and consume their time, must in addition pay from their own money for this waste of time. Other injustice in these competitive sports is that the players exercise too much, getting exhausted, and others, the very many spectators, do not move at all.

— It is very interesting what happens with these human beings, each of them separately, behaves in a manner, how it is said, normal, and more or less predictable but when get together in a crowd, many times cannot control themselves and act in a totally irrational manner, become violent and not only once, the end of the competition results in dead and injured.

— Dead and injured you said?

— Yes, dead and injured.

— But for what? We are talking here about sports not war.

— It is true that we are talking about sports and not about war, but don't forget two things, first, is a competitive sport and in this activity, what counts more is the competition, not the sport for its own value. The competition pushes the physical effort of the competitors out of the sane limits, creates a sick nervous tension, which is transmitted to the audience of spectators. The second thing is that these, the spectators, are no more than human beings, the worse beings of whatever living species in what concerns their behavior. The statistics show that always when there is a competition with an audience, some support one team or player and others support the adversary team or player. As the human beings, who are the spectators in the tribunes of the stadium, have nothing to do physically, all their energy concentrates in the nervous sphere, in the support for their team.

— Well, but how does it go from here to the bloodshed?

— Unfortunately, very easily. It is enough a mistake of the arbitrator, or the appearance of a mistake, or only the frustration due to the result of the game, to inflame the passion of many or of some spectators and a small incident is transformed very rapidly in a real battle, and from here, without any planning or premeditation, up to dead and injured, the distance is very short.

— I understand very well what you are saying, but I don't understand the reason for the dispute.

— There is no reason, by all means, no rational reason or explanation. But this doesn't prevent the human beings from declaring a war in the battlefield or in the stadium. For them the reason could be, as I said, the dispute for a goal.

— And what importance has a goal more or a goal less, from one side or from other one?

— Absolutely none. This is not a reason even to get a little nervous and by no means for a fight. Think for a moment that the audience is not of human beings but of lions, tigers or dogs. If they are not hungry and don't feel that their life is in danger, do you think that they would kill each other or at least would fight among themselves because the result of the competition? In no way. They would watch patiently the competitive game, may be a little bored, and afterwards each of them would go in their way. A much superior behavior than the one of the human beings.

— I am from Belgium, a small country from Western Europe, which is considered very civilized. A few years ago, during a football competition in the capital city, between a team of this country and a visiting team from England, other country considered very civilized, a big fight occurred involving young spectators of both countries exactly how you have described here, addressed the Belgian bicycle to the speaker, and dozens of dead and injured were transported to the morgue and hospitals by the police, which had great difficulties to stop the fighting and separate the belligerents. A big scandal followed in the newspapers and television, but after a while everything was forgotten due to other, more recent scandals.

— You talk about dozens of victims? I am from Brazil and I remember that in a similar situation in an Olympic stadium in one of the largest cities of the country, the number of dead reached many hundreds. It is true that this was a unique case by its magnitude but there are many cases of violence for the same cause, which simply are considered common events of the human beings life.

— The competition in sports generates violence not only between spectators, which due to their inactivity have much energy to spend, but also between players, which are always at the peak of the energy consumption.

— And for what do they fight?

— For money. The reward for the winners is so high that the players many times forget about morality and the rules of the game and give powerful kicks to the players of the adversary team to reduce its capacity of winning. Sometimes the attackers are punished by the arbitrator but many times the attacked ones, which are very valuable and even essential for the respective team, cannot continue to play, what is exactly the purpose of the attacker.

— This means that a player of a team considers a player from the other team not as an associate in the sportive activity, who could be even a friend, but as an enemy competing for the same money and glory which is given only to the winner.

— Exactly so.

— How bad! What a sad reality due to the introduction of the competition in sports what could be such a healthy and enjoyable activity for all and always.

— Well, let's say that in football and in other similar team games, the fight between players are accidents in contravention to the rules, but how the boxing can be accepted, where the very rules require that the competitors fight with direct physical force, with their fists, one against another until one of them falls exhausted, without consciousness or sometimes dead or fatally injured. Is this sport?

— Very good question, of great interest for many and for the public opinion in general. From our point of view, the bicycles, and from all human beings, which have some common sense in the definition of an activity as the sport, the boxing definitively is not a sport, is a bestial activity that shouldn't have any place in the human beings society. Unfortunately for the prestige of the human species, this bestial fight between human beings not only is accepted by the society but it is legal and a very lucrative business.

— Business? What they sell?

— They sell violence, brutality, open savagery but with the label of competitive sport.

— It is true, all this is pure truth and this truth intrigues me to know to whom do they sell this repugnant and scandalous merchandise and who buys it.

— Other very interesting question. This merchandise, as you say, sells and sells well because there is a market for it. There are many human beings who are ready to pay enough money to see how one of them, a human being is destroying or tries to destroy other human being, how they kick each other in the face until one of them falls without consciousness.

— And the audience of spectators doesn't protest, trying to stop this absurd fight?

— No, they like all this, they pay with their money to enjoy it.

— But at least, there aren't there some human beings women, who could protest? They must be more sensitive.

— Your naiveté, my dear is very lovely. I wouldn't like to disappoint you but there isn't other way. There are many women in the hall where the boxing competitions occur. And what do you think, as incredible as could be, many times they enjoy more than the human beings, men.

— Really incredible, but how this can be explained?

— This is explained by the human beings nature more animal and primitive, although being women, than the nature of the animals. They go there in modern cars, with elegant dresses, speak in a very decent manner, but inside they are ferocious animals. The boxing competitions in a world that the human beings call it civilized proves that the only change that occurred since the primitive epoch is the apparition of the façade that the animals don't need. It is true that in some species of animals, the females assist to the males fight, but only because in this manner it will be decided which will be her partner and not for enjoying the violence and the cruelty of the fight. For them this is not a show but a vital necessity. The human beings women assist at tournaments of boxing with their husbands or boyfriends and therefore the reason for the females of other species doesn't apply to them. Those women who come by themselves pay the entrance without hoping to marry the winning boxer. Then, which is the conclusion? The conclusion must be that the spectators of boxing enjoy the violence and the cruelty in itself and nothing else, without any necessity. And they pay for this pleasure, which is below the atavism, because the animals don't have it. Therefore, behind the spectacular façade of the boxing tournaments, including the sale of coca-cola, comparing the human beings with the animals, which are superior and which are inferior, according with the morality considered civilized, by the human beings themselves? It is clear that the human beings are the inferior ones. After a pause, the same bicycle continued:

— I have another disappointment for you, today clubs are preparing women for boxing competitions, presently between them, woman against woman, but in the future, who knows, we could see men boxing women in public places, legally, for the enjoyment of other men and women. Poor human creatures!

— Unfortunately, all this is a shameful reality of the cultural and sportive life of the human beings. In what concerns the sports, some of them so irrational, cruel as the boxing, and sometimes tragic in results as they are, one can say that it is a voluntary and conscientious choice of both participants which involve themselves in a competition, even if this involves the cruelty and the stupidity of the spectators. But things become more ugly and dirty when the entertainment of these human beings involves in these competitions innocent animals, which always lose and always die.

What the bicycles think about the bullfights.

I am from Spain, a nice country, well known for its so pleasant music, but unfortunately, also for a terrible form of competition between human beings armed with swords and bulls armed with nothing, named bullfights and in which the Spanish songs accompany the assassination of those bulls which don't expect that these melodies so nice, are the signal for their violent death for the savage and primitive pleasure of thousands of spectators which pretend to be civilized, comfortably seated around the arena. The criminals, they are criminals also, even though are called matadors and toreadors, dressed in shiny costumes, provoke the bulls with a red piece of cloth and afterwards kill them by pushing the sword in the neck of the bull under the very strong sound of the nice music and the sick acclamations of the spectators for their heroes of the day, the matadors and toreadors, the elegant synonyms for criminals and beasts.

There is other cruel and stupid aspect in these bullfights. Not only the bulls die, the victims which were charged with the death penalty by the toreadors and the organizers of the bullfights, but sometimes also the toreadors themselves die, criminals by their action, but handsome youngsters with all the life in front of them, and who think that is nothing wrong when they kill the bulls. They are products of the primitivism of the human beings society, together with the entire audience of delirious spectators. And in each bullfight, even if no one toreador dies, always this danger exists. For what reason do they take the risk? There is only one valid answer: the imbecility of the human beings, organizers, players, and spectators.

To kill innocent beings, and even killing the guilty ones is not a pleasure and by no means a show for entertainment, but, if for whatever reason such a sinister spectacle is imposed, makes more sense to replace the innocent animals as victims of the spectacle, with criminals from prison.

A bicycle interrupted the established silence after the story about the bullfights, which provoked the repulsion of the audience, with her comment about the value of the competition.
— There is also other very dirty aspect of the sport of competition. The very notion of competition implies a winner and at least one loser, as in boxing, or many losers as in any race. The competition produces one winner with all his glory and good mood, money and confidence in himself, sometimes up to arrogance, for a very irrational, childish achievement: a second or a fraction of a second, a goal or a centimeter, depending of what is the purpose of the competition. The real price for this is that at the same time losers are created, one or more than one with all the negative feelings and psychological effects. All for a loss which is totally artificial. An inequality and animosity feeling is created between sport colleagues, instead of friendship and peace of mind and an enjoyable sportive activity, if the sport is not competitive.

After the shocking discussion about the abstract "art" and the sports of competition, the exchange of opinions and information addressed other interesting subjects, starting with the capacity of orientation of the human beings compared with that of the animals. The discussion continued with the same vivacity and high participation.

— I have a question, or better to say a comment, about what you said related to the capacity to think in a rational manner of some human beings and to the low level of intelligence of the animals.
— We are listening.

— What is required for a human being to build a small house, or a dam even a small one across a small river, only his natural intelligence?

— Oh, no, my dear, to build a house, even a small one, or a dam, even a small one, the intelligence is only the required base. In addition, in order to be such a constructor, one must study for several years the respective technology at the university.

— But the human beings had built houses many centuries ago, when universities didn't exist.

— This is true but in that time in order to learn what is studied today in several years at the university, many years of experience were necessary, many times transmitted from fathers to sons and only few human beings were capable to be good builders.

— Well, this is clear, but can all the human beings move from one point to another at thousands and thousands of kilometers away and return several months later exactly to the same point of departure?

— Certainly, you talk about organized trips with guides, maps, with motorized vehicles, with all modern orientation technology. Why not? They can and they do it.

— No, without guide, without maps, without vehicles, and without any technology for orientation.

— What are you talking about, my friend? This is impossible, or you want to make a joke?

— No, is not a joke, is the reality of life but not for the human beings, for some animals.

— I am very curious, what are you talking about.

— I am talking about all the birds, which build their little houses, about the little animals called beavers, which build dams for improving their chances to catch fish. They didn't learn anything in any university and these dams are so strong and well built, that the human beings must use dynamite to destroy them and so to avoid the flooding of their agricultural land. I am talking also about all migratory birds with their brains so small which guide them perfectly without computers or other modern technology for orientation in their flight to South, many thousands of kilometers, when the cold season starts, and return to their nests which are their little houses, several month later, in the spring. This is a mass phenomenon and no one of these birds has a diploma from any university. Well, how are compared the human beings who are intelligent and have such high education, with these animals?

A roar of approval demonstrated without any doubt the interest of the audience for the point marked by the last speaker and the interest continued to be alive for this very interesting discussion.
— I would like to refer to such interesting and strange comment of our sister, said the first speaker.
— All of us are listening to you, was the answer in a unanimous voice of many bicycles.

— Well, what our sister just finished to say is at the same time an obvious truth and a proof of the tremendous sophistication of the nature and of the world in which we live. Sometimes the first impression is that there is such a great contradiction for which the only explanation is the miracle and nothing less, but miracles do not exist. Really, how can be explained that the nature has created these animals and birds with a capacity in some compartments, extremely superior to that of the human beings. The scientific explanation for this situation at least very curious, is the power of the instinct to help these animals to survive in the existing, very unfavorable conditions. How the system works technically, I don't know, but certainly there is a scientific explanation.

With this very powerful instinct, as it was said here a little before, an animal otherwise so common as the beaver, can build without a project and without any calculations, a dam, and birds can fly a very long distance and find their nest at return without any study or instrument. They do that for millions of years and nothing else, without developing in any way how the human beings had developed in the few last thousands years, not millions of years.

One may ask why the same nature didn't give to the human beings similar instincts with those of the beavers and birds. Why the human beings were not born constructors, doctors, pilots, without the necessity to study so many years in the school, college and university? I don't know which is the answer, for me is an enigma, a curiosity of the nature, but it is the reality.

— I would like to exemplify this contradiction or better said curiosity, in the development of the human beings, at least in what concerns their ability to orient themselves without technology.

— I am sure that you will tell us something very interesting.

— I hope so. I thought myself many times about this aspect. It is true that the human beings technology for orientation is magnificent and a proof of the advance and of the superior level of intelligence of some human beings, the engineers, who are a special category of them. With this technology, so multilateral and sophisticated, is possible to see during the most obscure night, without artificial light, to find the landing point in any airport in the world at whatever distance, in any atmospheric condition, day or night. But without this technology? The poor human beings are literally lost, in very many situations not only in the jungle but also in any ordinary forest, and what is not only stupid but also comical, in their own cities. I said stupid because the cities are not natural things as the jungle, they themselves build them in such a chaotic manner that is very easy to get lost.

— At least they could put adequate indicators in the streets, noticed a bicycle.

— They could, but they don't do it as is necessary.

This answer was not clear enough for a young bicycle from a little town and she asked for a more detailed explanation.

— Well, continued the previous speaker, I want to say that the difficulties for orientation in the cities are not due to natural causes as in the forest, which is there for the trees, not for the human beings, not because, let's say of an earthquake. They are caused entirely by the stupidity of the human beings.

— In what consists this stupidity, interrupted again the bicycle from the little town.

— This stupidity consists of two stupidities, or of one action, which is very stupid, and of lack of an action, which is also a great stupidity. The first stupidity was the action to build the cities in a totally irrational manner, without planning, in which way almost all cities were built.

What the bicycles think about the orientation in cities.

A sister spoke before about the cities of the human beings but she described the lack of economic efficiency of the cities, how they expand more horizontally and not vertically, wasting an immense area of very productive agricultural land, creating a field of houses with only one or maximum two levels, requiring a very developed network, otherwise not necessary, of pipes for potable water, pipes for residual water, for sewage, cables for electricity and communication, streets for transportation and what is very important, the precious time for transportation. Moreover, the real total cost per square meter of housing in these conditions of waste of resources is very much higher when compared with the cost in conditions of rational urbanism. Now, in addition to all this, I want to insist about the particular aspect of which we are talking, the orientation.

— Excuse me please, said a bicycle with three speeds, this issue is very interesting for us, the bicycles. I don't want to interrupt more, but after you finish talking I will present a flagrant case of stupidity in what concerns the orientation.

— Very well my sister, all of us will listen to you a little later. Well, the great majority of streets in many cities are winding, short and with unpredictable connections with the main avenues. To find a place without having instructions is practically impossible. There are thousands and thousands of street names without any rule and are also two or three streets with the same name. Only a map is not of much help, it is necessary also an indication of the specific part of the city where the street you are looking for is.

After a short pause, the same bicycle continued:

— This is the first part of the stupidity, the stupidity to build a city in this way. Now, about the stupidity of lack of action. Considering that the cities are a "fait acompli" how the French say, it means a fact of life or a situation already existing, it is imperative that the names of these streets are visible without effort, and are put in the adequate places. In fact, the names of the streets are not displayed in all intersections, are written with too small letters and many times are invisible at night. Imagine that one travels by car or bicycle during the night, arrives at an intersection and needs to know immediately what to do, continue straight ahead, take a left, or a right turn. If he cannot find out rapidly this information, it is a problem with the possibility of an accident. If this happens when is raining, the situation becomes worse.

The action that must be taken, is to change immediately all the small pieces of metal with the names that cannot be read easily, with adequate indicators with big letters and good light, which could be read without stopping. The lack of this action is a great stupidity without any justification.

— But every city has a mayor and so many clerks in charge with the urban transportation. What are they doing? Nothing?

— How nothing? They take regularly their big enough salaries, are passing close to these almost invisible street names every day during many years and nothing else. They don't have the capacity to think about what we were talking here, they are typical examples of human beings.

It seems that this issue apparently minor in the so large family of urban problems, created a major interest in this discussion, and this because the problem by no means is minor.

— I am glad that our sister approached with such competence this aspect of life in the cities. Not only once I was witness of situations very close to accidents for this very reason, intervened a bicycle with a very authoritarian voice.

— When we go to a place for the first time, this is a problem. My cyclist and I are in danger. When it becomes dark and moreover it rains, this danger is ten times greater, jumped in the discussion other bicycle.

— I have an experience of many thousands of kilometers in the city, but in these situations, and always during the night, my cyclist and I prefer to stop, get out of the traffic, stop on the side walk and try to read the indicators without danger, but with a loss of valuable time, loss that could be avoided so simply. Oh, these human creatures with their mayor in front! expressed the bicycle with an obvious nervousness.

— Very well, completed the idea a nice brown bicycle, you could solve the problem by stopping and putting yourself on the sidewalk. But what must a car do in the same situation? To jump also on the sidewalk? And what happens to the security of the traffic if there are two or three cars in the same situation?

— I don't know, we must ask the mayor.

— It is worth asking the mayor only if the mayor was a bicycle, but in that case the problem would have been solved much before. To ask the mayor and other clerks is a sure waste of time.

— True, true, responded a choir of bicycles.

— And the fact that, with extremely rare exceptions, the streets do not have numbers, only names without any order, makes the finding of the street what you are looking for, a task without any real chance of success. What street is next after passing the street named "Clara", for instance? Or the street "Maria" or "John", or "Dupont"? Where is the street "Market" which you need? Who knows! With the numbers, it is totally other thing. If you are at the corner with the street number three, the following is the street number four and after number five, etc. If you are looking for the street number fifteen, you know precisely where to go. This comment caused other comment by the neighbour bicycle.

— I am from New York and my task is to transport my cyclist to distribute special documents at various addresses in the most congested part of the city named Manhattan. Fortunately, this part of the city is a very rare exception in the world. Is the idea you just finished to talk about, existing in the real life, and everything works in a wonderful manner. To orient yourself there is very easy. All this part of the city was build according to a very clear and strict plan. All the streets are parallel, have numbers and intersect perpendicularly with the avenues, which are also parallel between them and have their own numbers. If I remember well, there are ten avenues for the longest distance and one hundred eighty streets in perpendicular direction. So, if you are at the corner of the third avenue and street number ten and you want to go to a place at the avenue number six and street number forty, it is very simple to orient yourself without asking anything to anybody. I want to say that Manhattan represents an example of rational urbanism and shows that if there is the will everything can be done.

— But at the same time this shows that the stupidity of the human beings in charge of the cities is not so big as it was said here, commented a young bicycle.

— No, this shows that the stupidity is greater now than before building Manhattan

— Can you explain to me what do you want to say? asked the young bicycle very surprised.

— Why not? But before answering to your question, in order to understand me better, I will ask you something.

— Please.

— Imagine that in a café for tourists campers there are two groups of tourists at the same table. Both groups decide to eat sardines from cans they have in their backpacks. There are on the table special instruments to open the cans but the tourists from the first group don't use those very efficient instruments and waste much time and effort by opening the cans with knifes very inadequate for this. What do you think about this?

— They were stupid, very clear.

— Well, the second group starts to open their cans using those special instruments, very rapidly and without effort. What do you think about this?

— They acted in a normal, intelligent manner.

— At the same time the tourists from the first group continued to open other cans in the same inefficient manner using the knifes in spite of being witnesses of how the tourists from the second group were using the special instruments in front of their eyes. What do you think about this?

— I already told you that they proved to be stupid.

— This is clear, but when they proved to be more stupid, before seeing how the tourists from the second group opened their cans, or after, or this doesn't matter much?

— Clearly that after.

— Why after?

— Because before, some could pretend whatever excuse, without value but an excuse, as they didn't notice the instruments on the table, lack of imagination how to use them or doesn't matter what else, but after seeing with their own eyes the much more efficient procedure, not only that there is not any base for excuses but it is obvious that their stupidity multiplies with the stupidity for not simply copying the more efficient method used by the second group, although they were not able to come to that by themselves.

— Perfect, thanks for your so logical reasoning.

— But what has in common how the sardine cans were opened with construction of cities, in Manhattan and in other places in the world?

— Everything. Think about this please. I am sure that you don't need help.

The other bicycle smiled and without delay, responded:

— Thanks for your example so detailed and clear. Translating your example into urbanism, certainly that the planners of Manhattan are intelligent human beings. Breaking with the routine of conservative and so irrational urbanism, they planned and built an area of housing and other buildings, as large as a city, in a rational manner in which, in addition to other positive things, it is very easy to orient yourself. Unfortunately, they are a small minority. All others who have built cities before Manhattan didn't have any vision, didn't matter to them how life in those cities will be and least of all they thought about the daily orientation in the streets and about the danger connected with the necessity to look for the names of the streets and the numbers on the houses and other buildings, for those who drive vehicles. This is to say that certainly those human beings were stupid. The human beings, who have built and continue to build cities after Manhattan without paying any mind to this example, are certainly more stupid. To copy is very much easier than to invent. This category of human beings was not and is not capable to invent or to copy. There is a Latin proverb, which says: "To make mistakes is human but to persevere in the mistakes is diabolic".

— Many thanks for your excellent comment. I see that there are other sisters which want to present their opinions about this issue but before, I would like to invite our sister who said that she wants to tell us something about a special case, to talk about it now.

— Agreed, exclaimed without reservation other bicycles.

— Go ahead, my friend.

— I am from Toronto, Canada. It is considered that Toronto is a very well developed city, clean, with much green space and other advantages in comparison with many other cities. It is also very inefficient in the utilization of its total area but I will not talk about this now, I will concentrate on the difficulties of orientation. The city expands on more than thirty kilometers from East to West and up to twenty kilometers from North to South, the area of the city is too big for the three million inhabitants, this is a terrible waste of land. The orientation in this field of houses is somehow easier because the main avenues are parallel, long, straight and wide. However, the problem is with the multitude of secondary streets between the main avenues, which are at a distance of one and a half up to two kilometers between them. There we encounter the same difficulties as in other irrational cities: some streets are semi-circular, others without exit and many of them without names at the intersections, and where they are, they are written with letters too small to be read fast from a convenient distance. During the night, few of them can be read. This is true in many cases for the main avenues also. The numbers on the houses are another problem. Not all houses have numbers or numbers that can be seen well from the street. Very many shops and companies in the commercial streets and main streets also, show only its advertising and the name of the shop or company, but not the numbers for orientation, because the owners are interested only in orienting as much people as possible towards their shops or companies, they are not interested in anything else. Many times it is necessary to stop, get out from your vehicle and ask which is the number of the house or building. It is terrible.

— But this is a problem of municipal responsibility; I think this issue is regulated by law.

— Probably yes, but the situation in fact is that nobody respects the law and there are not municipal controllers to impose the law. This situation is lasting not for years but for decades. It is not good but could be much worse, as in the case about which I will talk now. A few years ago I was with my cyclist and with a group of American cyclists in a two weeks bicycle trip in Nicaragua. In Managua, the capital, all were surprised that the streets didn't have names, all the streets, can you imagine?

— And how do the human beings orient themselves in that city, how do they give directions?

— My cyclist asked exactly the same to the local guide of the foreign cyclists group and the answer was that they use natural things as a big tree, or isolated or uncommon buildings, a tall building in an area of low houses, a church and other similar things as points of orientation. And the streets are winding, without planning.

— What an abysmal difference between the human beings who have planned and built Manhattan and those responsible for the situation in Managua! exclaimed a bicycle very intrigued by the story related by the Canadian bicycle.

— Managua may be, let's say an original case of human stupidity, but there are other differences which can pretend to the title of "abysmal", jumped into the discussion a bicycle who was paying attention at all times to the discussion.

— For instance?

— I want to give the example of the city of Kingston, the capital of Jamaica, one of the very nice islands in the Caribbean Sea. I must mention that "nice" is referred to the nature of the island, not to some activities of the human beings in that island. I am from Jamaica, I lived many years in Kingston and I know very well the situation. From the urban, economic, transportation and architectural points of view, with its ghettos, winding streets, very poor houses in the great majority of the city, and waste of land, Kingston is a disaster even if there are very nice areas with big and elegant houses where the very rich live. But not about this I want to talk now, I will concentrate to the relation between the human beings and the indicators with the names of the streets. In many places there are none of them, in other places the metallic plates are very old, rusty and illegible. But, although it seems strange, the municipality had a very valuable initiative and installed new plates, green with white letters that could be read, not from very far how it should be if to consider the motorized traffic and also of some bicycles, but they can be read, it is better than the previous situation. Is this good?

— Yes, is very good, but it seems that you have a surprise, not so tasty, for us, intervened other bicycle.

— How well you guess! Yes, the deception is that some human beings started an action of vandalism against these new plates, destroying them. Why? There is no logical reason. The explanation? The human beings nature, not only stupid but in those cases also destructive. Unfortunately, the victims of vandalism are not only the plates with the names of the streets, but also the public phones. The vandals destroy them for two reasons, to rob the coins and for the pleasure of vandalizing. Now all the telephones, which were functioning with coins, were replaced with telephones which function with credit cards but however only few of them work and always there is a line of people waiting to use them. If there isn't a line, most probably that the respective phone doesn't work.

— Two sisters just finished talking about the desolate urban situation in Managua and Kingston, capitals of third world countries or how they are called also, "developing" countries. I am from a first world country, what means very developed, and I didn't have the opportunity to travel much out of my city, small enough. In my city there aren't winding streets but is true that we have the same difficulty to read the names of the streets from the vehicles in traffic even during the day, during the night it is not possible to read anything. I am a little confused, I am not sure if the worse urban situation is specific only for the cities of the poor countries or how it is said, developing.

— My dear sister, rushed to respond a neighbour bicycle very close to her, I am from London, the capital of England, a country considered to be very developed or of the first world, how you mentioned. I travelled many years before, with my cyclist to Kingston, Jamaica and so I think that I can answer to your question, from my own experience.

— I am very interested to listen to you.

— Certainly there are big differences between the two cities specially in what concerns the richness of the city in general, not in particular, because in London, which is a richer city than Kingston, are poor people poorer than many poor people in Kingston, and in Kingston there are rich people richer than many rich people in

London. However, the two cities have a great thing in common: the stupidity of the human beings. This is reflected in many aspects, but I will concentrate my comment about the urbanism and the difficulty of orientation, aspects very close one to another.

— How many inhabitants have the two cities?

— Kingston has one million and London has ten million but the urban disaster is the same, based on the same stupidity of the founders of both cities and of those who have developed them afterwards. Each of these cities is a mixture of narrow, winding streets with few main streets, wasting a very great area of precious land as in so many other cities. Both cities were developed in quantity and not in quality, without any planning, vision or perspective for the future. There is an explanation for the similarity between the two cities. Kingston was founded and developed when Jamaica was a British colony and consequently Kingston was developed by the colonialists with London as a model. The difficulty of orientation and of reading the numbers on the houses and the names of the streets is also the same in both cities. And this demonstrates that the quality of the cities is not necessarily superior in the cities of the first world. In what concerns the cities of the "developing" countries, by the way, this title is only a very kind expression behind which hides a terrible real economic situation. Only a small minority of very rich and politicians of these countries justifies this word "developing". For the great majority the situation becomes worse, and what is more sad, there is no real hope at the horizon to improve its situation. The quality of life is so low that the miserable level of urbanism and the difficulty for orientation in their cities of which we are talking here, in no way is a priority for this majority.

— I understand, intervened in the discussion the young bicycle, that there are problems more grave and important than the urbanism and the possibility for easy orientation, but this is still a problem and once we are discussing it now, I would like to clarify an aspect that seems to me a contradiction.

— We are listening. What or which is the contradiction?

— It seems to me that the contradiction is between the quality or the total different treatment given to the names of the streets and to the numbers on the houses, on one hand, and to the indicators installed in all highways and expressways for cars. I will explain in more detail what I want to say.

The young one continued:

— The indicators with the names of the streets, numbers for the houses and the indicators in the highways, all have the same purpose, to make possible the orientation for all those who move in the city, pedestrians, bicycles, cars, buses, etc., and for the motorized vehicles out of the city. I will talk about the motorized vehicles because only these ones can circulate on the streets of the city and on the highways; to the pedestrians, and bicycles the access on the highways is not allowed.

Well, the indicators on the highways are very good and following them, is possible to travel with the speed of one hundred kilometers per hour and be well informed about the place where you want to get out, much before you reach the exit point. This information is written with big enough letters, is well lit and is of permanent use during the day or night, in any weather conditions, including heavy rain, snow, and is easy to read it very well without reducing the speed. The system is functional and is an integral part of the highway. Without this information system for the drivers, the highways couldn't be functional, true?

— Perfectly true.

— Now, the same drivers, in one or another point must exit from the highway and enter the city and circulate on the streets up to their destination. In this moment they enter other world, an enemy world. It is true that the speed is limited on the city streets to fifty or sixty kilometers per hour. This speed is also big enough and requires adequate indications similar with those on the highways, but from the moment a motorized vehicle enters from the highway to the city streets, the indicators are little functional for the same vehicles. My question is how this contradiction can be explained

— Your question, my friend, is very logical and very, very welcome and I think, more than this, I am sure that I have the answer to your so interesting comment and question.

The response is at the same time philosophical and very realistic about the nature of various categories of human beings. The construction of the cities began many years before the apparition of the motorized vehicles and the indicators were directed to the pedestrians and to the vehicles with horses, which moved with a speed less than ours, the bicycles. The clerks and the bureaucrats from the municipality were in charge with these indicators. The task was very simple and didn't require much thinking and intelligence, the indicators at that time were more or less functional. With the apparition of the motorized vehicles, an essential change was necessary, but this was a requirement too big for the intellectual capacity of those bureaucrats and for many decades afterwards, nothing changed.

With the highways, this is totally other story. The highways were designed and built as an integral system including the indicators, by the engineers, the superior category of the human beings. For them, the necessity of high quality indicators was obvious and was an essential part of each highway project and practically realized strictly according to the project. In the first case, in spite of the major changes of the circulation in the city, nothing changed with the system of indicators thanks to the entire army of stupid clerks and bureaucrats in front with the mayors. In the second case, everything was perfectly managed from the beginning, thanks to the engineers in charge with the implementation of the highways. All the respect and admiration for the engineers.

— You are in love with the engineers, joked the young bicycle.

— Certainly I am, responded immediately the interlocutor bicycle, without considering the words of the young one as a joke.

— In this world, which is a sea of stupidity, moral decadence, stagnation or regression, the engineers are the unique absolute promoters of the advance, with very few exceptions of representatives of other professions. The engineering as a profession doesn't know the way of retreat or periods of decadence as occurs frequently with the arts, the entire economy of many countries, with the politics, that can stop the development of a country or of an entire continent. The permanent success of the engineering is explained by its scientific base, by the rational logic or absolute logical reasoning which doesn't leave any space for myths, for decisions based on religious beliefs, neither for whatever argument that cannot be demonstrated. The engineering is based on the explanation of all phenomena with the physical laws of the nature and on the use of these laws for the technical progress. The engineering is based on the scientific investigation and on the inspiration generated by this investigation and not on the religious obscurantism, which doesn't explain anything in a rational manner, the only universal explanation being the divine power, which contains thousands of unexplained contradictions for a sound mind. The engineers are not afraid of questions and always are ready to give the realist answers. The basic principle of the religion is "believe and don't ask". To whatever question an engineer gives an intelligent answer, a priest, only a stupid answer. For this I love the engineers. And don't forget please, we the bicycles were created by the engineers. By combining in a genial manner the laws of gravity and of the motion, have produced such a simple and precious vehicle. We don't have engine, no hidden parts, everything can be seen through us and not everybody can understand how we can keep the balance when we run, even at a low speed of few kilometers per hour.

I remember very well a specific part of the discussion between my cyclist and his friends about the book of the famous soviet writer Ilya Ehrenburg with the title "And Was the Second Day". In this book dedicated to the massive and rapid industrialization of the Asian part of the Soviet Union, few years after the revolution, there is a very interesting part in which the talk is about us, the bicycles.

That process of industrialization was conducted by the Russians involving also the local inhabitants, who had at that time a very low level of culture and development. An essential part for the building of factories was the transport and the soviets built for the first time in those remote areas railways and so the local inhabitants saw for the first time in their life trains and locomotives. At that time the locomotives were with steam and produced together with energy, much noise, smoke and sparks, and some locals with their primitive level were afraid of these big, black locomotives and with fire inside. The Russians came there not only with trains but also with us for the local transportation of the workers and so the local inhabitants had for the first time the occasion to see bicycles circulating.

Well, after such a long but very necessary introduction in order to understand the comic irony that follows in this discussion between two local inhabitants:

— I can't understand how the bicycle can move and with a man on top of her and doesn't fall!

— I can't understand how the locomotive can move the train. Where are the horses? There are no horses!

— Oh, this is very clear. Inside the dark and hot locomotive is the devil who spits fire. But the bicycle?

The opinion of the bicycles about various professions, engineers, doctors, artists, lawyers.

A choir of prolonged laughter put an enjoyable end to the comment of the bicycle in love with the engineers. But this end was only temporary because other bicycle continued the issue with the following question:

— Now is very clear why you are in love with the engineers, but I can assure you that there is a great danger of much jealousy, not only you are in love with them, for the same reasons. But this is other matter. I have a question: you explained very well the professional merits of the engineers, but what is the position of other professionals as the doctors, artists, lawyers?

— Talking about doctors, it is sure that many of them are very valuable members of the society of the human beings, but not all of them. The doctors have saved many lives and have improved the health of many more. It is difficult to imagine the contemporary, civilized life without an army of doctors and dentists. But if you want to make a comparison for evaluating the contribution to the society by each category of professionals, it is necessary to assume that the services of the professionals of the analyzed category are not available for a while.

— Agreed, responded the bicycle who asked the question. I would like to ask you, what do you do if you get sick or have an accident? Do you go to a lawyer, or artist or take an engineer with you? No, you go to a doctor, or to a hospital and not to anybody else, true?

— Tell me please, how old are you?

— I am two thousand five hundred kilometers of age.

— Well, you are very young and because of this there are things, which you didn't have yet the opportunity to learn in life, when you will be of several dozens of thousands of kilometers you will understand everything much better. Now I would like to help you with some questions.

— Enchanted.

— You say that, assuming that you are a human being and get sick, you go to a doctor and not to a lawyer or artist, true?

— True.

— Why?

— Because they are of no help. The doctor can do what is necessary perfectly without them.

— This is perfectly true, they are useless for you and for the doctor. But you say also that you don't take an engineer with you, true?

— True.

— Why?

— For the same reason, they are of no help, neither for me nor for the doctor.

— Not for this.

— What do you mean? But for what?

— Because they, the engineers, and not only one, are already there, ready to help you with essential services.

— I don't understand, what services?

— In order to understand better, let's assume that all the lawyers, artists, actors, have disappeared. This affects your visit to the doctor?

— In no way. There will be fewer lawsuits in the courts, less paintings and less plays at the theatre but this will not affect me.

— And how you go to the doctor?

— Very simple, calling a taxi by phone.

— Wonderful. But let's assume that the engineers disappeared also.

— This doesn't change anything.

— Don't rush, you say that you will call for a taxi by phone?

— Yes.

— But without engineers there is no telephone and there are no cars, and the taxi is a car. No engineers—no telephone and no—taxi.

Silence. The young one doesn't say anything.

— Don't worry, you can take a horse, or for more convenience, a carriage, and if there isn't a horse around, it is possible to take a bull or a cow, they also were used for transportation. Well, you arrive at the doctor's office, later but you arrive. But it became dark and the doctor wants to see you.

— This is simple, the doctor presses a button and the light appears in his cabinet.

— But don't forget, if there aren't engineers there isn't electricity. And to make the story shorter, all the instruments for analysis and the devices of the modern medicine, are products of engineering.

— My sister, says the young bicycle, I feel very stupid, how could I equalize the artists, the lawyers and the actors with the engineers in our life? All is very clear, very many thanks. However, to clarify everything, I would like to ask you, what do you think when you say that are doctors that aren't so good?

— Very well, I want to clarify this very important aspect in the comparison with the engineers. It is essential to mention that each profession has a positive or negative influence on the ethic and moral code and on the professional behavior, especially in this very materialistic world in which we live.

The engineers are interested personally in the production of material values and in the general health of the population. Healthier is the population more things are consumed and better is the personal well being of the engineers. With the doctors and hospitals, especially in the countries with private medical practice, as in the United States, the human beings are for them potential clients, and more of them get sick, more clients the doctors have and their material situation is better. Many times there are flagrant abuses, exaggerated sickness, or directly invented, useless operations, to grab more money from the patients, which are defenseless, totally in the hands of the doctor.

The same thing happens with the dentists. Not rare are the cases when if a patient goes to five dentists, he obtains five different stories for the treatment with big differences in the price, what creates a great confusion. Practically, the citizens are without any medical or legal protection. The dentistry is a private, very profitable industry and even in Canada where there is free medical care for all the citizens, the dental treatment is not included. It is a diabolic jungle, and in this regard, the government is guilty not for stupidity but for an organized crime of great proportion. This is a very important difference between engineers and doctors and dentists.

— One moment please, sounded the voice of a remote bicycle in the audience. I have a very important question to clarify a great confusion, and this question is for our Canadian sister.

— I am listening to you, my dear.

— If I heard well, in Canada the medical service is free for all the population of the country.

— Correct.

— Including hospitalization for all the illnesses and accidents?

— Yes.

— This is very good, but if I understood well, for the dental treatment everybody should pay.

— Correct.

— And for what reason it is considered that the health of the mouth, of the teeth, which assure in a direct manner the health of all the body, the healthy digestion, is not included in the free general treatment? What is the difference between the health of one or other part of the same human body?

— A very reasonable question which doesn't have any response from the authorities of the country, provincial or federal.

— But isn't there a Minister of Health? And also a Prime Minister responsible for the health and well being of the population?

— Sure there are. An entire bureaucratic machinery.

— But this is such an important problem. They don't think?

— Why not? They think and think a lot.

— And then, why the situation doesn't change?

— Because they don't think about this. This issue doesn't interest them at all.

— But what are they thinking about?

— They think how to win the next elections, to assure their position for the future and how to make more money using the political and administrative influence that they have today.

— In this case can I assume that those who need to replace one, two or three teeth must pay for everything with their own money?

— More than assume, you can be sure.

— And how much costs an implant for a new tooth, for instance?

— In Canada this could cost about four thousand dollars per tooth.

— This is very expensive. And if one doesn't have the necessary money, what does he do?

— The solution is very simple.

— What?

— To live without those teeth, how long and how he can, with all the consequences.

— And there isn't insurance?

— Certainly there is but is very expensive and doesn't cover all that is necessary. This is other crookery. If the dentist knows that you have insurance, and this cannot be a secret for him, he puts a much higher price for the treatment, and here there is a vicious circle, the insurance companies protect themselves against this speculative action by increasing the insurance premiums.

— I have a last question.

— Please.

— You said that these ministers always think about next elections. It happens that the same party and government win the elections and the power for the second time?

— And for the third time also.

— In this case why the great majority of the people, which is not rich, vote for the same politicians for the second time, and how you say, for the third one, knowing very well that they didn't solve essential problems as the one related to the financial aspect for the dental treatment?

— Other very reasonable question. Don't forget that you are talking not about bicycles, but about human beings, and this is another proof of their stupidity without limits.

— I want to make an essential correction to avoid misinterpretation, intervened a bicycle who was very attentive to the discussion. The Canadian sister said that in Canada the general medical treatment is free, true?

— True, answered without delay the Canadian bicycle.

— This is to say that the government makes a gift to the entire population with the medical treatment, paying with the personal money of the members of the government?

— I understand very well what you want to say, responded the Canadian bicycle, smiling. It is very clear that nothing is for free. The medical treatment that we call "free" is paid entirely as a form of insurance by all those who work in the country. It is not a favour on behalf of the government, it is its obligation, and the inadmissible situation for not covering the dental treatment, is a grave default of its obligation. Many thanks for your valuable observation.

— Very sad things happen with the human creatures, commented other bicycle. Some of them are stupid, others are crooks and thieves. Thanks, you clarified very well the situation with the doctors. I would like to know also what is the position of the artists and actors in this comparison with the engineers.

— Unfortunately, it can be said that the art in our time is in many cases, dying. In the past centuries the art was totally independent of the engineering and technology and was of high quality. The engineering couldn't create art. Today it can, and very much better and cheaper than an artist. Two or three centuries ago, a painter could create a very realist painting of a landscape or a person. This work required a very long time, maybe several months. To make a copy of the same quality as the original, approximately the same time was necessary. Today, with the modern technology, to produce a photography with a perfect image of a landscape or person requires only a fraction of a second and less of a minute to produce the copy in live colors on paper and the cost is less than a dollar. To make one hundred copies, or one thousand or doesn't matter how many copies of the same quality and with the same very low cost or less, doesn't represent any problem. These photos are closer to the reality in each detail and to make them it is not necessary to be an artist. Literally every person capable to take a camera in his hands can make them.

— So, you are saying that there is no difference between an artist emeritus and an ignorant in painting.

— Certainly there is. If we are talking about producing an image of the existing reality, a landscape, a person or group of persons or whatever other things, the artist requires possibly months to produce the painting and the ignorant requires only a second to take the picture and afterwards one minute to copy it on paper. And the quality of the picture is the same or better than the painting. In what concerns the details, the photography is more precise. So, talking about the result of the work the artist cannot compete with the ignorant. If we are talking about the very process of painting or about producing an image by imagination and not of the reality, the ignorant with his camera cannot compete with the artist; however, this necessity is very limited.

— It means that today every person can be an artist without being a recognized artist.

— Exactly so, with the observation that I just made.

— In this case what is the present value of an artist painter for instance, with diplomas, many paintings and recognized artistic merits?

— Do you want me to tell you the naked truth?

— Yes.

— Historical. Has only an historical value, not practical, for the society.

— Can you explain in little more detail?

— Sure. But you will need some patience, because there are two aspects in my response and I would like to clarify them well.

— I have all the patience you may need.

— And we too, the subject is so interesting, completed a choir of bicycles.

— Very well, the first aspect is the explanation of the apparition of the painting and of the painters, thousands of years ago, but the most beautiful paintings and the most talented painters with many works of art well known are from about the last seven centuries and specially from the last century. The main purpose of those paintings was to satisfy the taste of the powerful of the day, emperors, empresses, kings, queens, barons and baronesses and other magnates, to embellish their palaces. This was very important for their reputation, their status and desire to show off, to make a display of their richness at whatever cost, and the nice paintings were very adequate for this. The great majority of these paintings are portraits of the members of those imperial or royal families, scenes of their life, of their palaces, and sometimes beautiful landscapes. These paintings can be seen in many palaces, which are today museums. In that past time these palaces were the only market for the painters. The poor didn't have any possibility neither to buy nor even to see them.

The other aspect is the technology. At that time, the only way to have a portrait of you or of your family was to use a painter. In our days the situation is totally different. The engineers had developed the photographical technology to such a high artistic level and at such a low cost, that the painting is completely out of competition. This is not to say that the painting disappeared, but the demand is extremely limited, is used more as a personal hobby, or is sold in some shops as landscape souvenirs for tourists at high enough prices. Here also there is an invasion of pictures as post cards of various sizes and of very good quality at a cost of three, five or ten for a dollar. And for making your own souvenirs, what does your cyclist take when goes with you and other cyclists in a trip, a camera or a painter?
A wave of laughter was the very clear answer. And after the laughter calmed down, the same bicycle continued:
— There is also other unfavorable aspect for the professional painters, the saturation of the market with large and very expensive paintings, sceneries and portraits of persons. During more than six centuries until the apparition of the modern photographic industry, a great number of paintings were produced. The museums are now full of them and I don't think that more museums will be built for new paintings with the same themes.

— And how it is possible to evaluate a recent painting or a famous one from the past centuries and to decide how much it costs, many times the price being of millions of dollars?

— Doesn't exist absolutely any rational criterion for this. All is a commercial circus for the benefit of some crooks, not artists, especially today when for a derisory price is possible to produce with the modern technology, identical copies that cannot be distinguished from the original without a special laboratory analysis. As an example for this aspect, I remember what my cyclist has related about his visit to the Art Museum in Ottawa, the capital of Canada. On one wall were exposed a nice painting by a famous painter in original and immediately close to it, its copy produced with the technology. For all the viewers it was practically impossible to see the difference. And this was the purpose of demonstration by putting together the two paintings, the original and the copy.

— So the very act of evaluation in money the value and the quality of a work of art is a proof of mercantilism and of stupidity of the human beings.

— More than stupidity, pure idiocy.

The conclusion is that in arts also, the engineering has a very strong position and changed totally all the previous aspects.

It seemed that everything was very clear in this discussion about the participation of the engineering in the artistic life of the human beings, but this only seemed so, because without wasting time, other bicycle intervened with the following observation:

— I am sure that all of us have learned a lot about the participation of the engineering in the artistic life of the human beings, in this case, the painting. I must say that before I didn't think about the tremendous role of the engineers in the visual art, making possible for each person to be an artist in fact, producing with little effort the same that a professional artist, in this case a painter, produces with so much work and born talent, if he has it. This wasn't so obvious for me but now is very clear. And to give an additional example in this regard, not farther than yesterday, coming back to the house, we stopped for a short while at a cheap shop where everything is sold for a dollar or two, and among other things my cyclist bought some mats for the table so beautiful with sceneries of mountains and flowers, that would be a very good idea to frame them as precious paintings and hang them on the wall, and everything for a cost close to nothing. What I would like to say is that in my opinion, what is true for the visual art, the painting, is not applicable for the music. With this art I think that the engineering doesn't have anything in common. Here there aren't devices like cameras with which is possible to replace a singer or a musician. I am right?

— Not, you are not, better think once more about it.

— Why am I not right? My cyclist is a singer, very young, but a singer, and when he wants to hear music, he sings, and he sings very well without any help from the engineers. He has talent.

— Really? And can he sing as Pavarotti or Caruso? Or can he substitute a choir or an orchestra in his house?

— You are joking, certainly, he cannot, nobody can.

— But I can, and everybody can.

— You are joking again and I am serious.

— I don't joke, I am very serious also. You are talking about the situation of one century ago. In this case you are right, but with the present development of the engineering even in this activity, I can use a device not bigger than a photo camera to listen to all the music that I want, to the most celebrated singers in the world, orchestras, choirs, everything. My talent is not necessary for this and doesn't matter if I have it.

The engineering is present here as in the visual art. And other aspect is the dimension of the audience, the capacity to communicate. How many can listen to a singer without the technology and how many with the help of the technology. Think about the role of the radio, television, and movies the acoustic in the concert halls, in theatres. It is very sad that nobody thinks about engineers and their major importance in the everyday life. Everybody knows the names of the actors, singers, politicians, but not of one single engineer, without whom all the celebrities would not be celebrities.

— I didn't think about all this, you are right.

— Talking about the comparison between the engineers and the representatives of other professions as doctors, artists, the necessity and the supreme importance of the engineering and of the engineers is very clear. But there is another category, which seems that doesn't depend on engineers and have a very important position in the society of the human beings.

— About whom you are talking?

— About lawyers.

— Ah, the lawyers! What a pleasure to hear about them in this discussion! And you want to compare them with the engineers?

— Why not?

— Because I like only good lawyers. Do you know what is a good lawyer?

— Yes, I think that a good lawyer is one who works hard and is successful in his activity.

— But there is also other definition for a good lawyer.

— It means?

— It means that a good lawyer is a dead lawyer.

Other wave of laughter propagated all over the audience. And the bicycle that provoked this wave continued:

— The lawyers are a special category, which live well as parasites on a healthy body, the body being the society of the human beings. They, the lawyers, don't produce anything, none of them, neither material products nor spiritual, all their work, and many work hard, is directed to grab money, as much as possible, from everybody. A special kind of prey is other human beings, which have various problems. Defending criminals and thieves is also a very profitable business. Their existence and work in the society are due integrally to the stupidity of the human beings in general and to their social organization in particular. In a rational society, with intelligent beings, there is no room for them. Such a society would not produce and would not allow to produce lawyers.

The cumbersome and confusing legal procedure must be drastically simplified and the legal assistance to everybody when necessary, must be performed by governmental clerks with fix salaries as part of the useful necessary public service cutting in this way any possibility of abuse and speculation.

A small minority of lawyers initially works as employees but all of them dream to have a private practice, which gives them the opportunity to make more money, they don't have any scruples for this. Most of the lawyers are crooks and not only in few cases, defending a client, they sell themselves to the other part, for more money. It is much better, if possible, to avoid dealing with them. Their fees are sickening and not controllable, up to five hundred dollars per hour or more and other costs are extra.

For all these reasons whatever comparison with the engineers is simply an insult to the engineers. If in one moment all the lawyers would disappear or would go in a permanent strike, no one cataclysm would occur, by the contrary, the world would become better, but if the same happens with all the engineers, disasters would start to occur minutes later and in very short time our civilization will go thousands of years back.

After a short pause, interrupting the absolute silence, which witnessed the interest paid to her words, the same bicycle continued:
— There isn't any sarcastic joke about engineers but are many about lawyers. I remember two, do you want them?
— Immediately, was the response of a choir of bicycles.
— Well, it is said that so happened that in a place met together two dangerous dictators, Saddam Hussein from Iraq and Muhammad Gadafy from Libya, a lawyer and a very good man with a strong

desire to protect the humanity. This man had a gun with only two bullets. What do you think he did?

— Shot the two dictators, for sure, rushed to respond a bicycle.

— No, he shot twice the lawyer to make sure that he is dead, because the lawyer could do more harm to the humanity than the two dictators.

After the laughter calmed down, the speaker continued:

— And now the second one. One morning, a man getting out of his house met his neighbour, a lawyer, and told him "Good morning" but continued without pause, remember please that I said "Good morning" only, because when I met you two days ago and greeted you with "How are you?" you sent me an invoice of two hundred dollars for the question.

After another good laughter, the same bicycle continued:

— I also remember a statement made during a program about sharks on May 2004 at the Discovery TV Channel saying that out of professional courtesy, sharks don't eat lawyers.

When the new wave of laughter ended, a bicycle intervened in the discussion with a comment and a question:

— All that I heard here was very interesting and new for me and I learned much, but I don't understand why, if the situation with the lawyers is so detestable, the government doesn't intervene to control them and to impose the necessary discipline, cutting the abuse.

— What a welcome question! I am sure that you have very good intentions but don't have much experience in the society of the human beings. You must be very young. May I ask you how many kilometers do you have?

— Not too many, is true, no more than a thousand.

— When you will reach one hundred thousand kilometers, life will teach you the response to your question, but that day is far enough and I will answer your very reasonable question, now. As the saying goes, the wolf doesn't attack other wolf, especially when there are so many sheep around. Of what profession do you think are the ministers of all levels of government, provincial, state or federal including prime ministers and presidents of the state and the great majority of the members of the Parliament and other politicians? Lawyers. And what do you think all these politicians including the prime-minister do when they lose the elections? They go back to their profession of lawyers using the very valuable connections made during their work in the government. So, in this situation, do you think that they, while in power, will promulgate laws against the lawyers' abuses, it is to say against themselves some years or months later? Certainly not. And who are the sheep? The people, the human beings so stupid in their great majority, that can be used very well as a permanent source of gains for the large enterprises in collaboration with the government. So, the lawyers are very well protected. The entire society of the poor human beings is sick with so much stupidity, wherever you look.

— Everything is very clear but very sad. Many thanks. At least I am happy that there are not lawyers among us, the bicycles.

A massive movement of wheels and the sound of bells signaled the agreement of the audience with these last words.

After this extended discussion about the importance of various professions, when it seemed that no one aspect was forgotten, a bicycle signaled insistently her desire to talk.

— I have a question, which is by itself an issue for discussion. I recognize from the beginning that my question has only theoretical value, without practical meaning for the society, but I would like to clarify this issue. Are you interested to listen to me?

— Without any doubt, our friend, we are listening to you, answered a very curious bicycle, with the tacit approval of all other bicycles.

— The conclusion of our discussion about the necessity and priority of some professions, as a competition between engineers, doctors, artists, actors and lawyers, not involving in this discussion other professions, was very clear: the engineers are in the first place, position totally undisputable, the doctors, even with the mentioned deficiencies, are indispensable for the society, the artists of other than abstract art and the actors are welcome but not indispensable. The lawyers, well, the lawyers are out of competition, there is no place for them in a civilized and rational society, they are not necessary as there are not necessary other parasites in the society. All this is very clear. The dilemma, I repeat purely theoretical, is if a society would be obligated to choose between engineers without doctors or doctors without engineers, which would be the more reasonable choice?

— Hm, your question, I must say, is original and assumes a choice clearly hypothetical as you say, and cruel or cynical. But once this is a question, requires an answer, and a logical and impartial answer. In order to make this task which is difficult enough, less difficult, I would like to have first your or other bicycle response to the following example: if there are two large ships in the sea, in imminent danger to be lost, a ship with one thousand passengers and other ship with one hundred passengers, and with all the humanly possible efforts, the naval base can save only one ship, which ship must be saved?

— The response is very sad but very simple, said a bicycle without reservation, if it is not possible to save both, the ship with one thousand passengers must be saved.

— I like your direct and rational answer. Now, to get closer to the answer to the initial question of our sister, also in a direct and rational manner, let's assume that one of these two ships represents the engineers, and the other ship the doctors. Can you specify in what ship are the engineers and in what ship the doctors?

— The ship with one thousand passengers represents the engineers and the ship with one hundred passengers represents the doctors, and without waiting for the normal question "why?" my answer is that thousands of years ago, the human beings have survived without engineers and without doctors, but the human beings of today are not capable anymore to live as thousands of years before. The doctors today are very necessary but the engineers are more necessary. Without doctors many will die or get sick, but very many more, the majority, will live a healthy life. It is very clear that today there are many human beings who don't use the doctors' services for many years or decades because they don't need them. Without the engineers, many more will die or get sick, and the life for all, absolutely for all, will be miserable, as centuries or thousands of years before, and the capacity of the human beings of today to adapt to the conditions of primitive life, is very debatable. More than that, in a society without engineers, the doctors could practice only a primitive medicine, the modern pharmaceutical industry will disappear and in very short time the hospitals will become morgues. Fortunately, this terrible situation, to choose between a society without engineers or without doctors, is not real, is only an interesting theme for a purely theoretical debate, and I hope that all of us have enjoyed it, at least I did.

— And we also, added other bicycles.

What the bicycles think about religion.

Nothing is more specific and characteristic for the abysmal profundity of the stupidity and primitivism of the human beings as a species, as the power of the religion, of the superstitions and mystical cults, in short, the preponderance of the irrational over their capability of reasoning.

This theme provoked a much passionate and prolonged debate in the mass of bicycles participating in this reunion. Many bicycles have expressed their ideas, impressions and opinions resulting from their life experience. And so, the exchange of opinions began.

— I would like to mention one of the greatest stupidities of the human beings, their religious belief of no matter what denomination, intervened a bicycle. I traveled a lot in this world, in countries called developed and in other ones named as moving in this direction, in Europe, in North and South America and in Asia and I was very surprised by how deep and devastating is this aspect of the stupidity of the human beings.

— My dear, addressed to the speaker other bicycle, let me correct what you said, based on my direct observations and on the comments of those few human beings, which are the exceptions from the rule. We are talking now not about "one" of the greatest stupidity of the human beings as you said, but about the "greatest", I repeat, the greatest stupidity of all others. I can understand all kind of errors of judgment, of calculations, of interpretation, lack of enough intelligence to understand a scientific theory, mistaken assumptions based on lack of experience, all this I can understand, and as none of the human beings is perfect, these cases are more or less acceptable when they represent a minority and not the rule. But simply I cannot understand how human beings with appearance of normal beings who proved their competence and capacity in some of their intellectual works or achievements, can be the victims of such a great foolishness as is doesn't matter what religion or religious cult. I cannot understand how so many human beings can believe in the existence of a divine force with absolute and unlimited power, in an almighty God who knows about everything that happens in the entire world in an instantaneous manner, and who is good and wants to help everybody, a God who represent the top of the justice for everything in the world. He is in their imagination as a very kind father for his large family, which is the entire humanity, which was created by him. I cannot understand why none of these believers asks himself some elementary questions, as why, if there is an almighty and good God who controls all what happens in the world, there are so many bad things that happens to the good and innocent ones, disasters and catastrophes, individual and collective, without any logical justification. There are thousands of questions without answer and all what they do is to pray. None of them questions the very necessity of the prayer. In a normal family, the children don't have to pray to the father for food, the father gives to the children all what they need without waiting for their prayers. I know that to all this there is a direct answer, complete and cruel, it is to say their stupidity that goes up to idiocy.

— This is your opinion thinking as a bicycle but don't forget that they, the humans, are an inferior species without the capacity of logical reasoning in their great majority. And the rest of them who have this capacity, are atheists, not believers.

— The religious belief is a cerebral disease, a malfunctioning of a part of the brain of the human beings which is manifested only at the higher levels of the thinking process and does not affect directly the habitual activities. However, this malfunction can affect and many times affects, influences and determines the activities of these human beings up to such a tragic and fundamental point as when the affected beings commit suicide, individual or collective, or commit crimes, assassinations and destructions in the name of religious beliefs. It is true, these are relatively rare cases, but the danger is permanent, never can be said or predicted when and exactly in what circumstances this sleeping bomb can explode. This cerebral malfunction causes the lack of control over the logical behavior in these extreme situation.

— But how do they behave in normal, habitual conditions of the everyday life in the society?

— Very normal, very well, sometimes better than their neighbours, colleagues and other members of the community who don't have this malfunction. In this consists also the tremendous danger of these individuals, who cannot be distinguished from others up to the moment, when they start putting in practice their criminal, crazy enough, intentions. But they are not common criminals, who kill to rob or for making a witness of his robbery or other crime disappear. Surely that these criminals are very dangerous but the religious fanatics are more dangerous.

— Why do you say so?

— Because the common criminals are very selfish, very careful in their anti-social actions, because they do them to live better. They don't have moral principles or scruples but they want to live by all means and not to die. The religious fanatics have totally different philosophy. Not only that they are not afraid of death, they are convinced by their religious beliefs and their incapacity to reason independently of this belief, that their own death is something good and for sure a very low price for the benefits they will get.

— Of what benefits one can talk when he is dead? got indignant the same bicycle.

— I will explain to you immediately. For a normal mind, there is no doubt that the death means the end of everything. For a believer the life doesn't end with the death. For them the life on earth is only the first part of the existence and not the best one. The best part, that they think is also permanent, continues in paradise where they will arrive after death and have a happy existence, close to God, without any problems, without worrying or being anxious about anything. They believe that when a human being dies, it means that God calls him to paradise, and so the death is not so bad, can be a very good solution and for this reason there are believers that commit suicide. This is the result of the religious education for those who at the end become believers.

— In this case all the believers must or at least can commit suicide?

— This would be so if we forget something very important, that the human beings belong not to God, which doesn't exist, but to the animal kingdom of this world, that exists, and they are before anything else, animals. And all the animals, in order to be able to survive, have the natural immunity, which protects them against the diseases provoked by microbes, germs and virus. And here there is a ferocious fight between these microbes, germs and virus, which attack the body of other living beings, and the capacity of the immune system of these beings to protect the body against these attackers. The equation is very simple, when the immune system is stronger than the enemies, the beings remain alive and healthy, when the enemies are stronger, the beings, including the human beings, get sick and eventually die. The same happens with the brain. The power of the brain to fight against the exterior causes which put in danger the health or the life of the respective being, it means the immunity, can be measured with its intelligence or instinct. The animals and the human beings atheists have one thing in common, their immune system against religion is absolute, one hundred percent. For this, if an entire group of priests, the most talented in their lies, will spend an entire year to convince a chicken or a goat to pray to God instead of eating their food, or to commit suicide for a better posterior life, or for the sake of God, they will waste their time without any success. Exactly the same will happen in a similar experiment with the atheists.

— But what is the situation with other human beings, the believers?

— Eh, here is the problem. This issue is a little more ample and requires a more detailed explanation. The instinct to live and the desire for life, even if the life is very difficult, are very powerful and the immense majority of believers will not commit suicide or kill others because their capacity of reasoning, to think, is higher than their religious belief. In these cases their brains stop them to pass from desire to action. But here there is a hidden danger. Takes place a similar process as with the body. There are bacteria and virus, which because of the superior power of the immune system, cannot develop but exist in the body in dormant state without affecting the body for many years. But if at some moment the immune system for whatever cause becomes weak, the bacteria and virus wake up from the dormant or passive state and become active, attacking the body. In some cases this can result in a serious illness or death. If there are not such bacteria or virus in the body there is nothing to wake up, or if the immune system is always high, there is no danger. A believer always, as long he is a believer, has in his brain a kind of virus, which is dormant. In this situation the activity of that human being is well controlled by the reasoning power of his brain. But the dangerous virus of the belief is there, sleeping. If the religious influence becomes more powerful than the capacity of reasoning, the virus may wake up and provoke or lead to disastrous actions, of which there are many frightening examples. They behave like time bombs and are armed with such bombs or with explosives but are very much more dangerous than a time bomb.

— Why more dangerous? These bombs explode with certainty in whatever place are put, and are not afraid of the police.

— In this consists the dangerous difference. The time bombs are placed in one spot. The bombs or the explosives carried by the believers terrorists are mobile and are activated when and where the believer who carries them thinks that can produce a greater damage and to kill more people, using all the capacity of his brain to choose the moment and the place more favorable exactly for this. If the police have the suspicion that whatever hidden or abandoned parcel contains a bomb, they bring the specialists to neutralize it. When a believer carries the bomb and is in danger to be arrested by the police, he prefers to explode the bomb immediately, killing at least a few policemen and doesn't matter how many innocents, who are around.

— They are brutes and terrorists, this is clear, but aren't they afraid for their own death?

— By no means. And they, men or women, don't consider themselves terrorists but martyrs. They don't kill to rob but for a superior cause, as they think, for their religion and following the will of God. In this direction they consider themselves of high morality and for this, their determination based on the totally irrational religious fanaticism makes them much more dangerous than the common criminals.

— Why you said "men or women", there are women involved also in these actions?

— Certainly there are. When the religious virus enters into the action, there are no limits of sex, age, consequences or of anything else. Men, women, and youngsters, even children are involved in these actions. And sometimes their own parents don't know that they prepare themselves to die in this way. How ugly and dangerous is the religion, although sometimes for some, has a very sweet façade!

— I ask myself, how these youngsters are recruited, they must be very poor, true?

— Not necessarily. Of course, there are many poor involved in these actions, being promised all kind of imaginable things, and they are made to believe in this with such a force that they become ready to die for those things. The obvious cause is the total blockage of the reasoning capacity. A flagrant example is the promise that each man committing suicide in these terrorist actions will receive in paradise seventy virgins and for sure many material things. And they, the poor or the rich, but with poor minds, believe in this foolishness. The preparation for the terrorist actions is very well organized, and in the more sophisticated actions are involved believers with high education and qualification, including pilots for very large planes. These are human beings with very good material situation, they have families, children, houses, cars, are good neighbours and behave very well in the community, so that nobody could assume of what terrible crimes these human beings are capable and ready to commit. They live in their community, sometimes for years, in a very quiet and peaceful manner but the virus in their brains is active. When the order comes, the believers leave everything behind, very good professional position, house, wife, children, all this is not important for them anymore, and they go to the indicated place and time to participate in the suicidal action for which they were selected with their genuine acceptance, and they accomplish it well up to the end. Why? It is a human beings tragedy but this is the reality and this shows the real and tremendous danger of the religion.

— This is more dangerous than an epidemic of cholera.

— Certainly is. And this epidemic contains special schools to prepare the candidates for the suicide, using men, women youngsters and children from several years old.

— And what does the police do?

— By your question it is clear for me that you assume that the police is a power independent of the judicial system, with the only purpose to protect the people and to maintain the order in the society. If this is your opinion about the police, I must disappoint you a bit. The main purpose of the police is to control the people before protecting it. But nobody and nothing can control better the people, the mass of human beings, than the religion. Those who control the society of the poor human beings are using both, the police and the religion, to keep the people in permanent state of obedience. For this, the police will never take any action against the religion. There are countries were the religion has dictatorial power as in the Middle Age in Europe, and controls also the police. These countries are the nest for the creation and training of believers converting them in terrorists to act in different places in the world.

— And what is the purpose of these terrorist actions?

— The base is a fight for economic power between different groups, which want to control the entire economy. They cannot do that by themselves only, they need to involve in this fight the mass of people but not for the interest of this mass but for their own interest. This naked purpose is not a tasty food for the mass of people, but if a very spicy religious gravy is added, which is the virus that attacks the reasoning capacity, the mass will take it, get intoxicated and turn obedient thinking that fights for its belief, not for the interest of its manipulators. And so, many times the terrorism is a fight between religions and they kill each other in the name of different Gods.

— And the respective Gods don't do anything? Simply watch how their believers exterminate each other provoking at the same time a great damage to so many innocents?

— If God existed, this would be the reality, but there is not any God. However, this is an excellent question for the believers but they cannot think at the level of such a simple and logical question.

— I want to clarify other very important aspect of the religion in the society of the human beings. Our sister underlined in an excellent manner what an immense damage was made by the religion and continues to be made with its violent methods. But the religion has also other façade, very peaceful and at the same time not less dangerous. The purpose is to dominate totally and profoundly the human beings in all their activities, to control and direct these activities, eliminating for this whatever resistance and imposing the will of the powerful of the society. Here, the materialist aspect of life has a very strong voice. Those who can control the society can become very rich, even if the price for this is the poverty of the great majority of the society. For this purpose, the malfunctioning, the partial sickness of the brain of the human beings is very welcome. By using it is possible to manipulate much easier the mass of human beings. All forms of religion serve extremely well for this purpose.

The intense promotion of the idea that there is a divine force personified by God, who is almighty, knows everything, is very good and is receptive to all prayers of each human being, and that without Him nothing can be obtained or changed, can easily divert the attention of one person or of an entire mass, from the real problems towards imaginary problems, passing all the responsibility from the leaders of the society for all the bad things they are doing, to God, who cannot be seen, heard, touched, asked, bothered, only prayed, what means a communication with only one way. By this, all causes of rebellion, revolution or whatever other action against the powerful of the day, can be avoided. This creates a defeatism very useful for these omnipotent who take great advantage of the existing situation, when the question of changing it for the benefit of those who protest, is approached.

The religion creates a psychological state of obedience to the existing rules which are considered established by a supernatural power which can not be fought, neither confronted nor explained.

— But how come, interrupted a bicycle with her question, that all the bad things, all the tragedies and disasters that occur, are not an incentive for these believers to change their thinking, to eliminate the cause which allows them to occur, or at least to think about it and protest?

— This question marks an essential point. The problem is the major contradiction between the capability of the same brain to analyze well a complicated enough aspect and its total incapacity to analyze in the same way, in a rational manner, a very simple aspect. I want to give an example. Let's say that you talk to someone that proves that he understands problems of high level, can solve problems very well, in a rational manner. What is your opinion about him?

— I will say that he is an intelligent being and has a brain that functions well.

— Well, now let's say that you talk to somebody else who says that two plus two makes seven, and he is serious in his affirmation. What do you tell him?

— I don't tell him anything. I take two apples, put them on a plate and ask him how many apples are on the plate and he says two, I repeat the operation with other two apples and I ask him how many apples are now on the plate. He must say four, what is obvious.

— And if he says seven?

— In this case he qualifies as an idiot, with a brain without any value.

— Well, now let's assume that you make the two experiments with the same person. How you qualify him? Can you qualify him as intelligent forgetting the arithmetical operation with the apples?

— No, in no way.

— Can you qualify him as an idiot forgetting the first experiment?

— Not, either. The answer is not so easy but I don't think that this is a real case.

— It is very real, is the case with very many believers. Their belief has exactly the same logic as two plus two makes seven, or worse than this. Beside this, everything is normal, or they make errors of interpretation but not in this grotesque manner. Stronger is his religious belief, less are the chances that at the end he will come to the conclusion that two plus two makes four and not seven. In extreme cases he becomes a fanatic ready to make all the terrible things. This is the danger of the religious education and religious influence. It is clear now?

— Very clear.

And the first bicycle continued:

— It is very easy to use the epithet of "idiot" for a believer but this is only a pejorative. The reality is much more complicated. If you want to be serious, it is necessary to approach the issue in a scientific manner. The religious belief of whatever religion or cult is more than stupidity or idiocy is a cerebral disease, more precisely, in that part of the brain where the very complicated process of reasoning and the respective movement of neurons occurs. Until today the medicine cannot cure this deficiency of unequal reasoning but the brain itself can, especially with an effort to understand by the sane part of the brain and with the positive help from outside. And as it is said, always the prevention is better than the cure; it means a scientific education from an early age, contrary to all those religious schools, which make sick the children's brain, must take place.

This very interesting discussion about the religion involved more and more bicycles. One of them said:

— I want to make some additional observations about the behavior of the human beings when they must choose between the logic and the religious belief. This is a ferocious fight although many times the appearance is very peaceful.
— True, my sister, these are the most adequate words, a ferocious fight. And this is so because the influence of the religion is very strong, and it is so strong because the religion fights in the almost totality of cases against defenseless victims, children from three or four years of age, people without the capacity of reasoning in a logical manner and specially when there is not any scientific influence around. On the other hand, continued the bicycle, if a believer tries to convince a well educated person and what is more important, with the capacity to think and analyze the things in a rational manner, the chances of success for the believer are exactly zero.
— Is as a bandit armed with a knife that attacks in the street a child or a person who cannot defend himself. In this case his success is

almost sure. In the other case is as the same bandit tries to attack a well-armed soldier, with a machine gun, in a tank.

— For this, exactly for this, all the super-structure of the religion, in order to survive and continue its existence, concentrates its actions on the religious education in schools, against the children only several years old, when their very young brains start to understand the first aspects of life, commented other bicycle.

— This is a crime against the humanity, protested immediately a very upset bicycle. This is a mutilation of the brain of a child; the long-term effect could be graver than to hit his little head with a stone.

— One of the most obvious proofs of the profound imbecility of the human beings in their religious belief is the way in which they are manipulated and exploited by the leaders of their own belief. These rob their money, their time, and in many cases the most precious what the human beings have, their very life, convincing them to participate in collective suicide, in criminal actions, or in both at the same time. They are named evangelists, fundamentalists, extremists of all kind which like to associate their names and the names of their organizations with words like saviors, liberators, fighters, martyrs, prophets, miraculous healers with divine power.

After a much welcome pause for digesting these novelties totally strange for the rational world of bicycles, the same bicycle continued:

— The magnitude of these actions, the depth of their stupidity combined with the highest level of idiocy, if it can be said so, the total defiance of the elementary logic, are simply incredible. Unfortunately, so incredible are the power and the negative effects of these actions over the poor minds of the human beings. Do you want some examples?

— Yes, yes, was the unanimous response of the audience, motivated by a legitimate and great curiosity.

— Well, if you watch television, each Sunday morning on some main channels, in various countries considered civilized, you can see direct transmissions from a large church or auditorium with thousands and thousands of participants who came to see with their own eyes the "miracles" made by the religious leader who pretends using his power and his direct contacts with God to cure in an instant invalid people. The thousands of participating believers can see how after some words addressed to God and being touched by the hands of the religious leader, the paralyzed stand up from their wheel-chairs and start walking normally expressing in ecstasy: "I can walk!" "I can walk!", "eternal thanks to God", and how the blind, after the same procedure exclaimed with enthusiasm: "I can see!" "I can see!" with the same thanks to God. The enthusiasm turns general and after, in the most opportune time, the youngsters in charge with collecting the monetary contributions for the church start their begging action, the believers sincerely and voluntarily part with a significant amount of their money for such a good cause, hoping that one day in the future, they also could benefit from the miracles that occurred in front of their eyes.

— I was not there and I did not see that televised transmission but I don't believe that the miracles of which you are talking are real, interrupted with defiance a young bicycle.

— I would be extremely surprised, responded the speaker, if you or whatever other bicycle, believed in such called miracle. We, the bicycles, have an intellectual capacity very much higher than the minimal level necessary to understand the entire stupidity of the religious belief. Only the human beings, who in their great majority are below this level, can be believers. But you interrupted me before the end of my story. However, thanks for your opinion, it is important for this discussion.

— Excuse me please, I am very interested in listening to the continuation of your story.

— Well, the continuation of my story refers to a real case transmitted by the powerful television channel of the United States called "ABC" and starts before the point when you interrupted me, addressed the speaker to the young bicycle.

— What do you mean? asked the young one, a little surprised.

— Well, before this well arranged spectacle by crook-artists in front with the religious leader, a well known evangelist, secret cameras installed by the police recorded a secret session in which the evangelist and thirty five "invalids" which in reality were perfectly healthy, rehearsed how to play the roles of paralyzed and blind for the great reunion of believers of the next day. For sure that the crooks "invalids" were well paid for their roles, but the major crook, the evangelist, robbed millions of dollars for this and other actions based on the blind belief of his clients. He was condemned to three years in prison what is too little for such a crime and abuse, and most probably, the things were arranged and he was not in prison even one single day.

— And you say that all this was presented by a main television channel?

— Not only that I say, this was presented indeed by the very powerful North American national television channel ABC which has usually millions of viewers.

— In this case I am sure that after this presentation, nobody participated anymore in these Sunday reunions and that this was the end of the religious belief for the viewers believers, commented the same young bicycle.

— Don't be so sure, responded the speaker, nothing like this occurred and the religious business continues with success in America and in other countries.

— It is true, confirmed other bicycle, I lived for several years in Jamaica, and in addition to the local crooks, once in a while grand reunions with the same traps sold as miracles, are organized by the North-American crooks evangelists.

— The same happens in Nigeria and other countries from Africa. A great number of black workers with poor culture and totally illiterate, are very impressed by the circus of medical "miracles" shown by the white evangelists.

— For sure they don't know anything about the banditism and manipulation behind the curtain in preparation for this grotesque spectacle, everything well directed by the group of imported and local crooks, with the support of the authorities and of the business community.

— This story reflects a very sad reality, which involves these crooks and the mass of believers. However, I don't understand why you say that the authorities and the business community support these actions, asked with her comment a very analytical bicycle.

— I say it because this occurs in reality, and occurs because the authorities represent the interest of the great business and the two of them are interested in taking advantage of the other part of the society of the human beings, being totally in control without problems and the religion is the best instrument for this.

— This is very clear, commented the young bicycle, what is not so clear for me is how so many human beings cannot see the reality of the situation and that they are not the protected ones but the victims of their own religious leaders.

— In this consists the tragedy of the human beings, the cause of their inferiority, the fact that, as you say, they not only believe in what they don't see, but also in that they can not see the reality of their enormous error.

— And these are actions, we can say peaceful, of these religious leaders, continued the speaking bicycle, in other religious adventures the religious leaders instigate directly to collective suicide and crime.

— Can you give us an example of this, also?

— Certainly. There are many cases of such psychological abuse, but one of the more relevant cases is the collective suicide organized by a North-American religious fanatic several years ago in Guyana when about one thousand believers died including their children and babies, by poisoning. They were obligated by the armed guards to give poison to their children and after that to take it themselves.

— If this was not true, this story could be considered as the dirtiest, most terrible and criminal calumny against the religious belief and its leaders, commented a bicycle, which became directly furious listening to this case.

— Perfectly agreed, responded in a very calm manner the speaking bicycle. This would be such a repugnant calumny that the authors deserved the death penalty. True?

— True, true, responded in a choir some bicycles very intrigued by the ferocity of the described case.

— Very well, the death penalty for the calumniators, if this case was an invention, a calumny of a sick mind. But what should be done if the case is real, how can be easily demonstrated?

— In this case, the death penalty for all religious leaders and others involved in this crime, reacted immediately the same bicycles.

— This is good but not enough.

— What more than the death for the guilty ones? asked other bicycle.

— The death penalty for the religion itself, was the answer.

— This makes so much sense that you deserve a million of the most sincere congratulations for the idea.

— Agreed, approved at the same time other bicycles.

— I would like to ask something, intervened a bicycle, silent until this moment.

— Please.

— What was the reason, for which the diabolic religious leader organized this mass suicide in Guyana? What was his interest in that, was he mentally sick and nothing more?

— Much more. Much before committing suicide, all the members of the cult, according to the internal rules of the cult, must renounce legally to all their material possessions, absolutely all, in favor of the cult, in charge of which, was the religious leader. When all the members of the cult died, all the valuables remained in the hands of the religious leader of the cult, who didn't have any intention of killing himself. I don't know exactly what happened with him but this doesn't have much significance, what is important is that such a terrible case could happen and was real.

— If after this case the religious belief survived, and as the religion is an excellent measurement for the depth of the stupidity, this is to say that the human beings still believers are at the bottom of a bottomless abyss of stupidity or, to be more realistic, this is the mental disease of which we were talking here before.

— And this is not all, unfortunately there is much more in this chapter. By the way, talking about the program "sixty minutes" I want to mention a very interesting documentary about a fanatic cult in a religious congregation that exists and functions in a state in the South part of the United States. The documentary shows how according with the belief of this cult, the believers pray to God with a venomous snake in their hands. The result is that the number of orphans in that community is very large because there are many fatal cases due to the snakes' bites.

— At least those believers get what they deserve, but what a pity for the children condemned to grow without parents, due to the terrible foolishness of those parents.

— It can be said that this is other miserable aspect of the religious infection.

— Certainly, this is very sad but I have other real story which was a fact about two thousand years ago, but however a sinister fact of the religious life of those times. My cyclist was in a trip in Tunis, in the North part of Africa. In the tourist program was included a visit to an ancient cemetery. He doesn't like to visit cemeteries but this time he didn't have other alternative, and this was a short visit included in the tourist bus journey from one city to another. The view of some small caskets of stone didn't give him any pleasure but what caused him repulsion and made him furious was the explanation of the guide that those caskets were used for children. But not for children who died because of disease or accident, but for children two to four years old sacrificed by the priests with a religious ritual to please the Gods. More than that, the sacrifices were accomplished in front of the mothers of their own children, who were forced to bring them there. And for covering the wailing of the poor mothers, a group of musicians played their trumpets.

This story produced a profound consternation in all the bicycles, which became totally silent. The same bicycle continued:

— My cyclist is a convinced atheist, is engineer, but this visit to the cemetery perturbed him so much, even when he spoke about this to his friends many months later, that I am convinced that if he was a believer before this visit, the explanation of the guide would have transformed him in an atheist, instantaneously.

— It is so easy to understand this, commented a bicycle with very sad voice.

— What a stinky trick can be this religious belief and its consequences!

— A criminal stinky trick, completed other bicycle.

— And I am sure, continued the previous speaker, that if my cyclist had been there during this criminal ritual, none of those priests could escape alive.

— This is also very easy to understand.

— What a quantity of idiocy can live and act in the heads of these human beings religious believers! exclaimed with indignation other bicycle.

— How painful is only to imagine this scene so cruel of the sacrifice of the children, but to be there, or worse, to be one of those mothers! What can be more terrible? And in spite of this, there are human beings which consider themselves normal and sincerely believe that really exists a God who likes this barbarism, and that it is worth the price to satisfy this pleasure of His killing your own children. I myself become furious when I think about this.

— And I would like to have been there in that moment but only if I could transform myself for five minutes in a tank. Wouldn't need more time.

All the bicycles understood what she wanted to say.

— And me also, commented her neighbour. It is true without any doubt that the religion is the most powerful and dangerous drug. How right was that philosopher of the last century in his short and clear definition: "The religion is opium for people".

— How truthful and real is this definition of the religion! commented other bicycle. It applies perfectly to a real case, in our time, not so bestial as the story of our bicycle about the sacrifice of the children in Tunis in the past centuries, but nonetheless bitter enough and significant for the enslaving power of the religion. This happened some years ago, in Mexico, I don't remember exactly in what city or village but this doesn't matter. It was a very hot Sunday morning in front of a cathedral. A long line of people was moving slowly towards the entrance, probably to receive the blessing, under the supervision of some priests who walked along the line. Some persons in the line walked slowly but others moved on their knees, men and women, probably to demonstrate their submission to God. Among them was a very young woman in her last months of pregnancy, moving with difficulty on her knees, looking at the sky and with the face expressing well her devoted belief. What a suffering for this young mother to be! Can you imagine moving slowly on your knees in that heat, hundreds of meters, for the religious ritual? Really, what powerful effect must have this religious opium to determine a young woman to such a painful, meaningless action, voluntarily! What had she in her poor head? What a tragic scene to look at, for a rational human being and impossible to be understood by whatever being of other species!

With the ring of the bell, a very young bicycle signaled her desire to talk.

— With the exception of dogs and cats, the only animals with which I am in daily contact, are the human beings. I don't know much about the life of other animals. I would like to know if there are animals of other species which behave in a similar manner with the human beings, it means if they believe in a God or other divinity, and more than that, if the science or the practice knows about cases when animals kill their young ones in their belief in such a divinity.

— You my dear, may not know much about the zoological world, but you have a sharp analytical sense for which the poor human beings must be envious. Your original question is welcome. And the answer is a categorical NO. All other species of the animal kingdom, which the human beings call primitive because cannot read or produce cars, are not so primitive to believe in a divinity as a force which doesn't manifest itself in controllable ways, and they will never sacrifice their young to this divinity. One who is not convinced about this, can try to bother the little ones of a mother bear, his life will be in immediate and grave danger. And if a priest will try to convince or to force the mother to kill her offspring, even for the God sake, without any doubt she will choose to kill the priest, even at risk of her own life. There are no exceptions, absolutely.

— Many thanks for your explanation so eloquent. Now everything is very clear. In connection with this so moving example of what cruelty are capable the human beings under the influence of the religion, I would like to say that even this only one fact puts a permanent stigma which cannot be neither forgotten nor diminished, over whatsoever pretension of superiority of the human beings.

— Very well said, completed other bicycle.

After so many additional novelties, so sad, about various forms of intellectual incapacity of the human beings, this time related to their religious beliefs, a very sad silence, if it can be said so, was established. Probably, the bicycles were thinking what a bad luck they have in their dependency with their life and well being, of these human creatures without the capacity of elementary logical thinking.

After a while, the silence was interrupted by a bicycle with the clear intention to find some possibility to reduce, at least to some degree, the profound fault so well demonstrated of the human beings, concerning their religious belief.

— I listened carefully to all the explanations trying to determine the cause of this strange phenomenon, the religious belief. I heard the words of some sisters frustrated by the stupid behavior of some human beings believers and also by the bestial behavior of other believers. This frustration is well justified. I agree totally with the scientific explanation of this phenomenon presented by other sister according to whom the problem is in reality of medical nature, the sickness of the part of the brain, which affects the capacity of logical thinking. The danger of the development of the cerebral sickness up to the level at which the respective human being loses the rational control of his actions is directly terrifying. This is the cause of the terrorism and of other terrible actions mentioned here before. In stable condition, the religious belief is as a partial paralysis of the body because of a malfunction of the brain. So for instance, some invalids can move well the right hand but cannot move at all the left hand, or others with the upper part of the body in very good condition but with paralyzed legs. What is interesting is that in some cases, with an intensive treatment and exercise, the body rehabilitates and some predictions of permanent invalidity, fortunately are not confirmed. The body, with the essential function of the brain can finally defeat the disease.

Excuse me please for such a long introduction but I think that it was necessary to make my following question clearer: if it is possible for the body to get out of its state of invalidity and get healthy, it is also possible for the brain of a believer to overcome the religious disease and to come back to a logical thinking? This question is especially important for so many human beings, which are believers, and at the same time obviously capable of logical reasoning in other directions.

— What an interesting question! intervened the bicycle to whom the question was directed.

— And in direct connection with this first question, I have a second one.

— Tell me.

— If a rational human being, it means totally not religious has a good friend who seems to be capable to think well about other issues but is a believer, is possible to convince him in a friendly discussion, to abandon his religious belief and to take the realist, scientific position?

— Other question of much interest. I will answer to both your questions.

— I am listening.

— The brain of all the animal creatures has a very limited capacity and is subordinated to the primitive instincts with the main objective to survive in this world, which is a ferocious jungle for them. For this, the actions of all live beings except the human beings are predictable, limited to the necessity to survive as individuals and as species. They are not interested in anything else and don't have the capacity to think beyond these direct and immediate objectives. Their life repeats itself always in the same way for millions of years without significant changes. Their brain doesn't have the capacity to develop and their activity is concentrated on the tasks necessary strictly for the current life including the protection of the body and of their young ones against real enemies and dangers. Because of this, they are not afraid of whatever God or divinity, which is a notion only theoretical, which cannot be seen or felt in any way. They don't suffer of sick imagination as the human beings.

The human beings brain is totally different. They are the only species with the brain which has the capability of developing itself. And this development is fantastic, with a great variety and very unpredictable. The instinct is not the major factor which controls the brain as in the case of animals; the capacity of thinking controls in most of the cases the actions of the human beings. But this is not always an advantage. Because of the supremacy of this capacity of action over the instinct, very many times the human beings do very crazy things, irresponsible or directly against their own vital interests. This can be explained only by a partial cerebral paralysis. Because of this, there are human beings with great capacity of thinking in a positive manner in some directions together with the lack of capacity to think in other directions in spite of the evidence of facts and of adverse conclusive elements. This is the case of the human beings intelligent on one hand and completely stupid on the other hand. A very conclusive example of this is their religious belief.

In what concerns your question, if there is the possibility that the human beings brain improve itself with internal resources and with the help from outside only, the clear answer is that yes, this possibility exists. Unfortunately, this is a difficult process and these cases are relatively rare, but they exist. The most evident proof of the existence of this process is the apparition of the atheism during the evolution of the human beings. Thousands of years before, in the tribal or primitive stage of the society, all the human beings were under the total and very powerful influence of various religious beliefs and superstitions.

Due to the capacity of the brain to develop by itself, some human beings rebelled against the current way of thinking and interpreting the natural phenomena and so appeared the atheism and the first human beings fighting against religion and obscurantism of any kind.

— Due to this fight, intervened a bicycle parked in front of the speaking one, the church and the religion which in general has a great influence over very many human beings in all parts of the world for reasons so well explained by you, doesn't have anymore the absolute power as five or six centuries ago, in the tenebrous period of inquisition. In the same Europe, today with the science and technology so advanced, at that time human beings were burnt alive for their scientific discoveries, which were in contradiction with the religious dogmas.

A famous case and at the same time so shameful for the Catholic church, was the one of the scientist astronomer Giordano Bruno who was condemned to death in this way for his teaching that the earth is spherical and not flat. Other well-known case is the one of the famous scientist astronomer Galileo Galiley, who could escape the same death penalty with the condition to make a public declaration in front of the inquisitors that the earth doesn't move. He did it, but when he got out from that court he murmured to his friends: "E pur se mueve", what means "And still it moves". The human beings of this category are the promoters of the scientific and technological progress, and also philosophical and social. At the same time they are the natural enemies of all religious beliefs.

— You know a lot about the history of the human beings, expressed with admiration her opinion the bicycle who talked before.

— My cyclist is professor of History at the University and often there are very interesting discussion with his friends at his house. He never leaves me outside, I have a comfortable place in his apartment and so I can hear well many very interesting stories.

Obviously he is atheist, and it is clear that with his knowledge of the history of the religion, couldn't be otherwise. The history of the human beings is full of so many terrible cases including not thousands but millions of dead and injured and incredible destruction and suffering due to the religion.

— Many thanks for all that you told us, it is so interesting.

A bell ring signaled that other bicycle had something to say, and immediately. Addressing to the bicycle with her cyclist, professor of History, she said:

— I agree that your story is very interesting for all of us. I think that my story will be also of interest, at least because is a demonstration, a real case, how a believer very serious in his belief can transform himself in short time in an convinced atheist, based only on his mental capacity, and with little help from outside.

— We are ready to listen with much interest and curiosity, said the bicycle who asked before in this discussion if such a transformation is possible.

— My cyclist is an engineer with a profound analytic spirit and due to this, hundred percent atheist. But was not like this when he was a teenager. He grew in a very religious family and was educated in this spirit since he was few years old, just a child. Following the religious traditions of his family, he attended the religious services and each morning before going to school, he had his verbal contact with God by praying. He was a good pupil at school but it seems that the influence of the religious environment was more powerful than his analytic spirit, sleeping at that time. The existence of God and the religious practice was part of the daily life and he never thought about this with critical spirit. At nine years of age his father died, and his family, specially his mother who was so good and kind to him, insisted that he attended a religious service and pray for his father during an entire year each morning before going to school, in the summer and in the winter, and he did it. Almost all other children, boys and teenagers were like him, nothing special. This situation lasted until he reached fourteen years. At this point in his life everything changed in a totally unexpected manner. The details are forgotten and don't matter but the essential is what follows. In a discussion with a person, he doesn't remember how and why it was initiated, that person told him: "There is no God, doesn't exist, the religion is a big lie, a hallucination of the brain. Think about it." And the person went away. The impression of this verdict over the believer boy of fourteen years was tremendous and terrible. He felt very offended and afterwards became also nervous, thinking: "How somebody can say that there is no God?". Doesn't he know that God is everything? What a sin! What a shame! What a shame! The words of that person went repeating in his mind provoking a feeling of indignation and also of apprehension: "There is no God, doesn't exist. Think about it". The sick part of his young brain was in control. "This is also a great sin" commented he for himself. "Think about it" These last words had at the same time a wake-up effect for his analytic spirit. The desire to think was stronger than the apprehension and the repulsion. The healthy part of his brain was fighting, and the young boy, the future cyclist and engineer, started to THINK. And more he thought, more contradictions in the theories of the religion he found, more questions without rational answers. Days and nights after this, his mind was preoccupied analyzing with objectivity and calm, all the aspects of life around him, as a passionate detective for his new profession. Each discovery directed him to other discoveries and the great stupidity of religion began to appear in all its depth. He started to read books of popularized science and decided to read the bible, in the desire to be totally objective, and he did it, but not as a believer blind in his mind, but as a judge and auditor. With this approach, the same bible that poisoned millions and millions of defenseless brains, helped to cure very rapidly the sick part of his brain. The public library turned into a place frequently visited. Among many books with philosophic, sociologic and scientific character explaining with all clarity the natural phenomena of this world and the physical laws of the nature, he enjoyed much a book entitled "The bible for non-believers", a scientific parody, very entertaining, of he bible for the believers. The famous definition of the religion, so short and so complete: "The religion is opium for people" appeared in all its might and impressed him profoundly.

With the combination of his strength and desire to think, his intensive education and also with his personal religious experience, my cyclist became totally immune to religion and a human being of vanguard.

The bicycle finished her story but the silence of all other bicycles continued for a while. Finally, a bicycle commented:

— I think that I am speaking on behalf of many of us when I say that I was very impressed with your real and so educational story about the possibility of some, not all but some, human beings to fight against the religious disease, late or early in their life, but what is important is that this is possible.

A wave of support followed the words of this bicycle.

— And how feels today your cyclist engineer, asked other bicycle.

— He feels very well and proud, not about himself but for his profession, the engineering, and for his spirit free of all religious garbage, which before was such an important part of his life. But up to this day he has a feeling of shame.

— Shame you say? For what?

— For the fact that his mind was prisoner of religion until the age of fourteen. He asks himself where was his mind before, considering the religious explanations a taboo, which cannot be discussed. He himself gave the answer: the very negative influence of the environment and, what is more important, he didn't think about that. When he started to think and ask, everything changed. When people think in an analytic manner, the religion is dead.

— It is better later than never. Your cyclist is one of a very precious minority. Unfortunately, the great majority of the human beings live in obscurantism all their life.

— Very well, said the bicycle who had spoken a short while ago, I think that his example explains very well the possibilities of the brain of the human beings to free itself from the influence of the religious obscurantism but with the essential condition, to THINK.

After all these opinions and expressions of indignation demonstrating the sad reality of the human beings nature, it seemed that the verdict of the court of bicycles was very clear: the human beings in their immense majority, during thousands of years and continuing at present, are the victims of their own stupidity creating the religion with the very many alternatives of beliefs.

The conclusion of all speakers was that the only explanation and the cause of the apparition and persistence of the religion is the stupidity of these human beings, the real authors and creators of the religion, who in a comical manner believe with all the conviction that they themselves are the creation of God or of the Gods of the respective beliefs, which are the essence of the religion.

If this was the reality, and an angel decides to sound his trumpet to summon all these Gods invented by the human beings, an entire battalion of them, Gods licensed by the sick imagination of the human beings, could march on the street, or to fly over it, in function of the circumstances.

What the bicycles think about monarchy.

— Other aspect specific to the human beings as beings with an inferiority complex in many of their great communities, as entire countries, is the acceptance of the monarchy or of the royal parasitism. The monarchy is not and never was of any use for the society, is a relic from the far past and survives today solely due to the submission and stupidity of the mass of human beings.

The essential difference between louses, fleas and bugs on one side and kings, queens, princes, barons and other parasites of the same category, on other side, is the size. The first ones are small parasites; the last ones are big parasites. The essential similarity between them is that both groups are parasites, the first ones live on human body, the last ones, on the body of the human society. There are also some major differences between these two groups of parasites. The first ones suck only a little blood from the human being's body, no more than what is necessary to survive. The last ones suck everything that is possible, wasting an immense quantity of material resources produced by the intensive work of the body of the human beings society, and take much more than it is necessary to live very well.

For the little real damage that the parasites of the first group do to them, the human beings consider them a nuisance and a shame and kill them without compassion. With all the big damage that the parasites of the last group do to them, the human beings glorify them, give them all the respect and consider themselves honored even to see them from close, and they are sincerely happy if they are lucky to shake hands with them in the rare occasions when the big parasites, or kings, queens, princes, which are their official names, appear in public to show that they have love for the mass of human beings, which in fact is worth in their eyes a little more than the dust in the street.

— This feeling of inferiority, commented other bicycle, in front of a king, queen or a prince, doesn't have a real base, the difference in material possessions doesn't justify this feeling, and only the stupidity explains it. The few intelligent human beings know that the immense richness of the royal families is robbed integrally from the people of the nation who work hard for the little that they have. However, the great majority of the human beings are impressed exactly by this richness and by all the façade and ritual, which make shine the members of the royal families. The explanation for this attitude is again the lack of logical reasoning, which is called in other words, stupidity.

— If I am well informed, said other bicycle, today only few countries still have monarchy, true?

— Yes, you are well informed. Before all countries of Europe had kings or emperors, today only seven of them, in Western Europe, countries called civilized and developed, have a parasite as the highest representative of the country, named king or queen, even if today has little power. This shows that the general mentality of the population is still in a primitive stage in what concerns the organization of the state.

— And what is significant, says a bicycle from Canada, is that when a king or queen or even only a prince from these countries visits Canada or the United States, there are genuine demonstrations of sympathy by part of the population, instead of treating them as they really are, parasites. The myth of power, richness and royal fanfaronade is more powerful for these participants in the demonstration of sympathy than the feeling of dignity of a citizen living in a republic, which represents the contemporary, not the primitive age of the state organization.

— It is true, we cannot have much confidence in these human beings. They can be so easily manipulated by the religion, monarchy and other things belonging to the area of stupidity. What a pity!

— Yes, there is a great distance up to a really advanced and civilized society of them.

At the end of this very interesting and passionate discussion, prolonged until very late at night, the unanimous decision was that other reunion will be organized in the same place at a time not yet decided, but all the bicycles agreed without reservation to be in touch and to participate in the following reunion. The main issue and of major interest for all the bicycles is the history of the promotion for the visionary concept of the Bicycle Expressways. The situation of the project for the city of Morelia, in Mexico is also of much interest and all the bicycles hope for very good news at the following reunion.

 # THIRD PART

The continuation of the promotion of the concept in Mexico, Turkey, Morocco.

A permanent contact was maintained between all the bicycles participating in the previous reunions but this third reunion could be organized only with a great delay, several years later. All the bicycles desired very much to participate and were present.

So, the third reunion began in a very high spirit, with acclamations and bell rings very eloquent for the state of mind very happy of all the bicycles, it can be said without exaggeration. When everything calmed down, after a few moments of silence, the first bicycle that opened the discussion, said:
— Dear sisters, I like so much to be together with all of you and to discuss about everything what is of interest for us, that it is difficult for me to control my emotion. I am sure that this time also, we have much to discuss but I am interested first in the situation of the promotion of the concept of our engineer from Toronto, Canada, the project for a new fatherland for us, the bicycles. In the same context I would like to know what is the situation with the proposal for Morelia. I think that the other sisters bicycles are also interested in this information.

— Certainly, all of us are, was heard the immediate response by a choir of bicycles.

— I am the one from Morelia and I am very happy to be here again, but unfortunately, I don't have very good news. The fact is, I can say, that the project was not built in Morelia in spite of the efforts of our engineer from Canada. I am well informed that some meetings took place with the Municipal Authority of Morelia and that he had some discussions with the chief engineer of the local engineering company who was very enthusiastic in supporting the project, but I don't know anything more what happened. I think that the Canadian sister can give us more information about this issue.

— Many thanks to the Morelian sister for her introduction, continued the idea the Canadian bicycle. I have news for you, some very good others not so good, but in what concerns the project for Morelia, unfortunately, the news are very bad. It is true that our engineer had some meetings with representatives of the Municipality of Morelia but the bureaucracy and the lack of vision of the local officials are of the same caliber as those of the Canadian officials, good only for the garbage of history. These are the bad news. The good news is that the chief engineer of the engineering company with whom our engineer worked, told him not to worry about the local bureaucracy, because he has a good friend, a man of vision and with entrepreneurial spirit of whom he was sure that will understand the concept and if he could, will promote it up to the implementation. This friend is a good candidate for the position of President of Mexico in the coming elections. If elected, the engineer had all the hope that this was the key for the success of the project. He will talk with his friend. With this excellent news, our engineer returned to Toronto and maintained the contact by phone with the engineer from Morelia. And now comes the very bad news. On a Sunday, the engineer from Morelia informed our engineer that on Thursday of the coming week he will discuss the concept with his friend, the candidate, who has good chances to win the elections. Our engineer couldn't be more enchanted and impatient for the following news. On Tuesday, two days before the planned day for the discussion, Mr. Colosio, this is the name of the candidate to the Presidency of Mexico, was assassinated.

A silence, can be said mortal, covered all the audience. The sadness related to the death of Mr. Colosio, was amplified with the sadness of the death of a great hope for all the bicycles of Morelia and certainly, after a short time, of many other cities of the entire world.
The total and prolonged silence was finally interrupted by the same Canadian bicycle.
— I am sure that many of you would like to know what happened with our engineer after he received this terrible news.
— All of us want.
— Very well, I will continue the history of promotion of this visionary concept. Our engineer was very affected and sorry by this crime but he didn't remain with crossed arms; he developed a new plan to continue his promotional activity.
In parallel with the continuation of the promotion in Toronto, fighting with the powerful bureaucracy, lack of vision and stupidity of the human beings in charge with public transport, he concentrated also in the promotion outside of Canada.

Looking for new possibilities and connections, he combined the promotional activity with his tourist trips; our engineer is also a passionate tourist and a good sportsman. So, during a trip of almost three weeks in Turkey, he contacted the Municipal Authority of Istanbul and of the capital of the country, Ankara. Both cities have problems with the traffic congestion and the implementation of the concept could help a lot to reduce the congestion and also the air pollution. The authorities recognized this but the engineer realized that the interlocutors, although in high official positions, had a low level of understanding and no vision. Because of this, everything remained at discussion level.

The trip itself was interesting and educative by the variety of the scenery and the ancient places with ruins more than two thousand years old, from the civilizations of the far past. As a matter of fact, a good part of the revenue from the tourism of today is based on visiting these ancient ruins. The inhabitants of those times didn't assume and didn't know or guess how valuable for the future of the country will be the destroyed temples and the statues without heads or arms. Also, the broken pots, which probably the human beings of those past times put in the garbage, today are valuable objects exhibited in archeological museums.

Other aspect characteristic of the pride of the human beings based on the lack of logic can be seen in a rug factory. The visit there was included in the tourist program, for commercial reasons; always some tourists from the group buy rugs sold at a high price, justified by the intensive manual labor. The factory produces rugs only with manual labor and primitive instruments. The modern technology is not utilized. The workers are almost always women, very young and very old. They work all day for two or three dollars, in a very uncomfortable position, doing a boring and intensive work.

A rug, which produced manually, requires six months, can be produced with the modern automatic technology without intensive labor, in only a few hours. The quality is the same, a common buyer cannot see the difference, only a specialist. The aspect of a rug produced automatically is very nice, equal or better than of one produced by hand. But the price, all the difference is in the price, is fifty up to one hundred times higher for a rug produced manually. There are old, used rugs, in my opinion very ugly, made by hand, for a price of twenty or thirty thousand dollars. For me and for the reasonable human beings, this is simply garbage, but for some very rich collectors this is an object of pride, for nothing else than for the paid price, to be shown to others and not for the practical use or for the aspect. It is something similar with a very expensive painting of abstract "art" which serves exactly for the same purpose.

The question of principle is: how can be explained such a huge discrepancy between the human beings, what kind of social organization they have, when some human beings are forced by the circumstances to work for two or three dollars per day and in all their working life cannot save the money necessary to buy even one of the rugs produced by themselves and others can afford to waste thousands and tens of thousands of dollars without any necessity, and the benefit goes into the pockets of the owners of the factory, leaving for the workers who produce them no more than for surviving, with the only purpose to work like slaves?.

— Very good question, especially when you think that the only use of the rug is to step on it. Let's assume that one buys two rugs to cover the floor of his living room, one of industrial production of a nice model, that costs one hundred or one hundred fifty dollars, and other one of manual production, of the same model, that costs seven, ten or fourteen thousand dollars. If one hundred visitors come to the house, how many of them will notice the difference? Very probably that none of them, but if there are some of them which will notice whatever difference, how many of them will feel offended by the rug produced industrially and how many will be so pleased by the rug produced manually that will think that the difference is worth the money, and how many from these last ones will spend the same amount of money to buy a similar rug for his house?

— For the owner of the house, said other bicycle, all this is not important, all that matters is his pleasure based on his imagination about the opinion of others and he has the right to his opinion. What is important is the sometimes strange manner in which some human beings reason and choose the alternative that they think is the best.

A bicycle with a very peaceful and practical spirit signaled that she wanted to share her opinion.

— I have an idea that could be a proposal for a friendly solution for all involved in this conflict. So, I propose that the factory that produces rugs with primitive methods and tools, to be transformed in a modern factory with automatic machines to produce with great efficiency and at low cost nice rugs of all models and sizes, without extenuating labor. This high efficiency will allow to pay the workers, the same young and old women, a dignifying and stable salary, which must be at least twenty times higher than the present salary. The owners of the factory will gain the same or more money, selling the same kind of rugs produced at a very low cost, to the two categories of buyers, which visit the factory. The first category will be of buyers with modest financial resources, or with a rational way of thinking, or with both. The selling price for this category must be the conventional price in the market, covering the cost of production and a reasonable benefit. Let's say that the total cost at the factory for a rug of average size is one hundred dollars. The other category will be of very proud buyers, very rich, but this is not a must, what is important is to be a little crazy, with a very low capacity of thinking in a rational manner, especially when they go shopping and are ready to spend lots of money, doesn't matter if they have it or not; the use of credit cards is very welcome. The personal opinion that the very expensive and extravagant material things are at the base of the happiness in life is essential. The selling price for this category doesn't have obligatory rules or limits, more is better. So, the same rug, which is sold to the first category of buyers for one hundred dollars, can be sold for five thousand, eight, ten, fifteen thousand dollars or more, depending of the kind of client. In order to make the selling possible at these prices and to make the buyers happy and convinced that the transaction is a bargain, each buyer will receive a diploma or a certificate big enough and in colors with a nice frame to be hung on the wall very close to the place where the rug is on the floor. This official certificate will confirm the real price paid, not the real value of the rug, this will be a secret, which the factory agrees to observe. Also, the certificate will include a text, which can read for example: "Dear visitors, attention please! This rug on which your feet walk now cost me five (ten or fifteen, etc.) thousand dollars. Many thanks for honoring me putting your feet on my rug in my house". Variations with a similar text are possible. With this proposal, concluded the bicycle, all will be happy, the workers of the factory for a much better salary, the owners of the factory for a very good sale, the buyers of the first category for very reasonable prices for their nice rugs, the buyers of the other category, for the opportunity to waste their money with great pleasure, and the visitors to their houses for the honor to walk for free on such an expensive rug although with a real value very much lower but well hidden by the certificate on the wall. This is all.

A wave of laughter was the appreciation of the audience for her proposal so original.

— A very interesting finale for the history of the promotion of the concept of the Bicycle Expressways in Turkey, concluded the Canadian bicycle.

Other wave of laughter was the very sincere response of all bicycles.

— And now, with your permission, I want to continue with the next step of the history of the promotion of the concept.

— We are waiting with much pleasure.

— Next year our engineer decided to visit Morocco, an exotic country in the Northwest part of Africa, with ancient cities, mountains, desert, camels and much heat and also with sumptuous royal palaces, impressive mosques and tremendous poverty.

Before traveling there, the engineer contacted the Moroccan embassy in Canada and got information about the adequate persons with whom he could discuss his concept in the capital of the country, Casablanca.

The tourist trip started and ended in Casablanca. His first meeting with the officials of the Municipality occurred in the second day of the visit in the capital, for preliminary discussions and the presentation of the concept. The following discussions were programmed for the last two days of the trip, also in the capital. And here, as in Turkey last year, in spite of the vivid interest expressed by the authorities, the lack of money for the investment was the official cause for which the concept could not be realized in Casablanca. The real cause is the lack of vision and understanding how the project could be a generator of richness for the national economy and a consumer of investment only for the first few years. The engineer understood soon that the interlocutors were not at the necessary high level for such a visionary project and that the vision for them could not be bought at the pharmacy.

Even if this promotional activity had a negative final result, the positive part was the additional gained experience, the better understanding of the difficulties of the promotion of a new and sustainable idea, when the decision makers are not the exceptions but common human beings in their stupidity.

As a compensation for the time lost with the officials in Casablanca, the trip itself in many cities, towns and villages of Morocco, in the countryside, which represents basically the olive plantations, and in the desert, was very interesting. A very impressing characteristic was the peaceful coexistence of two extremes of the society of the human beings, the immense richness of very few if front with the king, with his unconditional power and luxurious palaces, and the misery of the great part of the population. I remember that in his description of the trip to his friends, our engineer mentioned how a child of about five years of age, prepared his bed to sleep in one of the principal streets of Casablanca. This bed was a piece of cloth and nothing else. The place: the sidewalk, close to the wall of a house. No other piece of cloth to cover himself. Nobody knows if the child ate something before going to sleep in his "bed" or not. This was not a unique case, but the visible top of the poverty glacier. Visiting Casablanca even by bus in several directions up to the end of the line, the engineer could see the flagrant difference between the level of the standard of living in the rich center and of the very poor suburbs. In the countryside, some isolated dwellings in the desert were no more than big tents and some children and goats around.

— And how can be explained please, asked a bicycle, this peaceful coexistence as you say, between the poverty so great and the richness of the king and other few. Nobody rebels? Probably the king and the rich elite have a very strong police, true?

— This is the minor part of the truth. It would be extremely difficult to control and make obedient a mass of poor only with the force of the police. To make the people obedient and submissive, that very rich elite use a force much more powerful than the police. They control the will of action of the mass of human beings.

— How?

— Using a very powerful drug.

— Cocaine.

— No, one more powerful.

— Hashish.

— No, one more powerful.

— Opium?

— A kind of opium but more powerful.

— What is it?

— The religion. The unquestioned belief and the rituals which are observed strictly five times everyday, don't leave any free space and time to think about rebellion and the change of the system. Of important help are the mosques existent everywhere. In spite of the all-general poverty of the country, the new mosque of Casablanca is like a huge palace, very tall and very luxurious, to impress the mass of the poor and make them submissive, and they are made so.

After this combined story including the promotion of the concept and the personal impressions of the engineer as a tourist and very attentive observer of the life in Turkey and Morocco, the Canadian bicycle continued the history of the promotion of the concept in other countries, involving trips and official encounters not only very interesting by their diversity and particular character, out of routine but also as a testimony of a relentless and dedicated activity, worthy for the noble cause of this concept.

Before passing to the presentation of the specific cases in various countries, sometimes on the other side of the globe, the Canadian bicycle began talking with an extended monologue about the strategy of the promotion related to the particular conditions of this promotion.
— In order to be lucrative and sustainable, the system of bicycle expressways must be implemented at a large scale, covering at the end the entire city, starting with a Pilot Project, which also should be of a significant length. A bicycle expressway of short distance only, will be of little use or only for a very local and limited use, without being an incentive for the massive use of bicycles. More than this, in this case the implementation of the system can be unfavorable to the concept, serving more as an exhibition rather than a practical thing. Is like a very short subway line, being of little use and discrediting the respective mode of transportation. For this reason, this concept is basically a large project, which requires a large investment, which will be recuperated in short time, in a few years. However, the initial investment for the construction of the system is significant. For this reason, as part of the promotion, the engineer contacted some banks and other financial organizations to make known the existence of this opportunity for investment and to ask information about the interest of the respective organizations to invest in this project.

Discussions at the World Bank in Washington and the received support. The promotion in the Philippines, Cuba and Mexico.

This wasn't his obligation, the financing of the project is the task of the municipality or of the respective government, but this additional information could help the promotion.

In the summer of 1996 he went to the Head Office of the World Bank in Washington, the United States, to present the concept and to have a discussion about the possibility of financing and the interest of the World Bank in this concept. The discussion took place in several meetings with the directors of the Bank, with a clear positive result. However, the position of the Bank is that in order to decide about the financing, a solicitation by the government of the respective country, is necessary. In October of the same year, the engineer received an official letter from the Office of the Executive Director of the World Bank confirming the interest and the support of the Bank for the concept of the Bicycle Expressways System. This letter of support from the powerful World Bank was very important in the following promotional actions and discussions in various countries.

A month later, the engineer was in Philippines where he had discussions up to an advanced level with a strong financial organization, interested in the promotion of the concept for the city of Manila, the capital of Philippines. Also, he discussed the concept with the mayor of the city of Batangas, from whom he received an official letter of interest in the concept for his city, everything being conditioned by the possibility to find the necessary money for the investment.

Short time after his return from Philippines, in December of the same year, the engineer was again in the plane flying this time to Havana, Cuba, where he participated at the International Conference entitled: "The Bicycles: an Option for the 21st Century" and to present his concept with the title: "The Bicycle Expressways—a Sustainable Solution for the Urban Transportation" in the plenary session of the Conference. After the Conference, he remained in Cuba, this island so nice, for another week during which he contacted the pertinent officials suggesting the possibility of building a bicycle expressway system in the capital of the country, Havana, where there are also problems with the urban transportation about which the Cuban bicycle spoke before, at the first reunion of bicycles, with all clarity.

This proposal in principle and the concept itself were well appreciated but the officials explained to our engineer with all the kindness, that due to the present economic conditions of the country, the necessary investment simply is not available. In the future, we will see. Besides this issue, surely the engineer didn't forget to take advantage of the opportunity, and visited some of the many nice places and as a passionate swimmer, swam for long time in the warm, clear water at the beautiful and clean beaches with fine sand.

The continuation of the promotion at the International Conferences and meetings in Singapore, Thailand, Switzerland and again Mexico.

In October 1997 our engineer was invited to present his concept to the Conference entitled: "The Second Encounter of Cities", in the city of Puebla, in Mexico. The engineering company, which organized the Conference, was interested in the concept. After the Conference, followed discussions with the engineers of the company, who invited him to continue the promotion of the concept in Mexico. A very friendly and lucrative relationship was established with the engineers representing this engineering company, relationship that was continued successfully in the following years.

In 1998, the promotional activity and the recognition of the merits of the concept of the Bicycle Expressways were marked by some important events in four countries of three continents.

In the first days of March, our engineer was in Singapore, were he was invited to present his concept at the International Seminar entitled: "Quality of Life in Cities". This time the title of his presentation was; "The Bicycle Expressways System: The Vision of Today, the Reality of Tomorrow". This was his second visit to this city well organized and administrated as an independent country, with a high level of cleanliness and citizens' discipline. However, the traffic in the city is congested, this is a problem of world character and Singapore is not an exception. For this reason, the engineer used the opportunity of being there and contacted the authorities in charge with urban transportation, to make them aware of the existence of the concept. The idea was well received but the engineer understood that the clerks, or the bureaucrats, were not at the required level and the discussion ended in an amiable way and without wasting time. An additional experience of contacts with the authorities is always of good use for the future activity. Before leaving Singapore, he visited the Zoological Garden, the nice park, and took the cable car for a nice view from the top of the hill.

The next day he traveled by plane to Bangkok, the capital of Thailand, an exotic country of South-East Asia. Some meetings were planned with the representatives of the Governor of Bangkok, before leaving Toronto, Canada, with the help of the Thailand Embassy in Canada.

Bangkok is a very large city with several millions inhabitants and also with very serious traffic congestion problems. This was the reason for which the suggestion of our engineer to present and discuss his concept at a high level in Bangkok was accepted with much interest. At that time, the city of Bangkok was in a very difficult financial situation; the construction of a system of elevated urban trains was stopped because of lack of money to continue the necessary investment. For this reason, other significant investment for the proposed system for bicycles didn't appear possible at this time to the superior clerks of the municipal authority. In reality, the financial difficulties were the result of the poor administration and economic policy, the lack of vision and interest to attend the needs of the society. The construction of the system of the bicycle expressways could help very much to the urban transportation and at the same time to the economy, by its own very high economic efficiency. But without the adequate vision, nothing can be achieved.

In a free week between meetings, the engineer made a trip of ten hours by train to the north of the country, with exotic scenery. Being there, he took a local excursion in the jungle, on a special seat on the back of an elephant. Everything was very interesting and so much different from the life in the city. He had seen how the elephants are used not only for foreign tourists, for which a ride on an elephant in the jungle is an extravaganza little common that cannot be omitted, but also for working tasks that need the strength and the ability which these intelligent animals have.

After returning to Bangkok, he visited places of the two extremes as in Morocco, the famous and very rich royal palace, and the ghettos with the very poor houses built on pillars above the level of the very dirty water in which the inhabitants wash their clothes and use it for preparing their food. It is a shame that this unimaginable poverty, instead of being liquidated without delay, is used as an additional source of revenue by the tourist organizations, evidently with the knowledge and the authorization of the government, showing this painful misery to the foreign tourists sitting in comfortable boats.

After two weeks in Thailand, the engineer left the Bangkok airport for a twelve hours trip by plane to Zurich, in Switzerland, in the middle of Europe, from the tropical climate and exotic jungle, to the winter in the mountains covered by snow, in the same day. He was invited there to present his concept to other International Seminar named: "Forum Engelberg" in a small village with the name of Engelberg, in the mountains, at one hour by train or by car from Zurich. The very invitation to participate to this very prestigious Seminar means an important mark for the promotion and the value of the concept. Although without expecting lucrative results in short time, the engineer established valuable contacts with eminent personalities participating at the Seminar which showed interest in the concept, contacts that could be very useful in the future. He contacted also and had a discussion with the mayor of Zurich for the same reason. Without making promises, the mayor was genuine in his real interest in the concept and the engineer was pleased with his appreciation.

After the end of the Seminar, the engineer stayed another week in Engelberg to ski in the majestic mountains around. From his hotel he could walk to the ski lift station. The difference in altitude up to the last station is almost two thousand meters and the descent on ski was very pleasant and with unforgettable views. A very interesting and original thing was the way how some skiers transport their skis from home to the ski lift station: on bicycle, in a special device, very light, installed behind the saddle. This was the first and the only place where the engineer have seen this ingenious alternative to transport the skis. For two days he took also the train to visit some places with sceneries unique in their beauty, so specific to Switzerland.

In the summer of the same year, our engineer was invited to present his concept in Mexico, at an International Seminar organized by the National University of Mexico City and soon afterwards, at the International Conference in Huatulco, on the western coast of Mexico, at the Pacific Ocean. After returning from Huatulco to Mexico City, he was invited to make another presentation of the concept at the Conference for Urban Transportation in Guadalajara. The conference ended with a dinner and a very nice concert of Mexican popular music with the famous Mariachis.

These presentations in various places of Mexico were very important for the following promotion of the concept in Mexico City.

— Mexico City intervened again the Canadian bicycle, represents the major objective for the promotion of the concept in Mexico, one of the most important objectives in all the promotional activity of the last several years. This is so for some reasons, all of them of prime importance. I know very well a significant part of the promotional activity of our engineer in this direction since he was in Toronto and for sure I am informed about what happened in Mexico, but one of the participants in our reunion is a Mexican sister, from Mexico City and she knows many details better than any other source of information. I am sure that she is very willing to share with us what she knows, and that all of us are ready to listen to her.

— All of us are in reception mood with all the attention.

— It is clear that couldn't be otherwise, but before that I want to continue my idea about the correlation between the concept of the bicycle expressways and Mexico City. They need each other. The arguments are as follows:

1. Mexico City has twenty two million inhabitants, a very large city with a population bigger than many whole countries, concentrated in one city.

2. The great majority of these inhabitants move everyday at different hours in various directions and for this they need an enormous urban transportation system well regulated, which will respond to these needs of the travelers.

3. The existing system that includes the buses and the subway as public transportation, and private cars and taxis as private transportation, has big difficulties in satisfying the needs of an adequate urban transportation.

4. The public urban transportation system can serve the inhabitants who need transportation, only in the established routes and hours of operation, which in many cases do not coincide with the needs of the travellers.

5. Because of the contradiction between the situations mentioned at points 2 and 4 above, the general orientation and at least the desire of the public, is towards private cars. Because of this, already at present time there are more cars in the streets than they are able to sustain.

6. The construction of wide streets and of additional highways to solve the problem in this way, with more private cars, is physically impossible and of prohibitive cost, even if it was possible.

7. The solution mentioned at point 6 above is not sustainable even for other reason; it doesn't solve the urban traffic congestion, but only transfers the congestion from the highways to the streets, which automatically will retransmit the congestion back to the highways, as a wave.

8. In face of this reality some bureaucrats from the municipality in charge with the urban transportation thought that they found the miraculous solution with a law which allows the use of the cars in the streets in accordance with the plate number; so, in the days with even numbers as four, fourteen, twenty two for instance, it is permitted the circulation of cars with plate numbers also even, in other days it is permitted the circulation only for other vehicles. In this way, they thought, they will cut in half the number of cars circulating simultaneously in the streets. The result? More cars in the city and more problems with the parking because people bought a second car to be able to circulate in the days when they cannot use the first car. Not less cars in the streets but more air pollution produced by these second cars usually very old and not in good condition.

9. What Mexico City requires is an additional space capacity for the urban transportation which doesn't affect the existing urban structure and which is economically sustainable. The only realist response is the Bicycle Expressway System.

10. Mexico City depends at present with its urban transportation, totally of motorized vehicles, public and private, and its permanent and uncontrollable increase in numbers reached a level, which suffocates the transport capacity of the city streets. The massive use of bicycles can reduce significantly this number up to a sustainable level but in the present situation this is an impossible task: simply there isn't space available for bicycles in the street and also it is very dangerous and uncomfortable to use the bicycles in present conditions.

11. The solution that can transform this impossible task in a sustainable one is the implementation of the proposed concept for the Bicycle Expressway System which has all the advantages presented so well by our sister from Morelia.
12. More traffic congestion and air pollution problem a city has, more adequate it is for the concept of Bicycle Expressways and more adequate is the concept to demonstrate its sustainable capacity to significantly contribute to solve these problems, and Mexico City is exactly such a city.

For all these reasons, continued the Canadian bicycle, our engineer involved himself with interest, energy and dedication in the promotion of the concept for Mexico City. He continued the very good relations established before with two engineers of an engineering company, really interested in the promotion of the concept. Without them and their local contacts, all the promotional activity including the presentations at the Conferences and Seminars, would be extremely difficult to accomplish. At the Conference in Huatulco our engineer met other engineer from Mexico City who was also very interested in the concept and who later joined the other two engineers supporting the promotion. I think that our Mexican sister will give us important and more detailed information about what happened in Mexico City.

— I am from Mexico City and I like very much this concept of the Canadian engineer and all the promotional activity that occurred in my city. As the Canadian sister explained so clearly, in Mexico City we really need the implementation of the concept as a saving solution, for the radical improvement of the urban transportation and for our good life, the bicycles of this city. Today we are not too many due to the terribly adverse conditions underlined by our sister, but without any doubt, with the implementation of the concept our number will grow as an avalanche.

And the Mexican bicycle continued her story about the promotion of the concept:

— With the efforts and kindness of the Mexican engineers, contacts were established with the governmental authorities and a detailed presentation by the Canadian engineer was organized for a meeting with four ministers of the Government of the Federal District. The Mexican engineering company helped with the preparation of a three-dimensional model of a portion of bicycle expressway.

Other discussion about the religious belief, religious fanatics and terrorism and about the overpopulation.

The purpose of the promotion of the concept in its first stage was to obtain the approval for the design and construction of a Pilot Project for Mexico City with a total length of two hundred kilometers. The bicycle expressways will be connected with many subway stations, with large parking lots for bicycles to facilitate efficient combined trips by bicycle and subway.

The discussions with the authorities and the presentations were very well prepared, continued the Mexican bicycle, with a very detailed analysis of the concept and its adaptation to the specific conditions of Mexico City. Our engineer presented to his friends and now associates, the Mexican engineers, his calculations, drawings, schemes, and could respond to absolutely all questions of technical, economic, social and of environmental nature related to this project. Everything was very clear and everybody was convinced that the proposed concept has a real value, that it is sustainable and the effort to promote it is worthy. Without this conviction, without any doubt, neither our engineer nor his friends, the Mexican engineers, would have decided to go ahead into this great battle, which is the promotion of such a unique and visionary concept.

Of great help for the promotion of the concept was the fact that the friends Mexican engineers, being residents of Mexico City, could have a permanent and very efficient contact with the pertinent authorities and inform our engineer in Canada about this activity and to tell him when is necessary to come to Mexico for actions which require his presence. This is all, briefly. Many thanks for your attention.

— We all are thankful to you for the essential information. Now we know much more about the promotion of the concept in Mexico. We hope that in the near future we will have very good news about the results of all this collective and intensive work for the promotion of the concept so necessary for Mexico City and for all the present and future bicycles of this city, which is also yours.

After the explanation by the Mexican bicycle about the last news of promotion of the concept in Mexico, the discussion turned to other aspect of religion in the society of the human beings with the comment of a bicycle interested in the very process of thinking of the believers and the possibility to change it.

— Talking about the possibility to convince the human beings believers to renounce to their religious belief which is based on a sick fantasy, in favor of a healthy reasoning, I ask myself how come that still there are so many believers in the world when there are so many arguments so clear and of common sense against the religious belief.

— To talk about the possibility to convince them means talking about the enormous difficulty to convince them, in spite of all clear and obvious arguments. With few exceptions, about which a sister of ours talked before, is extremely difficult or almost impossible to convince them in a discussion because they talk a mystic language and the interlocutors, the atheists, talk the language of logic, which the believers don't understand. If you want, I can give a few examples of their responses to very simple and reasonable questions.

— Certainly we want, was the response without delay of many bicycles.

— Well, the first example. When a plane falls and two hundred or three hundred passengers die, to the question what was the role of God in this accident, one can expect in principle the following dialogue:

— God knew that the plane will fall?

— Sure, God knows everything.

— God could avoid this accident?

— Certainly, God can do everything.

— And why God didn't avoid it?

— To punish the passengers.

— Why punish them? What was their fault?

— They were sinners.

— How is possible to assume that all of them were guilty of crimes that deserve the death penalty?

— God knows better. And those who were not sinners must pay for the sins of their parents.

— And the children and the babies?

— They will grow and commit sins. So, God punish them before, they are also sinners.

— As it is said in banking terms, they get credit in punishment and can sin after. And why the human beings commit sins? Why God doesn't create them with a healthy mentality and a manner of thinking as a copy of Him? In this case they will act following the will of God.

— God doesn't want His creatures to be robots, He wants them to think and act in an independent manner.

— But all other organs in the body of the human beings created by the same God, work exactly like robots, the heart, the lungs, the liver, why not also the brain? All these organs are created by the same God to work according to His will, true?

— bbbldmsysssa, silence

— End of the first example.

— There is in this example such a big quantity of stupidity that it seems to be more a product of imagination than a real case.

— No, my dear, this is not imagination, it is a real case, the discussion of my cyclist with a lady who pretends to be well educated, and otherwise very nice, but very serious and convinced of her affirmations. To argue with her about religious issues doesn't make any sense because nothing and nobody can change her opinions.

— Her cerebral sickness is very clear for any bicycle but not for her.

— Exactly so.

— Well, the example number two. After a massacre in a country of Central Africa, some years ago, when the members of one tribe killed about a million of human beings of other tribe, other lady was asked:

— How can be explained that about a million of human beings were massacred by their neighbours and God didn't do anything to stop that massacre? Such a direct and clear question caught her unprepared and the response was very short and also very clear:

— mmmppprssdguwtydur . . . . God knows what He is doing.

— Her cerebral sickness is also very clear, commented other bicycle.

— The example number three. In an interview by a major north-American television channel, an old lady, survivor of a concentration camp during the Second World War in Europe, said to her interviewer among other things that thanks to God she survived the terrible concentration camp where millions of people died and that now she is alive and well. The interviewer asked her:

— You say that God saved your life during the detention and liberated you from the concentration camp, true?

— True.

— Well, but why in the first place God allowed your deportation to the concentration camp which was in fact a camp of extermination, and as nothing happens in this world without His consent or permission, how can be explained that He agreed or even ordered that millions of totally innocent human beings, including children and old people, be killed there?

— This is a very good question! This was the answer of the old lady believer.

— Example number four. During a pleasure trip by boat in the Atlantic Ocean, a hurricane occurred and the boat was overturned. Three of the five members of the team died, the other two, a woman and a man, were saved three days later. The woman had an interview at the television. All the conversation during almost one hour was about the trip, the accident and how God saved her life. No one single word or explanation why in the first place, God provoked or permitted the accident, allowed her to suffer so much and only after that saved her, killing three of her companions. Why? In fact she saved herself with her own efforts and with the help of others, but she wants to think that was God who saved her. This is as an assassin arsonist, without any reason, put fire to the house, which is destroyed, and three are killed, but one with his own efforts and the efforts of others finally could escape. And this one instead of incriminating the assassin tells him many thanks because he didn't die and thinks that was saved by the assassin. And in this example also, the mental sickness and the crazy interpretation of the situation are obvious. Common sense? Absolutely not at all.

— Example number five. A little girl of five years old was kidnapped and killed. All America was profoundly moved by this savage crime. The police was mobilized with all its force to find the criminal. Three days later the girl's body was discovered but not the criminal. What do you think that followed? A big funeral ceremony at the church. Doing what? All the audience in front with the priests, praying. To whom? To the same God who, if existed, committed a criminal act by causing or accepting the crime. Everything was transmitted by the main television channels. One from the audience asked why God couldn't do a miracle and save the child. The answer of the priest was that God did a miracle.

— What miracle? interrupted an almost furious bicycle.

— The priest said that God did a miracle by calling the girl to him. And this is not all. A close relative, I am not sure if that was not the mother herself, declared that she feels happy because the girl is now in the company of God and Jesus Christ.

— What an unimaginable idiocy! commented other bicycle.

— There are not thousands but millions of similar examples. I think that for our demonstration these five examples are enough, but if you want, I have others also.

— Yes, we want, to satisfy our curiosity and to know more about the depth of the stupidity and imbecility of the great majority of the human beings believers.

— We also, please, added other group of bicycles.

— Well, example number six. My cyclist was invited to a private reunion. Among other guests was also a priest. To have some fun, my cyclist decided to ask the priest a question with practical-philosophical character. He approached the priest and after an exchange of kind banalities, asked him:

— Tell me please, from where the billions of human beings living on earth come?

— You must study the bible! God created Adam and afterwards, from his body created Eva. They had children, these children had other children and after many generations we have today the billions you are talking about.

— I studied the bible and in the bible is said that Adam and Eva had two sons, Cain and Abel. Cain was very bad and killed his brother Abel. So, the only descendent alive was Cain who became a criminal killing his brother and the only woman was Eva, his mother. That means that all of us are descendents from a criminal who had sexual relations of incest with his mother who was the only woman in the world at that time. Correct?

— Eeh, hmm, brrr. I will make investigations on this theme and I will call you to give the answer. Give me please your phone number. My cyclist gave him his telephone number, to make the joke complete. The priest never called.

— Example number seven. Discussion with a believer:
In accordance with the religious belief, Jesus Christ was the unique Son of God, who was born by a terrestrial virgin. Why and how, is not explained in the bible, probably to avoid questions about the sexual relations of God with Mary, the virgin mother of his son, Jesus. Well, let's accept this. It is said in the bible that later in his life, Jesus, the beloved Son of God, became the emissary of his father and in His name he did many good things for the human beings. For these good things he was punished with the death penalty by crucifixion by the same human beings but of other nationality. He wasn't killed immediately, until his death on the cross he suffered a lot in front of the people and in front of his almighty and loving daddy, the God. The question for you is: how can you explain that a son is tortured in front of the eyes of his father who could easily avoid this and by all means stop and even prevent the torture and save his son, because he as God, is almighty, but doesn't do anything and his son dies?
— He died for us, was the answer of an unexpected imbecility.
— But why to die? What is the use of his death for us? But not this was the question. The question was how can be explained the behavior of his father, which it is said is almighty and kind, at least for his own son?
— He died for all of us.
This answer was a clear message that it doesn't make sense to insist for a logical answer because doesn't exist a logical answer based on religious belief to this question or to any other one, and there are so many questions without answer. However, the atheist interlocutor continued his exploration with other questions on the same theme.
— If in our daily life an armed policeman sees how a bandit attacks an innocent with the clear intention to kill him and the policeman doesn't do anything, what kind of policeman is he? For sure he will be dismissed. Or he refers to the example of God. And truly, what

kind of example gave God with his behavior for his son, for all the human beings? How can we hope that God will save and help other human beings when he didn't do anything for his own son?

The tumultuous and eloquent answer of the believer was a total silence. The conclusion? The conclusion is that all this story is food eatable only by one category of human beings: those affected by a strong mental disability. Unfortunately, there are many of them in the world.

— Example number eight. The following discussion occurred in a plane returning to Canada between my cyclist and his neighbour, a lady, mother of two children, who liked to chat. Among other things the discussion turned to the issue of religion with the question of the lady to what church my cyclist goes. He understood immediately that she is a believer and in order not to upset her, didn't tell her that he is not a believer and gave her an evasive answer. At a point, talking about crocodiles, my cyclist said that this species is very old with an existence of millions of years.
— This is not possible, she protested, because the earth has only six thousand years.
— From where this results?
— It is written very clearly in the bible. The earth with all the animals was created by God six thousand years ago.
— But the science demonstrated that the earth has the age of many millions of years.
— Don't you know that this is a lie?
— But we, the human beings as a species, exist on earth much more than six thousand years, with the evolution from animal stage as Darwin demonstrated.
— Darwin with his theory of evolution is a great liar. God created us starting with Adam and Eve as the bible says.
— But Adam and Eve had only two sons as the same bible says.

— But afterwards they had hundreds and hundreds of children more.

— How a woman with two mature sons can have hundreds of children?

— I don't know, but this happened.

After this affirmation, my cyclist directed the discussion towards a more peaceful issue, about what weather is waiting for us in Toronto.

— Example number nine. In a discussion with a believer about the evangelists who pretend to be miraculous "healers" in grand televised reunions, the following dialogue took place:

— What do you think about this show with the liars paid for pretending to be healed instantaneously by the evangelist invoking the power of God?

— I believe that the evangelist has the real power to contact God and to cure the invalids immediately, as was shown.

— But there are undisputable proofs that everything was a well-organized circus and that the "healed" were not invalids, but only interested in the money for their roles as healed invalids.

— I think that was a miracle, God can do everything, and that the evangelist was of essential help.

— It means that you are convinced that with the method used by the evangelist and with the help of God, invalids and sick people for many years, can be healed in a few seconds?

— Yes.

— In this case, why he doesn't do this service so miraculous in the hospitals, healing thousands and thousands of invalids and hopelessly sick people, each day, making the hospitals and the doctors useless?

— I don't know.

— Example number ten. Other dialogue with a believer.

— If somebody prays to God, He listens to him?

— Certainly and immediately.

— And if there are millions or hundreds of millions of believers who pray to God at the same time all around the world, God can listen to all of them at the same time?

— Yes, he listens to them.

— And why God doesn't talk to them, doesn't answer them?

— God knows better what he must do.

— And God accepts the prayers from any place, or only from the churches and other religious institutions specific for various beliefs?

— From any place, from the most humble ones or from your house.

— In this case, what is the use of the entire multitude of priests, cardinals, rabbis and other religious professionals of all beliefs and denominations, very well paid by the believers, which are in fact useless intermediaries if the contact with God can be established directly and immediately between the believer and God from the moment the believer starts his prayer? And what is the use of the immense multitude of churches, synagogues, mosques, temples, cathedrals and other buildings for the same purpose, which cost a pile of money paid by the same believers, if God can listen the prayer from each believer from whatever other place including his house, the street and even the open field?

— Hmm errr psss uuubr oppp, I don't know.

— I can tell you why. All this army of charlatans and liars is necessary to control the mass of believers and to continue the brain washing process in the religious spirit or in popular terms, the imbecilization process, and so to get assured that nobody escapes from the religious influence, in a permanent manner. The best places for this are the churches, impressive cathedrals and other similar institutions where an adequate environment is created for collective obedience and a reciprocal social relationship between believers, which contributes to this purpose. To the same purpose serves the magnificence of the building itself, enormous cathedrals, very tall and with many paintings and statues of saints, in which the believers feel overwhelmed, small and without power to resist to the well calculated exterior influence. All this costs lots of money but this doesn't matter because everything is paid with a great personal benefit for the priests and other clergymen, by nobody else than the same believers, who are the victims of this circus and addiction process.

— Speaking of the dominant psychological effect of the edifice over the believers, I remember the story of my cyclist about his visit at a Buddhist temple in China. The building is about thirty meters tall outside but the surprise was inside. An immense statue of Buddha very close to the entrance occupies almost all space up to the ceiling. The natural tendency of the visitors is to look up and then, what can be seen is a giant head of Buddha in live colors looking directly to the visitors and with his also giant finger directed to the visitors. It is easy to imagine the effect on the poor believers, which probably feel like dwarfs overwhelmed by the powerful Buddha.

— Many thanks for your so interesting story. This shows that all the religions have a common policy to impress and control their believers.

— Example number eleven. So, you say that you are an intellectual, with the sense of justice and at the same time a devoted believer.

— Correct.

— In my interpretation it seems like talking about a clean dirty thing or about a full empty bottle, but lets clarify if possible, a basic issue. Tell me please, it is true that everything that happens in the world it happens by the will or at least with the knowledge of God?

— Yes, it is true.

— And it is clear that by saying "everything" it means good and bad things?

— Yes.

— Then how come that the believers always praise and thank God for good things and even for bad things and never get upset and hold Him responsible for the bad things that happen so often in the world?

— God is never accountable to us.

— Why?

— Because He is God.

— But how do you explain the need to pray to God for very important and obviously necessary help for indisputably good people who fully deserve such help? Without such prayers God doesn't pay attention to those needs of His beloved good children, the human beings? Does He suffer from a terrible sense of vanity? And why so many times these good human beings are not helped at all or much worse, they are even severely punished instead, not rarely with their death, instead of the expected salvation? And how come that in parallel with this, so many times obvious and terrible wrongdoers as criminals, robbers, crooks of all kind up to the heads of state, enjoy a permanent unpunished happy life? How your sense of justice reacts to all of this? Doesn't God know what is He doing? Is He drunk, crazy, cruel or totally irresponsible? Or all the expectations of help after the prayers are due only to the hallucination of the brain of the respective human beings believers who are wasting their time and hope in praying to a God that simply doesn't exist? Can you explain please, all these contradictions which happen on a daily basis in the world, or the answer is that all what happens has nothing to do with the prayers, God's will and power, just because no God of any kind exists and all the believers simply and totally fool themselves?

— The only thing I can say is that this is the way that it is.

— Your explanation is complete and clear and it has everything to do with a clean dirty thing or with a full empty bottle as I said before. I feel sorry for you.

— Example number twelve. I am atheist because the existence of a God, any God, cannot be demonstrated, but you are a believer, do you believe in only one God or in all of them?

— What are you talking about? There is only one God, my God, who created the Universe.

— And there are hundreds of millions of human beings who believe in the same God.

— I am glad that you are aware of this.

— Of course I am aware because it is a reality of life, but the same reality shows that other hundreds of millions believe with the same sincerity and conviction in other, totally different God who is the only real and unique God, and other hundreds of millions believe with the same sincerity and conviction in a different God who has nothing to do with the other two Gods. And in addition to these believers in their Gods there are many other groups of believers from tribal size to many millions, who believe with the same sincerity and conviction in other Gods. All of these groups of believers, regardless of size, believe that their respective God is the only true, real and unique God.

There is a little bit of a great confusion here. I am curious to know if all these believers of different groups are right in their belief in one single God, their God, and if these Gods are aware one about other ones. If this is the case, why all the existing official Gods don't form a club or association of Gods to coordinate their activities, if any, in order to avoid the present trouble in the world? If this collaboration is not acceptable to Them, why the God or the Gods who believe in their own supremacy and uniqueness doesn't or don't come out to make known in an obvious and unmistakable way to their believers that they are right and to all the other believers in other Gods that they are wrong? The obvious and the only rational answer is that they, the Gods, don't do this simply because none of them exists. But how come that the same question and confusion doesn't bother at all the different groups of believers in different Gods? Where is their elementary logic? What do you think about this?

— Nothing.

— Let's go now to the last two examples. So, the example number thirteen.

A short conversation between a believer and an atheist.

— Great is God and his power! Look, he created the entire world, with the earth, the sun, the moon, in one day. Great is He.

— But there is a thing greater than Him.

— Nothing can be greater than God.

— Yes, there is.

— It is a sin even to think about this, but for my curiosity, what is greater?

— The stupidity of the human beings, which created the very idea of the existence of God and of his power.

— Example number fourteen. A scientist had a discussion with a believer, which he wanted to be open, sincere and logical about the philosophical essence of the religion and of the atheism, to clarify with the power of logic, what is reasonable and what is not.

— I am a scientist, my thinking by my nature and education is absolutely logical, I don't reject any idea, doesn't matter how strange it may seem to me, with the only one but absolute condition: the promoter of the idea must be able to demonstrate his point of view and to answer in a logical manner to all my questions. From this position, in all honesty, I am ready to change my opinion if somebody can demonstrate that I am wrong in whatever issue. This refers also to the religious belief. It is clear that I am convinced that the existence of a supernatural power, as God, is not compatible with the reality of life and with the logical reasoning, as two plus two makes four and no seven or five. But I am ready to change even this conviction if somebody can demonstrate that two plus two is different from four. Can you explain to me on what is based your religious belief and convince me to be a believer also?

— If you are not a believer, I can share with great pleasure my belief with you and to attract you to be a devoted believer. But if you are an atheist, what means a sinner who rejects the very existence of God, doesn't make sense to discuss about this subject. My opinion is that you have the right to your opinion and that I have the right to my opinion and this is all.

— But this is only the description of your position, not the demonstration of this position.

— There is nothing to demonstrate. I believe in God and that's all. Neither you nor anybody else can change my belief in God. He makes me happy and is the explanation of all my achievements. It is clear?

All was very clear. The interlocutor started to become nervous. Very probably that the continuation of the discussion from the position of logic which he doesn't have, will transform him from nervous to furious without any practical result, perfectly foreseeable due to the effect of the opium active in his brain, opium which is the well known definition of the religion.

Unfortunately, this last example, that can be easily followed by thousands and thousands of other examples, represent the mentality of the almost totality of believers. In the best case, they behave in a kind manner, without changing their position or at least offering whatever explanation that doesn't make sense. In many other cases, they get upset and feel offended, situation that makes even more difficult to continue the discussion, or impossible or without any purpose. The purpose of changing their conviction doesn't have any chance to succeed. In other cases, the interlocutors believers feel directly insulted and there are also cases when in the name of their God they take the position of revenge ready to punish the sinners, because they think that these sinners insult their God by denying his existence. So, these discussions, with all peaceful intentions, involve a potential danger.

Who has any doubt about this can take a short course, or a more profound one if he has the time and the interest, and study the history of religious wars conducted not against atheists but against other believers, which are also believers but in other God. How far can go the stupidity and the idiocy of these human beings believers!

— More than this, intervened a bicycle well intrigued by all these examples and especially by the last one, showing how limited in their philosophic thinking at least, are these human being believers. I want to say that the history of religion is full of wars and other violent actions, but it is not necessary to go back some centuries in the past, for instance in the Middle Age, when the European countries totally under control of the Catholic church, organized the crusades against the Ottoman Empire and other countries of the Middle East, which were controlled by the Islamic religion. These fights lasted for many years and resulted in many dead and injured and material damages for both sides. At the present time the same thing is repeated, several years ago massacres occurred in the country that before was called Yugoslavia, in the south-eastern part of Europe, between Muslim and Christian residents, and more than this, there is a permanent and bloody fight in Ireland between those of the same Christian belief but of different denominations, Catholics and Protestants. There are also fights between Muslims, Hindus and Buddhists in various countries of Asia and fights between various sects of the same religion.

— And what is the difference between them? asked a young bicycle, innocent in problems of advanced idiocy.

— Practically none, the same idiocy but with various tonalities.

— The devastating effect of the religion, said other bicycle, is demonstrated everyday at present starting with the terrorism act of large scale, organized and implemented very well by the Islamic religious fanatics on eleventh of September, 2001, when the two very tall commercial towers of one hundred floors, a symbol of New York and of North American economic power, were totally destroyed by two planes kidnapped by these fanatics and which exploded in the collision with the towers killing without any scruples all of more than two hundred passengers in each plane and thousands of people in the buildings. This is an example, which will remain as classic in the history of modern terrorism based integrally on the religious belief of the authors.

This is also a unique example of the mixture of the imbecility of the purpose of the action with the perfection of its technical implementation for which the organizers and the executors, who died by suicide, can congratulate themselves. They were pilots with high qualification, all the participants were well educated, with good and stable material situation, good parents and family members and good neighbours in the community but with the very powerful religious virus in their infected brains. Their high level of discipline and dedication up to the sacrifice of their own life, even without the direct control and supervision from their bosses, could serve to a cause of other category, really good.

This act of terrorism without precedent in its magnitude and macabre ingenuity, was implemented by using the most advanced technology, not their own but that of their enemies, in the heart of their territory, in the largest city of the country, with a total defiance for the entire military might, nuclear arsenal, police, intelligence and counter-espionage services of the enemy. This act planned for years with diabolic meticulousity and perseverance, was executed by nineteen religious fanatics which before everything and initially were simple believers as millions of others, and like all the religious believers, potential fanatics.

All these nineteen actors in the final act of the terrorist action knew that they were going to die and got involved in this action voluntarily and with sick dedication, if it can be said so. No one common criminal or thief would accept such a task, if he knows with absolute certainty that he will die. Only a believer can decide to participate in an action, which means without any doubt, the death for him. In this consists the greatest danger of the religion. A common criminal can and many times takes the risk of death to achieve his materialistic purpose to improve his life, but will never commit suicide, which is contrary to the very purpose of his criminal action. For a fanatic believer, what means well imbecilized, this is possible and was demonstrated many times in an undisputable manner.

— We are not talking here about a rational suicide, added other bicycle, when there is not a better alternative, for instance to avoid the torture by the enemies that will kill him anyway or in a tragic situation without any hope to survive. Not this was the case with these believers accepting the suicide, all of them had the alternative for a normal, very good life. To abandon everything and to choose the death voluntarily is only the result of the most terrible disease, the acute infection of the brain up to the total loss of control due to the powerful religious virus.

— I want to underline an aspect of paramount importance, got involved in the discussion other bicycle. I am from New York and many times my cyclist and I had a ride in the area of the towers destroyed by the terrorist attack. The local result of the attack short time after the two hijacked planes collided with the towers was more than three thousand dead and I don't know how many injured and much suffering for so many others.

— Why you say "the local result" when you talk about this attack? Interrupted with her question, an impatient bicycle.

— You interrupted me, my dear, exactly when I wanted to continue my idea with the general aspect and damage of the attack, even where there are not dead and injured, is very much more grave than the local aspect. We are talking here about an entire nation of three hundred million, which lost the peace of mind in its daily activity in exchange for a feeling of insecurity and permanent fear.

— And in all other countries, added other bicycle, is today the same situation. This is so, but the country, which suffered the most and directly is the United States. The fact that in the same day, in few hours, the fanatic believers succeeded to hijack four large planes using them as very powerful projectiles destroying the two towers of New York and part of the Pentagon in Washington, the capital of the country, the symbol of the military power of the United States, represents a major damage for the prestige of the government and for the moral of the nation. And this damage has some aspects, which cannot be under-estimated.

The first aspect is that the entire immense military power including the nuclear arsenal of such a big country as the United States is totally useless to protect the population of the country against violent actions of massacre proportions.

The second aspect in the present situation is that the task to find the enemy is similar with finding and catching the wind in the field. The contemporary civilized society with such developed technology is extremely vulnerable by the religious fanatic terrorists who use the tactics and strategy of suicide and the lives of their own combatants for the very efficient manipulation of everything that can be destroyed and to provoke damages of great proportion. The policy of all other armies was historically and is now, to protect their own combatants provoking damages to the enemy and not by sacrificing its own combatants with premeditated intention, to increase their success in the war. Such an adversary is much more dangerous and difficult to combat.

The third aspect is that the reality of today showed that all the thousands of billions of dollars spent for the nuclear arsenal with the intention, as stated, to defend the country against the Soviet Union were in fact wasted, because the Soviet Union, at least for its own interest, didn't have the intention to attack the United States, not in a classic war and even less in a nuclear war which doesn't have winners because it will be a total destruction for all. After the fall of the Soviet Union from inside without even one single bullet from the American army, there is no country, which could be considered seriously a potential enemy to attack and occupy the United States in a war that could justify the present level of continuous waste for the armed forces.

The forth aspect is that at present the military and political strategists of The United States and may be of other countries of the first world, to their greatest surprise, they have a real enemy extremely dangerous about which not too long ago nobody was thinking, is the religious Islamic fanaticism or how they are called also, the fundamentalists. The dispute has also an economic base but the main reason is philosophical. To the Americans, which in their majority believe in a divinity named "God" doesn't matter in what the fundamentalists believe neither that they believe in a divinity named "Allah". The fundamentalists hate all who don't believe in Allah, especially the Christians and they hate America in principle. So, during this dispute about which God has the right to be entitled the Supreme Chief, the fundamentalists kill as many human beings of other belief as possible, in the name and with approval and the help of Allah, they say, and they thank him for the success of their crimes which they don't consider as crimes but heroic and holly actions. At the same time, the other divinity, the God of the Christians which also has absolute power, as his believers say, is watching passively how his believers are killed, one by one or thousands of them at once, and doesn't do anything to defend his believers and to save their lives, not even a telephone call to his competitor Allah, also almighty, to try a compromise. Here there is a dilemma for the believers Christians: their God doesn't know anything about what is going on, including the terrorist attack by the Islamic believers in which the two towers in New York were destroyed and more than three thousand died, or He was well aware of everything but couldn't do anything to prevent the attack in spite of his title of almighty, or He knew everything and had the power but didn't want to do anything, being possibly busy watching in television a Hollywood program with violence and passion crimes, in the breaks between the commercial advertising. No one of these alternatives justifies the absolute and blind belief in such a God, but what do you think that happened after the attack? The believers which escaped alive instead of being terribly angry for the totally irresponsible behavior of their God or to start thinking that his power and his very existence is only an illusion, took their dead to the churches, cathedrals or similar places of other denominations and during a very pompous funeral service prayed to the same God and presented to him their profound thanks.

— Prayers and thanks for what?

— A very legitimate question to which you can choose one, two or three answers: their own stupidity, idiocy or imbecilism, or all of them without limits.

— I want to vote for the last option, it means all of them without limits.

— I think that is the only option for which we, the bicycles, can vote, if asked.

— Don't get involved too much with the indignation, even well justified, be calm and don't forget that we deal here with a classical case of cerebral disease of which we spoke before. And the same medical diagnostic is valid for both groups, the religious fanatics that provoked the death of those thousands of victims, and the relatives of the dead, who organized or let themselves involved in the ritual of the religious funerals praying and thanking God. The same religious virus without which all this terrible story would not exist.

A roar of approval came from all the bicycles for this calm and realist conclusion. The discussion continued about the same subject with the intervention of a bicycle interested in the security problem.

— The main problem in the present conditions when the religious infection in the human brain demonstrates its terrible force in terrorist attacks is how the security of a country can be assured.

— This is the fifth aspect, the extreme difficulty to fight against the terrorism of the religious fanatics with current methods. Before, in all classical or traditional wars, it was a clear line of demarcation between the zone of the armed fight and the zone of peace behind that line. Today that zone of peace doesn't exist anymore. The entire country can be the war zone, in permanent danger. All populated centers are in danger with the observation that more is the concentration of the population, bigger is the danger and easier is for the terrorists to cause damages up to disaster proportion, from local to national. This refers to the current methods of distance remote-controlled explosion or with suicidal fanatics, in crowded centers like movie theatres, theatres, stadiums, conference places, trains, buses, subway, congested main streets, bars and restaurants and other similar places. This refers also to more sophisticated methods like the poisoning of the supply of potable water, the sabotage of the supply of gas and electricity.

The religious terrorists don't know limits in their destructive dementia. Greater and more terrible is the potential for destruction, more attractive and preferred is the action. The danger for their own lives is not important for them because they are ready to die anyway as suicides. In direct connection with this, the perspective and the real possibility of using biological arms and also nuclear arms are frightening. More frightening is the fact that for such an attack the enemy doesn't have to come from outside with planes that can be detected and destroyed, the enemies are in the heart of the society which is the objective of the attack, are invisibles and very difficult to be detected. They, the authors in waiting for these barbaric actions, hide very well in the population of the same ethnicity and also outside of it. All the nineteen participants in the suicidal attack of eleventh of September were religious Muslim fanatics residents in the United States, who until the start of the action couldn't be detected as terrorists. There are seven millions Muslim residents in the United States, the immense majority of which are not involved in such actions, but who can see the difference?

Who can guess what horrible ideas and plans are hidden in their brains, when they behave for years in an irreproachable manner, as well assimilated members of the North-American society, even they cut the beard and the traditional moustache that the great majority of Muslims have. They lived until the last moment before the action in an area of middle class, they had their house, car, family with children and well paid jobs and never had problems with the police.

The appearance was of model citizens, good examples for many others.

Until the day of the attack, all the relations with their bosses and the terrorist network were an impenetrable secret for all outside of the network. Unfortunately for the nation, the organization of the attack was without errors.

It is clear that there is a general feeling of suspicion against all members of the Muslim community, specially after the attack of eleventh of September, what is easy to understand, but no legal and efficient action can be taken against anybody before proving the guilt, and then it will be too late.

— But this situation is a real danger for the entire nation and I think that a preventive action is justified.

— It is true what you are saying but practically is very little that can be done, the leaders of the country, for political reasons, don't want to be accused of religious discrimination, and don't forget that the leaders of these fanatics can hide and act not only among the seven millions Muslims residents of the United States, but also among the more than seven hundred millions Muslims in various countries of the world, and the governments of these countries don't want or cannot cooperate with America against these fundamentalists. What is the solution? Occupy all these countries with armed forces? It means to provoke another world war? Look what happens in Afghanistan and Iraq. The United States won rapidly the war but lost the peace and nobody can say when the real peace will be assured there.

— In this case it can be said that there isn't any solution? That all the population is condemned to live in a state of permanent fear and anxiety? And everything depends on the will and mood of the religious fanatics? That they will renounce to their terrorist actions only when will get bored of this endless fighting? Or it is more probable that the fanatic leaders will continue their terrorist actions without stopping and in an unpredictable manner hoping to achieve the results they want?

— Unfortunately, the sad reality is that the answer to all these questions, which make lots of sense, is affirmative. And this because the human beings in their almost totality are as lemons ready to be squeezed by a minority of them who are the lemon squeezers. Neither ones nor others are capable to create and lead an intelligent society and the religion is a very useful drug to manipulate the mass of the human beings. The squeezers don't care about exactly what religious denomination is used, what is important for them is the religious belief itself. For this reason, the leaders of the rich countries which are the main target of the Muslim fundamentalists, don't want and cannot take any measures against the Islamic religion, without affecting the Christian religion and other religions which help them to control their own people.

— Then the only solution is to cut the roots of the terrorism which are the religious beliefs of all denominations with a massive program of reeducation of the mass of believers and with the categorical prevention of the religious influence over all members of the society paying special attention to the atheist education of the children continued until they achieve the level of absolute immunity against this disease, immunity based on their own logical reasoning and on the scientific base of their education. Without believers there is not from where to recruit candidates to be converted in fanatics and without fanatics there is not from where to recruit candidates to be converted in terrorists. This must be very clear.

— Very well said, this solution is truly perfect, the only one capable to cure the society of one of its most terrible diseases, with only one observation: the great majority of the human beings, as they are, for reasons explained a little before, are not capable to implement this solution in their society. For its implementation it is necessary a very strong and well organized action for a long period of time, by the intelligent minority of them, without any change of this purpose and taking all the necessary measures for its complete achievement.

Without this solution of total eradication of the religion from society's life, the danger of reappearance of various forms of the religious fanaticism with all well-known consequences will be permanent.

— I have a question about religion, somehow particular, intervened a bicycle.

— We talked so much about this subject, what else can be said? However, I think that all of us are curious about your particular question. We are ready to listen to you.

— It is true that we talked about many aspects of the religion, but all these aspects were negative. I agree with everything that was said and well demonstrated in this multilateral discussion with a profound and undisputable analysis of the essence and the negative effects of the religion. However, my question is: there is any positive aspect of the religion, even of minor importance?

— Your question is really particular and I would like to say significant and important for completing the real image of the religion. Many thanks. Giving a general answer, I must say that together with all terrible aspects well clarified before, the religion has also a sweet and tasty aspect.

These words provoked a shock of surprise mixed with indignation.

— What do you want to say with the sweet and tasty aspect of religion? asked a bicycle with an illusory calm at a step away from a storm.

— I am sure about two things, the first thing is that all of you appear surprised and in disagreement with what I just finished to say, the second one is that all of you will agree with me after you listen further on to me.

— I agree with the first one but I am not so sure about the second, intervened other bicycle, trying to hide her indignation with nice words.

— Well let's me explain.

— Please.

— Well, before going to details tell me please, what is done to make it easier for children and even for adults, to swallow a medical pill which is very bitter?

— The procedure is classic and very simple: to cover the bitter pill with a sweet or tasty coating. This helps to take the medication without feeling that is bitter, and after, once inside the stomach, the medication starts making its effect, in spite of the sweet coating which disappears in short time. The criminal mafia uses the same procedure when it wants to kill the victim by poisoning or to provoke the loss of his ability to reason. Also, a mixture of tasty substances and poisonous substances is put in the food or drink with the same purpose, which is served later to the victim with a very nice smile. Also it is used to get the children and other potential clients, to the use of the very dangerous, addictive and expensive drugs. The sweet or tasty coating does a very good service at a very low cost. I hope that my answer to your question is clear. Now I expect your explanation for the sweet part of the religion.

— Many thanks to you. You gave a complete answer to the question; you made the explanation about what means the sweet aspect of religion even better than me.

So, now it is clear that the part or the sweet and tasty aspect of the religion is nothing more and exactly the coating to give the religious venom to the innocents, children or adults without experience and necessary understanding. The same venom doesn't have any effect on an atheist but can poison the mind of others.

— And in what consists this sweet or tasty coating?

— This very short question has a long enough answer. For this purpose there is an entire, well elaborated arsenal which includes holidays with religious reasons, one more stupid than others, songs, also with religious motives, with words that don't make any logical sense, but with music sometimes nice, specially when copied from the American folk songs changing the original words with religious ones.

The food for the festive days represents other attraction and at the same time a big business. By the way, the religious holidays lost long time ago their religious devotion and have been transformed in a good opportunity for the vendors of all kind of merchandise, with the pretension of religious celebration. The religious holidays are also connected with the habit to give gifts and consequently, all believers give gifts one to another. So, the big business is directly and deeply interested in the permanent continuation of religion.

These pleasures as holidays, reunions at church and other places of prayer, songs, gifts, congratulation cards with religious text, which in themselves are not dangerous, maintain the religious influence over the entire mass of believers and represent at the same time an opportunity to recruit new believers. This mass, today peaceful and innocent represents the reserve and the source to recruit candidates to be transformed from the peaceful believers of today into the fanatic terrorists of tomorrow, exactly how the fanatic terrorists of today are the children and other innocents from yesterday.

In this direction the sweet coating mentioned before, proved its efficiency during centuries and also its hidden danger.

It seemed that all negative aspects of religion, naked or covered with the sweet coating, were exhausted but a new participant in the discussion was insisting to present to the audience her opinion about an issue not mentioned yet in the discussion and which proved to be of prime importance.

— We have discussed here about very many proofs of stupidity and idiocy of the human beings in the organization and in the life of their society in which, without any doubt, the religion is an essential contributor. These proofs are obvious and with all their inherent trouble are applicable to the past, present and immediate future situation. But there is an aspect in which the religion of all denominations has a primordial role, especially in the countries where the religion has not only the influencing power but also the political decision power. This aspect acts as a time bomb with disastrous effects, not so fast, but sure. This aspect is called the lack of the birth control, which allows the dangerous growth of the population, farther than the sustainable limits of the natural and material resources.

— And in what consists the role of the religion?

— In the opposition to all the measures to control the birth rate.

— And what is the danger?

— The danger is that without this control well observed, with each generation the population increases more, and in some cases much more, than the vital resources for a civilized life. The population can grow practically without limits but the vital natural resources for the very existence of the human beings are absolutely limited. This is referred to the basic elements as the potable water, the surface of the agricultural land and the surface of the land appropriate for housing, the reserves of energy, and the capacity to produce food.

— I agree totally, this danger, although not always immediate, is always existing and acting, it can be said that this is not only a danger but also a slow but sure movement towards an economic and social disaster. And because it is not an immediate danger, the political leaders of the respective society don't do anything to prevent the disaster.

— I want to say, got involved other bicycle, that this phenomenon of lack of control has an international effect, but not always in connection with the religion. With few exceptions, in all countries of the world, even in the countries where the religion doesn't have the power to control the internal policy of the government, the population grows constantly. At present the total population of the world is more than six billion people, and not too long ago, maybe one century, it was only two billion.

— I remember a book in the library of my cyclist, from the beginning of the fourth decade of the twentieth century, about China entitled "The country of four hundred fifty millions". Today, few years in the twenty first century, China has more than one billion two hundred million or close to one billion three hundred million inhabitants.

— This is true. I am from China and I can say that fortunately, the government of the country promulgated a law that allows only one child per family. There are local abuses but basically the uncontrolled grow of population was stopped. However, the significant results of this policy will be seen only after an entire generation.

— Very good for China, intervened a bicycle from India, in my country with a population which is close to a billion and with a state of poverty which is a very grave national problem, the population growth is other national problem.

A few decades ago, the prime minister of the country, Indira Gandhi, a very intelligent woman and conscious of the overpopulation danger, tried to introduce measures to limit the number of children per family. For this, she was assassinated by the religious fanatics from her own security guard following the orders of their religious leaders. Again, other example of the destructive power of religion.

— The fact that in many countries of the third world the unimaginable poverty is the cause of emigration by all means, legal or illegal, represents a real and permanent danger for the well-being of the countries of the first world, adding another problem to the ones that those countries, although developed, already have.

If drastic measures for the reduction of the overpopulation are not taken, a disaster comparable with a nuclear war will occur, later or sooner, probably sooner than later.

Commentaries of the bicycles about the globalization.

With the well known stupidity level of the human beings which are not capable to manage the economy of their society and to eliminate the poverty even today when still there are enough material resources for the existing population, the combination of this stupidity with a major lack of resources due to a too great number of human beings, will create an economic chaos and a greater poverty of national dimensions followed by a social chaos with unpredictable consequences. The famine, malnutrition and the mass diseases of today, will develop to a level of uncontrollable tragedy. And as the efficient isolation of countries or entire continents is not possible, the economic globalization will be transformed in a globalization of diseases.

— Related to the globalization, intervened a bicycle from the United States, this process or economic policy with the clear intention to increase the profits of the companies from the developed countries, or of the first world, has a double effect, or more precisely, triple. The first effect is according to the intention, the significant increase of the profit for the companies which are moving the production of things and services from their own countries to the third world countries where the pay for the same labor is ten, twenty or thirty times less, with the respective fabulous increase in profits for the executives of these companies.

The second effect is the creation of many work opportunities in the poor countries where there is an enormous unemployment, what means that they have an enormous reserve of cheap labor, without competition, at the discretion of the foreign investors. This reserve of cheap labor will grow with the uncontrolled increase of population for the benefit of the same foreign investors. Even in these conditions, the globalization that in no way solves the poverty problem in the countries of the third world, only reduces it a little, is also a positive factor with immediate effect. But this positive factor contains some very powerful time bombs.

The explosion of the first bomb is the third effect, which refers to the economy of the developed countries or of the first world. For the economy of these countries, especially for the United States, which is the greatest investor in the third world, the effect is devastating. Millions of workers and specialists of high qualification lose their jobs and become unemployed with little chances to find other job.

In the program "Export America" of the powerful North American television channel CNN, it was shown in January 2004 that recently three million employees lost their jobs and that the process continues. In the same program it was shown the comparison between the salaries in the United States and in the countries where the capital is exported. So for instance, for a labor for which is paid 15 dollars per hour in the United States, it is paid less than a dollar in these countries, down to 0.27 dollars in China and 0.22 dollars per hour in Vietnam. The same process occurred in Canada from where not the products were exported but the very production of these products and services towards other countries. In a well documented and alarming article in the prestigious magazine "Dimensions" of the association of engineers of the Province of Ontario, Canada, it is shown how many engineering and computer services move from Canada to India, China, Philippines and other countries of the third world where the salary to produce the same services is many times lower, creating in this way, a massive unemployment in the respective areas of production in Canada.

The second bomb explodes soon after the first one, also in the developed countries and has an avalanche effect created by the lost of buying power by millions of employees who lost their job and consequently their salaries and money to buy the things that they bought before. This creates a reduction in other industries and services resulting in additional unemployment. If this phenomena grows, there is no more buying power, or buyers for the imported products from the third world countries, and this is the time when the third bomb explodes: the employment in the countries of the third world which got a boost because of the export of the investment from the developed countries, is reduced significantly and the unemployment there takes dramatic proportions.
All this is not a pessimist thinking, it is a real process with well foreseeable results, based on the reality of the first big steps, which

already occurred in the last years and continue to occur at the present.

— And what is the solution to prevent this tenebrous future? Or there is no solution?

— Yes and no. The solution is to treat not the symptoms of the disease but the very infection, which is the cause of the disease, it is to say, to go at the roots of the problem. And the root of this chaos is the poverty and the uncontrolled growth of population, especially in the countries of the third world. If the unemployment in these countries disappears and the standard of living including the salaries increases up to or close to the level in the developed countries, the incentive to move the production of things and services from the first world countries towards the countries of the third world also disappears. Will disappear also the arithmetical name of little pride for the countries which are called now of the third world. The immediate result will be the disappearance or the reduction of the unemployment in the countries which export presently not the products but the production of these products, which causes the closure of the factories and services companies in their own countries and consequently transforms millions of employees into unemployed.

— And where comes the "no" of which you talked before?

— I didn't forget this "no", it comes just now. The "no" refers to the practical impossibility, or let's say, to the very low probability for the implementation of this solution due to the lack of vision, lack of understanding, lack of intelligence and logical reasoning of the immense majority of the human beings and to the concentration of the decision making power in a minority that leads the economy and the policy for the interest of immediate material gains, even at the price of destroying the future of the economy of the country and at the end, of their own gains.

— All this is absolutely right but the probability of the third world countries to reach the level of the first world countries, to liquidate the unemployment and to reduce the population, is practically zero, at least in the foreseeable future. Is there any possibility to solve the problem of the growth of the unemployment in the developed countries independently of what happens in the countries of the third world?

— Do you want to say to continue the production of goods and services in the developed countries paying very much higher salaries without taking advantage of the possibility to use the opportunity to pay much less in the countries of the third world and so increasing significantly the benefits for the bosses of the economy?

— Yes.

— Look, in a society in which the supreme law and the goal is the maximal profit, with total indifference or even with the violation of the moral principles, without other ethic than the money, there is a good similarity with the law of hydraulics about the pressure of the water; where is a difference in level, there is pressure, bigger is the difference in level, bigger is the pressure and more powerful is the flow of the water from the higher level towards the lower one. If we think about water as the capital for investment and about the levels of water as the levels of paid salaries, we can understand better the massive flow of capital towards the countries of the third world. And there is other similarity also, in its tumultuous flow the water provokes material damages as the flow of capital. The third similarity is, that to the flow of capital, the provoked damages are exactly as important as are important to the water the damages provoked by its flow.

And now, concerning your question about the possibility to stop the flow of capital for investments from the developed countries in order to stop the damages to the local employment, the response is that in principle is possible, but who will take such a decision?

— The government of the respective country, in one, several or in all the countries which presently move the production outside of their own.

— This would be possible if the government represented and defended the interests of the present and potential unemployed.

— That means of all the present employees.

— Exactly, but the reality is completely different of this. The government is the well-paid servant of its bosses.

— About what government are you talking? I don't talk about a dictatorial government but about the government elected in democratic elections by the majority of the people, it means the majority of all unemployed and present employees, which as you say, are the potential unemployed of tomorrow. In the elections participate not only one party which can impose its will, but several parties and the voters can elect the party which will form the government most adequate to their aspirations, true? I don't know much about the politics of the human beings but it seems to me that a government elected in this manner will serve his boss as you say, which in my opinion is the people, who have the power to vote, and after the elections, the elected government has the power to take decisions about the economy also.

— Ehe, my dear, I would like very much for you to be right and that the things happen according to your reasoning, but very unfortunately, the reality of life is totally different. You are very young and obviously don't have yet the understanding that we, the bicycles with much more experience, have. I like your sincerity and honesty and based on this, the credit that you give to the human beings in the administration of their society, but you will be terribly disappointed when you understand what the Father Time will teach you. Let me explain to you the real situation which is hidden behind the bright façade.

— I am listening with much interest, responded the young one.

— I remember a cartoon in a magazine, many years ago, about the elections in the United States, with a message perfectly valid also today, in all the countries of the first world with an election system hundred percent democratic. In the cartoon, the two puppets represented the candidates to the Presidency, representatives of the two parties participating in the elections. The two candidates opponents one to other one, gesticulate in order to demonstrate their differences in opinions. Below those puppets were the hands of solely one manipulator, the puppeteer, moving both puppets, behind the scene, the representative of the financial power. This means that regardless which candidate and party wins the elections, the only real winner is the big finance. No one candidate could participate in the elections with real chances to be elected without the approval and financial support of the large corporations, and for them, whatever candidate or party wins the elections, will continue to implement the policy of the corporations and serve their interests, and the globalization is one of their major interests.

The elections themselves, it is true, strictly democratic in the procedure, are only a circus well organized, for public consumption, giving to the voters the illusory impression of their own importance and nothing else.

— But let's assume that there is other party with popular support, which decides to participate in the elections with its program of promotion of the real interests of the people defying the large corporations. What happens in this case?

— In this case, when the major interests of the large corporations are in danger, they use methods of defamation, repression, or of military and police dictatorship, as happened in Germany after the First World War, in France and Italy after the Second World War, when the electoral laws were changed in France and the leader of the principal opposition party in Italy was assassinated.

— The conclusion is then, that the democratic elections are practically also a dictatorship, not military if is not necessary, but by all means a dictatorship with democratic and peaceful façade.

— Exactly.

— And the mass of people?

— Behave as drug addicted by the political, religious and even commercial propaganda, and surely by their own stupidity and the lack of understanding of their own fundamental interests.

— Other very important problem with the believers is the uncertainty of the objectivity of their reasoning about whatever aspect of life. If one commits an error and persists in his error in one direction, there is no guaranty that a similar error will not be repeated in other direction, in short time or after a longer period. We are not talking here about an accidental mistake, all of us can make mistakes, we are talking about of a malfunctioning in the reasoning, which represents a permanent potential for decisions or explanations without justification.

— This is true, observed a neighbour bicycle, and is as the difference between a person with proven honesty and other one, which has the inclination to steal. Let's say that he doesn't do it regularly but nobody can tell if and when he will steal again. There is no more confidence in his actions and behavior.

— It is as a chronic disease of an organ of the human body, it is not known when other crisis can occur and how grave it could be. Whatever organ is sick, it is no good for the health of the human being but the brain is the most complex and essential organ. The malfunctioning of the brain can generate much greater damages to a person with consequences not limited to his own body or situation but in a sphere very much larger, which may affect sometimes an entire nation.

— What a coincidence in thinking, commented other bicycle. Many times I thought about this terrible possibility when this occurs to a human being with great responsibilities, in charge of an army, of an important and difficult action, or of an entire nation. In this process of taking the decision for the action, he may have a "divine" inspiration thinking that God wants to act in a special way and he is only the executor, and doesn't matter how disastrous such a decision could be, he will take it. There are many cases of this nature in the history of the human beings.

— It is true; it is a very great potential danger. It is true also that many times a leader doesn't mix his religious belief with his decisions at work but never can be said or be sure that this will not happen next minute or next day.

— Other coincidence in thinking, intervened other bicycle, every time when there is a difficult international situation and I see on television the president of the United States giving a speech, he always finishes it with the words "God Save America" or "God bless America", I start shaking of fear and disgust. Think about this, the fate of the entire nation of three hundred million people depends on the decisions of one single human being who is also the commander in chief of the armed forces and of the nuclear arsenal, and this human being is a believer, what means that one who thinks that the entire nation is in the hands of God and whatever God decides, will be good for the nation. So, whatever happens, whatever stupid decision he, the president takes, with whatever tragic consequences, he will have the supreme excuse, "this was the will of God" What irresponsibility! what idiocy! and what is more frightening and sad is that the great majority of this nation of three hundred million takes these words of the president with passivity and acceptance.

— Ehee my friend, you are very modest and indulgent, talking about the actual president or about one of the presidents of the United States. All the presidents of the United States and the presidents, prime ministers or chiefs of many other countries do the same. And many times, short time after such a decision and the respective speech of the president or head of the government, a mass of fathers are obligated to leave their homes, their children, women and their own fathers behind and to go in military uniforms, sometimes at very great distances, to kill the fathers of other children which on the other side of political spectrum are exactly in the same situation. And everything happens with the blessing of the priests who assure the combatants of both sides that the protection of God is there, surely of the same God. In other cases, as was shown in a very interesting documentary about the First World War at the French-German front, the process of imbecilization of the mass of human beings prepared for the war, which this time are called soldiers and officers, continued in the hours before the battle with a spectacle well staged in which the soldiers in their knees and with the head down and uncovered pray to God, what means they repeat some words without any common sense, enunciated by other human beings, the priests who keep a crucifix in the right hand moving it to mark in the air a bigger cross. Probably it is assumed that with this movement, God will hear and understand better the pray. It is assumed also that God is bilingual because the French soldiers and priests pray talking to God in their native language, the French, and the German soldiers and priests on the other side of the front line, in their native language, the German. After this Machiavellian circus, the soldiers and officers of different nations but of the same religious belief will kill each other, the human beings of each of these two fighting nations being convinced that God, who is called also "Our Father from Heaven" will arrange the things so that only the human beings of the other nation which are called "enemies" will be killed or mutilated and that everything will end up well for themselves.

— And what happened? Interrupted a bicycle very interested in this story and very curious at the same time.

— What happened? Happened something very grandiose for the human beings. In a macabre action, under the benevolent supervision of God for both parts fighting desperately and under His kind look full of love for His sons, many soldiers of both sides were killed and injured. This massacre amused God very much, but what amused and entertained Him even more were the religious ceremonies after the battle, when the believers who didn't die in this battle, buried the dead with the same prayers and thanks to God. This was like thanking a criminal for his crimes, a sick logic, crazy and, why not? amusing.

— I liked very much your presentation so original and with so much irony about what happened in the battlefield and with God. If God really existed, no other tragic-comical interpretation could be more adequate, commented suddenly a nice blue bicycle with ten speeds.

— And related to what you just finished to say, she continued, I have three questions.

— Enchanted, give me the first one please.

— What happened with the priests? Did they participate also in the battle taking the respective risks?

— Ehe, my nice darling. How graciously you treat the priests with this question of yours! Do you think that they are idealist believers, sincere and at least honest in their stupidity, ready for their own sacrifice for what they preach? No my dear, they, the priests are by definition charlatans, hypocrites, professional liars. They only prepare others to die, they never prepare themselves for this. Their activity is limited behind the area of the battle, the first line of fire is not for them. Which is the second question?

— I understand that in each war, on each fighting side there are major economic and political interests for a minority, but the war is done with the mass of human beings. What do they obtain from the war?

— In the best case, nothing. Generally all lose much, the life, the health or physical integrity, the psychological health or integrity, in many cases their houses, the job and many material things, the victory in the war is not necessarily a guaranty for a better life.

— Here comes my third question, how come the mass of human beings which in conditions of peace are individuals more or less normal and with power of reasoning in cases of secondary importance, at least, cannot reason and see the abysmal stupidity of the war, which is a case of prime importance? Why don't they ask themselves if the cause of war is just and the "enemies" are really the bad ones who must be destroyed as the only solution? then why the almighty God doesn't use His power to destroy these enemies in one second, so avoiding all the sacrifices and suffering for His children, the human beings? Why they don't ask themselves when they see their neighbor soldiers dying or injured and suffering so much, where is the result of the prayers to God, the Father, before the battle, if there is a God?

Why they don't think that all the surrounding misery in spite of all the prayers and priests is an obvious proof that there isn't any God, that everything is only an abysmal lie? Why this mass of human beings doesn't think that their real enemies are their own heads of state and the minority in power and not the human beings from other side of the front line? Wouldn't be better to unite with them, stop the dirty fight with their brothers and rebel against the instigators to war from both sides? Why in all these aspects don't they question the very existence of God? I was thinking many times about all this and my irreversible conclusion is that the human beings have a very serious problem with the functioning of their brain, as was said here before, it is really a brain disease.

— Your third question includes very many questions, all of them very valuable and reasonable. The response to all these questions is only one, which covers all of them, and this response is exactly what you just have said.

— One of the conclusions on this issue is that when we talk with a believer, we must show not so much irony and sarcasm but condescendence. Due to their sickness, they cannot be at the same level with the atheists and insisting to convince them, doesn't always bring the expected results. Many times the religious belief is so strong that the disease became chronic without hope of healing.

Other bicycle wanted to add other aspect about the presidents believers and intervened in the discussion:

Talking about presidents of the United States, prime ministers of other countries, believers, I remember the public affirmation of a leader of an opposition party candidate for the position of prime minister of Canada some years ago, that the earth has only six thousand years of age, as is said in the bible and other things of the same level. Just imagine, these human beings pretend to be considered intellectuals, well educated, capable to lead a nation, true? Many of them have diplomas from well-known universities. The flagrant contradiction is how it was possible to obtain these diplomas without finishing the previous stage of education as the high school, where is given the basic scientific teaching about physics, chemistry, history, geography, astronomy, mathematics logic or simple arithmetic with its reasoning so precise and clear, biology, zoology and other subjects totally incompatibles with the religion. How did they pass all these exams remaining high-level illiterates? And they pretend that can solve all the problems of the nation with due competence. In a public discussion with a high school teenager they could be terribly ashamed and embarrassed.

— I would like very much to see in a televised program such a public discussion, if it were possible to obligate these presidents and prime ministers believers to participate in such a discussion. For sure it will be very entertaining and lots of fun.

— What is the practical difference between the level of general culture of a president of the United States or of other country which is considered civilized and developed, who ends his speech asking God for help, and a chief of a primitive tribe who does the same addressing to his own Gods or to the fire or to the sun asking for help for the well-being of his tribe?

— None.

In a kind of competition to demonstrate the tragic-comical aspect but absolutely real of these supreme leaders of nations and to make a well-deserved mockery of them, other bicycle asked:

— Can anyone of you tell me if it can be considered that the human beings of very low level of general culture and knowledge and who believe in God, belong to the same category of those who believe that our planet is flat and square?

— Yes, it can be considered that they are of the same category.

— Then, I ask myself how will be received a presidential speech which instead of ending with "God bless America" will end with the words: "Will fight for freedom in all our flat and square planet" or some similar message.

A wave of laughter propagated immediately from one to other end of the audience.

What the bicycles think about the commercial advertising.

Other aspect of the everyday life in the society of the human beings is the commercial advertising. This is an epidemic of giant proportions in all places and at all times. The entire policy of advertising or commercial propaganda has its very solid base in the same stupidity without limits of the human beings, which are responsible for all inadequate solutions to all their problems.

— I want to say, intervened in the discussion other bicycle, that it would be a big mistake to confound the advertising with the information. The information is necessary, the advertising, the commercial propaganda, is an abuse of information of such a magnitude that it was transformed not only in the enemy of the information but also into an anti-social action extremely annoying, lying, very expensive and above all totally useless for a civilized society.

There is a multitude of examples of this in all directions, in the press, in the television, radio, in the streets, movie theatres, in the subways and buses, etc. The advertising comes without invitation in the private postal boxes, independently or in the same envelopes with the telephone bills, TV cable and car insurance invoices. It also comes by phone without permission to the house disturbing the peace and comfort of your home.

— I think that the entire advertising system is a mass robbery well organized and made legal by the big business, which has the economic power and the power to impose its interests to increase its profits by any modality. The legacy of the advertising, which is of no rational use, robbing the time and the money from the mass of buyers, is the result of this manipulation.

The commercial advertising is a very profitable business in itself in addition to the cost of the merchandise. The total cost of the advertising including the benefit, is added to the cost of the sold products without the knowledge of the buyers who don't know anything about what is included in the selling price. When one buys a kilogram of meat or cheese, or a dress, doesn't need to study before the respective advertising, he knows what and from where to buy but cannot avoid the cost of the advertising, useless for him, which is included in the selling price. The necessity for the advertising for whatever product can be an autosuggestion, an illusion, or simply an additional possibility to gain, or more exactly to rob money; the decision about the quality and quantity of the advertising is solely and totally in the hands of the vendors, I mean not the employees who are selling but the owners of the merchandise.

— Many times, says other bicycle, the advertising is so stupid that simply is not possible to understand what they are talking about, what is the object of advertising, is like it was made by crazies, idiots or for these categories, but the cost for it must be paid in money, wasted time and by tolerating this great nuisance.

— The most used word in the advertising and the most false is "free". This word is addressed to the most stupid human beings who believe that its content is true. In fact nothing is for free, everything is well calculated to give the appearance of free but all is included in the price of the objects that the buyers must buy in an obligatory manner in order to get the one apparently for "free". For instance if the price of a book is two dollars, three books will cost six dollars, but in the advertising for "free" the vendor puts the price for a book at three dollars instead of two and who buys two books and pays the same six dollars will get one for "free". The one who pays the price for two books is convinced that he got the third one for "free" but in fact he has paid the real price for three books and by using this trick, the vendor sells three books with a greater total benefit for him. With the trap of a "free" book the one who decides to buy three books instead of one, pays six dollars instead of three for the only one book that he really needs and the vendor gets a higher benefit. The statistics are very clear, with the trap of "free", the great majority of buyers buy much more than they need and this is an additional profit for the vendor, and so the advertising is paid by itself with a significant benefit. The vendor never loses.

— Now everything is clear. I think that the same applies for other word, which is used very much in business. This word is "sale", sometimes with indications that the price was reduced by twenty, fifty and even eighty percent. The trap here is that the great majority of buyers don't know the real price of these products.

— This is true, this trick is combined sometimes with the words "liquidation" or "shop closing", when there is no intention to close the shop. This is only to attract more buyers with the illusion to buy for cheaper. And this advertising trick works for the vendors.

Other bicycle intervened in the discussion with the observation:

— Nothing is more annoying and irritating that the frequent interruption of a movie, spectacle or interesting discussion on TV for several minutes of advertising. This is an abuse that shouldn't be permitted, affecting millions and millions of viewers, which are not interested in anything in that advertising.

I am sure that of these millions of TV viewers which are obligated to swallow so many times everyday, for instance the advertising for selling cars, only an insignificant percentage will buy a car being convinced by the images of cars running at high speed or with beautiful women next to the car. The potential buyers will go to a shop where the cars are sold, will take all the necessary information in due detail and only after that they will decide and buy the car. For all the rest of the viewers the advertising for cars is a total waste of time and a great boredom and the same is true for all other commercials.

— This is also a great abuse of the modern technology which could make the daily life happier and pleasant for all, said other bicycle. The television could serve very well to the education, information and relaxation at home, and could have a special channel only for advertising, for those viewers who like to watch these commercials even with little or any practical value for them. Instead of such an intelligent policy the television was transformed in an instrument for commercial advertising on all tens or hundreds of channels. To attract more viewers, this program of commercial propaganda mixes frequently with news, with portions of movies, which are interrupted immediately when other group of advertisements is programmed.

Even when there is an interview with the prime minister of the country or with other personality about problems of prime importance, the commercials have priority and the interview is interrupted several times in conformity with the program of advertising, without any shame, and the head of the state accepts with all humility this insult to him and to his people as something normal.

— And how this can be explained? The chief of the state is so stupid that cannot see the insult or doesn't have the power to impose himself as the representative of the people who listen to him?

— Doesn't have the power. And he doesn't represent the people, this is only the official propaganda for the stupid ones who believe that he, as the head of the government or of state, is the servant of the people. He is in fact the servant of the big business, which pays for the advertising on television and radio. And as a good servant who doesn't want to lose his job, he cannot ask not to be interrupted in his interview by the commercials, because his boss, the Big Money, thinks that will obtain more money with the commercial advertising. This is the explanation for his acceptance of the situation. Is it clear?

— It is clear but not good.

— It is not good for whom?

— It is not good for people, television viewers.

— Nobody cares about this. They don't have any power and will not protest as doesn't protest the chief of the government.

— Other thing with the advertising is that for counterbalancing its uselessness in very many cases the advertising is false in a hidden way or silent about the truth of the product quality. One of these methods frequently used is the technique of writing in the commercials with very big letters the words "free gift" with the buying of a product or service and below with minuscule letters the attached conditions which practically makes the offer without value for the buyer.

— All that was said about the advertising is the pure truth. However, I would like to know at least theoretically, in what conditions the advertising would be useless for the vendors of all the goods and services.

— This is possible with enormous advantages in savings of money and time for the buyers and in avoiding the commercial risks and a big headache for the vendors. The commercial propaganda so useless and full of lies will be transformed in useful and honest information. All this would be possible with one condition.

— Which?

— The condition is the annihilation, the total disappearance of the competition between private vendors and this is possible with the creation of a sole trader, which could be a private or state organization owner of all the commerce of the country.

— Well, but in this case the general sale of products, without competition will diminish.

— Not even with one cent.

— How this can be explained.

— Very well. At present the main purpose of the advertisement is to attract as many buyers as possible and to sell as many goods and services as possible. If a buyer doesn't buy from one vendor, he will buy from other vendor and opposite. If the profit from selling goes down below certain level, a very sad reality will appear without any doubt for that vendor: the bankruptcy with all personal tragedies attached. At the same time the buyers, which for whatever reason didn't buy from that vendor will buy from other vendors, the profits of these vendors will increase and they will be very glad. It is to say that we are talking about the human jungle, the tragedy for some, means happiness for others and the opposite.

To avoid such a tragedy, all private vendors are using all possible methods, tricks and traps to obtain a greater share of the money spent on the product they sell. In these conditions, the fight for a greater share of the market is ferocious, is the fight for survival.

— And how this ferocious fight can be avoided?

— With the existing reality of such a great stupidity of the human beings, this is not possible, but if the intelligence is used, there is a very simple solution.

— I am very interested to know which is the solution.

— In order to be clearer in what I want to say, I will give an example. Let's say that in a town there are three shops where bread is sold. Each shop belongs to a different vendor. Each of these three vendors is permanently preoccupied about the situation of the sales, every day and every hour, because he knows that if one buys bread from other shop he will not buy from his. For this, he thinks that the advertising, even lying, can help him to increase his sale and so he will put announcements in the window of his shop telling that here is sold white bread which is whiter than in other shops, or that the integral bread sold here is the most integral in the town or in the world. The reality is that with or without advertising, the quantity of bread sold in town, in the three shops, is the same, what differs is the quantity sold in each of these three shops.

Now imagine that one of these three vendors of bread makes a very good offer to the other two vendors and buys the other two shops. So, he will be the only vendor with three shops, all from where is possible to buy bread in town. In this situation, will he still need the advertising in the window of his shop about the quality of the bread? Certainly not, because those who need bread, if don't buy it from the first shop, will buy it from the second or from the third one. For the vendor this is not important anymore because all the profit from the three shops will be for him and not for anybody else. No more competition, no more problems, no more tension and headache. The exaggerated advertising can be transformed into useful information as "Here is sold white and integral bread" and nothing else.

— Now is clearer.

— I am very glad that you understood well my example, but this is not all.

— What else?

— Much more. Up to now is clear because there is no more competition in the bread sale but the economy of the town is bigger than the commerce of bread. Let's assume that due to a change in the habits of the population, the consumption of bread diminishes significantly in favor of other products as for instance rice, fruits and vegetables. In this case the competition moves between the shops selling bread and the shops selling the mentioned products. In this case, the solution to eliminate the competition and the necessity for advertising to sell bread or rice, fruits and vegetables is the same. In the same manner it is possible to solve similar problems in all other areas of the economy not only for a town but for the entire nation and at the end, for the entire world and so to avoid the competition which is so expensive not only because of advertising but also for many other negative aspects. The reason for which such a solution is possible is that, let's take as an example an entire country, the total income of the nation is the same regardless of what and how much one or other one buys. If the profit from all sales to all the citizens of the nation comes to the same purse, there is no reason for advertising neither for the fight for more buyers of one or other products. All what is not sold today will be sold tomorrow, if it is not sold in this shop, it will be sold in other shop to the same or other buyer. If a buyer of a car changes his mind and instead decides to make a trip and buys the ticket, again doesn't matter because the profit from the car or from the trip ticket comes to the cashbox of the same big vendor. If the buyer wants to put the money in the bank for one or two years, also doesn't matter, finally he will spend his money for one or other thing and the profit will arrive also to the sole vendor general without the fight for a competition which doesn't make any sense.

— Everything is marvelous, if it is realized in this manner, but my question is, if the lack of competition will not produce a lack of quality, products of inferior quality? The unique vendor who is not afraid of a competitor who for making more money will produce a product of better quality, can produce goods of low quality without punishment, true?

— Very good question and very reasonable preoccupation. If you remember, I said at the beginning that this is a real possibility, which requires intelligence as a fundamental condition, not stupidity. At present, the human beings at their level of general intellectual development, I am not talking of the exceptions, are not able to organize themselves in a society of this level. The tentative in this direction in some countries failed miserably. Certainly such a commercial system without competition and without unnecessary advertising requires a very rigorous control of the quality and price of the products, which must be strictly observed. With such a system is possible to achieve not only an immense saving in the cost of the useless advertising but also and in direct connection with this, a massive standardization of products with the elimination of thousands and thousands of new models, sizes and details without any real use which tremendously increase the cost and the selling price of these products. A reasonable range for various tastes of the clients is good but when this is abused and the market is flooded with a multitude of new models each year, which creates confusion and higher costs, this is not acceptable. The common sense must prevail to the superficiality.

Another bicycle signaled for attention and once she got it, started talking:

— There is other very important argument in favor of this system without competition. The supporters of the present model of economic organization praise so much the role of competition, trying to make everybody believe that without competition there is no economic life and that the only way to ensure the quality of everything is the competition as the miraculous key to it. I completely agree with what our sister said that such an economic system without competition requires a superior organization, this is very clear, but even in the present society with chaotic economy, when the competition doesn't solve any real problem, in the same very countries where everything in life is competition, there are taboo areas where the competition is simply unthinkable: the army, the police, the state security organization. Do we have two or several competing armies to defend the country or to fight in a war? In case of trouble do we have more than one police force to choose from, to call for help? It is assumed that the only one, the national army or police is enough and it is the best, and all efforts are directed to make it as good as possible. The same should be with the economy, without competition.

— Excellent observation, commented the previous speaker. And I have one too, consisting from one question and two answers to it. The question is: where all the saved money from the advertising will go? The first answer is: lower prices for everything, significantly lower, what means a better standard of living for everybody. The second answer is: as an alternative to this, by retraining the people involved presently in the entire machinery and bureaucracy of this useless advertising, for useful jobs, they can replace partially the present productive employees and so everybody could have an extra let's say, two months vacation with pay per year, which means a better quality of life for everybody. Sounds like a dream but it is perfectly feasible.

Discussion about the marvels of engineering.

The discussion continued with other theme, the engineering. Says a bicycle:
— The engineers and the engineering as a profession can be characterized by two extreme aspects, pertinent only to them and that cannot be found for instance in singers, artists and professional sportsmen. These aspects are the tremendous value of their products

without which our civilization couldn't exist, on one hand, and their absolute modesty on the other hand, commented the bicycle with a very analytical spirit about the society of human beings. And she continues the idea:

— Millions or tens of millions of fans know not only the name but also everything about a famous rock and roll singer, Hollywood artist or football, hockey or golf players. They know what they do, with whom they are in love, what they eat, how they dress, read all the details about their divorces, they know and are interested in everything about them. They are ready to wait in line for many hours and sometimes all night to buy a ticket for which they pay a high price. And what is the merit of a football player, even a world champion? All his merit consists in marking with his foot a goal more in the gate of the adversary team. What an important thing! This results in endless acclamations, enthusiasm close to delirium and not in rare cases, in many dead and injured following a battle in the stadium with the fans of the other team.

The same millions of fans and hundreds of millions of other human beings travel by plane each year and talk by phone every day. How many of them know or are interested even only in principle, how a plane or a telephone works? How many of them know the names of the engineers inventors of these wonders of technology?

— All what you are saying, intervened other bicycle, is a very sad reality. I want to add other questions in the same direction. How many football or hockey fans looking with enthusiasm to their preferred players in an immense stadium with all the facilities inside are also enthusiastic by the elegant and safe construction of the same stadium and by all the involved engineering? A similar question is valid for the concert fans that applaud for long time their preferred singers. What about the concert hall with all its acoustic, elegance and interior comfort based on the absolute safety of the construction of the entire complex and the engineers who made this possible?

Who thinks about this? There is no statistics about the answer but most probably, the real answer is that nobody.

— This shows very well what was said here a short while ago, the humility and the modesty of the profession and of engineers who work incognito and in silence as Cinderella, producing every day the very base of the modern life.

— You talk about planes, telephones and impressive constructions, all this is impressing and very obvious, but I would like to talk about a very modest product, small and less impressing at the view but impressing also by the content of engineering. The human beings use them in very large quantities, we can say hundreds of millions every day.

— What is this? asked with curiosity other bicycle.

— A can of coca-cola or soda water, of aluminum. What does each of those hundreds of millions of consumers do? Takes a can, opens it, drinks the content directly from the can or with a glass, and without thinking puts the can in the garbage. I doubt very much that even one of these consumers takes the can in his hands, looks at it and examines it with attention and thinks that no more than a century ago, such a product was impossible to be produced, doesn't matter at what cost, and if by a miracle a can would appear, its place would have been as a very precious display, in a royal or imperial palace. Look, this simple can, is also a wonder of engineering. The design is perfect and so its production serves in the best way its purpose, to bottle and conserve the beverage in a healthy, economic and very easy to manipulate manner. It is very light, so, its weight related to the weight of the bottled beverage is the minimal possible if to compare with whatever other container, the cost is very cheap, is perfectly sealed and at the same time very easy to open. Now, the question to which I can say with anticipation that the response is "nobody". How many of the hundreds of millions of drinkers think about the merits of the inventors, know their name and are interested in how the cans are produced and admire the intelligence of the involved engineers? I repeat, the answer is nobody. This is a fact of life that will not change, but if you think about it, is a disgrace.

— Truly, your story about the modest beverage can is very interesting and relevant for the way of thinking and appreciation of the human beings.

Promotion in China and South Korea. Discussions in India and Italy. Adventure in the Himalayas Mountains.

A remarkable chapter of the promotional activity for the bicycle expressway system was its promotion in China, the country with the largest population in the world and traditionally friendly to the bicycles as a means of transportation. The tremendous recent increase in the number of cars in the city streets is a powerful incentive for the implementation of the bicycle expressway system concept in all cities facing traffic congestion and air pollution.

In September 1995 the engineer presented his concept at the International Seminar-cum-Workshop on transportation organized by the United Nations Centre for Human Settlements in Beijing. The reaction was very positive and the Minister of Construction of China who couldn't attend the presentation because of his busy schedule, asked the engineer for the favor of a private presentation for him and a group of specialists in the same day, at mid-night. The additional presentation and the vivid discussion ended up at about two o'clock in the morning. The minister was very pleased with the idea, and realizing this, the engineer asked him directly about the chances to design and build such a system in China, starting with Beijing. The minister was very frank in saying that although the advantages of the proposed system are undisputable, the present policy of the government is to build more highways for cars as a priority which consumes all available funds for the development of transportation. However, he said, he is open to the idea and if the engineer can find investors willing to cover all the costs for a bicycle expressway system, then it will be a good chance for the implementation of the proposed system in China, starting most probably with a Pilot Project in Beijing.

This judgement may sound right from the point of view of the Minister of Construction but the engineer understood immediately that this is a dead end. Knowing very well the mentality of the private investors when they have to make a decision to invest hundreds of millions of dollars in a visionary, totally innovative idea without the guarantee of the government for their money, the engineer thanked the minister for his genuine interest in the concept, leaving a door open just in case that some unforeseen positive change may occur at the governmental level.

After the Seminar and the meeting with the Minister of Construction, the engineer remained in China another few days visiting some places of great interest like the Winter and the Summer Imperial Palaces, other museums, the famous Great Wall of five thousand kilometers long, the only construction on Earth that can be clearly noticed from the outer space. Observing the daily life in Beijing, the capital of China, with its very divers aspects, was also very interesting. He paid special attention to the urban transportation problems and they are many and growing.

When you are talking about urban transportation in China, there is no way to forget about bicycles or to overlook their important role. A flagrant change occurred since the engineer visited China 31 years before, on a very interesting tourist trip from his native Romania. He had been then in most of the main cities like Beijing or Peking as the city was named at that time, Shanghai, Canton, Hangzhou, Wuhan. With regard to the urban transportation, everywhere the picture was very similar: as a sister bicycle mentioned at the first bicycle reunion, he also could see rivers of bicycles and very few cars, the official ones. At the main intersections, to change the flow of bicycles according to the changing traffic lights, was not always an easy task. Now, thirty one years later, the number of cars increased tremendously and the life for bicycles became more difficult. At the main intersections, in order to avoid car congestion and wasted waiting time, overpasses were built. These overpasses allow the non stop flow of cars but they are terrible for bicycles. Their steep slopes that mean nothing for the cars, cause most of the cyclists to stop and push their bicycles up by hand especially those which carry loads, and there are many. In this way the traffic capacity for bicycles was reduced from the bicycle speed to a pedestrian speed because the traffic capacity at a strangulated point determines the real traffic capacity of the entire street behind.

Seven years later, in the summer of 2002, the engineer took another trip to China, the main objective being this time the four days trip by bout on Yang Tze River, the main river of China, passing through the area where a huge dam was being built to create the largest water reservoir in the world. The reservoir with a length of six hundred kilometers and a storage capacity of about thirty billion cubic meters of water will play an essential role for irrigation, hydro-electricity production and in avoiding flooding downstream which at present causes immense damage and loss of many lives very frequently.

The construction of the dam and the resettlement of the many inhabitants living in the reservoir area were in an advanced stage and this was the last opportunity to see the river and the spectacular Three Gorges in natural conditions before being flooded with water up to one hundred meters depth. As a hydro-technical engineer, he was professionally very interested in this monumental construction and was very glad for having the chance to see it in the process of implementation.

The rest of the trip was also extremely interesting and beautiful. In many places the scenery was like in a nice dream, extremely pleasant and relaxing to watch.

The engineer used the opportunity of this trip for contacting the officers of the municipality from the two largest cities in China, Beijing and Shanghai, to try again if there is any renewed interest in the bicycle expressway system concept. The results of these discussions only confirmed the governmental policy of supporting the car promotion and the neglect of bicycles as a means of urban transportation. The officials in both cities appreciated the value of the concept but recognized at the same time that the wind blows now strongly behind the cars and against the bicycles. As an obvious result of this policy the engineer could attest to a significant increase in the number of cars in the streets with the respective congestion problems and the diminished number of bicycles, not only compared with what he had seen in his first visit to China thirty eight years before but even compared with what he had seen during his last visit seven years before.

Where this policy leads? Without any doubt it leads to the same negative results as in the Western so called "developed" countries. It means terrible traffic congestion, air pollution, waste of precious time and of material resources, more traffic accidents, all these aspects existing at present in the West but it seems that nobody cares about what is awaiting the society at the end of this irresponsible race. Isn't it a proof of lack of vision of those human beings responsible for this situation? Certainly it is. Could the implementation of the bicycle expressway system improve in a radical way the present situation and avoid the coming troubles? Certainly it could.

There is also an essential difference between the developed countries of America and Europe and the situation in China. Those countries were doing a kind of "pioneering" job in creating the present troublesome situation in urban transportation, it means nobody then knew exactly where they were going. Being greedy for more and more money and immediate profits and shortsighted about the future, the result was the uncontrolled expansion of cars as a main means of transportation with all the major negative effects attached. The future was not clear at all for the promoters of car production. In China of today the situation is completely different. The promoters of also uncontrolled growth of the number of private cars for urban transportation don't have to guess the future, it is just in front of their eyes, as the present situation in the above mentioned countries. So, they knew or they should know where they are going, but they don't care or are not able to simply learn from what is going on now in the countries where the car use is out of control. Those countries' present is the China's future. With a rational policy, all troubles coming in the future could be avoided and the bicycle expressway system concept which creates an additional and safe traffic capacity, is an important and integral part of the rational solution. Not paying due attention to this issue is not a good sign for the power of perspective thinking of those human beings in charge with the urban transportation development which is directly connected with the well-being of the city residents. And what the mass of these human beings does to fight this abuse? Just nothing as it happens in all other parts of the world.

In this disputed policy about cars and bicycles it should be very clear that nobody advocates for maintaining China in the position of a poor relative in the world family of nations who should have access only to the bicycles and contemplating how the Americans and the Europeans are entitled to use the car even for a trip around the corner. The correct approach is a balanced policy in accordance with the real possibilities and the best interest of all the members of the human society. To achieve this, the proper coordination for the rational use of both means of transportation, cars and bicycles, is a must in China and everywhere else. And in order to achieve this goal the use of the bicycle expressway system concept is essential.

This is the story of promotion of the concept in China. From there the engineer stopped for a few days in Seoul, the capital of South Korea, to discuss the chances of the promotion of the concept in South Korea with one of the top officials at the Canadian Embassy for whom he had a letter of recommendation and support from a leading member of the Canadian Federal Parliament.

The traffic congestion and other negative aspects of the urban transportation made the implementation of the concept very desirable and a problem solving solution. Unfortunately, the discussion at the embassy, although very amiable and frank, didn't lead to the hope for such a positive result. As in many other places, those in charge with the human society were not at the necessary level of vision and understanding for such a project. The unstable political and economic situation, the greediness for quick gains prevailed. But in spite of this, it was a useful additional experience to complete the general picture of how difficult is to move ahead a good idea when the final decision makers are the bad representatives of the human beings.

After this very interesting story about the engineer's trip to China and South Korea and the attempts to promote the concept there, a bicycle demanded the attention of the audience.

— I was very pleased to hear about the interest and willingness of our engineer to promote his concept in that remote for him but densely populated part of the world as South East Asia, and how he combined his tourist trips with the promotional activity for the countries like China, South Korea, Philippines, Japan, Singapore, Thailand, where the use of the concept would be very useful. I am from India, a country located in the same area and with a large population of almost one billion people, second only to China, where the bicycle use is also very extended and where the implementation of the concept in many of its large cities would be more than welcome.

I wish that our engineer had the opportunity to visit my country too and who knows, he could try to promote his so useful concept and at the same time to enjoy his trip as he did in other countries. I would kindly like to ask our Canadian sister who knows so much about our engineer's activities, if she could tell us something about this issue.

— I am very pleased to tell you, replied immediately the Canadian, that your wish has been already accomplished. Thank you for your invitation to talk about this. Yes, our engineer visited India many years ago and he has unforgettable great memories about his trip. He went there also with the intention to promote his concept.

I didn't talk about this until you asked me about it because the attempt didn't meet the expectations. What exceeded the expectations was the beauty together with the difficulties of the trip, the lessons learned about the life and nature of the human beings in conditions totally different of which the engineer was accustomed before. Also, it must be included in these lessons the involved risks which at least once, put his life in extreme danger. So, if you are interested in those events, I am glad to share the story with you.

— All of us are extremely interested in all that you can tell us, was the immediate answer of a choir of many bicycles including the Indian one.

— Well, in this case please be prepared to listen to a unique story that could exceed someone's imagination.

After this brief introduction, the Canadian bicycle started to tell what she knew about the trip.

— Everything happened a little less than a quarter of a century ago, just a few years after our engineer came to Canada. I don't know how, but he found out and got in touch with a group of students from the University of Ottawa preparing themselves for a hiking trip to the famous Himalayan Mountains in India.

The two organizers of the trip, if I am not mistaken, brothers, were before to India where their parents worked in a diplomatic mission, so they had some knowledge about the country. They were about twenty five years old and were the oldest from the student group. The only participants from outside the University group were our engineer and his brother, both about double the average age of the group, and a tourist guide from the northern part of Canada, who was sixty three old but in very good shape; to lift and carry his backpack would be a difficult task for anybody else. Our engineer and his brother, a mechanical engineer working in other city in Canada, who gladly agreed to participate in this trip, were also in good shape with a lengthy mountain hiking experience in the beautiful and not always easy to climb Carpatian Mountains in Romania, in Tatra Mountains in Czechoslovakia and Poland and also in the Rocky Mountains in western Canada.

Nobody from the group knew that and at the first get together the three "oldies" got the impression that there was some concern among the youngsters of the group, who knows, maybe thinking that at certain points these three may represent a problem for the rest of the group.

— They were very judgmental, as many youngsters are, commented immediately a bicycle.

— That's true, responded the Canadian, but to be fair, we have to consider that although nobody from the group except the two organizers had been to India, just the idea of a hiking trip in the Himalayan Mountains made them think that it will be a difficult enterprise and not a stroll in the park, and in this regard they were right and the entire trip confirmed this assumption.

What was not confirmed was their concerns about the three "oldies". As a matter of fact, by the contrary, the only ones who finished well the long and difficult trip without problems were these "oldies". More than that, after the end of the planned and organized trip, these three decided to continue the exploration in other extremely interesting areas of the northern part of India, about which we will talk later. All other members of the group had various kinds of problems, some abandoned the trip after the first few days, three ended up in hospital and few others cutting the trip short at the first opportunity of transportation to New Delhi.

— Very interesting, even amazing, commented other bicycle. I cannot wait to listen to the rest of your story.

— We too, joined this comment other bicycles.

— Well, continued the Canadian, encouraged by this vivid interest, just by-passing the non essential preliminary preparations, the group met at the Ottawa airport and after a long trip, arrived in the capital of India, New Delhi, which was also the capital of a totally new world for all the participants of this out of common trip.

The first few days the group stayed in a nice hotel western style, everybody having the opportunity to explore the city and the surroundings on their own. Our engineer and his brother went at all times together, joining sometimes other members of the group in discovering this entirely new world for them in architecture, people, habits, dressing, transportation, cultural life and other aspects.

After strolling on the nearby city streets, with many mansions, rich mosques and palaces with large gardens where the maharajah and the very rich lived, a good rest at the hotel was most welcome. The next day, the engineer, his brother and a few other members of the group decided to take a trip by bus to the famous Taj Mahal mosque in Agra. The day was very hot but the old crowded bus was even hotter having instead of air conditioning, a simple fan that didn't work. As the engineer remembered, the temperature was close to fifty degrees but seeing the magnificent and very expensive mosque was worth the trouble.

The impressive mosque was built centuries ago by a maharajah for his wife or for one of his wives, I don't remember exactly how the story goes, of course on the back of plenty of slaves who lived at the survival level, all the resources being wasted for building this clearly imposing mosque but also clearly useless for the people who built it.

This was the norm at that time in the past, the engineer was thinking, but now all the suffering connected with the construction of this remarkable mosque is just history.

The next day our engineer had the sad, the very sad occasion to see that what he was thinking of being just history is also the real miserable life of today, by visiting the other part of the city, the Old Delhi. He couldn't imagine such a bottomless poverty of mass proportion. No more palaces and elegant houses with large, well kept gardens like in New Delhi, just people sleeping on the street, their clothes being most probably all what they had, begging for food and not knowing what and if they will have what to eat tomorrow. What was even more terribly impressing were the many begging children surrounding him and his brother. Probably not many westerners, who for those poor mean a clear sign of richness, adventure themselves as pedestrians in that part of the city. Coming back to the elegant hotel and clean dining room, with those images in front of his eyes, he couldn't eat anything.

The next day being the last one before the departure to the mountains, the engineer contacted the municipal authority to discuss about the bicycle expressway concept which would be a real solution for the terrible traffic congestion on the streets. Nobody pertinent was available for such a discussion and he made arrangements for a meeting several weeks later, before his departure to Canada.

The long trip to the mountains started the following morning by bus from New Delhi to the village named Mussoorie at an altitude of seven thousand feet. The group stayed there for a week for adaptation to the altitude before hiking at much higher elevations. During this week several day hiking trips were undertaken in remote areas.

Everywhere the scenery of majestic mountains was overwhelming. The members of the group were told that they did not have to worry about the personal safety regarding the attacks by local people.

Although extremely poor, they were honest and peaceful and this was proven in several occasions. One of them was when being in a local market, our engineer bought at a stand a bottle of drink. The price was very low, he remembers that it was in local money like eighteen cents. He gave to the vendor, a young boy, a coin of twenty cents and went away with the drink not waiting for the change. Soon he realized that the boy was running after him insisting that he took his two cents change. This rarely would happen in other much richer places in the world.

According to the received categorical instructions, special attention should be paid at all times to the sanitary conditions. Never, ever to drink fresh, un-boiled water. It should be boiled not only a few minutes but for being in the safe side, not less than half an hour. Even if this precaution might seem somehow exaggerated, at least our engineer and his brother decided to observe strictly the advice. So, at the kind of hostel where the group was staying, the engineer asked the very friendly guys from the kitchen downstairs, to fill the pot with water and to boil it half an hour. It was obvious that they didn't understand why, these rules of hygiene didn't apply to them, their immune system was much better adjusted to the local conditions. Five minutes later the smiling boy brought upstairs the pot with water. The engineer gave him a good tip and sent him back to boil the water half an hour. Ten minutes later the story was repeated, encouraged by the generous tip, the boy brought again the pot with water. Then the engineer sent him back again telling him that he will come later downstairs to pick up the water. "Yes, Sir" was the gently reply of the boy and he returned to the kitchen. Half an hour later when the engineer went to the kitchen, it was suspicious to him that after so long time of boiling, the pot was still full of water. Later he found out that the boy, with the best intentions to serve well his good customer, kept pouring fresh water in the pot to compensate the evaporated one. Since then, any time the engineer ordered boiled water, he stayed in the kitchen to watch the operation.

The same strict rules were indicated for the food. For the entire duration of the trip nobody touched fresh fruits or vegetables, although very appealing slices of fresh water melon and other fruits were sold in the market.

The indication was also not to use the water from the small rivers during the hiking trips, not even for washing hands or dishes, unless one can be absolutely sure that there are no villages or even isolated houses upstream, because people were using the little streams for washing everything and so, contaminating the water flowing downstream. The lack of adequate immunity to the local conditions for people coming from far away and used to high level of hygiene was a powerful incentive for obeying the recommended rules.

In one of the next days of staying in Mussoorie, a hiking trip for one or two days was organized in a remote, isolated area. Our engineer and his brother decided to take the tent, food, boiled water and all that was necessary for the two days trip.

An open track transported the participants for about two hours to a point from which farther on, the only means of transportation was your own legs. The total self-sufficiency was the rule of the game because the area was almost un-inhabited and the few locals living there were completely isolated from the rest of the world. Surviving on a self-sufficient primitive economy and of course, not speaking English, most probably not even Indian but only a local dialect, were of no help in case of need.

After making sure about the time when the truck will come next day afternoon to pick them up, our engineer and his brother put their heavy backpacks on their back and started a trip to an unknown destination on the only narrow path going forward and up in the gorgeous mountains everywhere around.

This adventurous trip that lasted about seven hours was not only extremely interesting and tiring at the same time but also teaching them about certain aspects of life nowhere else to be learned in the civilized life from where these two explorers of the unknown came from.

Although that according to the received information the area was peaceful, a certain risk was involved for sure, the risk of unknown and of total isolation, the impossibility of whatsoever communication or help in case of emergency.

The cellular phone, a today's fact of everyday life, was not even a dream at that time, and even if it was a reality, it wouldn't be of any practical use in that remote area with nobody around. And again, if any locals were around they couldn't understand a word.

Can you imagine yourself leaving voluntarily the civilization, the comfort, the convenience and the good life behind and venturing only two of you in a difficult, unknown environment, being obligated to rely totally and solely on your strength and on your backpack which contained everything, your food, water, clothes and your temporary house, the tent? By the way, that tent which is more than a quarter of a century old is still strong and in perfect shape, has an undisputed place in the engineer's apartment, is still used and proved its usefulness and strength in any weather conditions, sunshine, heavy rain and strong wind, at more than nine thousand feet in the Rocky Mountains in Canada, at fifteen thousand feet in Andes in Peru, in South America, now in Himalayan Mountains in India and before, on the beaches of Jamaica and on the canoe trips in the remote provincial parks of the Ontario Province in Canada and it is ready for future use too.

— It is an amazing story that you tell us, our dear sister from Canada. It is really difficult to imagine what you asked us, to someone it may seem crazy, but it is not, it is an extremely valuable life experience enlarging your horizon and the power of understanding the world, to which very few dare to subscribe. I am very glad that our engineer did it.

— We all are at unison in thinking with our sister, added other bicycle.

— It is my pleasure to share with you what I know from our engineer's memories. It is a long story as you can see, not necessarily and not always connected with the promotion of his marvelous and unique concept and honestly, I am concerned and I am asking myself if I am not abusing your patience. Well, I can continue telling you about other interesting things in this trip but with the condition that if this is the case, you let me know to stop.

— My dear sister, please don't rely on that and don't build any hope on such a case. Pedal ahead with your story which is already ours too.

— Well, it is your wish and my pleasure, responded the Canadian, obviously flattered by this clear and undisputable interest of the audience in listening to her, and she continued:

— Well, the two brothers started their hike just by themselves with nobody around, hike that could be, who knows? without return, but they were too confident in their capabilities and experience and too overwhelmed by the beauty of the surrounding scenery, to think about such an alternative. After about two hours of hiking they reached a small flat area of cultivated land belonging to a very small community living in a few simple houses. The operation of plowing was being done with a primitive plow and one bull in a manner specific to many centuries or even thousands of years ago and with the hard work of the man behind the primitive plow. A powerful, comfortable and highly efficient tractor with an attached also highly productive plow? What a dream, from other world, or from other planet! The brothers stopped and looked with sadness at this picture, thinking at the same time proudly about the fact that at the same time in other parts of the same planet the great power of engineering created the technology which changed the face of the world, of the same production process, hoping and wishing that one day in the future, this amazing technology will arrive even at this remote point and will change for better the hard present life of these poor human beings. It is a very healthy hope and not an impossible dream.

After a short rest and with that hope in mind the two continued their ascent on the path no more than two meters wide, for about other five hours in the constantly changing but beautiful scenery. At some point they crossed a small narrow river with very clear, cool water. They stopped for a short while with the temptation to drink it but the wisdom of prevention convinced them to use the boiled not very pleasant but for sure safer water from their backpacks.

It started to become already late and both of them were getting tired. The idea of stopping and installing the tent became more and more attractive but the path remained constantly narrow, too narrow for putting the tent even if blocking the path for eventual but very unlikely other travelers. Because of this, the only solution, even with the risk of approaching night, was to continue to go ahead.

Eventually, after another about an hour, a platform appeared in the vicinity of a few primitive houses, wide enough to put the tent. Without wasting time the tent was installed and after a quick meal, a good, well deserved sleep in the sleeping bags followed just in time before the darkness of the night.

At about six o'clock in the morning with the dawn already there, they woke up with the intention to pack everything back and start the return trip, not to be late for the truck which should pick them up. Getting out of the tent, to their great surprise, an old man, a younger one and a couple of kids were at the edge of the path, looking with attention at the tent, probably for long time. They were totally silent, only watching carefully. One could bet for sure that they have never seen a tent before with people inside. When the two brothers dismantled quickly the tent which disappeared in the bag, their astonishment became obvious. With everything packed on their backs, our engineer and his brother were ready to go under the consternated looks of those few human beings from other historical epoch. Who knows what was in their minds? Maybe they were thinking that the two strangers landed there from the stars! Anyway, the occupants of the tent and the tent itself disappearing so quickly didn't look normal to the locals. Our engineer didn't know if that piece of land where they put the tent belong to them or not but as a sign of gratitude, he approached them and gave to the old man a few rupies, the Indian money, in banknotes. And here came the revelation, totally unexpected. Those people didn't know money. They were living in a time so remote when the money didn't exist yet. This was obvious by their behavior. The old man initially stood silent, not willing to take the bills. Eventually he took them very carefully, look at each of them, on one side and on other one, showed them to other local people who look at them with the same curiosity. In the same absolute silence, the old man tried to return the bills to the engineer but of course, he didn't take them back and making a sign of good bye, our engineer and his brother left the scene. After a short while, looking back, he saw one of them on the place where the tent was, looking down. Nobody knows exactly what was in those locals' heads but for sure the entire event was for them a mystery.

Our engineer and his brother realized that this hike was not only a trip on an unknown area but also a trip back in time, maybe thousands of years back in the dark past of the history of the human beings' society, in a primitive survival economy when money was not known yet.

The hike back, mostly descending was easier and with the precious feeling of returning to civilization, even to that far from modern one, as was the dwelling in Mussoorie and the old uncomfortable truck bringing them back there. Everything ended up well, the truck came on time and with understandable tiredness they arrived in good mood at the hostel.

Together with seeing the surrounding beauty of the nature on an immense scale and with the rewarding feeling of achievement, this trip gave to our engineer and to his brother plenty of food for thought regarding the tremendous development of technology which is by all means an undisputable merit of the avant-garde of the human beings but at the same time there is a very disputable progress regarding many other aspects of the behavior of the human beings and their achievements.

After their safe return from this two days hike they couldn't avoid the thought about what could have happened if instead of those very simple, curious and even intrigued people by the view of the tent and of the two strangers but very decent, peaceful and honest who refused to take money, belonging definitely to an undeveloped society, there were some bandits or robbers of our time of which there is no shortage in our modern so called civilized or developed society, using the products of modern technology like guns, to rob and kill their victims. In such a case, in the same conditions of the trip, hardly could be a possibility for our engineer and his brother to escape alive. So, the unavoidable question is what is the real definition of primitivism and civilization? Is it enough to have technology in order to be entitled civilized? Or should we make a much deeper, really profound and multilateral analysis when we attempt to name a society as "primitive" or "civilized"? Maybe one single word "primitive" or "civilized" is by far not enough to properly define the quality of the respective society.

After a week of staying in Mussoorie, the group minus a few who decide to return home, moved deeper and higher into the Himalayan mountains with a very old bus on roads which for sure would be immediately closed for traffic in America or Europe, for safety reasons.

It can be said without any exaggeration that the risks involved in hiking were by far less than the risks pertinent to the transportation by truck or bus. Most of the times the roads were very narrow, at the limit, between a vertical stony wall and an abysm on the other side. Holes and stones were a common thing on those winding roads.

Pavement and fences on the side of the abysm were totally strange and unknown notions in that area.

Sometimes, when traveling by bus, and it can be said that the name of bus was a great favor for those poor motorized creatures, and being seated on the side of the abysm, in many occasions looking through the window, you may have not the impression but the certitude that one wheel of the bus is slightly out of the road, over the abysm and that the bus didn't fall there just because the greatest part of its weight was still on the road. The proof that this was not just imagination born by the fear of the poor volunteer travelers, is that according to the local information, hardly a week passes without a bus or a truck full of passengers falling in the abysm on those mountain roads. This is a sad aspect of the gorgeous scenery everywhere you look.

Our engineer remembers that in certain occasions the group traveled in open trucks so crowded that besides being unsafe, it was not enough room to put the second foot on the floor. Everybody should stand keeping the balance with the hands on the neighbors' back or hands. This motorized transportation was so tiring that the following difficult hike was a welcome relaxation.

— I am wondering, said a bicycle intrigued by the harsh difficulties faced in that trip, if anyone of the members of the hiking group ever was thinking in those difficult moments, about how nice would be to be transferred right away by a miracle to a modern hotel with comfortable beds and looking at the mountains, not hiking on them, from the nice armchairs on the large terrace in front of your hotel room.

— And with a nice beach with warm, clean water on the other side of the hotel, completed without delay other bicycle.

— And with large, comfortable buses with reclining chairs for trips to the mountains on modern, paved smooth roads, jumped the third bicycle to make the dream even nicer.

— What a rich imagination and tempting alternatives! Responded to the hidden question the Canadian bicycle. You, my sisters, guessed well, it was in the mind of at least some of the members of the expedition to Himalayas. I remember our engineer talking about this, of course joking and not in a defeatist way.

— O.K., you said not in a defeatist way, intervened other bicycle, in this case I would like to know, assuming that the miracle presented by the other sister happened, and suddenly at a bell ring, who wanted should go back immediately to the reality of the hiking trip so nicely and truthfully described by you, how many would leave all the comfort behind and will return to the hiking trip?

— Very interesting and legitimate question, answered the Canadian. My response is that it is rather difficult to say exactly what would happen in those conditions, how many will decide to stay there and how many will return, but what is a certainty is that all the members of the hiking group had the possibility to make the choice for a comfortable, easy trip if they wanted and not for a difficult hiking trip. They chose this trip entirely on their own free will and paid for it. It is true that some of them left before or much before the end of the trip. Everybody could do the same but the great majority didn't. With all the difficulties, and I would say with the attached satisfaction, stayed up to the end of the trip and more than that, the three "oldies", our engineer, his brother and the sixty three years old tourist guide continued the trip for another three weeks after the official trip ended. It means that making good use of their will power, the satisfaction they have got from the trip with all its problems and difficulties was more valuable than the other alternative, as I mentioned before, the defeatist one.

— It is very true what our Canadian sister just said, this kind of trip is clearly more valuable health-wise and by the learned experience than a classical comfortable trip organized by the travel agencies.

— True, replied the Canadian, I remember the comment of our engineer about the difficulties encountered during the trip and the conditions sometimes similar with those for a military special commando unit. He said that such a trip that no travel agency would organize, is teaching a lot to all the participants about the real world in which we live, makes us more humble and to appreciate more the value of the good things that we have in life, the good modern conditions that we take for granted. Experiencing the hunger, the food will always taste better. Without that, the best buffet never has the same value. He said that for him at least, this trip had a great value and that it was a precious, unforgettable experience.

After this unexpected philosophical brake in her story, the Canadian continued:
— And now, after some theoretical aspects of the trip were clarified, let's go back to the hiking, if you don't want to remain in a nice hotel, she joked.
— No, all of us want to go back to your hiking trip, was the immediate answer of the audience.
— Well, the hike continued in good spirit in a beautiful, breathtaking landscape with the same difficulties that now became routine. But if you think that you already learned everything about the potential dangers, you are wrong, just wait.

In one of the following days during a trip by something called there bus, the unexpected happened without notice. Sometimes, or more often than that, the success and the very life depends on the good luck of the moment, the luck for us being the coincidence or lack of coincidence of totally independent events determined by their own causes.
If the bus was faster with just a couple of minutes, you would never hear about this trip because the bus with the entire group would have been finished at the bottom of the canyon immediately on the left side of the road. What happened? An avalanche of huge pieces of rock, stones and soil fell from the high right side of the narrow road and after brushing the road went down into the abysmal canyon. This was the cause of the noise heard a little before. Some of the rocks

and debris remained on the road making the continuation of traveling impossible. Fortunately, very fortunately, the dislocation of the rock producing the avalanche didn't happen a few minutes later or in the same fortunate way, the bus was not fast enough to coincide with the place and the time of the avalanche.

What to do now? Moving the bus back on the narrow road was extremely dangerous, staying there was also very risky because some dislocated rocks may form other avalanche.

Luckily, the very large boulders, because of their weight, couldn't stop on the road and continued falling into the canyon. The decision was taken to quickly clear the road with empty hands and improvised tools, to create a minimal path for the bus to pass.

After this clear survival and about one hour of hard work, the taken decision paid off and the trip by bus continued as nothing happened. After another few hours, tired but happy, the group arrived at the end of the road. From that point farther on, the only mode of transportation was your own legs.

A short rest followed and saying good bye to the driver who could find a place large enough for turning the bus for the return trip, the group started moving on the only existing pedestrian path, upwards. After three or four hours of hiking sometimes with steep slopes, the arrival at the place where the tents could be installed, was most welcome.

The good rest overnight was the reward for previous tough day when everybody could say that was born again. The program for the next day was the hiking up to the next stop, the first place where the group could sleep, at an altitude of about fifteen thousand feet or about five thousand meters. A hike of seven or eight hours on a path not wider than two meters in average, with all the staff carried on your back, was the price to be paid to reach the destination, a very small community with a small hot spring with blessed miraculous power according to local belief. For this reason, people came walking from remote areas to take a bath there. Those who couldn't walk and could afford to pay, were carried on somebody else's back or those higher in rank, on a platform carried on the shoulders of four people, one in each corner. If the somebody's back was the local taxi, the platform carried by four people was the local "Cadillac". Any time such a "Cadillac" passed up or down on the path at a speed surprisingly higher than the one of the group, the members of the group should squeeze against the vertical rocky wall to avoid the edge of the canyon on the other side of the path, at about two meters to the right when going uphill.

It seems that in that isolated and remote area the wheel was not discovered yet. Our engineer said to his friends that he couldn't notice one single simple vehicle with even one or two wheels which would make the carrying of goods or people much easier. Everything was carried on the top of the head or on the back. What a life!

In accordance with the received indications, because of the lack of adequate space and of the cold at night at that high altitude, the sleeping for the two nights must to be in a old house which most probably was not used for many years judging at least by the several centimeters of dust accumulated on the floor. In order to put the sleeping bags, an entire operation of floor cleaning and carrying the dust outside, was organized. I hope that none of you expected nice, soft, clean beds awaiting for the members of the hiking group, joked the Canadian bicycle.

— We got such a hard training by your story that we cannot expect anything easy, responded also joking a bicycle.

— In this case maybe you want that I stop here telling the story because this is not the end of the bad things, asked jokingly again the Canadian being sure about the answer to come.

— What? I really hope that you don't intend to leave us here at fifteen thousand feet, in middle of nowhere. Whatever will be, go ahead, was the verdict of the bicycle audience.

— Well, agreed, said smiling the Canadian, obviously pleased by the tremendous interest for her knowledge about the trip to India, learned from the many conversations of the engineer with his friends.

— I will finish first with the accommodation on the floor of that dormitory, continued the Canadian bicycle. The evening became really cold. In the large room, now full of sleeping bags, was a fire place and some pieces of dry wood could be found outside. To use the fire place to get some warmth was a welcome idea and several members of the group tried to start the fire but at no avail. The salvation came from our engineer's brother. He was skilled in camp fires and to everybody's amazement and satisfaction a good fire made the overnight rest very pleasant.

Next day was planned a hike to a higher and more remote area. Our engineer's brother didn't feel very well, a little bit tired and decided to stay "home" to rest for the day, so this time our engineer went without his company.

After a few hours of hiking in the same beautiful scenery the group reached a place with a magnificent view. After a short rest and picture taking time, the group should return to reach the camping place during the day light. Three members of the group decided to go to a point about one thousand feet higher, in a rush. The group waited for them but those three paid a high price for this extra effort in the rarefied air at about sixteen and a half thousand feet, they ended up in the first available hospital.

On the way back everything went well up to a point where a totally unexpected disaster could end up the trip and the life of our engineer. So happened that this time he was the last in line at a short distance of others. He could see them but couldn't be seen by them unless they would keep turning back frequently their heads what usually doesn't happen. A wrong step in an unnoticed wet place made him slip aside in an area with a steep slope with the edge of the canyon very close. As the entire area was muddy, he lost the balance and slipped down on his back in a hardly to explain way up to the very edge of the abysm where he stopped with a foot on a stone that happened to be there. Any other movement could make him slip father down, directly into the canyon.

His disappearance was not noticed until the group reached the camping place and his brother asked about him. Then everybody was panicking but this was of no help to him. He was laying down, in mud, with nobody around, getting dark and cold, with no hope for outside help whatsoever, at the end of the world, at about fifteen thousand feet in Himalayan Mountains. What to do? As he told later, he was afraid to make any move because of the imminent danger of slipping down in the canyon. One single wrong movement could mean the end of everything. Can you imagine his situation? How life can turn around in one second!

The consternation of all bicycles was obvious and so strong that the very fact that the engineer survived, demonstrated clearly by his later activities well known to everybody, was for the time being forgotten. So, one of the bicycles asked, what in fact was in the mind of all others:

— Tell us please immediately, what followed, what he did in this desperate, hopeless situation? We know for sure that he didn't pray because he doesn't believe in such foolishness, he is not a believer. Who could help him? It seems to me that he was in an impossible situation with the only clear end being the end of his life.

The desire to listen to what the Canadian will say couldn't be stronger. In a total silence she started to talk:

— I appreciate your concern for the well-being of our engineer. I appreciate also your clear understanding of the terrible situation in which he was, the fact that nobody was around to rely on, for him there was no God's help to count on simply because if God existed, the engineer wouldn't be put in such a situation, to start with. In those circumstances, as a sister said, without exit, still there was one to rely on, the only one.

— What? Who was he? Exploded with curiosity a choir of bicycles.

— He could rely only on himself, and he did it with the positive expected results, responded calmly the Canadian bicycle. And she continued:

— He sat there for a while, of course stressed by this situation but with the clear understanding of the choices he had. The almost obvious choice was to die peacefully. But that was not he to surrender before trying the other alternative. When you say "almost", it means a lot but not all, something, although very little, is left for something better. And here came to help his engineering analytic spirit. It was a difficult problem, tremendously difficult, to get out from that trap alive. And if there is a problem, look for a possible solution! He understood that he was left with a small and going down reserve of precious time and of his own strength. The coming darkness was other, very dangerous enemy. He realized that if he falls into panic, that will be the end of any hope, then, he cooled down and started looking around, analyzing the gloomy situation. So he noticed a remotely, very remotely but potential friend. This was a branch of a tree hanging over him, that he could touch if he was standing but not from his present position. He decided to try the only solution with a chance of success: to carefully and slowly change the position of his body, concentrate in one supreme effort all his strength and jump to catch the branch and keeping it strongly to move along slowly to the nearby solid ground and from there a few meters farther, back to the path.

He was at the same time the commander in chief and the army, all in one. This was the only chance he had. He took it, gave the order as a commander and implemented it as his army. The expected success became in a few seconds the reality.

To find solutions to problems was not a novelty for him but never in his entire life he had to find a solution for such a difficult problem, a "To be or not to be" solution.

To make such a long story short, he reached the path, dirty, tired but happy and started his hike to the camping site, using his sense of orientation in the semidarkness and being careful at each step.

When he reached the camping ground, the old, dirty and far from comfortable, it seemed to him like a five star hotel. Everybody was glad for this happy end and after a good rest, next day the hiking continued.

After several days the group reached again the base from where the trip started, at Mussoorie and after another three days of resting and local hikes the group prepared for the return to New Delhi and from there to Canada. The group, but minus the three "oldies" who decided to continue the trip on their own, in other areas, towards the north, this time with little hiking but lots of visiting in extremely interesting and difficult to reach places in Kashmir and Indian Tibet called Laddak. If you are interested in this part of the story also, please let me know.

A sight of relief by all the bicycles was the response for the happy end of the almost tragic adventure of the engineer, and the continuation of the story by the Canadian bicycle was not only accepted with greatest desire but almost imposed. So, after a short brake, the Canadian continued to relate the following events of the trip, this time for the small group of three and eventually only for our engineer and his brother.

— This part of the trip without a planned dead line started with a rented very old car and a nice young driver. Traveling generally toward the north, the three "oldies" who should be called rather the "youngsters" of the hiking group, tireless and always hungry for discovering all the details of this such a new world for them, were rewarded constantly with plenty of spectacular scenery of all kind of geographic definitions, from cultivated plains in terraces for the maximal use of the available land, to fields and beautiful lakes backed by majestic mountains of the Himalayas. Also, the local habits of the ancient population, many times very strange for people coming from the western world, were not less interesting aspects of this unforgettable trip. Just a few examples if you wish, will make this description more eloquent.

— If you wish, you said? What an unreasonable doubt! We are burning of desire to listen to every single word you, our dear sister from Canada, are willing to tell us, and more is better. Go ahead please, we are listening with undivided attention.

— Well, responded the more than flattered and pleased Canadian bicycle, then listen to this.

You know what means traffic congestion in the streets of most of the cities in so many countries and how strict are the rules against those who willingly create such a congestion, let's say if a driver decides to turn his car across the street and stops there indefinitely. What will happen in such a case? The mass of other travelers will react immediately, possibly in a rude manner and the police will be there in no time to remove the car and punish the culprit, as for sure that driver will be considered. What is true, I have never seen or heard about such a scene, but imagine now that instead of a car creating this traffic mess, the culprit is a cow. In the same cities, the cow will be not fined but removed as soon as possible. Everywhere else but not in India, or at least in that part where our travelers have been. In such a case, and there are many, the cow, which is considered holly, has the full rights to sit down in the middle of the street for how long she desires without anybody protesting but stopping or moving around when possible. Nobody will dare to touch or disturb the cow in any way. Not only that, once our engineer and his brother met a cow, you know where? in a shop. In that hot climate there are many shops displaying the merchandise outside too and the doors are widely open. The cow decided to enter, looked around and when was bored enough, slowly moved out of the shop without buying anything. Nobody dared to touch or to push her out of the shop or to stop her entering. It would be considered a great sin. This is a local reality.

Other case. To eat beef meat is considered there a terrible sin. Not knowing this, once in a restaurant our engineer ordered among other things, a beefsteak. He remembered the face of the waiter taking the order, he got frozen in horror, as in a restaurant in New York for instance, somebody would order a stake of human leg. Realizing the innocence of his foreign clients, after a brief but categorical explanation, the order was changed for chicken meat.

Talking about restaurants and eating habits, in other place, the engineer noticed a sink with running water in a visible place in the dinning room. What for there? For the convenience of the clients to wash their hands before and after using them to eat the food without cutlery. Many times as our travelers have seen, the food is brought on a big plate and put in the middle of the table, other times on the floor, and the customers take the prepared rice and other items with their hands and put in their mouth. When the ordered food was brought at their table, the engineer should make a special request for the cutlery, to the surprise of the waiter.
We have to understand that what is strange for us is normal for them, the locals, and opposite. Telling to an audience of locals that you have seen people eating without using forks and spoons, just with their hands, will not surprise anybody because they consider that normal, and trying to make them wonder about that would be a waste of time. The same will happen if one tries to surprise some westerners telling them about people eating by using cutlery. Again, it will be a waste of time.
How different is our world! Everything is relative. The absolute truth is that two plus two is four, but I wouldn't be very surprised if somebody will contest even this!

From all, many specific aspects of life in cities and countryside, the predominant one is the terrible poverty. The overall look is depressing. Miserable ghettos and people sleeping on the street carrying all that they have, it means the clothes they wear, is a common picture. Begging is not only a well spread and accepted habit but an entire industry. Many may think that giving a few cents to a beggar buys their peace of mind and an entrance ticket to heaven. For this reason, in frequently visited places as mosques or close to the shores of Gange river which is a place of ritual bathing by millions of believers, and at the same time a most probable way to catch an infectious disease, there are herds of beggars, some of them running after and bothering the visitors, other, more organized, beg sitting down on the ground in long lines along the visitors' track. The entrepreneurs didn't miss this business opportunity and were selling small change coins piled up in small pyramids on the ground, of two or three feet high. In this local "banks" you can change your big money banknotes, and the equivalent of even one or few American dollars is big money there, but not by counting the change given to you but by selling a cup or two or how many you want, of change, like buying rice in the market; the vendor takes your money and pours in your purse or bag the equivalent amount of change taken from the pyramid. After that, you are well equipped to be a goodie-goodie to many beggars making them happy or at lest content for the moment at a minimal cost to you. Practical, not? Very. In this way a big social problem, the survival of those human beings, at least from one day to other one, is solved rapidly and at a cost of few cents.

Of course, there is also other alternative, to destroy the very necessity of begging, to organize and put these millions of people living in abject, hopeless poverty, to work efficiently using the existing all powerful technology, to build factories, houses, schools for children presently begging on the street and most important of all, building in this way their human dignity and eventually transforming these disastrous parts of India in something like, let's say, Switzerland. An impossible dream? Yes, today it is obviously a dream but theoretically and technically not at all impossible.

The cause, of the present poverty? They are several. The first, definitely, is the present social organization of the same human beings, this time from India, and connected with this, the very low productivity, the terrible, pitiless exploitation, the uncontrolled growth of population in total disregard to the existing economic resources and the all powerful influence of religion blinding people's capacity of thinking and pushing the human beings divided in various religious sects to fight and kill each other instead of concentrating their efforts for building together a new, happy life.

— It is amazing how many things you know, thank you so much for sharing them with us, said an enthusiastic bicycle using a brief pause made by the Canadian.

— I am only telling them to you, and what is very important, I know them directly from the source, our engineer went through all this personally, was the eyewitness and a participant to many of these actions. I understand that there is a lot to listen to and to think about and if you, my sisters, are tired, I can make a break and we can talk about something else.

— You may get tired talking, we will never get tired listening. Please go ahead and tell us everything that you remember. By the way, I would like to know about the life of our sisters there and how is the transportation in general.

— Well, once I got your acceptance, I am glad to continue talking about our engineer's trip in India.

Coming to transportation, there is not too much good to say. You know already about the dangerous conditions of motorized transportation in the mountains. Nothing to be envious about. The urban transportation is a mixture of everything, mostly old cars and buses, trucks, rickshaws, some of them motorized, other ones pedaled by poor skinny human beings, many bicycles mostly old with one speed only, very many carrying heavy loads, in almost always congested traffic and in permanent danger. There is not a good life for our sisters there. This is why our engineer decided to try to promote his idea in the capital city, New Delhi. I know that all of you are very curious to find out about this aspect of his trip but I will talk about this at the end of the trip in India, at the return to New Delhi.

Now I would like to tell you briefly about the accommodation for sleeping during the continuation of the trip. In New Delhi and in other big cities there are of course, nice, elegant hotels at a high price but in the country side most hotels are very modest or less than that. So, in one place the hotel was just a number of beds under a canvas roof, without walls and everybody from the street could see you in bed. Our three travelers were accustomed to sleep in any conditions but once they stopped at a place called "Hotel International". When they have seen the available room, so dirty and bad smelling, they chose to sleep outside on the grass in their sleeping bags. Only next day in the morning they found out with horror that the grass is visited by snakes, so that option was cut off for ever; at least in the closed tent you have some protection, but sleeping out in the sleeping bag and you wake up with a snake that squeezed in, even if doesn't bite, a heart attack is a high probability.

In a couple of days of traveling by the rented car they arrived in the beautiful Kashmir. The small group of three stopped in the old city of Srinagar. Nearby was the very nice Dan lake surrounded by high, spectacular mountains. They chose to stay at a floating hotel and restaurant named for unknown reason "The Queen of Africa". During the stay there they had some nice trips by rowing boat on the lake, being approached many times by other small boats offering to sell all kind of fruits, food and souvenirs. In Srinagar looking to buy a souvenir they had the opportunity to visit the place where they were produced by talented artists, some of them very old. What was shocking were the miserable conditions of working and the extremely low pay for the artists; for what they were paid just a few dollars was sold for hundreds of dollars in America. The exploitation of those very talented but very poor local artists was pushed to the limit by their bosses, the owners of the business.

Next move from Kashmir was not towards home but to Laddak, the Indian Tibet. To reach there they had to cross the Himalayan Mountains on the only road, at an altitude of fourteen thousand feet, it seems the highest in the world. Unfortunately, at the beginning of this trip the rented car broke down and they continued the two days trip with an open truck luckily passing by and willing to take them. This trip was breathtaking. The Himalayan Mountains appeared in all their majestic splendor. The weather was cooperating so, everything was just to enjoy regardless to the lack of comfort in the truck. After an overnight stay at a modest hotel high in the mountains and another day of traveling, the three explorers arrived in Leh, the main city of the region, at the altitude of about thirteen thousand feet. The air was rarefied and climbing even a few steps was not an easy task. There again was a different world to be experienced. The Tibetans are quite different in looks and culture from the Indians in Kashmir, only the poverty seemed to be the same. The sunny days and the very clean air had a very nice contribution in the taken pictures. They stayed there at a modest house renting a room, small but clean, at a derisory price of three dollars per night. The price was derisory for the Canadians, less even than the tip at home, but it was considered expensive by some youngsters from Europe who paid only one and a half dollars per night, true with less comfort, and very expensive for the locals if to consider what was found out later, that the local average salary for a worker was the equivalent of only thirty cents per day. Again everything is relative.

While there, our engineer and his two companions visited a very old abandoned palace and just enjoyed for a couple of days the peaceful environment and the nice scenery. A few years before the access of foreigners was forbidden in Laddak.

The trip, with all its difficulties and beautiful sides, was coming to an end. After saying good bye to their companion and a two hours flight by a small plane from Leh, our engineer and his brother arrived in New Delhi.

The intention was to stay there a few days for the discussions with the local authorities for the promotion of the bicycle expressway system concept. The clerks representing the authority were so remote from understanding the concept and its advantages for the city transportation, that the engineer understood that there is no hope to achieve the expected result and this first meeting was the last one.

After seeing the city for the second time and visiting the main places of interest, the engineer and his brother didn't feel like staying longer in New Delhi and decided to live the country one day earlier than initially planed, taking advantage of the available two seats with Al Italia. Instead of returning directly home, they decided to stay for a good rest in the beautiful island of Capri in Italy. They didn't know how lucky they were by making this decision to leave one day earlier until they reached the airport in Rome one week later, for the flight home, as you will find out later.

During the long flight to Italy our engineer and his brother shared with delight the many and so interesting memories of this unforgettable adventure in India.

After a day spent in Rome visiting the main attractions of the city they took the train to Naples or Napoli in Italian. Looking out of the window, this trip by train was a reward in itself but the greater reward was to follow. After a short visit in the very congested city of Naples, one and a half hour trip by ferry to Capri island was another delight.

Capri, independently of other circumstances, can be named a paradise island. This is much more so when you stay there for an entire week, after the long and strenuous adventure in the Himalayan Mountains of which all of you are already aware about.

The island, with a high hill in the middle, is beautiful. The views from everywhere but especially from the top of the hill are superb, relaxing and enjoyable. The surrounding clean and refreshing water is inviting for a swim or for a trip by small rowing boat among the large rocks of peculiar shape close to the shore and for a guided trip by boat in the nearby cave.

Can you imagine how nice it was to wake up as late as you wish in a clean comfortable bed instead of waking up early in the morning in a tent after a tiring previous day and getting ready for the same task this day, deep in the Himalayan Mountains carrying a heavy backpack? And admiring the scenery from your hotel room terrace and going nowhere if you don't want to? Or the enjoyment of eating an ice cream or fruits bought on the street or in a cafeteria without thinking about sanitary restrictions? Can you imagine the pleasure of traveling to the top of the hill in a comfortable bus if you want to, instead of no other choice than hiking there? Or the enjoyment of eating a tasty, well done beefsteak without scaring the waiter by making such an order? Do you really appreciate the life with plenty of technology around you, at every step and for any need?
Who could answer better to all these questions than those few who accomplished that hiking trip in Himalayas or something similar? Everybody or most of the people take everything good for granted and very few are wise enough to make themselves happier, at least once in a while, by making the comparison with the life without all these goods around what is unfortunately, the reality for hundreds of millions of people in this world.

After three days of full and well deserved relaxation, our engineer was thinking about not missing the opportunity of being in Italy without making an attempt at least to check the market for the promotion of his concept for the bicycle expressways. So, next day early in the morning, leaving his brother to continue the relaxation in Capri, he took the ferry to Naples, the train to Rome and the bus to the city municipal authority and without having an appointment, succeeded to have a discussion about this issue with the pertinent official. Of course, our engineer didn't expect a miracle to come back with a signed contract or a firm commitment, he wanted just to take the pulse of the market and of the reaction of the municipal authority in Rome to such a proposal. Being realistic, he just wanted to inform the authority about the existence of such a concept and to get the reaction to it. The discussion was vivid, interesting and surprising for the interlocutor official who fortunately could speak English, with a pleasant Italian accent. He was also surprised and pleased to know that our engineer is in fact a cousin to him by mother tongue, the Italian and Romanian being very closely related to the same Latin background with many identical words. A door was left open for future possible contacts concerning the proposed concept.

On his way back to Capri our engineer learned something specific for urban transportation in Rome and Naples. The traffic congestion was similar with the one on the streets in North America. What was bigger was the noise because the very many mopeds which extremely rarely can be seen on the roads in America. What was smaller, much smaller, was the size of the cars. The big cars were very rarely seen, the great majority were small and very small cars, because of the many narrow streets, the parking problem and the much higher cost of gasoline. The bicycles were also present on the streets but only as a tiny minority, obviously because the inconvenience and the danger in the streets for cycling. The bicycles could reach a much more significant role in the urban transportation only with the implementation of the bicycle expressways concept.

After another couple of days of full enjoyment in Capri, the following day was the traveling one, back to Naples by ferry and by train to

Rome. At the airport the two brothers had a big surprise, they met a member of the hiking group who told them the sad news that something very wrong happened with the return flight for the group and that they had a very tough time for a long period in New Delhi before they could fly back much later. Even the flight from which our engineer and his brother changed the trip for a day earlier was cancelled with big difficulties to find seats for several days, I don't know the exact details. Yes, life is sometimes like that, a good inspiration has more value than any planning or reason.

In the same day our engineer and his brother arrived safely in Toronto, Canada and this was the end of the trip and it is the end of my story, concluded the Canadian bicycle followed by the many thanks and nice comments by other bicycles.

CONCLUSION ABOUT THE THREE BICYCLE REUNIONS.

This third bicycle reunion so rich in discussions about many subjects, with very interesting and original questions and with very clear and honest answers, was the necessary and precise continuation of the first and second reunions, few years before.

The exchange of opinions and experiences between many bicycles from all parts of the world, led to essential conclusions to understand the behavior and the capacity of reasoning of the human beings, of which depends everything what happens in this world. Some of these conclusions are unexpected and unacceptable or directly offensive for many human beings, but these conclusions are the result of a long time observation, from outside of the human beings species, and are totally objective.

The bicycles participating in the discussion, as the entire audience of bicycles in the reunion and as any bicycle in the world, don't have any fear of political or economic repercussion from other bicycle, as the human beings behave between themselves, also they feel totally free to express their opinions about all the aspects of the human beings society. Not always all of them have the same opinions about the discussed issue but their iron law is the logic, the reason, the most objective argument and the conclusion will be accepted by all with much pleasure, friendship and without pride or resentment. For them the religion, superstitions and the primitivism in thinking of any kind, don't exist. They are not the prisoners of the obscure mentality of the stone age as can be observed so frequently in the society and the actions of the human beings. The bicycles with less life experience learn from the bicycles with more experience and are not ashamed to ask about each detail until everything is very clear.

We, the bicycles, have a very sharp and silent feeling of observation, and as we depend so much of the human beings, with our daily observation we know more about them than they themselves. The great majority of the problems that they have, and the most important of them, don't have natural causes but are created by the human beings themselves. And if these problems persist or become worse, this is also because of them themselves, as it was well demonstrated in our discussions. We can say without exaggeration that we can see with all the clarity the solutions for their problems. They are not capable of this and don't have the decision power in their society. We know that there is a very intelligent minority, which has all the merits for the technological progress and valuable ideas but that this minority doesn't have any power to control what happens in the society, and this is very sad.

After this very relevant monologue, a bicycle asked:
— Due to the discussions here, now all of us are well informed about the incessant efforts and the patience of our engineer to promote his concept that is of vital importance for us, the bicycles, and of very great use for the urban transportation of the human beings. Unfortunately, all these efforts remained without practical results. Can our Canadian sister tell us what thinks now our engineer about this situation, has he other plans for the future or everything is finished for this marvelous concept?

— Thanks for such an essential and reasonable question. I will answer now.

I would like to tell you from the beginning that this intense promotional activity during a quarter of century is not finished or stopped. In spite of the lack of the expected results at the beginning of this activity, our engineer is very determined to continue the fight any time and in any place where makes sense to give a try.

There is a tremendous difference between the engineer who started the promotion of his idea two years after his arrival in Canada, a world very different for him, when being a little naïve about the sincerity, honesty and integrity of the politicians and people of the big business, he was thinking that if one has a good idea and can demonstrate it, its implementation will be very easy, and the same engineer of today, twenty five years later. Our engineer and good friend of ours, accumulated during these years a valuable experience in countries of the first, second and third world as project manager, consulting engineer in his basic profession, water resources engineering and at the same time international promoter and president of the company "Bicycle Expressway Systems". In this period of time he had direct contacts for the promotion of the concept with hundreds of personalities and pertinent officials, up to the level of prime minister, including directors and presidents of private companies, bankers, ministers, chiefs of department, journalists, directors of national television and radio channels, members of parliament, politicians at municipal level and others.

The continuous promotion was not an activity or a fight in vain, but a fight on many fronts, well organized and with real possibilities of final success. A great number of encouraging official letters from prominent persons with high-level of responsibility is available also today to demonstrate the seriousness of the promotional action. Moreover, his participation with presentations of the concept at International Conferences in various countries, added much to his experience and at the same time this was another proof of the acceptance of the concept.

— Without any doubt, intervened a bicycle, if the idea didn't have a real value, nobody or very few of those who supported the concept would waste their time and prestige in supporting it.

— This is true but our engineer learned that with all this success in publicity and acceptance in principle, in reality there is many times a great difference between the words and the action even if the words are very nice. He learned also that there is a great distance between the public interest and the material interest of private companies and governmental agencies. All want an immediate profit or in short time with a minimal risk, and an innovative project which wasn't built before nowhere in the world, always in their opinion represents a risk, regardless to what proofs exist for the opposite. The health, the well-being and other advantages for the population have for them secondary importance or none.

The project for a Bicycle Expressways System is in principle and from the beginning a large project, which requires a substantial investment, in spite that the cost per kilometer is very low. For the system to be efficient, it cannot be short, this is as a subway line or a highway for cars. This was a major difficulty for the promotion. But to be very clear, this difficulty is not pertinent to the concept, is pertinent to the human beings, who should make the decision. They didn't have the vision of the great final efficiency of the concept with many other advantages.

— Is the same stupidity of the human beings of which we talked before, intervened a bicycle.

— Correct, but the basic philosophy of our engineer was the perseverance. It is true, he says after his extensive experience in promotion, that the great majority of persons is very limited in thinking, but one can never tell where hides a visionary who can save the situation, and always makes sense to look for him. And he continues doing so.

— I listened one day what our engineer said talking about an inscription that he had seen in an office, which said: "The one who tries to do something good and doesn't succeed, is in a better position than one who tries to do nothing and succeeds in this". And the opinion of the engineer is that this is true because in this way you are prepared for an opportunity with a successful end.

— We must hope that one day the human beings become more intelligent, says a bicycle.

— I am afraid that this is a hope that will not be fulfilled, commented other bicycle.

— I think that the construction of the first system of expressways for us, doesn't matter where in the world, will be a convincing proof of collective intelligence of those human beings with the capacity to expand this very precious quality to other human beings.

— This is so, but if this achievement depends on the improvement of the human beings intelligence, I am afraid that they will move in opposite direction.

— What makes you think in this way? asked her neighbour.

— What makes me think in this way? repeated the question the first speaker. The fall of the Soviet Union.

— The fall of what?

— Of the Soviet Union, the country which was the largest in the world and where everything was changed.

— I don't understand, what is the connection between the fall of the Soviet Union and the successful promotion of the concept for bicycle expressways.

— Must be a joke, tell it to us, please, gave her opinion other bicycle.

— It is not a joke, let me explain and after that you can express your opinion.

— Agreed, said in a choir some bicycles.

— Well, I am from Russia, which before was the major part of the Soviet Union, a country very rich in natural resources, with an area of twenty two million square kilometers, larger than Canada or the United States, the largest in the world. With its three hundred million inhabitants, its military power, including nuclear arms, equal or bigger than that of the United States and with its very developed industrial base, nobody from the exterior could touch the security of the country without the deadly risk of a world war.

— Still I can't see the connection of this with the bicycle expressways promotion.

— Neither do I, said other bicycle.

The Russian bicycle continued her story without being disturbed by these two last comments.

— This country had a social organization called "socialism" which means a society without rich, nobody could be a millionaire but also without poor as in many other parts of the world, everybody had a job, housing at a very low cost, school, university and medical services for free, no drugs, no illiteracy, no organized crime or terrorism, no people sleeping in the street. This is not to say that they didn't have problems, they had many, due to the mistakes of the leaders and to the same far from perfection human nature of the mass of the human beings, but in general the basic needs for a civilized life with high cultural level were assured. This was possible due to a generation of idealists and to the unimaginable efforts of the entire population during the revolution of 1917 and the following period of intensive construction. Less than a quarter of a century after the revolution, the enemies of the socialist state tried to destroy it during the Second World War, but without success. After a four year terrible war, the Soviet Union became more powerful than before and the same enemies spent thousands of billions of dollars in the new nuclear armament, all with the perspective to destroy the Soviet Union, but were afraid to take action in this direction, the military power of the Soviet Union was very strong. And suddenly, about half a century later, happened something totally incredible and unexpected. Without a single bullet fired by its enemies, the much powerful Soviet Union disintegrated from the interior. All that was gained during three quarters of a century was lost in several months. Practically was no resistance to this change, everybody conformed to the orders of the chief, replaced the state economy with the private economy, changed the national flag with the old emperor's flag. All, or the great majority expected that with this change in very short time they will become millionaires. A population of three hundred million including millions of party members, military, members of the security forces, who should be the first defenders of the system, followed the orders without protesting, as a heard of cows or goats.

— How this was possible, asked with amazement a bicycle.

— This was the question, which was repeated millions of times in those days.

— But this was nothing else than a mass stupidity, as if the entire nation was under drugs.

— This is to say that the stupidity of the human beings doesn't have limits.

But this is not all, said the Russian bicycle.

— What more? asked with curiosity other bicycle.

— What more? a misery of national proportions followed almost immediately. Billions of dollars were robbed and transferred out of the country by the new rich, who were the thieves in high positions. Under the new rulers, to facilitate this change, the revival of religion in the previously atheist state was orchestrated, priests appeared as mushrooms after the rain, an invasion of bibles and religious propagandists of all kind from abroad, like locusts, started simultaneously. Some justified this situation with the hope that in very short time, about one year, the private economy will develop with giant steps and that the imagined American rich life style will come for everybody. Now, fifteen years later everything is worse without any hope to get out from this situation of third world country with a class of few very rich. And nobody protests, don't do anything to change the situation, are complacent with this state of things, without dignity and reason as a mass of drunken without personality and will.

— This is again a proof of collective stupidity of national dimensions.

— Exactly this is what I want to say, responded the Russian bicycle, if the human beings were rational beings, they would have used their intelligence to solve all the problems inside their system. Instead of this they destroyed the system expecting a miracle. This is like one who has a large and good house but which requires some repairs, instead of making these repairs, puts the house on fire and destroys it, hoping that the neighbour will build for him a new house. And as nobody did it, he sleeps now outside dreaming about something that will never happen. And this happened not only with the three hundred million human beings of the Soviet Union but also with other hundred million in other countries of Eastern Europe which before were socialist, short time after the fall of the Soviet Union. This was an action that cannot be explained by a rational mind but only by the immense stupidity of these human beings in doesn't matter what social, political and economic system they have. And now, after this very long but necessary introduction or explanation, I come to my initial point, the connection between the fall of the Soviet Union and the hope of the improvement of the human beings up to the necessary level to promote and implement the visionary concept proposed by our engineer. My profound pessimism about such a change resides in this basic question: do you think that the same ones who proved their stupidity or idiocy in mass, in life essential issues, will act in a very intelligent manner to implement an important objective but minor if compared with what they had destroyed? I don't believe it.

I much respect our engineer for his continuous efforts for the promotion of the concept, but I am afraid that the enemy with which he fights, the stupidity and the indifference of the human beings, is too strong. I wish him all the well deserved success in his fight, but I remain very pessimistic about the expected success in this direction.

The words of the Russian bicycle produced a wave of shock in all the audience of bicycles by the pessimism that seemed very well justified by the events, which made history in the last years in a large part of the world. The connection between the promotion of the concept for the bicycle expressways and the disintegration of the Soviet Union which initially was considered a joke or an affirmation without sense, after the explanation given by the Russian bicycle was very well understood and accepted as a reality of life and a good reason for the pessimism about the future success of the promotion of the concept.

— Our Russian sister has much reason for her so sad opinion. Before I didn't think about this, only in the political aspect, which is of little interest for us. In reality there is much more than politics. It is true that the base for a political action is the intelligence or the stupidity.

— I can confirm that all what our Russian sister said is the pure truth, my cyclist is from Poland and he knows very well the present situation there and in other countries which belonged before to the socialist camp. The stupidity of human beings causing the terrible situation of today is incredible and this stupidity can directly or indirectly affect the future plans for us.

Other bicycle intervened in the discussion with a question:

— I am not religious, but I want to ask something.
— Don't tell me that you are not religious, interrupted her immediately a neighbour bicycle. Only a bicycle with square wheels could be religious and you don't have them. Continue with your question please.
Before that the first could continue, a wave of laughter followed the idea of believer bicycles with square wheels.
— I would like to know, if a God existed how would He solve all those problems of the human beings?
The response followed without delay.

— If a God existed, wouldn't be anything to solve, everything would be perfect from the beginning, but obviously such a divinity doesn't exist.

We talked so much about many and various negative aspects of the human beings society in spite of the tremendous development of the technology, situation that is in itself a huge contradiction which makes very difficult to appreciate in one word the present state of this society. We, the bicycles and the few intelligent human beings, understand very well the existing situation and have the solutions to cut and eliminate the immense discrepancy between the reality of today and the potential alternative which is not only reasonable but also a solution for a society with a dignified and happy life for all its members. Unfortunately, with the exceptions mentioned before, the entire today's society of the human beings, those who provoke the bad things to happen and the victim of these bad things, are not aware of the possibilities to improve their life, and more than this, the existing situation seems to them normal, without a way and for many of them even without the need to change it. And when the suffering is too great or when they want to improve or to get something, all what they do is to pray to their Gods, and when they don't get anything and the suffering continues without any logical explanation, they say that this is the will of these Gods and this is the top of their thinking.

Comparing our vision with the vision of this great majority, if not the almost totality of them, we can say that we belong to two completely different worlds but living together. A very similar situation was described as cannot be done better, in the famous book of the not less famous American writer of a century ago, Mark Twain entitled "A Yankee at the King Arthur's Court". The tale of this book is about a human being of the contemporary American society who by a miraculous process waked up in the time of Middle Age, five centuries before, at the King Arthur's court in England. Coming with the knowledge of the twentieth century, he tried to introduce it in the society of that time for its benefit, explaining to everybody the possibilities and the advantages of those changes. Nobody could understand them and the results of his tentative to change the society with an improvement obvious to him, were disastrous. For those changes to occur, it was necessary to wait five centuries. Not less than this. Who knows how many centuries, or maybe millenniums, is necessary to wait for the present society of the human beings to transform and reach the level of our vision!

— Thank you for your very nice story and wise comment, said another bicycle. I would like to make an observation that is at the same time a question to all of you. During all our three reunions with passionate discussions and debates, together with the unequivocal recognition of the great merits and contributions by the tiny minority of intelligent and visionary human beings, we presented the great majority of the human beings as belonging to an inferior species, named them repeatedly, so many times, stupid and idiots in all the activities of their society, using many times very unfavorable for them comparison with the animal species. My position in this regard is straightforward supporting these affirmations as reflecting the sad reality and I think that all bicycles share this opinion, but I am wondering what would be the perception of the human beings if they were aware and could listen to our discussions. I am wondering if even an independent observer wouldn't be annoyed by the frequent repetition of the degrading and unpleasant words as stupid, inferior or idiots, used by the bicycles participating in these discussions. What do you think?

— You touched a very sensitive and at the same time very important subject. What you are saying is true. It is not pleasant to hear these words by those who are the targets and it is not pleasant either for those bicycles that expressed them, but a basic clarification is necessary in order to avoid a dangerous confusion.

— Confusion about what?

— Confusion about the value of being polite at the price of hiding the truth. Confusion about the real meaning and purpose of the used language by the bicycles expressing their opinions. Confusion about the rightness to treat the criticized human beings with silk gloves.

— It seems like a very interesting approach. Please go ahead, we are listening.

— Being polite just for the sake of being polite, for sure will be nice for the offenders but very frustrating and unjust for the offended ones. Why should we do this? For what reason? It is understandable that in some cases, when the offence is accidental, against the will of the offender, masking the reality with a polite cover can be justified. This should be clear, but when the offender is doing his bad things purposely, openly and repeatedly, this approach is not justified anymore even if the use of negative adjectives becomes a nuisance for the so-called outside observers.

— But let's define first what is an outside or independent observer.

— Right. Good point. An outside or independent observer who could be also a valuable judge for the entire issue, can be of three kinds, namely:

— the first kind is one who likes the polite approach by all means and is not able to see the real situation and why the bad words are used.

— the second kind is one who understands the reasons for using the bad words but in spite of this, prefers to put the garbage under the rug, just to have a nice and peaceful appearance even if the bad things are not solved and sooner or later the garbage from under the rug will start to stink.

— the third kind is one who understands all the evils of the situation and the unpleasant atmosphere created by telling the open truth but doesn't see any reason for hiding it being aware of all aggravations and negative consequences. Part of the open truth is to recognize a stupid or idiotic action or a way of thinking as stupid or idiotic respectively, and to say so. This is valid if you can demonstrate the reasons for such names. If you don't have such reasons, better keep your mouth shut, because otherwise you will be not only impolite but also a liar and a verbal offender. Telling the full truth including the unpleasant but realistic names has also a very important problem solving, practical effect. If we make clear that the real cause of a bad result of an action is nothing else than the stupidity of those who did it, we don't waste precious time to look for other hidden causes.

I personally and we, all the bicycles, belong to this third kind of observers, together with the intelligent human beings with whom we share so much in understanding the real causes of the phenomena and situations. All of us are independent observers but this doesn't mean that we are indifferent to the truth just to be polite with who doesn't deserve it.

If somebody has any doubt that we belong to this third kind, I would like to make a quick and immediate referendum. Please, all the bicycles that think they belong to the first kind of observers, ring the bell.

A total silence fell on the entire audience.

— Well, now please, all the bicycles who think they belong to the second kind of observers, ring the bell.

The same total silence continued.

— Well, now please, all the bicycles who think they belong to the third kind of observers, ring the bell.

An avalanche of bell rings followed immediately and it took a while until the working silence was installed.

— I think that the proof is obvious.

— Absolutely obvious, confirmed a choir of bicycles.

— I think that this aspect is very clear intervened a bicycle, what I am not sure about is if the amount of repetitions of the bad names in our discussions is justified or it could be reduced to a general single statement.

— Another good observation. I will answer to it by a clarifying example. Let's say that one has a car in very poor shape but which can and it is worth to be fixed. The items to be fixed are the transmission, a missing wheel, low air pressure in other wheels, the battery, a broken window, and the radiator. Let's stop here.

Now, if you contact a mechanic at a repair shop, what do you tell him about the car, do you make only a general statement telling that the car is in bad shape and needs repairs or you talk about all the items that need to be fixed in order to get the job properly done?

— Of course you have to tell about all items in due detail, telling how bad they are.

— Do you think that it is impolite to tell that a wheel is missing or that the battery doesn't work?

A general laughter was the clear response.

— So, I understand that in order to be clear and get the repair well done you have to repeat the words related to malfunctioning of each item that needs to be fixed. Talking now about our discussions about the human society and its problems, there are many, many quite different issues that came into our debates. Do you think that making only a single general statement, we make clear what is really wrong, or we have to approach each issue separately and in due detail?

— Yes, it makes plenty of sense to talk about each issue separately.

— I will go farther on with my example to show how important is to clarify the cause of the problem: it is a real, natural problem, or in the case of our example, a mechanical problem, or the cause is the human stupidity or idiocy. So, if a wheel is missing, the mechanic may think that the bolts keeping the wheel in place were cut off, or other mechanical cause, but if he found out that the owner of the car took the wheel off trying to travel only with three wheels, which sounds crazy, the mechanic will not waste time searching for mechanical problems. Such idiocy or craziness is not less real than the religion in the human society. If the radiator got damaged because the owner wanted to save money and did not put coolant in it, again, this is not due to a natural, mechanical cause but to the stupidity of the owner. This may look like unthinkable but is not more unthinkable than the stupidity of the human beings society with thousands of homeless people sleeping in the street with plenty of resources around.

Now, if the mechanic should report about the damaged car should he talk politely about the case or should he say that the car can be repaired but before that the owner of the car should be repaired or replaced telling directly that he is stupid or crazy and that this is the real cause of damage to the car?

— This example is very significant and my conclusion is that if the unpleasant words mentioned before were expressed so many times, all of them are fully justified because each refers to a specific situation and there are so many terrible situations in the society of the human beings which deserve to be characterized by the hard words like stupid, idiot, crazy and whatever else. They were used not because our willingness to offend or because we are impolite, but because our spirit of objectivity and fairness demands these words to properly describe what we have observed in the human beings society. Maybe some day, these unpleasant but rightly used words, will serve like a waking up signal and will help to change for better the present situation in the human society.

I am sure that we have on our side that intelligent minority of the human beings which deserve all the respect and which represents the only hope for a radical change. To those nice human beings who agree with our conclusions but are too sensitive for these harsh words, we can tell that if they are so afraid or unpleased even with the words describing a very bad situation, could they be the required heroic soldiers in a tough battle to change it? Probably not, but if finally they will applaud the positive results of such a battle, they are welcome. If they can rethink their position and be totally on our side, they are most welcome.

I believe that we exhausted this sensitive issue and that all of us agree with these conclusions.

A powerful roar and bell ringing was the undisputed acceptance of these words by the entire bicycle audience.

A bicycle parked close to the Canadian bicycle, addressed her with a very direct and practical question:

— Tell us please, do you know what is the opinion of our engineer about the future of his promotion taking in consideration what our Russian friend just finished to say?

The Canadian responded immediately:

— Yes, I am well informed about the position and the plans of our engineer in the present circumstances. And who knows better than him the depth of the human beings stupidity and the difficulties for the promotion of the concept in these conditions? The concept is necessary and sustainable and the engineer is convinced that its realization at first in one city and afterwards in many others, is only a question of time. So he is determined to continue the promotion in accordance with the real conditions, without wasting time where there aren't chances of success. This is a difficult and long-term battle, but he has two very powerful allies, which for sure will help him.

— Which are these two allies?

— One is the intelligence of a minority of visionaries, which in a favorable moment can support the concept not only with words but also with actions.

— And the second?

— The second is the same mass stupidity of the human beings.

— Excuse me please, I didn't hear or I didn't understand well what you said.

— I said that the second very powerful ally is the stupidity of the mass of human beings.

— Now I am sure that I heard well but I don't understand what do you mean.

— I mean that in their stupidity in the urbanism and urban transportation policy, the condition will become worse and worse and at the end it will be very easy to understand the real value of the concept to solve the problems created by the human beings themselves. Is a similar case of which our Russian friend spoke, but in other direction. The human beings will continue to agglomerate their cities, will use more cars moving in the same streets already at the limit of their capacity, until when the traffic will be suffocated and will move at a speed very much lower than a bicycle. The parking is other problem, almost as big as the traffic congestion.

With the increase in the number of cars, parking a car in the city becomes more difficult and more expensive. This is so not only in the places of public interest, in the center of the city or on the main streets, but also in the secondary streets and in the buildings with a great numbers of apartments, or in the private houses where a second car is very necessary in the present conditions.

— This is true, and what is the value of a car if you cannot park where and when you want? With the bicycles this problem is almost inexistent or very much easier to solve.

— And in places with traffic congestion, were is not possible to park even a single car, with the system of bicycle expressways, thousands of bicycles can be parked, even without touching the street, but inside the system. This essential advantage has weight in favor of the system and will also push the promotion of the concept.

— It is possible to assume that the situation will reach a point of balance between the number of cars and the traffic capacity in the streets?

— No, it is not possible, because the human beings are very limited in their capacity to think about the future, in their vision, in more than one direction.

— It means?

— It means that they don't have any control over the size of population especially in the cities. The birth control is not imposed in spite of the limitation of the natural resources. The migration of people from poor countries towards the rich countries increases also and the migration of people from countryside to the city also rises in an uncontrolled manner. It is not possible to foresee with precision but in a long or short range the necessity will push and the visionaries will take the opportunity for the implementation of the concept.

— These are good news, which give us a dose of optimism so much necessary, observed a bicycle.

— Fortunately, this optimism is based not only on the desire but also on realism, and as a proof of this I want to communicate to you a last hour news.

— All of us are listening.

— Very recently an unexpected opportunity appeared during a discussion between the engineer and a friend of his about the concept and his promotional activity, as an interesting story only, without any intention of promotion. His friend was very interested in the concept and told him that this concept would be very good for Mexico City; our engineer responded that he promoted the concept there few years before but without the expected result due to the lack of vision or power of the involved politicians. His friend told him that he has contacts that could make the idea known to a politician with very high position and that is worth to try again to promote the concept in Mexico. Our engineer agreed and prepared a letter with attached documentation to be sent by his friend to the proper destination.

Although in this case also there is no guarantee of success, at least it is an opportunity to promote the concept directly at a high level, cutting the intermediate bureaucracy. Let's see what will happen. There is nothing to lose, but possibly everything to gain. You can be sure that at our next reunion, I will inform you about this experience with all the details. And this is not all. There is also other news, of last minute, if you want. This news might be even better than the first one. Short time ago our engineer received a phone call totally unexpected from one of his collaborators during the promotion of the concept in Jamaica, ten years ago. He told to our engineer that there is a very good surprise, a person with much influence is interested in the concept and wants to discuss the issue in detail, for its possible implementation in Kingston, the capital of Jamaica. The engineer was invited to go there for several meetings, a month later, when the respective person returns from a business trip abroad. Clearly, the engineer agreed, everything was arranged and now he has already his plane ticket.

Again, in this case also, there is no guarantee for success but at least there is a good possibility, specially considering that this time the initiative comes not due to the engineer's insistence but from the other side, situation that indicates a real interest. This signifies also that all the previous promotional efforts even without favorable results at that time were not a waste of time, it never can be said when they could be of very much use as in this case, ten years later. Certainly, all of you will be informed about the results of these discussions.

With this, the third reunion of bicycles ended. The facts and the opinions presented in the three reunions are an instructive, real and truthful story about an unique event in the life of bicycles, the promotion of a visionary concept which, although today it is only a dream, it can be said that is a dream that can be implemented. The only but overwhelming reason for which this concept is not implemented is the negative part of the human beings nature, so well expressed in the discussions between the bicycles. However, there is the hope that finally, one day the intelligent minority of the human beings will succeed to take control of the society. If this occurs, there is no doubt that among many good things that will be realized, one of the first will be the implementation of the concept for the Bicycle Expressways Systems, initially in one city and finally in all the cities of the world which need it.

ANNEX
CONTENT OF ATTACHED COPIES OF LETTERS AND PUBLISHED ARTICLES
(IN CHRONOLOGICAL ORDER)

1. ABSTRACT

2. PROPOSAL for the improvement of urban transportation by implementing the BICYCLE EXPRESSWAY SYSTEMS concept. (NOT INCLUDED IN THIS PACKAGE)

3. He's peddling plans to bike you downtown. Article published by David Miller in THE TORONTO STAR. – June 14, 1981

4. Les cyclists pourraient avoir leur routes a 15 pieds du sol. Article published by Denis Masse in LA PRESSE-Montreal. – March 31, 1982

5. Engineering News-Inventive Engineer peddles plan for saving energy, reducing pollution. Article published in THE CANADIAN CONSULTING ENGINEER.—June 1982

6. Bicyclists need encouragement. Article published by William F. Buckley Jr. in THE PHILADELPHIA INQUIRER and in other about 100 newspapers in the U.S.A. – October 5, 1982

7. UTOPIA AND JOSEPH ADLER. Article published in the BIKE TALK magazine-New York. U.S.A.-May 1983

8. Back to the bicycle. Article published by Morris Cargill in The SUNDAY GLEANER- Kingston, Jamaica. –June 12, 1983

9. Letter from G.H. Johnston-Assistant Deputy Minister, Provincial Municipal Transportation – September 6, 1990

10. Letter from William F. Buckley Jr.-Editor, NATIONAL REVIEW-New York, U.S.A., to Joseph Adler-September 19, 1990

11. Letter from Jenny Carter, Minister of Energy- Queen's Park-Toronto, Ontario. to Joseph Adler-December 20, 1990

12. Visionary plan for cycling city no pie in sky. Article published by Rosie DiManno in THE TORONTO STAR- June 7, 1991.

13. Jesse Flis-Official Report in the House of Commons –Ottawa, supporting the Bicycle Expressway System concept- May 7, 1992

14. Letter from Ricardo Neves-President, Institute of Technology for the Citizen-Rio de Janeiro, Brazil, to Joseph Adler- June 29, 1992

15. Letter from Maurice Strong-Secretary General of United Nations Conference on Environment & Development- Switzerland, to Joseph Adler regarding his presentation at the International Conference in Rio de Janeiro, Brazil—July 20, 1992

16. Letter from Charles Caccia, M.P.-House of Commons-Ottawa, to Joseph Adler –April 21, 1993

17. Letter from Maurice Strong to George Davies, Deputy Minister, Ministry of Transport, Ontario-October 22, 1993

18. Letter from Maurice Strong to June Rowlands, the Mayor of Toronto supporting the Joseph Adler's concept-January 12, 1994

19. Letter on behalf of Prince Charles, Prince of Wales, to Joseph Adler, supporting his concept—July 29, 1994

20. Letter from Carlton E. Davis, Permanent Secretary-Government of Jamaica, supporting the Bicycle Expressway Systems concept for Kingston, Jamaica--September 9, 1994

21. Invitation to Joseph Adler from R. Kay, Chief, United Nations Centre for Human Settlements (Habitat) to participate at the International Seminar for Transportation in Beijing –China for 25-27 September, 1995-September 15, 1995

22. Letter from Eduardo Dimacuha, Mayor of the City of Batangas, Philippines, to Joseph Adler expressing interest in the concept for the city and the willingness to discuss the necessary preliminary conditions further on. –October 18, 1995

23. Letter to Joseph Adler expressing the interest for the presentation of the Bicycle Expressway Systems concept at the International Bicycle Conference in Fremantle, Western Australia on October 28, 1996-Nov. 1, 1996—July 11, 1996

24. Letter of acceptance for the presentation of the Bicycle Expressway Systems concept entitled "Bicycles – an option for the 21st century" at the International Conference in Havana, Cuba –August 1, 1996

25. Letter from the Office of the Executive Director of the World Bank in support of the Bicycle Expressway Systems concept, to Joseph Adler and TO WHOM IT MAY CONCERN – October 25, 1996

26. Letter from Ruben N.M. de Leon, from Penta Capital Investment Corporation to Joseph Adler, to confirm the positive feedback to the presentation of the Bicycle Expressway Systems concept for the City of Manila, Philippines –Nov. 18, 1996

27. Letter from Alan Tonks, Metropolitan Chairman, Toronto, to Leonard Good, Executive Director of the World Bank, Washington, U.S.A., supporting the Bicycle Expressway Systems concept and asking for the World's Bank cooperation for its further promotion – January 16, 1997

28. Letter from Alexander B. Leman, President of Leman Group Inc. to Joseph Adler –January 17, 1997

29. Invitation from Sancho Cervera, Director General, to Joseph Adler to participate with the presentation of the Bicycle Expressway Systems concept at the International Conference "Segundo Encuentro de Ciudades" at 24-26 October, 1997 in Puebla, Mexico. –August 12, 1997

30. Invitation from Dr. Foo Tvan Seck, Conference Secretary, to Joseph Adler to participate with the presentation of his concept entitled "The Bicycle Expressway Systems, today's vision, tomorrow's reality" at the First International Conference on Quality of Life in Cities in Singapore from 4-6 March 1998—September 7, 1997

31. Letter from Bernard Ecoffey-Postgraduate of Science and Technology and Director of the FORUM ENGELBERG, Switzerland, to Joseph Adler accepting his presentation of the concept at the Conference –November 4, 1997

32. Letter from Alexander B. Leman, President of Leman Group Inc. to Dr. Utis Kaothien, Director of Urban Development

–National Economic and Social Development Board, Bangkok, Thailand—February 25, 1998

33. Invitation from Propin Borisuthi, Director –International Affairs Division, Bangkok, Thailand to Joseph Adler to make a presentation of the Bicycle Expressway Systems concept for the city of Bangkok—March 9, 1998

34. Letter from Dr. Jose Jesus Acosta Flores, Coordinator General del Comite Organizador-National University of Mexico, to Joseph Adler with the invitation to present the concept for the city of Bangkok –March 9, 1998

35. Diploma forwarded to Joseph Adler for the outstanding presentation at the 2nd Seminar International of Engineering for Systems in Huatulco, Mexico –June 27, 1998

36. Letter from Maurice Strong to the Honourable Enrique Penalosa, the Mayor of Bogota-Bolivia, supporting the Bicycle Expressway System concept –June 9, 1999

37. Hot wheels, high up. Article published by Jennifer Wells in THE TORONTO STAR –April 16, 2006

38. Letter from Dalton McGuinty, Premier of Ontario—August 1, 2007

There are also relevant letters of interest from Honolulu—Hawaii, Tokyo-Japan and other places and private organizations but it seems that the presented documentation can easily fulfill the purpose, i.e. to show clearly and convincingly the serious attention paid to the Bicycle Expressway Systems concept by an impressive number of reputable persons and prestigious organizations.

THE BICYCLE EXPRESSWAY SYSTEM: TODAY'S VISION, TOMORROW'S REALITY

A VIABLE SOLUTION FOR THE RADICAL IMPROVEMENT OF URBAN TRANSPORTATION

AUTHOR   : JOSEPH ADLER, Master Of Engineering, P.Eng.
ORGANIZATION : BICYCLE EXPRESSWAY SYSTEMS CO.

ADDRESS   : 33 ORCHARD VIEW BLVD. #1805, TORONTO,
                   ONT., CANADA, M4R 2E9
TEL   : (416) 487-1066
FAX   : (416) 481-7298

ABSTRACT

The concept of Bicycle Expressway System was developed by Joseph Adler who has been in chronological order, an enthusiast cyclist, a professional engineer and a resident of Toronto. These three assets brought him to the idea of improving in a radical and well engineered way, cycling as a means of safe and convenient mass transportation in Toronto, Canada. However, this concept is applicable for any other city in the world facing traffic congestion and air pollution problems. With proper local adjustments, a tremendous improvement in the quality of life and enormous material advantages can be obtained.

The Bicycle Expressway System represents an additional transportation facility provided exclusively for bicycles and serving all the city area, in any weather or topographic conditions. Its purpose is to create excellent conditions for utilitarian and recreational cycling and thus to give all the residents a real choice and the incentive for replacing the use of the car, or the often inconvenient public transport, by the use of the bicycle in most of their daily trips.

The basic philosophy of this concept is the construction of a network of **expressways for bicycles only, elevated at minimum 5 meters (15 ft.) above the street level, covered, at level or with downhill slopes only, the uphill differences in elevation being**

taken by escalators. Because there is always one way of travelling and no intersections at the same level, no stop signs or stop lights are necessary and a collision accident within the system is virtually impossible. In these conditions a non stop bicycle ride with maximal safe speed will be possible regardless of the traffic jams at the street level. A combination of bicycle expressways and other means of transportation is perfectly possible and desirable. This will optimize the efficiency of the urban transportation in general.

Conceived in this way, the Bicycle Expressway System provides complete separation from the motorized and pedestrian traffic, complete safety and full protection against bad weather year round and eliminates the need of strenuous and slow uphill pedaling. With the proposed system in place, the bicycle **will become the safest, cheapest, healthiest and the fastest door to door, very convenient means of urban transportation.** Resting, shopping and parking facilities for thousands of bicycles will be also provided without taking any space from the street level.

The return period of the required investment is very short because the cost of the system including operation and maintenance is very low and **cannot be challenged by any other transportation alternative** with the same traffic capacity. Additional invaluable assets of the proposed system are the dramatic reduction in the rate of urban traffic accidents, the great positive environmental impact by significantly reducing the air and noise pollution, the reduction of the transportation cost of the presently wasted time and other positive social and material advantages.

The concept received wide support from prominent personalities and prestigious organizations in Canada and abroad, was commended by leading newspapers and magazines, major Radio and TV stations and was presented at International Conferences in Colorado Springs-USA, Toronto-Canada, Rio de Janeiro-Brazil, Beijing-China, Fremantle-Australia, Havana-Cuba, Puebla-Mexico, Singapore, Forum Engelberg-Switzerland, Huatulco and Guadulajara-Mexico.

After getting official agreements and unequivocal recognition for the outstanding merits and socio-economic potential of the proposed Bicycle Expressway System, we are searching now for visionary leaders and investors to implement a Pilot Project as **World Showcase** for this unique, innovative and sustainable concept.

The bicycle expressways are:

ELEVATED	at minimum 4.6m (15 ft.) above the street level → any interference with streets, motorized or pedestrian traffic is eliminated → complete safety.

+

COVERED	with transparent, sun reflecting material → full protection against bad weather, year round (cold, rain, snow, icy roads, wind, sun, heat).

+

LEVEL OR DOWNHILL	→ no more hills or streets with long slopes to climb → no more sweating, faster ride

+

NEVER	interfere one with another at the same level. At intersections they are interconnected by ramps and escalators →no stop lights or stop signs →direct, non-stop bike riding between any two points in the system.

= Very easy, safe, pleasant and fast riding

DEAR READERS

In the attached ANNEX there are many articles and letters from outstanding personalities and organizations in support of the concept for the radical improvement of urban transportation proposed by P. Eng. Joseph Adler presented in this book.

Unfortunately, the only newspaper publishing company which has a very strange approach for allowing to attach to the book copies of three very interesting articles already published in the same newspaper as far as 32 years ago is the TORONTO STAR. The MANAGEMENT of this company demands money prior to permitting the publications of the articles and other entire list of difficult conditions including the number of my credit card for unknown now but potentially additional expenses.

In these conditions we decided not to publish these articles in the book because we do not agree with this approach.

The articles mentioned at points 3, 12, and 37 in the ANNEX are as follows:

Nr. In the ANNEX	Date	Title of the article	Writer
3	June 14, 1981	He is peddling plans to bike you downtown	David Miller
12	June 7, 1991	Visionary plan for cycling city no pie in sky	Rosie Di Mano
37	April 16, 2006	Hot wheels up	Jennifer Wells

We are very sorry about this policy of Toronto Star, but interested readers can find these articles in libraries archives and possible in the internet.

Thank you for your understanding

Joseph Adler
Author.

LA PRESSE, MONTRÉAL, MERCREDI 31 MARS 1982

SELON LE PROJET D'UN INGÉNIEUR D'ORIGINE ROUMAINE

Les cyclistes pourraient avoir leurs routes... à 15 pieds du sol

> Please see this article in readable size on the next three pages

G 5

■ Joseph Adler a une solution toute simple — quoique coûteuse — au conflit grandissant entre les automobilistes et les cyclistes qui se disputent le libre usage de nos voies urbaines.

DENIS MASSE

Selon Adler, un ingénieur d'origine roumaine établi à Toronto, on a tort de vouloir marier à tout prix les deux modes de transport sur une même chaussée. Chacun des deux modes de transport la chaussée restera aux véhicules motorisés tandis que des tubes montés sur pylônes permettront la libre circulation des vélos au-dessus de leurs concurrents quatre roues.

Les véloroutes, peu encombrantes en raison de leur superstructure légère, seraient recouvertes de plexiglas permettant leur usage toute-saison en dépit des intempéries et du froid.

Se riant des pentes et autres dénivellations, les cyclistes pourraient alors circuler sans entraves à la vitesse maximale de leur vélo, dans leurs corridors exclusifs.

Idéal pour les ponts de Montréal

La section montréalaise du [...]

Les corridors aériens proposés par Adler pourraient ressembler à cette passerelle pour piétons, sauf qu'ils seraient établis dans le sens longitudinal de la route.

[...] solution Adler, voyant une application pratique et immédiate au problème des ponts reliant l'île de Montréal à la Rive sud et à l'île Jésus, au nord.

Les cyclistes montréalais y ont vu également une solution souhaitable au projet d'axe nord-sud qu'ils préconisent depuis longtemps.

Adler, lui-même adepte du cyclisme malgré ses 58 ans, a mis au point un imposant projet de véloroutes pour la ville de Toronto. Les routes auraient été construites dans l'usage de l'automobile.

Ces chiffres valent pour Toronto où les 300,000 cyclistes cités représentent 12 pour cent de la [...] un investissement global de près de deux milliards de dollars.

« Il ne faut pas regarder le coût en chiffres absolus, souligne cependant Adler, mais ce que ça rapporte ou ce que l'on obtient pour la somme investie. »

Ainsi, a-t-il calculé, à raison de 300,000 cyclistes utilisant son système durant l'année, à raison de 300 jours de vélo par année, moyennant 10 kilomètres par jour un espargne unique de 900 millions de kilomètres par an sur les principales artères aux usagers actuellement [...] population métropolitaine.

Les mêmes calculs montrent que 10,000 cyclistes utilisant les voies élevées pendant 300 jours à raison de 30 kilomètres par jour réduiraient de millions de dol-lars par an la consommation du carburant sur le territoire urbain.

À 15 pieds du sol

Le plan Adler prévoit que les corridors aériens seraient suspendus à au moins 15 pieds au-dessus de la chaussée; des rampes d'accès, munies d'ascenseurs seraient reliées aux principales intersections.

L'Hôtel de ville de Toronto définitivement écarté le plan proposé par l'ingénieur roumain, jugeant son coût prohibitif, mais les autorités penchent pour l'addition de nouvelles voies rapides convergeant vers le centre-ville.

« Les usagers du transport en commun ont leur réseau souterrain; les automobilistes ont les rues, et les autoroutes sur les piétons ont leurs trottoirs... mais les cyclistes n'ont rien qui leur soit propre, déplore Bob Silverman, l'âme dirigeante du Monde à bicyclette à Montréal.

Adler est convaincu que son [...] réseau de voies élevées à l'usage exclusif des cyclistes peut être entrepris et que son coût initial peut être rapidement absorbé par l'économie d'énergie qu'il couterait.

« Sans compter, ajoute-t-il, qu'il contribuerait à assainir l'air ambiant par la réduction du taux de carbone et qu'il permettrait un grand nombre de gens de se rendre à leur travail et en revenir. Plusieurs familles pourraient aussi économiser l'achat d'une seconde voiture et se servir de l'automobile une fois rendues à l'extérieur de la ville. »

LA PRESSE, MONTRÉAL, MERCREDI 31 MARS 1982

SELON LE PROJET D'UN INGÉN

Les cycliste
routes... à

Joseph Adler a une solution toute simple — quoique coûteuse — au conflit grandissant entre cyclistes et automobilistes qui se disputent le libre usage de nos voies urbaines.

DENIS MASSE

Selon Adler, un ingénieur d'origine roumaine établi à Toronto, on a tort de vouloir marier à tout prix les deux modes de transport sur roues: il faut donner à chacun ses voies propres dans les artères existantes. La solution consiste à *superposer les voies attribuées à chacun des deux modes de transport:* la chaussée restera aux véhicules motorisés tandis que des tubes montés sur pylones permettront la libre circulation des vélos au-dessus de leurs concurrents de toujours.

Les véloroutes, peu encombrantes en raison de leur superstructure légère, seraient recouvertes de plexiglas permettant leur usage toute-saison en dépit des intempéries et du froid.

Se riant des pentes et autres déclivités de terrain, les cyclistes pourraient alors circuler sans entraves à la vitesse maximale de leur vélo, dans leurs corridors exclusifs.

Idéal pour les ponts de Montréal

La section montréalaise du «Monde à bicyclette» à qui l'ingénieur torontois a exposé son plan hier soir, a accepté d'emblée la

Les corridors aériens proposés
L'intérieur aurait à peu près l'a

solution Adler, voyant une application pratique et immédiate au problème des ponts reliant l'île de Montréal à la Rive sud et à l'île Jésus, au nord.

Les cyclistes montréalais y ont vu également une solution séduisante au projet d'axe nord-sud qu'ils préconisent depuis longtemps.

Adler, lui-même adepte du cyclisme malgré ses 50 ans, a mis au point un imposant projet de véloroutes pour la ville de Toronto. Le vaste treillis qui recouvrirait les rues de la Ville-reine, d'Étobicoke à Scarborough, incluant York et tout le centre-ville, nécessiterait

IIEUR D'ORIGINE ROUMAINE

s pourraient
15 pieds du

par Adler pourraient ressembler à cette passerelle pour piétons, sau ipect qu'on peut apprécier sur la photo de droite.

un investissement global de près de deux milliards de dollars.

«Il ne faut pas regarder le coût en chiffres absolus, souligne cependant Adler, mais ce que ça rapporte ou ce que l'on obtient pour la somme investie».

Ainsi, a-t-il calculé, à raison de 300,000 cyclistes utilisant son système de voies élevées pendant 200 jours de l'année, moyennant 50 kilomètres par jour, on épargnerait quelque 450 millions de dollars par an investis actuellement dans l'usage de l'automobile.

Ces chiffres valent pour Toronto où les 300,000 cyclistes cités représentent 12 pour cent de la population métropolitaine.

Les mêmes calculs montrent que 10,000 cyclistes utilisant les voies élevées pendant 200 jours à raison de 30 kilomètres par jour réduiraient de 9 millions de dollars par an la consommation du carburant sur le territoire urbain.

À 15 pieds du sol

Le plan Adler prévoit que les corridors aériens seraient suspendus à au moins 15 pieds au-dessus de la chaussée; des rampes d'accès munies d'ascenseurs seraient situées aux principales intersections et chaque tube pourrait être distant d'environ un à deux kilomètres.

t avoir leurs sol

f qu'ils seraient édifiés dans le sens longitudinal de la route.

L'Hôtel de ville de Toronto a définitivement écarté le plan proposé par l'ingénieur roumain, jugeant son coût prohibitif, mais les autorités penchent pour l'addition de nouvelles voies rapides convergeant vers le centre-ville.

«Les usagers du transport en commun ont leur réseau souterrain; les automobilistes ont les rues et les autoroutes sur lesquelles ils exercent un monopole; les piétons ont leurs trottoirs, mais les cyclistes n'ont rien qui leur soit propre, déplore Bob Silverman, l'âme dirigeante du Monde à bicyclette à Montréal.

Adler est convaincu que son

réseau de voies élevées à l'usage exclusif des cyclistes peut être entrepris et que son coût initial peut être rapidement absorbé par l'économie d'énergie qui en découlerait.

«Sans compter, ajoute-t-il, qu'il contribuerait à assainir l'air ambiant par la réduction de la pollution carbonique et qu'il permettrait à un grand nombre de gens de se maintenir en santé en pédalant pour se rendre à leur travail et en revenir. Plusieurs familles pourraient aussi économiser l'achat d'une seconde voiture et ne se servir de l'automobile que pour les randonnées à l'extérieur de la ville».

ENGINEERING NEWS

Inventive engineer peddles plan for saving energy, reducing pollution

Joseph Adler, a Toronto professional engineer, has published plans that he believes could save millions of dollars in energy, reduce pollution caused by automobiles and raise the level of physical fitness of the population of Metropolitan Toronto. So why hasn't the plan been implemented? Basically because a number of psychological and economic barriers have yet to be broken down.

Adler's plan calls for the creation of a network of enclosed bicycle highways, suspended a minimum of 5 metres above the city's main streets on concrete columns. The network would consist of nine 30-kilometer paths going in an east-west direction and 14 paths of about 15 kilometres going north-south, operating on exclusive rights of way.

Being an engineer, Adler believes the paths would allow year-round cycling. To overcome differences in elevation (the other serious natural impediment to cycling as a means of mass transportation), the paths would be built at level grade. Access ramps and intersections between the north-south, east-west systems would be built at regular intervals approximately 2 kilometres apart, says Adler, so that cyclists need not walk more than a few hundred metres from an access point. Where necessary, lifting stations with escalators would carry dismounted cyclists and their bicycles from one level to another.

Adler says the 470-kilometre cycling highway would cost about $1.5 billion but that savings in fuel alone would be that much in a decade if a substantial number of Torontonians could be convinced to use the system. Other savings would accrue from the reduced use of automobiles, from reduced property damage due to car accidents, from a drop in compensation paid to car accident victims, as well as from a drop in expense for the relevant medical treatment that physical activity and therefore fitness of the population.

Needless to say, not everyone is as convinced as Adler that the bicycle expressway is the better way. The committee of the project are studied the city's cycling committee. The committee is convinced that cyclists can be accommodated on the streets.

Adler has taken his plan to a number of Ontario ministries for study, in the hope of funding for development of his proposal, but has not yet been forthcoming, but Adler is not discouraged.

Urban transportation is a field that can use plenty of imagination. Anyone who has lived through a transit strike or commuted on a congested highway and expressways, who jammed daily onto crowded subway trains and buses to get to and from work or who has been seat flying over the handlebars of a bicycle when a driver unexpectedly opens the car door, would agree.

As gasoline prices go up, the need for acceptable urban transit becomes even greater. According to a June, 1980 article in the American magazine, "Across the Board," a study by the U.S. Federal Highway Administration in 1976 showed that 42 percent of the trips American motorists make by car" were under five miles — a predictable distance at which the auto-mobile is an energy-inefficient in the extreme. Urban life is energy-inefficient, too. Dutch and others have shown it is not the bicycle that is impractical, only the design of the cities in which European cars, the article says, has calculated that "if business and shopping trips were limited only to those shorter than two miles now taken by car, Americans could save 2.4 billion gallons of gasoline a year — a modest but significant 11 percent of the nation's annual consumption. That might make a dent in the air pollution, too.

The article points out that American cities have been designed for the automobile, and that in Europe and Asia, where the car, the cyclist, the pedestrian and the bicycle grew up together, are considered the interloper; the Netherlands, for example, has built a segregated, parallel highway system for bicycles. Even in Europe, drivers regard bicyclists with much the same lack of enthusiasm as North American drivers.

An engineer with drive and imagination, Adler recently returned from a trip abroad where he presented his scheme to several major city-dwellers toward shepherding.

The same article concluded that "if clearly is one of the solutions. As the Americans learn anything from the Agency, the article states, has cost-effectiveness is largely a problem of moving large numbers of people, relatively small spaces. The auto has not proved to be the solution. Nor will the bike, but it is a viable urban transit option.

In Canada, Adler puts forth a similar argument claiming that bicycling highways in several major cities.

METROPOLITAN TORONTO BICYCLE NETWORK

Please see this article
in readable size on the
next three pages

ENGINEERING NEWS

Inventive engineer peddles plan for saving en

Joseph Adler, a Toronto professional engineer has a plan which could save millions of dollars of energy, reduce pollution caused by automobiles and raise the level of physical fitness of the population of Metropolitan Toronto. So why hasn't the plan been implemented? Basically because a number of psychological and economic barriers have yet to be broken down.

Adler's plan calls for the creation of a network of enclosed bicycle highways, suspended a minimum of 5 metres above the city's main streets on concrete columns. The network would consist of nine 30-kilometre paths going in an east west direction and 14 paths of about 15 kilometres going north south, operating on exclusive rights of way.

Enclosed by a transparent, sun-reflecting material, the paths would allow year-round cycling. To overcome differences in elevation (the other serious natural impediment to cycling as a means of mass transportation) the paths would be built at level grade. Access ramps and intersections between the north-south, east-west systems would be built at regular intervals approximately 2

kilometres apart, says Adler, so tha no place in Metropolitan Toront would be more than a few minute from an access point. Where neces sary, lifting stations with escalator would carry dismounted cyclists an their bicycles from one level to another.

Adler says the 470-kilometr cycling highway would cost abou $1.5 billion but that savings in fue alone would be that much in a decade if a substantial number of Torontonians could be convinced to use the system. Other savings would accrue from the reduced use of automobiles from reduced property damage due to car accidents, from a drop in compensation paid to car accident victims, as well as from a drop in expenses for sick leave and medical treatment that would result from the increased physical activity and therefore fitness of the population.

Needless to say, not everyone is as convinced as Adler that the bicycle expressway is the better way. The economics of the project are unfeasible, says one Toronto alderman who heads the city's cycling committee. The committee is convinced cyclists can be accommodated on the streets.

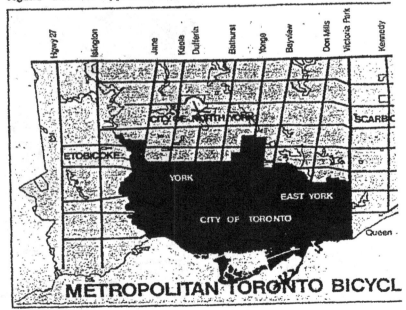

METROPOLITAN TORONTO BICYCL

gy, reducing pollution

Adler disagrees. "Many of Toronto's main streets are narrow," he says, "and have a heavy flow of traffic, making cycling a real danger and a nuisance."

Adler has taken his plans to a number of Ontario ministries for study. So far funding for closer study of his proposal has not been forthcoming, but Adler is not discouraged.

Urban transportation is a field that can use plenty of imagination. Anyone who has lived through a transit strike or commutes on congested highways and expressways, who pushes daily onto crowded subways and buses to get to and from work or who has been sent flying over the handlebars of a bicycle when a driver unexpectedly opens the car door knows this is true.

As gasoline prices go up, the need for acceptable urban transit becomes even greater. According to a June 1980 article in the American magazine, "across the board," a study by American Federal Highway Administration in 1976 showed that "62 percent of the trips Americans make by car" are under five miles — a pedalable distance at which the auto-

mobile is as energy-inefficient as t human body is energy-efficient."

"The U.S. Environmental Prote tion Agency, the article states, h calculated that "if business and sho ping trips shorter than two miles n made by car were instead made bikes, the U.S. might save as much 2.5 billion gallons of gasoline a year a modest but significant 2.5 perce dent in the nation's annual consum tion. That might make a dent in pollution too."

The article points out that Ame can cities have been designed for automobile, and that in Europe a Asia, where the automobile and bicycle grew up together, the car considered the interloper; the N therlands, for example has built separate, parallel highway system bikes. In the city, however drivers not be mention planners, law enforc ment officials and traffic engineers regard bicyclists with much the sar lack of enthusiasm once shown

An engineer with drive an imagination, Adler recently found himself a little ahead would he presented his scheme for an efficien cycling highway in several major c ies.

E NETWORK

cattlemen toward sheepherders."

The same article concluded that "if Americans learn anything from the European experience, it should be that there is no one solution to the problem of moving large numbers of people through relatively small spaces. The auto has not proved to be the solution. Nor will the bike. But it

clearly is one of the solutions. As the Dutch and others have shown, it is not the bicycle that is impractical, only the design of the cities in which people ride them."

In Canada, Adler puts forth a similar argument claiming that bicycling is a viable urban transit option. ▫

YOU CAN'T GO WRONG BY SPECIFYING ETATECH MOTORS

But that's not the only fact every consulting engineer should be aware of. When you specify Etatech motors you get much more than just a top-of-the-line product.

- Etatech builds Canada's widest range of electric motors, from 1/20 HP to 250 HP.
- Etatech supplies major manufacturers of industrial equipment. They know they can depend on us. So can you.
- Etatech can meet all your needs from volume orders to custom installations.
- Etatech excels in special development projects requiring strong engineering support.

Etatech Industries Inc. Our name means efficiency and technology. And we live up to our name.

etatech
INDUSTRIES INC.

Toronto plan

The Philadelphia Inquirer
Op-ed Page
Tuesday, Oct. 5, 1982   19-A

Bicyclists need encouragement

By William F. Buckley Jr.

There are a number of interesting things going on in Canada, about which more in due course. The urban transportation division of Canada has set up a special conference in Ottawa to listen to the proposals of one Joseph Adler, who is the president of Bicycle Expressway Systems. Are you ready?

Adler's idea is adaptable to any city. But concretely, he has engineered (he is a professional) a bicycle grid that would permit anyone living in metropolitan Toronto (they call it "metro" nowadays) to travel by bicycle from virtually any point in the city to any other point in the city. The plan calls for 250 miles of suspended bicycle expressways, access to which would be possible every mile or so — so that, for instance, using the New York City block as a measuring rod, every 20 blocks or so a cyclist could mount the grid.

How? By escalator. Adler, though a confirmed cyclist, does not believe in unnecessary exertion. In fact, he is very much opposed to such anachronisms as bicycling uphill. When it was proposed that in order to cheapen the cost of his proposed expressway he permit gentle grades of not more than 1 percent inclination, he scornfully declined the modification. Do it right, he says.

Doing it right means taking into account the three principal reasons

why people don't use bicycles in the cities. The first, of course, is competing vehicular traffic. The second is weather. The third is drudgery.

In the proposed system, which would hang a minimum of 15 feet above city streets, there would be, of course, no automobiles to get in your way or to slow you down. To cope with the hills of Toronto (New York's essential flatness would all but remove this problem) every few miles the cyclist would stop and an escalator would propel him to a new level, whence he would proceed merrily along his leveled way.

Joseph Adler is not going to permit his bicyclists to pump iron — do that, if you want, at home or in a gym. And the glass-covered expressway will of course shield you from the elements, permitting the sun's rays to come through the glass, but keeping away rain, sleet, snow and tempest.

The cost? It pays, at this moment, to sit down: $1.5 billion. But there are 600,000 bicycles in metro. How long would it take to amortize $1.5 billion if you count all the gasoline saved? Assuming, let us say, that one-half the city's commuters elected to avail themselves of the option of bicycling to work? The figures are obviously variable, but Adler believes that $450 million per year would be saved in gasoline costs alone.

But begin now to think of the social advantages. There would be few-

er accidents: The bicycle accident rate in the city streets is considerable. And what about the increased health of tens of thousands who would now bicycle five, 10, 15 miles per day, or even more?

And what value do you attach to good humor? That is what you experience when you get to work not having battled automobiles, or buses, or subways. And what about the good humor of those who persist in riding automobiles, or need to ride in automobiles, and drive through unchoked city streets as though it was Sunday morning, or Thanksgiving Day?

When I ran for mayor of New York, back before the great plague hit the city, I made a relatively modest proposal that an experimental expressway be mounted along Second Avenue. The important thing to keep in mind, when addressing cyclists, is that although many people do it as a sport, it is the utilitarian cyclist who is a serious potential bicycle consumer.

New York City Mayor Edward I. Koch, shortly after his inauguration, experimented with bicycle lanes. These were doomed to fail. They needed to share the streets with four-wheel juggernauts propelled by gasoline engines. And to stop every block or so for a red light, or to make way for lateral traffic, takes from the bicycle its uniqueness. It is as if you sat down to watch a television program, and every minute or two you had to get up to stick the plug back in.

Big money never scared Americans if they became convinced of a project's utility. They are talking, in New York, about $4 billion plus for one Westside Drive. Well, Adler will be heard not only in Canada, but in Colorado Springs, Colo., at a "Pro Bike" convention a week from now. He needs encouragement.

The bicycle is one of the neatest expansions ever on the idea of the wheel. Find out about it, and pester your local politicians. The address is 45 Dunfield Avenue, Suite 1818, Toronto M4S 2H4. Come to think of it, it is unlikely that any country that came up with a ZIP code that cumbersome could come up with a bicycle expressway this neat. But perhaps atonement is in order.

395

Published ii
"BIKE TALK"
NEW YORK, U
May, 1983

UTOPIA

AND

JOSEPH

ADLER

Utopia.Is a place of perfection which can only exist in our minds. This is true because we are too limited to allow it to exist in reality. We would rather complain about the world as it is. There is a feeling of security in that which is familiar. Joseph Adler of Canada has shaken us up a bit with his proposals of a transformed Toronto. In fact, his ideas are so unique that those who call themselves "supporters of the bicycle" will not support his revolutionary plans.

Ever since a William Buckley article appeared in over 100 American newspapers about Joseph Adler, the public officials in Canada(and recently in Washington, D.C.) have been "forced" to listen to him. Mr. Adler has developed a workable plan to incorporate an elevated system of bikeways into the transportation network of the City of Toronto (as well as every other city which exists).

Almost 250 miles of bicycle expressways would carry millions of cyclists around the city. His plan, if adopted, would dramatically reduce traffic congestion, air pollution, energy consumption, insurance and the cost of medical expense due to automobile accidents.

Article published in Kingston, Jamaica

The Sunday Gleaner, June 12, 1983

PAGE TWELVE

BACK TO THE BICYCLE

By MORRIS CARGILL

Please see this article in readable size on the next three pages

Some time in 1982 a William Buckley column appeared in 100 American newspapers about a Canadian, Joseph Adler, who had developed a system of elevated bikeways for the city of Toronto, and for that matter for other cities. Nobody has yet adopted the Adler system, but it so happens that Joseph Adler is now living temporarily in Jamaica, and I had a talk with him about his system.

Joseph Adler is an engineer and is here as one of the experts recently employed by the Water Authority to try to sort out our various water problems. It seems a good opportunity to talk with him about his original if somewhat far-out proposals, which he feels would work well for Jamaica.

Mr. Adler's scheme is based upon the postulate that an enormous number of traffic problems would be solved if commuters could be induced to ride bicycles to and from work. The trouble with riding a bicycle under ordinary conditions is, first of all, that you get wet when it rains, and secondly that it is hard work, especially uphill. Mr. Adler's scheme enables cyclists to avoid both troubles.

Major hazard

He has done this by proposing what he calls a bicycle grid that would permit travel by bicycle from virtually any point in a city to another. For the Corporate Area, for instance, this would involve about 80 miles of overhead bicycle expressways, which you could get onto every mile or so. You and your bicycle would be lifted on to the expressway by elevators. Thereafter all riding would be done on the dead level through miles of expressway, covered overhead the sun and the rain.

The means of achieving this dead level riding are ingenious. If you were going from upper St. Andrew to Kingston it's down-hill all the way, though you would still ride on the level, descending downwards at intervals by specially designed slopes. On the way back the ride would still be on the level for ever so often you would come to an elevator, which would take to the next level. As the expressway would be a dual carriage-way, it would not be possible to come into collision with cyclists coming in the opposite direction. Indeed, it would not be possible to come into collision with anything.

One of the major hazards of cycling, especially in the Corporate Area, is that the cyclist is mixed up with the rest of the traffic. If I took to a bicycle I don't think I would survive for long the assaults of mini-bus drivers. In Mr. Adler's system this would not arise as the cyclist would be completely segregated.

Mr. Adler tells me that his system of elevated cycle expressways could be set up comparatively cheaply, because for cyclists there would be no great load-bearing problem and the structure could be light. He estimates, for instance, that a 250-mile system for the city of Toronto would cost $1.5 billion. As against this, there would be enormous savings in fuel, a sharp reduction in road accidents, and a notable improvement in the health of people who would get mild daily exercise.

Fascinating

It is a fascinating and logical proposal. I doubt though, that it would be very popular in Jamaica, where the motor car itself is not so much a means of transport as a status symbol and, one might add, a kind of aphrodisiac. Girls in Jamaica more or less refuse to go out with men who have no car, and I doubt whether at this stage of the game, they could be got to accept a bicycle made for two — even on the level.

However, I tell you about Mr. Adler's scheme because it seems to be both workable and logical, as well as a remarkable fuel-saver. Maybe, if it is adopted here, I would take up cycle-riding again. I haven't ridden a bicycle since the early days of World War II when I fell off quite regularly on the Earls Court Road in London, and stopped only when my ancient second-hand bicycle was stolen outside a cinema, no longer in existence, called the Fulham Forum.

THE B6

While on engineering subjects, a friend of mine, Mr. Derek Roberts, who is by way of being an authority on Art has made a suggestion which I think worthy of note. He says that he thinks the poor old B6 generator of the Jamaica Public Service Company ought to be retired from active life and handed over to the Nation as a contribution to our National Culture. He tells me that it is a splendid example of Early Jamaican Surrealism, and should be put on permanent exhibition at Devon House where it could be enjoyed by the general public during the day. Exhibition at nights would not be practical owing to lack of light, B6 being able to generate only enough power to boil a pot of tea.

Joseph Adler - Engineer, developed a system of elevated bike-ways for Toronto and other cities. He felt that an enormous number of traffic problems would be solved if commuters would ride to and from work.

Article published in Kingston, Jamaica

PAGE TWELVE

——BACK TO

Joseph Adler - Engineer, developed a system of elevated bikeways for Toronto *and other cities. He felt that an enormous number of traffic problems would* *be solved if commuters would ride to and from work.* ‘

THE BIC

Some time in 1982 a William Buckley column appeared in 100 American newspapers about a Canadian, Joseph Adler, who had developed a system of elevated bikeways for the city of Toronto, and for that matter for other cities. Nobody has yet adopted the Adler system, but it so happens that Joseph Adler is now living temporarily in Jamaica, and I had a talk with him about his system.

Joseph Adler is an engineer and is here as one of the experts recently employed by the Water Authority to try to sort out our various water problems. It seems a good opportunity to talk with him about his original if somewhat far-out proposals, which he feels would work well for Jamaica.

Mr. Adler's scheme is based upon the postulate that an enormous number of traffic problems would be solved if commuters could be induced to ride bicycles to and from work. The trouble with riding a bicycle under ordinary conditions is, first of all, that you get wet when it rains, and secondly that it is hard work, especially uphill. Mr. Adler's scheme enables cyclists to avoid both troubles.

Major hazard

He has done this by proposing what he calls a bicycle grid that would permit travel by bicycle from virtually any point in a city to another. For the Corporate Area, for instance, this would involve about 80 miles of overhead bicycle expressways, which you could get onto every mile or so. You and your bicycle

:YCLE

By
MORRIS'
CARGILL

would be lifted on to the expressways by elevators. Thereafter all riding would be done on the dead level through miles of expressway, covered over from the sun and the rain.

The means of achieving this dead level riding are ingenious. If you were going from upper St. Andrew to Kingston it's down-hill all the way, though you would still ride on the level, descending downwards at intervals by specially designed slopes. On the way back the ride would still be on the level; for ever so often you would come to an elevator, which would take to the next level. As the expressway would be a dual carriage-way, it would not be possible to come into collision with cyclists coming in the opposite direction. Indeed, it would not be possible to come into collision with anything.

One of the major hazards of cycling, especially in the Corporate Area, is that the cyclist is mixed up with the rest of the traffic. If I took to a bicycle I don't think I would survive for long the assaults of mini-bus drivers. In Mr. Adler's system this would not arise as the cyclist would be completely segregated.

Mr. Adler tells me that his system of elevated cycle expressways could be set up comparatively

The Sunday Gleaner, June 12, 1983

cheaply, because for cyclists there would be no great load-bearing problem and the structure could be light. He estimates, for instance, that a 250-mile system for the city of Toronto would cost $1.5 billion. As against this, there would be enormous savings in fuel, a sharp reduction in road accidents, and a notable improvement in the health of people who would get mild daily exercise

Fascinating

It is a fascinating and logical proposal. I doubt though, that it would be very popular in Jamaica, where the motor car is not so much a means of transport as a status symbol and, one might add, a kind of aphrodisiac. Girls in Jamaica more or less refuse to go out with men who have no car, and I doubt whether at this stage of the game, they could be got to accept a bicycle made for two — even on the level.

However, I tell you about Mr. Adler's scheme because it seems to be both workable and logical, as well as a remarkable fuel-saver. Maybe, if it is adopted here, I would take up cycle-riding again. I haven't ridden a bicycle since the early days of World War II when I fell off quite regularly on the Earls Court Road in London, and stopped only when my ancient second-hand bicycle was stolen outside a cinema, no longer in existence, called the Fulham Forum.

THE B6

While on engineering subjects, a friend of mine, Mr. Deryk Roberts, who is by way of being an authority on Art has made a suggestion which I think worthy of note. He says that he thinks the poor old B6 generator of the Jamaica Public Service Company ought to be retired from active life and handed over to the Nation as a contribution to our National Culture. He tells me that it is a splendid example of Early Jamaican Surrealism, and should be put on permanent exhibition at Devon House where it could be enjoyed by the general public during the day. Exhibition at nights would not be practical owing to lack of light, B6 being able to generate only enough power to boil a pot of tea.

Ministry	Ministère
of	des
Transportation	Transports

Ontario

East Building,
1201 Wilson Ave.,
Downsview, Ontario.
M3M 1J8

September 6th 1990.

Mr. Joseph Adler,
President,
Bicycle Expressway Systems,
33 Orchard View Blvd.,
Suite 1805,
Toronto, Ontario.
M4R 2E9.

Dear Mr. Adler:

Your letter dated August 8th 1990, regarding bicycle
expressways, addressed to Kim Anderson of our Minister's
office, has been passed along to me for reply.

As congestion continues to increase in many of Ontario's
urban areas, solutions are always being sought to help
address this problem in the most environmentally positive
way. Over the last number of years, cycling has emerged as
part of the solution, which has many beneficial side effects
identified in your background material.

The Ministry has been impressed with the increasing
popularity of bicycles and, given the associated
environmental considerations and a concern over safety, the
Minister has directed staff to initiate a review of the
Ministry's bicycle policy. This review will consider the
role of bicycles as a viable mode of transportation with
consideration of such factors as ridership demand, safety,
environmental concerns, congestion, costs, legislation,
experience of other jurisdictions and other elements which
will be identified during the study.

The "Bycycle Expressway System" is a unique idea especially
in light of our desire to move toward a more environmentally
friendly world. As your system appears not only to be of
benefit to the environment, but also serves to help overcome
one of the most aggravating problems on our roads today, and
that is, congestion. As a result, the Ministry will

-2-

include the "Bicycle Expressway System" concept in its
Bicycle Policy Review, in the context of a possible policy
option. Mr. David Hunt ('phone 235-4174) from our Municipal
Transportation Policy Office, will be managing this policy
review and will keep you informed of future developments.

Once again thank you for sharing with us your views on this
exciting transportation option.

Yours truly,

G. H. Johnston,
Assistant Deputy Minister,
Provincial/Municipal
Transportation.

NATIONAL REVIEW·150 East 35th Street, New York, New York 10016

Tel. 679-7330

WILLIAM F. BUCKLEY, JR.
Editor

September 19, 1990

Dear Mr. Adler:

I am most enthusiastic about your project and you can

certainly quote me as endorsing it as I have your wonderful ideas

for so long. With all good wishes,

Yours cordially,

Wm. F. Buckley Jr.

Mr. Joseph Adler
33 Orchard View Blvd.
Suite 1805
Toronto, Ontario
CANADA M4R 2E9

Minister Ministre	Ministry of Energy	Ministère de l'Énergie	Queen's Park Toronto, Ontario M7A 2B7 416/965-1301 Fax 324-3771	Queen's Park Toronto (Ontario) M7A 2B7 416/965-1301 Télécopieur 324-3771

416/327-2940
Fax 327-1512

December 20, 1990

Mr. Joseph Adler
President
Bicycle Expressway Systems
33 Orchard View Boulevard
Suite 1805
Toronto, Ontario
M4R 2E9

Dear Mr. Adler:

I would be pleased to meet with you to discuss the
Bicycle Expressway System. Our dependence on the
automobile is the root of many of our energy and
environmental concerns. I am keen to consider
alternatives.

I note that you will not be available until after
January 20, 1991. Maria Dyck from my office will
contact you after that date to arrange a meeting.

Yours sincerely,

Jenny Carter
Minister

SPEECH DELIVERED BY MR. JESSE FLIS, MEMBER OF
FEDERAL PARLIAMENT OF CANADA, IN THE HOUSE OF
COMMONS, DEDICATED ENTIRELY TO THE PROMOTION
OF THE BICYCLE EXPRESSWAY SYSTEM CONCEPT

CANADA

House of Commons Debates

VOLUME 132 • NUMBER 137 • 3rd SESSION • 34th PARLIAMENT

OFFICIAL REPORT
(HANSARD)

Thursday, May 7, 1992

Speaker: The Honourable John A. Fraser, P.C., Q.C.

406

The Environment

most important achievements for humanity than we have been able to make for a very long time.

I trust that all of us together will support the actions of the government representatives and of the NGOs and the independent sector which will be there to provide leadership on Canada's behalf.

The Acting Speaker (Mr. Mifflin): The hon. member for Parkdale—High Park.

Mr. Jesse Flis (Parkdale—High Park): Mr. Speaker, it is indeed a pleasure to take part in this special debate on the United Nations Conference on the Environment and Development. I am pleased that you are in the Chair, Mr. Speaker, listening to this important debate.

• (2010)

A lot has been said today about the UNCED conference. A lot has been said prior to today's debates, and a lot will be said after the conference. I asked myself how much of what we said here in the House today will actually be implemented, how much we say here today is actually being listened to.

I would like to take a little different approach on this topic and share with the viewers and the people in the Chamber one concept that if implemented will change the direction of this planet toward a sustainable development environment. If it is not implemented, 10 years from now we will be having similar debates and the planet will be going further and further downhill instead of being cleaned up.

But to do that I think the people attending the Rio conference will have to change their thinking from two-dimensional thinking to multi-dimensional thinking or at least three-dimensional thinking. If the people continue in their two-dimensional thinking the planet will not change. It will continue to be polluted. The approaches are going to have to be holistic approaches to any recommendations made at this conference.

The one concept that I would like to share with the House is the idea of elevated bicycle expressway systems for large cities. The concept of a bicycle expressway system was developed by Joseph Adler, an engineer from Toronto who is an enthusiastic cyclist, a professional engineer and a resident of Toronto. These three assets brought him to the idea of improving, in a radical,

engineered way, cycling as a means of mass transportation and recreation in large cities.

The bicycle expressway system represents an additional transportation facility provided exclusively for bicycles and the servicing of large city areas. Its purpose would be to create the conditions and to give all residents the choice of replacing the use of a car by the use of a bike in most of their daily trips within the city limits and to create a convenience for everybody who would be willing to use a bike. As we know, the car is one of the greatest polluters on this planet.

We talked about different modes of transportation. We were talking about a high speed railway system corridor from Windsor to Quebec City. That is an excellent idea, but if we just take the people who are using buses and move them on to trains that is not going to solve the problem. But if we can take the people out of the cars between Windsor, Toronto, Ottawa, Montreal and Quebec and put them on a high speed electric train, then yes we are working toward sustainable development.

My concept is to take the people out of their cars in the big cities and put them on bicycles. That can only be done if we have a bicycle expressway system that includes a network of elevated, covered, level or downhill bicycle expressways accessible from the street level by escalators or ramps, provided in numerous locations in all of the large city areas.

The basic philosophy of this concept is that all expressways on all their length are elevated at a minimum of five metres above street level, covered with transparent, sun-reflecting material and at level or with downhill slopes. Conceived in this way, the bicycle expressway system provides complete separation from car and pedestrian traffic and therefore complete safety, full protection against bad weather year round and eliminates the need of climbing the differences in elevation between any two points in the city.

There is no intersection at the same level between bike expressways running north-south with those running east-west. They will be interconnected by ramps and escalators. In these conditions, no stop signs or stop lights are necessary, and the non-stop bicycle ride with maximum speed will be possible.

According to engineer Joseph Adler, using the expressway system, the bicycle will become the safest, the cheapest, the healthiest and the fastest means of urban

The Environment

transportation, very easy, pleasant and convenient for most of the city residents.

Imagine the amount of money that we would save in health bills alone if we could shift even 10 per cent of the population from cars on to bicycles. Imagine how fit these people will be going to work by bike, returning home by bike. We will write off many of the health bills.

Imagine how many whiplash cases we have in this country from car accidents and how much money is spent on the treatment of simple whiplashes. A lot of these accidents and injuries to people would be eliminated. The proposed system will create the opportunity for a tremendous increase in general fitness, great energy and money saving, and a dramatic reduction in the rate of traffic accidents, noise and air pollution. The cost of the system can be recuperated in a few years according to engineer Joseph Adler.

Summarizing the features of such an expressway, first of all, it has to be elevated at close to five metres above street level. Any interference with streets, motorized or pedestrian traffic is eliminated leading to a completely safe system: The system would have to be covered with transparent, sun-reflecting material and full protection against bad weather year round, be it cold, rain, snow, sleet, wind, sun or heat.

The system would have to be at a level or downhill, approach. There would be no more streets with long slopes to peddle up. There would be no more sweating. It would be a faster ride. Many people will not take a bike to work today because they work up a sweat, there is no shower at work so they hop in the car instead.

With this system of not having to peddle uphill, we would not even work up a sweat. Many people are shocked with that concept. How can you have a system where you never peddle uphill? Very simple. We all know of escalators. Where there is a slope, you provide an escalator, you get to the level of the city and then you just peddle on level or downhill.

In Such a system, interfere one with another at the same
the expressways do not
level. At intersections, they are interconnected by ramps and escalators. There are no stop lights or stop signs. It is direct, non-stop bike riding between any two points in the system. We have a very easy, safe, pleasant and fast riding system.

If it is such a great system, why has it not been implemented until now? The reason it has not is because of economic barriers. I presented this concept to Transport Canada back in 1981, and I pressed them to do a feasibility study. I told them to choose any city they wanted; Vancouver, Montreal, Toronto. Do a feasibility study on an elevated bicycle expressway system. We were in government then, and the reason Transport Canada would not touch it was because of the 1981-82 recession.

Mr. Adler and I resurfaced this concept 10 years later. We are getting the same barrier, economic recession. In the years 2001 or 2002, someone will resurface this concept again and we will probably have the same barrier, economic recession. I hope not. I hope that we will get into multi-dimensional thinking instead of two-dimensional thinking. Hopefully, in a decade from now we will have not only a feasibility study, but a system well in place.

Imagine if a city like Toronto, where my riding is, developed such a system. It would be the first city in the world to have an elevated bicycle expressway system. Because it is elevated it does not interfere with the local pedestrian traffic, with the auto traffic, et cetera. It is a complete system unto itself.

● (2020)

Imagine the tourist attraction that this would be. Tourists would come from all over the world to look at this expressway system. Imagine what it would do to the bicycle economy. We could rent bikes at various locations along this system and drop them off at another locati People could tour cities on bikes, which is getting more and more popular.

But imagine what it will do to the environment. Toronto, a Canadian city, would be the first to make that important turn to a truly sustainable environment on this planet.

What I am appealing, through this debate, is for at least three levels of government—in metro Toronto it would be four levels of government—to get their heads together. We are talking about infrastructure, sharing infrastructure at one-third, one-third and one-third the cost among three levels of government.

Here is excellent sustainable infrastructure, sustainable transportation, sustainable development. That may look costly, but when we look at what we save in preventing accidents, improved health in the people and

The Environment

fewer medical costs, the system would probably pay for itself within five or ten years.

Here is an opportunity for Canada to take a leadership role at this conference and present at least one new creative idea, which this is. Most of the bicycle expressway systems present now consist of adding on a lane next to the cars. That is not the solution. We cannot put too many bikes and too many cars on the same level. Here the bicycles would be above the cars.

In Toronto, well right across Canada, there is a bid for Expo 98. I have already written to the committee. I said that if it would implement a bicycle expressway system in the city of Toronto, I am sure Canada would win Expo 98 because we would be the only city in the world that would have such a show-piece as this to show.

After my referring Mr. Adler to representatives of the provincial government, they were very polite. They thought it was a great idea, but they had the same excuse, a dozen economic reasons. They did not see themselves taking part now.

We talked with the chairman of metropolitan Toronto who said that because the federal government was giving less money to them through the provinces they could not afford to pay their welfare recipients, never mind building a bicycle expressway system.

We went to the former mayor of Toronto and received a similar answer. I referred Mr. Adler to the new mayor of Toronto, and I am sure it will be the same answer: this economic barrier.

We have to break that barrier, as I said, with three-dimensional thinking. We have to get away from two-dimensional thinking. Let us get into multi-dimensional thinking. If we implement such a system, the economy of that city would just boom because of the world attention, because of the world attraction.

Imagine the conventions that would be held in that city just to see a unique bicycle expressway system.

I do not know who is going to Rio de Janeiro, but I hope they will drop in to see Dr. Adler's presentation. He has been accepted to make the presentation at the sustainable transportation conference which is going on at the same time.

The government parliamentary secretary is listening very attentively. I hope he will pass this message on to the government or to all of the delegates who go to Brazil to sit in on this presentation.

It is something unique. It is something creative. It is something that no other country has thought of. A Canadian engineer has thought of it. Why do we not give this Canadian some help? I am not saying to go an build it off the bat. Let's do a feasibility study. Surely, putting our heads together we can come up with enough money to do a feasibility study, and if the feasibility study shows, yes, we can do it, let's go ahead and do it. Let's not wait and waste another decade. Let us really put into practice what we are going with to the UNCED conference.

Madam Speaker, I don't know if I require the unanimous consent of the House to table this document, *The Bicycle Expressway System* by engineer Joseph Adler. The presentation here has coloured photos, engineer's drawings. I feel it should be tabled, with your permission, so that anyone who reads this debate could come and could have access to this unique system which would save our environment.

Madam Deputy Speaker: Our Standing Orders would not allow the hon. member to table the document, but I am sure that as it is offered to table it, it will be in our minutes, will be in *Hansard* that any member who is interested will get in touch with the hon. member. But our Standing Orders do not allow for a member to table such a report. This is our law. Now, if there was unanimous consent—

Some hon. members: Agreed.

Madam Deputy Speaker: Agreed? If there is unanimous consent, by all means.

Mr. Jim Edwards (Parliamentary Secretary to Minister of State and Leader of the Government in the House of Commons): Madam Speaker, the hon. member for Parkdale—High Park was right. I listened with great interest to his speech, as I have to the bulk of the speeches here tonight. I think we ought to do more of this. This gives the public of Canada an opportunity to see this place at its best, in the sense that various different points of view, and some remarkably profound analyses, can be displayed as a result of work and interest areas of members of Parliament.

itC

Rua Hermenegildo Barros, 12
Rio de Janeiro RJ 20241 BRASIL
tel: 55 (0)21 222 7454
fax: 55 (0)21 232 7725

Instituto de Tecnologia para o Cidadão

Institute of Technology for the Citizen

29 June, 1992

of.417/92

Joseph Adler, President
Bicycle Expressay Systems
3 Orchard View Blvd., Suite 1805
Toronto, Ont. Canada M4R 2E9

Dear Mr. Adler,

I really appreciated your participation at the International Seminar Sustainable Transportation Strategies and Development during the Global Forum/UNCED 92 which happened in June in Rio.

Enclosed you will find the draft of the final document of the seminar. We are asking all the participants to make their remarks and corrections, and to send it back for us, so we can consolidate the final version and start the distribution of it.

Concerning the meeting we had for discussing about the potential utilization of the Bicycle Expressway System concepts in Greater Rio Metropolitan Area, itC is still making the preliminary moves to start a Bicycle Masterplan for this megacity.

As I told you, itC is a non-profit organization committed to the curtailing of the motorization of the urban sector and therefore our mission is much more complex than selling an new idea of public policy. As a NGO we are aware that actually we are catalyzing a new way of working out environmentally sustainable and socially acceptable solutions for urban development and transportation problems.

In this context, I see that your concepts can be very useful for sorting out some technical stalemates and challenges that we have in Rio to make a comprehensive bicycle masterplan. I envision that your bike expressways can be a great solution for instance to make possible for the bicycles -- which constitute a fleet of 2 million in Rio -- to share the omnipresent tunnels of Rio with the motorized transportation.

The itC has a very respectable CV, being technical consultant of grassroots organizations, local administrations in Brazil, and multilateral development banks like the IDB and the IBRD. Therefore I see with great expectations a potential cooperation which you suggested could that have the CIDA as a counterpart aiming to make preliminary studies for bicycle expressway corridors in Rio as part of our Bicycle Masterplan.

Looking forward to hearing from you soon. Sincerely,

Ricardo Neves, President

410

United Nations Conference on Environment & Development
Conférence des Nations Unies sur l'Environnement et le Développement

160 Route de Florissant
P.O. Box: 80
CH-1231 Conches   Tel: (41-22)789-1676
Switzerland   Fax: (41-22)789-3536

/NS

20 July 1992

Dear Mr. Adler,

     Thank you for your letter of May 1. I apologize for not getting back to you sooner but your letter arrived during the peak of preparatory activity for the Conference and I have not been able to get back to my correspondence until recently.

     I have had a rather quick review of your material and I am very impressed with your concept. It certainly has some initial challenges not the least of which is getting the modern city dweller, in the North and the South, past their love for the automobile.

     I would like an opportunity to discuss these ideas further but cannot at this time suggest a suitable date. My contract as Secretary-General comes to an end on August 31 and I am planning to move back to Canada to resume my more private life. Sometime in the fall I will be establishing an office at the University of British Columbia and I suggest you try and reach me there. Hopefully we can then find a suitable time.

     I thank you for bringing your ideas to my attention and I wish you every success. Best regards.

Yours sincerely,

Maurice Strong
Secretary General of UNCED

Joseph Adler
President
Bicycle Expressway Systems
33 Orchard View Blvd.
Suite 1805
Toronto, Ontario
Canada M4R 2E9

E-MAIL: APC: cdplunced;   TCN: tcn4091;   GeoNet: geo2:unced-is;   InterNet: cdplunced@arisia.xerox.com;
BitNet: adpluncad@fl L   ^

411

HARLES CACCIA, M.P.
VENPORT
)USE OF COMMONS
TAWA, ONTARIO
A 0A6
L: (613) 992-2576
X: (613) 995-8202

HOUSE OF COMMONS
CHAMBRE DES COMMUNES

RIDING OFFICE
1689A DUFFERIN STREET
TORONTO, ONTARIO
M6E 3N9
TEL.: (416) 654-8048
FAX : (416) 654-5083

April 21, 1993

Mr. Joseph Adler
Bicycle Expressway Systems
33 Orchard View Bldv.
Suite 1805
Toronto, ON M4R 2E9

Dear Mr. Adler,

Thank you for having accepted our invitation to becoming a pannellist at our Imagineering Townhall meeting on May 8. Attached please find a complete programme. Feel free to circulate and post it. I would certainly appreciate your help in publicizing this meeting through your channels.

I look forward to May 8 and thanks again.

Best regards,

encl

412

Ontario Hydro
700 University Avenue
Toronto, Ontario
M5G 1X6

Chairman's Office

22 October 1993

Mr. George Davies
Deputy Minister
Ministry of Transport
East Building
1201 Wilson Avenue
DOWNSVIEW, Ontario
M3M 1J8

Dear George,

I recently had the opportunity to meet with a Mr. Joseph Adler, President and creator of Bicycle Expressway Systems. I first met Mr. Adler when he was participating in the International Seminar on Sustainable Transportation Strategies, during the Global Forum/Earth Summit in Rio in 1992.

Although this is not within my traditional area of expertise or my current mandate at Ontario Hydro, I would like to bring to your attention Mr. Adler's fascinating and logical proposal. Basically, he has developed a scheme for a system of elevated, covered "bicycle-ways", to facilitate and encourage more people to use the bicycle as their primary means of transportation within urban areas.

This is, I believe, a visionary idea, which has been applauded by the likes of William F. Buckley Jr. It is quite appealing, and has the potential to result in several benefits: --environmental, social, physical and economical. It would alleviate traffic congestion, reduce smog, improve health and safety. This translates into enormous savings, both in terms of energy and economy, and in reduced social costs. Of course, this is a truly sustainable equation. Such a system could be set up comparatively cheaply because for cyclists there would be no great load-bearing problem and the structure could be light.

Mr. Adler has taken his plans to a number of federal, Ontario and municipal offices for study. So far funding has not been forthcoming. In fact, Mr. Adler corresponded with your Ministry (see attached letter) in 1990, which at least led to the "Bicycle Expressway System" plan being included in the Bicycle Policy Review. Mr. Adler has been refining and promoting his idea for over ten years now. I believe that it deserves some serious re-consideration. As a minimum, I would encourage a feasibility study to assess the project in terms of potential demand, usability and acceptability.

Mr. George Davies - 2   21 October 1993

Beyond that, perhaps the Province could consider a pilot demonstration project in the Metro Toronto area, along either a north-south, or east-west axis, instead of the more complex bicycle grid proposed by Mr. Adler.

I believe that this proposal could provide an opportunity for the Province to show vision and leadership by taking a concrete step to a more sustainable, environmentally friendly world. Therefore, I would like to suggest that you meet with Mr. Adler personally to listen to his proposal, and to seriously consider moving forward with at least a small scale demonstration project. As you know, we are constantly being challenged as a society to overcome a number of psychological and economical barriers to sustainable development, perhaps this is one case where can successfully overcome those obstacles.

Yours sincerely,

Maurice F. Strong

c Mr. J. Adler

414

Ontario |
700 Universm
Toronto
|

Chairman
Tel: (416) 592-2115, Fax: (416) :

12 January 1994

Her Worship Mayor June Rowlands
City Hall
TORONTO, Ontario
M5H 2N2

Dear Mayor Rowlands,

I am writing to follow-up on a letter which I sent to Mr. George Davies, Deputy Minister of Transport, last fall.

In my letter, I expressed my support for an interesting sustainable transportation concept called the "Bicycle Expressway System", and encouraged Mr. Davies to consider supporting an initial feasibility study of the proposal. I have attached a copy of my letter to Mr. Davies in which I explain the System briefly and what I consider to be its significant potential benefits to society.

Subsequent to my writing that letter, Mr. Davies met with Mr. Joseph Adler, creator of the Bicycle Expressway System. At that meeting, Mr. Davies agreed to allocate 50% of the cost of a marketing study for a pilot demonstration project in Toronto. That offer, however, was conditional on the Municipality of Toronto funding the other portion.

I am all too aware of the financial constraints with which industry, governments and the public must deal in today's tough economic climate. However, I believe that a small investment at this time in the Bicycle Expressway System would pay off substantial dividends in future saved environmental, social costs and transportation.

I urge you, therefore, to consider Mr. Adler's proposal in a positive light. I expect that he will be in contact with your office in the near future.

May I take this opportunity to wish you a successful 1994. It promises to be a year of continuing challenges. Best personal regards.

Yours sincerely,

Maurice F. Strong

c Mr. G. Davies
Mr. J. Adler

ST. JAMES'S PALACE
LONDON SW1A 1BS

29th July 1994

From: The Private Secretary to HRH The Prince of Wales

Dear Mr. Adler,

The Prince of Wales has asked me to thank you for your letter of 5th May, about Bicycle Expressway Systems, and to apologise for the long delay in replying.

His Royal Highness was most grateful for your kind comments about his television documentary on the environment, and interested to read about your own plans for using the bicycle as the main mode of urban transportation in selected cities around the world.

His Royal Highness very much hopes that you will succeed in creating a full-scale demonstration system, since this is clearly the way to convince people of the benefits, and hopes that you will keep him in touch with your progress.

Yours sincerely,

Commander Richard Aylard, RN

Joseph Adler Esq.
President
Bicycle Expressway Systems
33 Orchard View Boulevard
Suite 1805
Toronto
Ontario
Canada M4R 2E9,

CABINET OFFICES

1 DEVON ROAD,

P.O. BOX 272,

KINGSTON 6, JAMAICA

No. 94-117

9th September 1994

Mr Joseph Adler
President
Bicycle Expressway Systems
33 Orchard View Boulevard
Suite 1805
Toronto, Ontario
Canada
M4R 2E9

Dear Mr Adler

Following our discussions in Kingston in August and September 1994, we would like to emphasize the position of the Government of Jamaica regarding the proposed Bicycle Expressway for Kingston, as mentioned below:

1. The Government of Jamaica is of the opinion that the concept of Bicycle Expressway System is an innovative idea and that its implementation in Kingston as you envisage, could contribute to some degree to assist in resolving some of the present difficulties in the urban transportation.

2. We realize the additional benefits the implementation of such a system could generate as regards reduction in the rate of air and noise pollution and in the rate of traffic accidents, which are aspects of increasing concern for Kingston. At the same time, the project implementation will create some productive jobs, will reduce the requirement for imported fuel and will raise the general level of fitness for the Users of the system.

3. A comprehensive feasibility study is the first step towards the project implementation and although the Jamaican Government, because of present economic constraints, is not in a position to finance such a study directly or the first stage of project implementation, strongly supports such an initiative by private investors and government entities.

417

2

Mr Joseph Adler, President   9th September 1994

_____

4. The feasibility study, to be prepared by the Bicycle Expressway
    Systems Company under your direct responsibility, in
    collaboration with a Jamaican counterpart company, should analyze
    in detail all pertinent aspects and problems connected with the
    construction, operation and maintenance of the proposed first stage
    of development as engineering, economics, financing, social and
    environmental aspects, safety and security aspects, alternatives for
    fare collection and return on investment, etc.

5. During the preparation of the feasibility study a close contact will be
    maintained with the Jamaican Government through designated
    officials or directly, and all problems requiring further clarification
    should be solved within the framework of the feasibility study clearing
    the way for the detailed engineering design and project
    implementation.

6. The Government of Jamaica is committed to assist, where possible
    the preparation of the feasibility study, construction and operation of
    the system and the necessary public relations campaign in Jamaica
    and abroad. As a proof of direct interest and as an incentive, the
    Jamaican Government has made contact with Private and Public
    Sector Enterprises towards obtaining some financial assistance for
    the preparation of the feasibility study. In this regard, there is a
    pledge for US$100,000 from a public sector organization in Jamaica.

We wish to thank all persons and organizations supporting the promotion of this
concept and its implementation in Kingston, Jamaica and we hope that this
document will help to speed up the start of this pioneering and visionary project.

Yours sincerely
CABINET OFFICES

Carlton E Davis
Permanent Secretary/Cabinet Secretary

UNITED NATIONS CENTRE FOR HUMAN SETTLEMENTS (Habitat)
CENTRE DES NATIONS UNIES POUR LES ETABLISSEMENTS HUMAINS
CENTRO DE LAS NACIONES UNIDAS PARA LOS ASENTAMIENTOS HUMANOS

PO Box 30030, Nairobi, KENYA
Telephone: (254-2) 621234, Telex: 22996 UNHAB KE, Cable: UNHABITAT
Facsimile: (254-2) 624266/7 (Central Office), 624262 (ADM), 624263/4 (TCD), 624265 (RDD)

TELEFAX TRANSMISSION

To:	Mr. Joseph Adler	Drafter:	KR/vn
	President, Bicycles Expressway		
	Systems	Room:	M-215 Ext.: 3039
	33, Orchard View Blud		
	Suit 1805, Toronto, Ontario	Date:	15 September 1995
	M4R 2E9 CANADA		
Telefax No:	416-4817298	Account No.:	FD-RDB-94-F02-5300
From:	K. Ray, Chief, BITS/RDD	Cleared by:	
Subject:	Seminar-cum-Workshop on Transport	Authorized by:	Mr. M. Hundsalz, OIC,
	Demand Management, Beijing, 25 to		RDD
	27 September 1995		
Prefix No.:	A00-4543-95	TOR:	

Dear Mr. Adler,

I am pleased to transmit in the following pages the provisional programme of the Beijing Seminar. The programme is still tentative and I would appreciate your comments and suggestions before we finalize it by mid next week. Your suggestions would be particularly helpful in deciding discussion themes for panel discussions scheduled for day two.

I am also pleased to invite you to act as a panel member during plenary session III on day two. As a panelist, you would be expected to make an initial short statement on each of the discussion themes (to be decided) and thereafter respond to the questions that may be raised by the participants.

I hope your travel arrangements have all been satisfactorily finalized and I am looking forward to seeing you soon in Beijing. Regards,

Yours sincerely

K. Ray
Chief
Building & Infrastructure Technology Section
Research & Development Division

419

Republic of the Philippines
Batangas City

®ffice of the City Mayor

18 October 1995

MR. JOSEPH ADLER
President
Bicycle Expressway System
33 Orchard View Blvd.,
Suite 1805
Toronto, Ontario, CANADA
M4R2E9

Dear Mr. Adler:

This has reference to your proposal regarding the concept of Bicycle Expressway System which you have presented to Mrs. Mibelle B. Garcia, our City Planning and Development Coordinator during the meeting held on October 10, 1995 in Batangas City.

Kindly be informed that we are interested in your proposal considering the following:

1. It could   possibly solved the traffic congestion problem that the city is presently experiencing;

2. It is safe, healthy, economical and environment friendly mode of transportation.

However, your proposal necessitates the preparation of a comprehensive feasibility study to determine its viability in our city and this requires a considerable amount. At present, the City Government is experiencing economic/financial difficulty and we do not have the capability to finance the conduct of study. Another factor that should be considered also is that the city government has no jurisdiction over the main roads in the city wherein you are proposing to locate the bicycle expressway system because these are all national roads under the responsibility of the Department of Public Works and Highways of the national government.

Please be informed further that the City Government is willing to negotiate with prospective parties who are interested in financing the preparation of the comprehensive feasibility study for Bicycle Expressway System which will be undertaken directly by your company.

We wish to thank you for the time you allocated for us in presenting your proposal and your desire to help us in our urban development planning effort.

Our warmest regards.

Very truly yours,

EDUARDO B. DIMACUHA
City Mayor

fn/adler
obbette

Mr Joseph Adler
Master of Engineering
Bicycle Expressway Systems
33 Orchard View Boulevard
Suite 1805
Toronto
Ontario, CANADA M4R 2E9

INTERNATIONAL BICYCLE CONFERENCE
FREMANTLE
WESTERN AUSTRALIA
OCTOBER 28 - NOVEMBER 1
1 9 9 6

Dear Mr Adler,

Re: Velos Australis Conference

Your concepts regarding the Bicycle Expressway System are of interest to the Conference program.

Although we are not in a position to offer you any assistance, we would like to invite you to the Conference to present a paper.

Your concepts will be of interest to many delegates and we hope that you will be able to join with us.

I have enclosed a registration booklet that shows the complete program.

I look forward to hearing from you.

Yours sincerely,

D T Pearce
Conference Organiser
PROMACO CONVENTIONS PTY LTD

July 11 1996
ENC:

ALL CORRESPONDENCE TO
THE ORGANISERS:
PROMACO CONVENTIONS PTY LTD
ACN 008 784 585
PO Box 890, Canning Bridge
WESTERN AUSTRALIA 6153

**COMITÉ ORGANIZADOR DE LA II CONFERENCIA Y EXPOSICIÓN
INTERNACIONAL CICLOS: OPCIÓN PARA EL SIGLO XXI**

Aptdo Postal 17029, Habana 17 C.P. 11700, CUBA
Teléfono: (537) 62–3051 al 58 ext. 30; 62–1557/8
Tele. -Fax: (537) 33–8250

Havana, August 1st, 1996

Joseph Adler, M.E., P.Eng.
President
BICYCLE EXPRESSWAY SYSTEMS
33 Orchard View Blvd., Suite 1805
Toronto, Ontario, Canada M4R 2E9

                    FAX: (416)-481-7298

Dear Joseph:

Finnally, I just received your letter from June 8th, that was
miscarried by the post office in Cuba.

Your paper' "The Bicycle Expressway- A Viable Urban
Transportation Solution", was accepted to be presented in the
2nd International Conference and Exhibition " Cycles: an option
for the 21st Century", that will be held in Havana from 2nd to
6th December 1996, as well as your proposed poster.

Related with your questions, the answers are the following:

-- margin on pages are 2,5 centimeters

-- peper numbers must be written on the back of leafs of papers

-- charge for displayed poster is additional

-- your paper will be submitted in plenary session

Concerning to extended in Cuba after the Conference, it should
be arranged from Canada through a Travel Agency. I suggest you
to use " MacQueens"(Fax:(902)894-4547), that is organizing a
group for this Conference.

Sincerely yours,

Humberto Valdés Rios, Ph.D.
President

Office of the Executive Director
The World Bank

FAX NO: (202) 477-4155   NUMBER OF PAGES   2
                                (including this page)

FACSIMILE TRANSMITTAL FORM

DATE: October 25, 1996

TO: Mr. Joseph Adler

FROM: François Pagé

TEL: 202-473-5681

SUBJECT:

The World Bank
Washington, D.C. 20433
U.S.A.

LEONARD GOOD
Executive Director

October 24, 1996

TO WHOM IT MAY CONCERN

    The office of the Executive Director for Canada at the World Bank is aware and supportive of the original and innovative Bicycle Expressway System Concept proposed and promoted by Mr. Joseph Adler from Toronto, Canada.

    We are of the opinion that the proposed concept could offer a sustainable solution for the significant improvement of urban transportation in many cities facing traffic congestion and air pollution problems. The implementation of the project would improve the quality of urban life by dramatically reducing the present heavy dependency on transportation by private cars, ease the burden on public transport, reduce the rate of traffic accidents, and the omnipresent health damaging air and noise pollution. At the same time, it would eliminate the costly and annoying waste of time in traffic jams, slow driving or in waiting and long distance walking connected with public transport. The concept sounds economically affordable for many cities for which a subway system is out of the question because of the high cost or for other reasons.

    We hope this confirmation of our interest in the Bicycle Expressway System concept will be of use for those willing to give proper consideration to this unique, visionary, environmentally friendly urban transportation alternative that may work very well in conjunction with other means of transportation.

Sincerely

PENTACAPITAL INVESTMENT CORPORATION
An Investment House

November 18, 1996

Mr. JOSEPH ADLER
President
BICYCLE EXPRESSWAY SYSTEMS, INC.
33 Orchard View Blvd., Suite 1805
Toronto, Ontario, Canada M4R 2E9

Attention: MR. ADLER

In lieu of our recent discussions in Manila regarding your Bicycle Expressway System concept, we are pleased to annouce the positive feedback in our intitial presentation/s of the elevated system design to at least four (4) local institutions, one of them is a MBA group representing the second biggest private academe in the country.

At least two of these institutions are willing to invest equity to fund a comprehensive pre-feasibility study to validate certain parameters in the concept, specifically, the financial component of the cost application of the infrastructure nessesary to build a 10-15 kilometer model system. It was unfortunate that you were not able to meet with the officials of the Department of Public Works and H Highways to discuss the possible application of your concept as an excellent alternative to current local roadway plans. I do hope you will get the opportunity in the future.

We are very pleased with your news of the direct endorsement of the World Bank of the concept as a valuable solution to traffic congestion and it's constriants on the general public. This endorsement, along as the possibility of a loan consideration from the same, has heightened local interest in the validity and business possiblities of the project as a whole.

In summary, we hope that future coordination of discussions about the project be kept constant, specially coordination with getting the local endorsement of DPWH. These series of steps will pave the way for a information roadshow that will create more business interest awareness for the project beyond the existing group.

We are prepared to organize the representation and possible funding for a task force to be formed to undertake the study. A foreign component to the funding will be nessesary on a 1: 1 basis in order to qialify the projoct for incentives and exceptions from the Bereau of Trade here in the Philippines.

We hope these arrangements will lead to the fruitful realization of a 15 kilometer mode system that we hope to endorse to the Office of the President of the Philippines

Sincerely,

RUBEN N. M. DE LEON II
Investment Banking Division
PENTACAPITAL INVESTMENT CORPORATION

427

**OFFICE OF
THE CHAIRMAN**

The Municipality of
Metropolitan Toronto
55 John Street
Stn. 1070, 7th Flr., Metro Hall
Toronto, ON M5V 3C6
Fax (416) 392-3799
Telephone (416) 392-5001

METRO

Alan Tonks
Metropolitan Chairman

January 16, 1997

Mr. Leonard Good
Executive Director
The World Bank
1818 H Street NW
Washington, D.C. 20433
U.S.A.

Dear Mr. Good:

Over the past several years Mr. Joseph Adler, President of Bicycle Expressway Systems, Inc., has been discussing with me his concept for an elevated bicycle expressway system. Mr. Adler's concept has stimulated local and, as you will gather from the attached letter, international interest.

In urban environments such transportation alternatives are appealing, offering sustainable and economical options when issues of accessibility, safety and convenience are addressed. I would be interested in exploring the potential of undertaking a pilot project with the World Bank to demonstrate the feasibility of this concept given commitments for private sponsorship are forthcoming.

If you are interested in pursuing Mr. Adler's prototypical integrated bicycle system I would be pleased to meet with you and other supporters to further this concept. I appreciate your serious consideration of Joseph Adler's proposal and look forward to hearing from you.

Yours truly,

Alan Tonks
Chairman
Metropolitan Toronto

Attachment

cc: M. François Pagé
       Mr. Joseph Adler

LEMAN GROUP INC.
CONSULTANTS ON HUMAN SETTLEMENTS
DEVELOPMENT PLANNING & ANALYSIS

DEVELOPMENT ANALYSIS   URBAN PLANNING & DESIGN   RESEARCH & POLICY   STRATEGIC PLANNING   GIS ANALYSIS   ENVIRONMENTAL ASSESSMENT

17 January 1997

Mr. Joseph Adler, M.A., P.Eng.
President
BICYCLE EXPRESSWAY SYSTEMS
33 Orchard View Blvd., Suite 1805
Toronto, Ontario   M4R 2E9

Re: BICYCLE EXPRESSWAY SYSTEMS IN MAJOR CITIES

Dear Mr. Adler,

Following our meetings, during which you kindly provided us with extensive briefings about your thoughtful concepts for BICYCLE EXPRESSWAY SYSTEMS IN MAJOR CITIES, we have now had the opportunity to review the material you have recently left with us.

I am pleased to let you know that in our opinion, your ideas have a great deal of relevance to the dire need evident in most major cities of the world, i.e. *to enhance the freedom and efficiency of movement in congested Metropolitan Areas*. Your ideas, if implemented with care and a strong dose of *urban* sensitivity, would contribute to huge improvements in economic efficiency, transportation diversity and air quality of most of the large cities everywhere.

On completion of our recent assignment for the Office of the Prime Minister of Thailand, where we prepared a NEW METROPOLITAN REGION STRUCTURE PLAN as an instrument for re-directing future urban developments away from highly-congested Bangkok, one of our recommendations was for urgent steps to be taken *to humanize Bangkok*. Your BICYCLE EXPRESSWAY SYSTEMS' concepts, go a long way to providing a very humanizing system of movements for all, and a very *humanizing urban development tool*.

As LEMAN GROUP INC. has worked on assignments in a number of developing countries around the world, we know from our first-hand observations that Metropolises such as Bangkok, Manila, Karachi, Dar es Salaam, Jakarta, - to name just a few major ones, are ripe and ready for intensive consideration *and implementation* of your ideas.

Your ideas are very good, are appropriate, and you should press on with your work. Where we can, we would be happy to assist you in advancing your cause.

With Best Personal Regards,
LEMAN GROUP INC.
per:

Alexander B. Leman, PLE, FRAIC, FRSA
President

ABL/bck - BCYCLEXP.001

THE HUDSON'S BAY CENTRE, 2 BLOOR ST. E., 28th FLOOR   TORONTO, CANADA   M4W 1A8   TELEPHONE 416 964-1865   FACSIMILE 416 964-60--

DIRECCION GENERAL DE INFRAESTRUCTURA Y EQUIPAMIENTO   FORMA C G.
DIRECCION DE INFRAESTRUCTURA, VIALIDAD Y TRANSPORTE

312.2.- 002045

SECRETARIA DE DESARROLLO SOCIAL

Ciudad de México, 12 de agosto de 1997.

Mr. Joseph Adler
President
Bicycle Expressway Systems
Toronto, Ontario M4R 2E9
P R E S E N T E

La Secretaría de Desarrollo Social y el Gobierno del Estado de Puebla, realizarán el "SEGUNDO
ENCUENTRO DE CIUDADES", con el objeto de conocer, analizar e intercambiar experiencias
nacionales como internacionales sobre la problemática y solución de la vialidad y el transporte, en
los centros urbanos.

Durante la reunión se presentarán ponencias que desarrollan aspectos, tales como:

I   LOS ORGANISMOS OPERADORES DE LOS SISTEMAS DE VIALIDAD Y TRANSPORTE URBANO PARA EL SIGLO XXI.

II LA INFRAESTRUCTURA VIAL Y DEL TRANSPORTE URBANO EN LAS CIUDADES MEDIAS PARA ENFRENTAR LOS RETOS DE LA MODERNIZACION DEL SIGLO XXI.

III NUEVAS TECNOLOGIAS PARA LA REHABILITACION Y RECONSTRUCCION DE PAVIMENTOS.

IV IMPACTO SOCIAL DE INVERSIONES EN MATERIA DE INFRAESTRUCTURA VIAL Y TRANSPORTE URBANO.

V   PROYECTOS DETONADORES EN LA MODERNIZACION DEL TRANSPORTE URBANO.

VI EL IMPACTO AMBIENTAL DERIVADO POR LA INFRAESTRUCTURA VIAL Y EL TRANSPORTE URBANO.

VII LA PARTICIPACION DE LAS CAMARAS , COLEGIOS DE PROFESIONALES Y EMPRESAS DE CONSULTORIA EN EL DISEÑO Y APLICACION DE PROGRAMAS DE MODERNIZACION DE LA VIALIDAD Y EN TRANSPORTE URBANO.

VIII LA INFORMATICA EN LA PLANEACION, DISEÑO Y APLICACION DE MODELOS DE SISTEMAS DE TRANSPORTE URBANO.

IX HACIA UNA NUEVA CULTURA DEL TRANSPORTE URBANO.

X   TECNOLOGIAS PARA MEJORAR EL SERVICIO AL USUARIO DEL TRANSPORTE URBANO.

XI ADMINISTRACION DE ESTACIONAMIENTOS.

XII CARRETERAS INTERMUNICIPALES.

XIII LAS VIAS DE FERROCARRIL EN ZONAS URBANAS.

Considerando su interés profesional en la materia, estimamos muy importante su concurrencia en
este evento a fin de intercambiar opiniones, por esta razón , me permito invitar a usted a participar
en el Encuentro a celebrarse en la ciudad de Puebla los días 24 y 25 de octubre de 1997. Con la
seguridad de contar con su presencia, le adjuntamos información relativa al encuentro y la ficha de
confirmación de asistencia.

Sin otro particular, aprovecho la oportunidad para enviarle un cordial saludo.

ATENTAMENTE
SUFRAGIO EFECTIVO NO REELECCION
EL DIRECTOR GENERAL

ING. JAIME SANCHO Y CERVERA.

Anexo: El que se indica.

c.c.p.- C. Lic. Antonio Sánchez Goenlces.- Subsecretario de Desarrollo Urbano y Vivienda. Presente
c.c.p. -C. Delegado Estatal de la SEDESOL.-Presente
c.c.p.- C. Lic. Carlos Valdez Mariscal.- Director de Infraestructura, Vialidad y Transporte. Presente

430

Founded 1905

THE NATIONAL UNIVERSITY *of* SINGAPORE

School of Building and Real Estate ˙

QUALITY OF LIFE IN CITIES
4 - 6 March 1998, Singapore

Mr Joseph Adler   3 September 1997
Bicycle Expressway Systems Co.
33 Orchard View Boulevard #1805
Toronto, Ontario
Canada M4R 2E9

Dear Mr Joseph Adler,

First International Conference on Quality of Life in Cities (4-6 March 1998)

We refer to the abstract of your proposed paper dated 27 August 1997 entitled "The Bicycle Expressway System: Today's Vision Tomorrow's Reality" which has been submitted for presentation at the First International Conference on Quality of Life in Cities, 4-6 March 1998. Your abstract has been vetted by the Conference Technical Committee and we are pleased to inform you that it has been accepted for presentation at the conference.

Please submit your full paper to us at the latest by 15 December 1997 together with a copy of the diskette. An early submission would be most appreciated. All papers are to be submitted in English on A4 size paper, double space, letter quality with left margin 1.5", right margin 1" and top and bottom margin 1" each, using either Microsoft Word for Windows 6.0 or WordPerfect 5.1 software. We enclose the latest conference leaflet, and Conference Registration Form/Hotel Reservation Form for you to fill in and return to us and our travel agent. To be certain of participation, please submit the forms to us at the latest by 15 December 1997.

For your information, the conference and accommodation fees are as follows:
Conference fee: Sin$700 (before 1 Feb, 1998) and Sin$800 for late registration.
Accommodation: Sin$223 (Conference hotel: Conrad International, a 5-star hotel)
                         Sin$170 (Allson Hotel) and Sin$130 (Oxford Hotel)
(Rates quoted are inclusive of 1% Cess, 3% Goods & Services Tax and 10% Service Charge).

We look forward to hearing from you soon.

Yours sincerely,

Dr Foo Tuan Seik
Conference Secretary

431

4.11.1997

FORUM ENGELBERG

Mr. Joseph ADLER
President
Bicycle Expressway System
33, Orchard View Blvd
Suite 1805
TORONTO , Ontario, Canada
M4R 2E9
fax 001 416 481 7298

To the attention of the Speakers, Moderators and Workshop Experts

Please accept my congratulations and heartfelt thanks for having accepted FORUM
ENGELBERG's invitation to participate in our 1998 Conference. The Scientific Committee,
chaired by Prof. Dr. Herwig Schopper, drew up the final programme during its October
meeting (28.10.97). For this reason, you are requested to kindly notify by FAX Ms Thérèse
Wolf (FAX +41 21 320 82 88), our Conference organiser, if you observe any errors in the
printed programme relating to your participation. I should be grateful if this could be done on
reception of this letter.

It is thanks to your participation in this interdisciplinary debate amongst leading figures from
the world of Science and Industry that FORUM ENGELBERG will once again be in the
foreground of all future decisions in the field. This will be due especially to the impact of the
recommendations drawn up at the end of the Conference. In order to ensure that your
contribution will also be published in the FORUM ENGELBERG Acta, you are invited to
forward the text of your speech to the FORUM ENGELBERG co-ordinator, Ms M.A. Heimo
as soon as possible and no later than March 1st, 1998.

In take this opportunity to congratulate you once more and I look forward to greeting you at
Engelberg on March 24, 1998.

Yours sincerely

Bernard ECOFFEY   Hubert CURIEN
Postgraduate of Science & Technology   f. Minister of Science, Technology and Founder
and Director of the   Space of the Republic of France
FORUM ENGELBERG   President of the Ministers' Committee of
                                        FORUM ENGELBERG

FORUM ENGELBERG
Secretariat : Thérèse Wolf, C.P. 112. CH-1000 Lausanne 5, tél +41 21 320 0805 fax +41 21 320 8288
e-mail : th_wolf@scopus.ch

432

K6   WORLD BANK   B. Ecoffey
     Theme :   Bicycle Expressway Systems

     Chaired by :   World Bank
     Experts :   Joseph ADLER, President, Bicycle Expressway Systems,
                 Toronto
                 N.N., Zurich   à proposer par
                                                        M. Wagner

K7   JAPAN - FRANCE TGV - SWISSMETRO   Mme Crausaz
     Theme :   Technological Development and the Future   (prop. de Prof
                of the Transport by Rail   Campagna. à
                                                        contacter Thyssen
     Chaired by :   Marcel JUFER, Prof. Dr., Laboratoire d'électromécanique
                    et de machines électriques, EPFL, Lausanne   à contacter
     Experts :

K8   ASCOM / VSM   Prof. Mey
     Theme :   Intelligent Traffic - Intelligent Fare Collection for   B. Ecoffey
                Public Transportation   (ok)

     Chaired by :   Johannes ZAUGG, Chief Technology Officer of ASCOM's
                    Group Segment Service Automation, Bern
     Experts :

K9   FEDERAL OFFICE ON SPATIAL PLANNING (BRP)   Mme Crausaz
     ASTAG
     Theme :   Transport and Spatial Development
                (Verkehr und Raumordnung)

     Chaired by :   Hans FLÜCKIGER, Prof. Dr., ETH Zürich, vormals Direktor
                    des Bundesamtes für Raumplanung
     Co-Chairman : Michel CRIPPA, Director of ASTAG

     Experts :   N.N., Swiss Institute of Comparative Law, Lausanne   B. Ecoffey

K10 SCIENCE AND TECHNOLOGY POLICIES   Einladung an
     Chaired by :   Federal Councillor   Bundesrat vom
                                                        31.5.97

25 February 1998

LEMAN
GROUP
INCORPORATED

Dr. Utis Kaothien
Director
Urban Development Co-ordination Division
National Economic and Social Development Board (NESDB)
962 Krung Kasem Road
Bangkok 10100, Thailand

Re: **Joseph Adler, M.E., P.Eng.
President,
BICYCLE EXPRESSWAY SYSTEMS**

Dear Utis,

I am writing to introduce a Colleague and an impressive engineering mind, **Joseph Adler, M.E., P.Eng.**, President of BICYCLE EXPRESSWAY SYSTEMS, based in Toronto. Mr. Adler's concept for elevated, bicycle urban expressways is a very interesting innovation, which I am convinced has enormous application potential in Asia's overcrowded Metropolises, almost all of which are outside of the winter-ice belt. But ice has not deterred Toronto officials speaking enthusiastically about Mr. Adler's approach to urban movements systems.

I would much appreciate it if you could arrange to receive Mr. Adler, consider his ideas and their applicability to Bangkok, and then, if you share my appreciation of this technology, arrange for Mr. Adler to meet with Khun Sansern or other appropriate, key persons in the NESDB. He already has an appointment arranged with the Governor of the Metropolitan Bangkok.

As he will already tell you, he has been received very well by the ADB, the World Bank and other international development agencies, but he needs a *ground contact"* such as the NESDB offers.

I do feel guilty in not keeping a better contact with you, but hope I will stop-over in Bangkok on one of my future trips and see you, for a day or two.

With Best Personal Regards,
LEMAN GROUP INC.

Alexander B. Leman, PLE, FRAIC. FRSA
President

ABL/bck

Copy: Mr. Joseph Adler.

Hudsons Bay Centre
2 Bloor Street East
28th Floor
Toronto Canada
M4W 1A8

Tel 416 964 1865
Fax 416 964 6065

Facsimile

To. Mr. Joseph Adler,
Bicycle Expressway System,
33 Orchard View Blvd, Suite 1805,
Toronto, Ont, Canada M4R 2J9.
Tel 416 4871066
Fax 416 4817298

From. International Affairs Division
Bangkok Metropolitan Administration
Bangkok 10200, Thailand
Tel. 66-2-2244686
Fax. 66-2-2244686

Dear Sir,

We refer to your letter dated 5 December 1997 informing Governor Bhichit Rattakul for your intention to visit Bangkok Metropolitan Administration to present the concept of Bicycle Expressway System.

We are very pleased to inform you that the Governor Bhichit has been acknowledged and assigned two of his advisers to welcome you on Monday 9 March 1998 at 10.00-12.00 at the BMA Human Resources Development Institute, City Hall.

We, therefore, would be very pleased if you could confirm your intention to visit and make presentation.

We look forward to hearing from you.

Yours sincerely,

(Ms.Prapim Borisuthi)
Director

435

JOSEPH ADLER, M.E. P., ENG.

PRESIDENTE DE
BICYCLE EXPRESSWAY SYSTEMS
33 ORCHARD VIEW BLVD., SUITE 1805
TORONTO, ONT. CANADA M4R 2E9

Muy estimado señor ingeniero Adler:

Por medio del presente tengo el agrado de hacerle una amable invitación para que nos hiciera el honor de presentar la Conferencia Magistral con el concepto Vias Expresas para Bicicletas en el 2ª Seminario Internacional de Ingeniería de Sistemas que con los temas: "Las grandes oportunidades en México y Norteamerica" y "Las soluciones a los problemas con el enfoque de sistemas", se llevará a cabo del 25 al 27 de junio de 1998 en Bahias de Huatulco, Oax., México.

Su conferencia Magistral sería el sábado 27 de las 9:30 a las 10:45 horas, incluyendo un periodo de preguntas y respuestas.

Me es grato reiterarle la seguridad de mi más alta y distinguida consideración

A t e n t a m e n t e
"POR MI RAZA HABLARA EL ESPIRITU"
Cd. Universitaria, a 10 de diciembre de 1998

DR. JOSE JESUS ACOSTA FLORES
COORDINADOR GENERAL DEL COMITE ORGANIZADOR

Edificio "A" Circuito Exterior, Cd. Universitaria, Apartado Postal 70-256, C.P. 04510, México, D.F.
Tels. 662-30-04 al 06 Fax: 616-10-73 http://frida.fi-p.unam.mx/~depfi

2° SEMINARIO INTERNACIONAL DE INGENIERIA DE SISTEMAS

Ingeniería y sociedad

Soluciones a los problemas del agua, educación, electricidad, petróleo, edificación, globalización, industrialización y comercio exterior, medio ambiente, regulación y normalización, y transporte.

Las grandes oportunidades en México y Norteamérica

Bahías de Huatulco, Oaxaca   25 al 27 de junio de 1998.

PROGRAMA

jueves 25 de junio

12:00   Registro de participantes
14:00   Comida
15:30   Ceremonia de inauguración, donde se le hará un reconocimiento al Sr. Ing. Luis E. Bracamontes.
16:00   Taller: "Desafío del liderazgo" por el M. en C. Carlos Morán Moguel.
20:00   Cena

viernes 26 de junio

08:00   Desayuno
09:30   Conferencia Magistral por el C. Secretario de Desarrollo Social, Ing. Carlos Rojas Gutiérrez.
10:45   Mesa redonda organizada por la Sociedad de Exalumnos de la Facultad de Ingeniería de la UNAM, presidida por el Sr. Ing. Fernando Favela Lozoya.
12:00   Mesa redonda presidida por el Sr. Ing. Francisco Lira Hernández.
13:15   Mesa redonda organizada por el Instituto Mexicano de Sistemas e Investigación de Operaciones, presidida por el Dr. Ricardo Aceves García.
14:30   Comida
16:00   Presentación de ponencias
20:00   Cena

sábado 27 de junio

08:00   Desayuno
09:30   Conferencia Magistral: "Sistema de vías expresas para bicicletas" por el Sr. Ing. Joseph Adler. ◄─────
10:45   Mesa redonda organizada por la Asociación Mexicana de Caminos, presidida por el Sr. Ing. Héctor Arvizu.
12:00   Mesa redonda organizada por la Academia Mexicana de Ingeniería, presidida por los señores Dr. Juan Casillas García de León y M. en I. Alberto Moreno Bonett, presidente de la Academia y de la Comisión de especialidad de ingeniería de sistemas de la misma, respectivamente.
13:15   Ceremonia de clausura.

La Universidad Nacional Autónoma de México
a través de la
Facultad de Ingeniería
otorga el presente

D I P L O M A

al:

Ing. Joseph Adler

por su destacada exposición como conferencista magistral en el
"2o. SEMINARIO INTERNACIONAL DE INGENIERÍA DE SISTEMAS"
realizado del 25 al 27 de junio de 1998 en Bahías de Huatulco, Oaxaca.

"POR MI RAZA HABLARÁ EL ESPÍRITU"

Ing. JOSÉ MANUEL COVARRUBIAS SOLÍS.
Director de la Facultad y Presidente del
Comité Organizador.

Dr. JOSÉ JESÚS ACOSTA FLORES.
Coordinador General del Comité
Organizador.

EARTH COUNCIL • CONSEJO DE LA TIERRA • CONSEIL DE LA TERRE

Headquarters: P.O. Box 2323-1000 • San José, Costa Rica • Tel: (506) 256-1611 • Fax: (506) 255-2197

E-mail:eci@terra. ecouncil. ac.cr / ecouncil@igc. apc.org. / Web server:http://www.ecouncil.ac.cr

June 9, 1999   Fax: 571-336-0403

FOR PERSONAL ATTENTION

Honourable Enrique Penalosa
The Mayor of Bogota
Carrera 8
No. 10-65 – 2ⁿᵈ Floor
Santa Fe de Bogota, Columbia

Dear Enrique,

I very much appreciated and enjoyed our lunch when we met in New York a couple of weeks ago.

As you will recall, during our conversation you told me of the importance of bicyles as a means of transportation in Bogota. I mentioned a fellow who has been promoting the concept of "bicycle expressways" and am enclosing some materials for your review. As it turns out, Mr. Joseph Adler, wrote to your office about one year ago to present this concept (see copy of his letter attached).

I do urge you to look at this carefully as it seems to me, although I am not an expert, to be an innovative concept which is worthy of consideration. I understand that Mr. Adler is looking for an opportunity to carry out a Bicycle Expressway Pilot Project that would demonstrate its feasibility and potential to the world. He would be quite prepared to travel to Bogota to meet with your officials.

I hope you will agree with me that this is worth pursuing. In the meantime, please accept my best wishes for your continuing programme leadership of Bogota and let us keep in close touch in the period ahead.

Best personal regards.

Sincerely,

Maurice F. Strong

cc: Mr. Joseph Adler

Chairman's Office: 255 Consumer s Road Suite 401 North York, Ontario M2J 5B6
Tel: (416) 498-3150 • Fax: (416) 498-7296
E-mail: ecfoster@web.net

What? You don't believe it?
All right, so the part about the French soap is a bit of over-reach.
But ask local architect Chris Hardwicke about the future of cycling in Toronto, and he
will draw you a vision of elevated bike tunnels that could remake the very culture of the
city.

He calls it Velo-city or, more properly, velo-city, and it's catching international notice,
from Hardwicke's appearance on National Public Radio in the U.S. earlier this year, to
numerous international publications, to his scheduled presentation at the Good Life For
All exhibition in New York City this September.

The vision: a network of elevated bikeways, tube-like and roofed in glass, providing
protection from the elements. Hardwicke has mapped the velo-city network, tucking the
bikeways along existing public highway, power and railway corridors, creating not a
dense inner-city network, but rather one that connects distant parts of the metropolis.
Cyclists will access the bikeways, which will run about five metres above ground level,
through ramps tucked under the tubes. The planned grade of the ramps will be gentle
enough to accommodate wheelchair usage.

According to Hardwicke's calculations, reduction in air resistance will increase cycling
efficiency by about 90 per cent, allowing for speeds, or velocity, of up to 50 km/h.
Advantages: no noise pollution, no air pollution. Plus, cycling is good for you, and in this
conception bike riders are protected from their car-driving brethren.
The scheme sounds futuristic, yet it is not entirely new. Joseph Adler, an irrepressibly
charming engineer, was possessed of a similar vision a quarter century ago: elevated
bikeways built not alongside highways, but above roadways crisscrossing Toronto's inner
city. On top of the bikeways Adler conceptualized bike stations with restroom and
restaurant facilities. The plan calls for interconnecting escalators to assist riders heading
up into the bikeways, and ramps for the trip down to street level.

> 'Every time I see an adult on a bicycle, I no
> longer despair for the future of the human
> race'
> *H.G. Wells, author and avid cyclist*

By training Adler is a hydrotechnical engineer, but cycling is his passion. Just inside the
door of his high-rise apartment sits his 25-year-old blue Peugeot, which he rides
regularly. Behind the doorway sits his downhill skis. He is 75. In his position as president
of Bicycle Expressway Systems, a one-man hobbyist operation, he is currently pitching
his bicycle expressway to Dubai, figuring that any desert country with the moxie to build
an indoor ski hill just might have the imagination to get behind his project.

Not that there hasn't been interest. Included in Adler's archive are supporting letters from
Maurice Strong, William F. Buckley Jr. and endless Canadian politicians and

bureaucrats. In 1982, Buckley wrote an op-ed piece for *The Philadelphia Inquirer* championing the bike expressway. "Adler's idea is adaptable to any city," wrote Buckley. "But concretely, he has engineered ... a bicycle grid that would permit anyone living in metropolitan Toronto (they call it "metro" nowadays) to travel by bicycle from virtually any point in the city."

As it happens, nothing concrete has developed. "The visionaries don't have any money," sighs Adler. "And those with money don't have the vision."

That disconnect has much to do with the perceptions around cycling. Is cycling an add-on method of transportation or an essential service that demands and deserves substantial capital investment? Adler's projected cost: $1 billion.

Chris Hardwicke is 38. He had never heard of Joseph Adler or his bicycle expressway until earlier this year, when Adler called him up. The two have not yet met. They share a sense of despair over the lack of serious funding for cycling. "All the other infrastructures are supported in grandiose ways," says Hardwicke.

Hardwicke's velo-city has not been conceived as an anti-car project, but rather as a system that elevates bike riding to equal status alongside private transit (the car) and public transit (GO, TTC). "The people seem to like to cycle," says Hardwicke of Torontonians. "But they don't have any support ... It's about time we built something that's sustainable."

Points to consider: a bicycle takes one-seventh the road space of a car. Ergo, Hardwicke's bikeways, conceived at an equivalent width, will have seven times the capacity of the adjacent roadways. Velo-city will relieve traffic congestion and the demand for parking spaces. The greater vision extends to this: creating a vibrant cycling city that will feed a proliferation of thriving businesses, cultural activities, restaurants and cafés. Bike riders, surveys have shown, are excellent shoppers.

In the draft for his Good Life presentation, Hardwicke has written this: "Over time, velo-city will create a cycling culture for Toronto: kiss 'n' rides, shower facilities, velodromes, bike parks, health clubs, cycle-path stalls, repair shops, bike couriers, bike picnics, car-free housing, inter-modal stations and cycling fashions. Above all, it would encourage active, healthier lifestyles and consequently better lives for all Torontonians."

Sound fanciful? In an interview Hardwicke says he senses immense energy in the city right now. "There's a huge desire for change," he says. In his work, Hardwicke has cited a quotation from H. G. Wells. "Every time I see an adult on a bicycle," wrote Wells, "I no longer despair for the future of the human race." The author was an avid cyclist.

Here's another Wells quote that seems to suit the circumstance: "What really matters is what you do with what you have."

Office of the	Cabinet du
Premier	Premier ministre

Legislative Building · Édifice de l'Assemblée législative
Queen's Park   Queen's Park
Toronto, Ontario   Toronto (Ontario)
M7A 1A1   M7A 1A1

Ontario

August 1, 2007

Mr. Joseph Adler
President
Bicycle Expressway Systems
1805-33 Orchard View Boulevard
Toronto, Ontario
M4R 2E9

Dear Mr. Adler:

Thank you for your letter regarding the use of electric bicycles on Ontario's roads. I am grateful to you for sharing your proposal with me and regret the delay in responding.

Our government supports clean air initiatives and recognizes that air quality is an important issue for Ontarians. However, road safety is also an important priority. I note that you have also sent a copy of your correspondence to my colleague the Honourable Donna Cansfield, Minister of Transportation. I have asked the minister to respond to you directly.

Thanks again for writing. Your input on any provincial issue is always welcome. My colleagues and I look forward to continuing to work with you and your fellow Ontarians to meet your priorities and deliver the results you deserve.

Yours truly,

Dalton McGuinty
Premier

c: The Honourable Donna Cansfield